PROFESSIONAL
FEATURE WRITING

COMMUNICATION TEXTBOOK SERIES
Jennings Bryant—Editor

Journalism
Maxwell McCombs—Advisor

BERNER • Writing Literary
Features

FENSCH • The Sports Writing
Handbook

TITCHENER • Reviewing
the Arts

FENSCH • Writing Solutions:
Beginnings, Middles,
and Endings

SHOEMAKER • Communication
Campaigns about Drugs:
Government, Media,
and the Public

STEPP • Editing for Today's
Newsroom

BOGART • Press and Public: Who
Reads What, When, Where,
and Why in American
Newspapers, Second Edition

FENSCH • Associated Press Coverage
of a Major Disaster: The
Crash of Delta Flight 1141

GARRISON • Professional
Feature Writing

FENSCH • Best Magazine
Articles: 1988

PROFESSIONAL FEATURE WRITING

Bruce Garrison
University of Miami

LEA LAWRENCE ERLBAUM ASSOCIATES, PUBLISHERS
1989 Hillsdale, New Jersey   Hove and London

Lawrence Erlbaum Associates, Inc., Publishers
365 Broadway
Hillsdale, New Jersey 07642

Library of Congress Cataloging-in-Publication Data

Garrison, Bruce, 1950–
    Professional feature writing / by Bruce Garrison.
        p.   cm.—(Communication textbook series. Journalism.)
    Bibliography: p.
    Includes index.
    ISBN 0-8058-0483-8
    ISBN 0-8058-0646-6 (pb)
    1. Feature writing. I. Title. II. Series.
PN4784.F37G37   1989
808'.06607—dc19   88-36937
                                                       CIP

Printed in the United States of America
10   9   8   7   6   5   4   3   2   1

Contents

PART III: THE PROFESSIONAL LIFE

Preface

Many sources of information go into a textbook. This book is a collection of a wide variety of perspectives of the author, other writers, editors, publishers, professors, and students.

This volume should be a solid tour of the world of newspaper and magazine feature writing. As author, I am serving as your tour guide.

The pages before you represent my own experiences as a feature writer, those of friends who are professional writers, and of my students who have become successful feature writers.

Critical to the success of the book is the contribution of others. There are 17 professionals—highly successful editors and writers—who have written material exclusively for this textbook to help you along in your development as a feature writer. Their advice in the foreword and the 16 chapters should hasten your metamorphosis from a student journalist to a published professional.

There are several points to note about the book before you start reading what's ahead. First, the book is geared to advanced student writers. You should have a foundation in writing basics from beginning writing and reporting classes to get the most from the material here.

Second, this book focuses both on newspaper and magazine feature writing. It looks ahead to feature writing in the next decade, but also explains how feature writing is done now.

This text emphasizes three aspects of feature writing: (a) introduction and writing skills/basics, (b) article types, and (c) the professional writing life.

In each chapter, you will learn from professionals and by example. In each chapter are excerpts and complete articles from some of the nation's leading newspapers and magazines, as well as from specialized publications, that illustrate points made in the text.

I have taken much of the material here from 13-plus years of feature writing and reporting classes at three different universities. I hope you will learn as much from it as I did putting it all together.

It was a project well worth doing, especially if it helps you get your first article published.

ACKNOWLEDGMENTS

There are many people who are owed gratitude for assistance in production of this work. My sincerest thanks go out to them and to my students, who have always been willing to lend a hand.

Thanks to:

Dean Edward Pfister for his assistance in providing the support of the School of Communication at the University of Miami.

Prof. Alan Prince, University of Miami journalism teacher and former travel editor and international edition editor at *The Miami Herald*, for his timely suggestions in editing the manuscript and for specific content suggestions on several chapters. His encouragement was instrumental in starting and finishing the project.

The late Prof. Warren Burkett, University of Texas, for his timely suggestions in reviewing the manuscript. His ideas, especially for the chapter on science and technical writing were quite useful.

Prof. Alice Klement, University of Miami journalism professor, former reporter for *The Miami Herald* and free-lance magazine writer, for her advice on the introductory chapter.

Dorothy Rosenthal, reference librarian at Richter Library at the University of Miami, for her assistance on reference works and research.

Appreciation also goes to *The Miami Herald* for permitting access to its computerized library data base, "Vu-Text." This courtesy made research easier and it certainly was a major time-saver.

Thanks go to a fellow Kentuckian and friend, Jay Ambrose, executive editor of the *Rocky Mountain News* in Denver for taking the time to read the entire manuscript and write the foreword.

Special thanks also go to Mariana L. Schenone, senior economics student at the University of Miami, for her assistance in typing, research, and other duties necessary in preparation of a manuscript. Similar thanks go to Astrid Romero, a University of Miami journalism student, for her assistance.

Gratitude also goes to Cecile Gauert and Shawna Serig, also University of Miami journalism students, for their comments and research during preparation.

Thanks go to the 16 editors who contributed "Direct Quote" for this project. Appreciation also goes to those editors and writers whose excellent works are published here with their permission: Donna Barron, Dave Barry, Art Buchwald, Laurel Leff, Linda Marx, Tom Moroney, Joe Nick Patoski, Donald L. Pevsner, and Maryln Schwartz.

And similar thanks to the following professional groups, publications, and publishing companies for their permission to reprint material here: American Society of Journalists and Authors, Inc., *Atlanta* Magazine, *Boston* Magazine, *Columbia Missourian*, *Florida Trend*, *Fort Wayne News-Sentinel*, The Hearst Corp., *National Geographic Magazine*, *Popular Mechanics*, Scripps Howard News Service, Society of Professional Journalists, Southwest Media Corp., The New York Times Company, *Texas Monthly*, *The Atlanta Journal-Constitution*, *The Boston Globe*, *The Chicago Tribune*, *The Dallas Morning News*, *The Hartford Courant*, *The Miami Herald*, *The Miami News*, *The Orlando Sentinel*, *The Pittsburgh Press*, *The St. Louis Post-Dispatch*, and *USA Today*.

Finally, thanks to Michi The Cat. Her faithful companionship during the long hours of writing helped a great deal. While Michi probably cannot read, her editorial opinions—expressed by sitting on manuscript pages piled on the floor, by walking on the computer keyboard, and by sitting on my computer's monitor—kept things in a real world perspective.

Bruce Garrison

Foreword

If you want to be a writer, write. That's the advice of one of the ancient Greeks. If you want to be a good magazine or newspaper feature writer, first read this book. That's my advice. It's advice based on examining *Professional Feature Writing* and finding first one nugget and then another until I finally concluded that here's a gold mine of solid instruction on how to go about one of the most exacting—and exciting—crafts in journalism.

Still, as Bruce Garrison points out, this business of feature writing is no easy matter.

My experience in more than 20 years of newspaper work is that plenty of people can develop into competent hard-news reporters. Relatively few develop into first-class feature writers. Although hard-news writing sometimes requires the comprehension of complicated, difficult issues, it is mainly a process of collecting facts and quotes and organizing them in a logical fashion in grammatical, simple English. Top-drawer feature writing ordinarily involves much more. It, too, may require comprehension of difficult issues, and yet the writer must do more than collect facts and quotes. A good feature writer must grasp the emotional context of an event, issue, or personality. He or she must have an unusual sensitivity to other people, to their feelings, to what motivates them. The good feature writer will have a highly honed sense of humor, a sense of perspective honed just as highly—and, importantly, a feel for language. This writer will have an eye for the telling detail and unusual descriptive power. This writer will know how to evoke moods. A hard-news story can be good and still be a bare-bones thing. No good feature is without flesh on its bones.

We don't do enough feature writing in newspapers these days, not the brilliantly imaginative stuff, anyway. To be sure, you will see many stories that are soft instead of hard. Too often, these are flimsy attempts at feature writing, news stories with a few feature elements thrown in. A real *feature* is a story with subtlety, nuance, and impact, a story that aims at the sort of epiphanies you find in the best fiction, a story that escapes the dreadful inverted pyramid, that is truly creative in its construction and expression. Such stories are rare. Too few editors press hard enough for them, and too few writers discipline themselves sufficiently to produce them.

If I am right in this observation, I am right about something shameful and negligent and ultimately self-defeating for the wonderful world of newspapers.

It's my conviction that the newspaper industry is in trouble right now. Newspaper penetration of households has been declining, and rather drastically, for the past two decades. The reasons are many: the advent of television, more mobile lifestyles, reduced newsholes, and a tradition-bound refusal to adapt content to a changing society, for instance. But surely one reason—a reason to some extent related to others I have mentioned—is a failure to connect with people's lives. And an important way to do that, a way to have relevance in the lives of readers, is to produce good features. I am not saying we should abandon hard-news coverage; I would fight such a notion to the death. I am saying that we should cultivate the art of writing excellent features that tell more than any hard-news story can every tell because they are not so limited in purpose or style. Editors, who are no more inclined to perish than any other beast in the woods, are rediscovering this truth, I think. Their publications will continue carrying a great many hard-news stories, but they will also make sure there is an ample offering of features that explore and elucidate and convey something more than unembellished facts. As this happens, the accomplished feature writer will be much in demand.

In this book, Bruce Garrison very methodically, very clearly, demonstrates the science of an art. He shows how a verbally equipped, alert, and industrious journalist, one who is prepared to make sacrifices for the sake of perhaps the best profession there is, can master the feature story. He discusses finding ideas and researching. He reviews the different categories of feature writing. I discovered rules, practices, and ideas here that I had once known but had forgotten and that I had never known at all, as well as concisely presented reaffirmations of writing principles I have long held dear. Those who study this book will profit from it, and may well go on to rewarding careers that will help the great journalistic enterprise to thrive.

Jay Ambrose
Executive Editor,
Rocky Mountain News
Denver, Colorado

I

THE BASICS

1

Magazine and Newspaper Feature Writing in the 1990s

Do you want to be a feature writer? Did you have an interest in the subject and think you would pick up a book and see what feature writing was about? Did someone out there tell you that you could write, that you might have what it takes?

If you want to be a successful professional feature writer, then you have to be willing to sweat. You have to be willing to live with frustration. You have to make personal and professional sacrifices. You have to be willing to work long hours. You have to be willing to take little or no remuneration in the beginning. You have to have a strong desire to publish your writing. If you think you lack the motivation or potential to overcome these obstacles, forget it. Pick another subject to read about. If you are starting a class, find the drop–add line. Think about another career interest.

If you are still reading after all that, welcome to the world of feature writing for magazines and newspapers. You might just have what it takes to be a feature writer, so read further to see.

It is important to emphasize the difficulty of being a successful professional writer these days. Yet for those who do have the drive and talent to succeed, the rewards can be great—both personally and professionally. Your first byline can be highly satisfying. The euphoria you feel from this accomplishment at any level, from student newspaper to major magazine, is equalled by little else in professional writing. And beginners do have a chance at making it. With the right idea at the right time, you can become a published feature writer early in your career.

But as Myrick E. Land (1987), professor of journalism at the University of Nevada at Reno, has said, success in writing "requires intelligence, imagination, talent, and persistence" (p. 1). This book will give you the basic tools for writing feature stories for newspapers and magazines.

What motivates you to be a writer? If you can answer that question by the time you finish this book, you might have the foundation for becoming a professional feature writer.

WRITING NONFICTION AND NEWS

You write to pass along information to your readers. You write to tell them what you have learned. They learn. They are entertained. They are thrilled. They are saddened. People react to what you have to say in print. At the same time, you have a tremendous responsibility to be accurate, concise, and timely.

You also have to know how to express yourself. This basic communication skill is your starting point in feature writing. You have to have the interest and you have to have writing ability. At some point in your life, you began to think of yourself as a writing-oriented person. And you wound up with this book, opened to the first few pages of the first chapter, wondering if you can write features for money.

But knowing you have basic writing interest and ability is not enough, according to literary agent Scott Meredith (1987). "To have basic writing ability and no technical knowledge, and to try to earn a living as a writer, is equivalent to finding yourself suddenly endowed with a large amount of steel, lumber, and bricks and, without any knowledge of architecture or building, setting out to earn your living building and selling houses" (p. 3).

DEFINING FEATURE WRITING

Most persons familiar with nonfiction writing for the mass media think of the conventional "straight news" or "hard news" topics and approaches—police and courts, sports, local government, or business—written to give the who, what, when, where, why, and how. These stories emphasize the important persons, the activities, current events, local and regional orientation, explanation of importance and nature of the event.

Feature stories go beyond this level. Feature writers can employ some "license" or flexibility and emphasize the unconventional or the different. Feature writers look for the story about someone who is not necessarily a newsmaker. Instead the story is about something or someone offbeat and entertaining. Feature stories are emotional, and they involve readers. They demand reader reaction because these articles can be serious or light, timely or timeless, funny or sad, joyful or joyless. These articles tell us much about the human condition. All you have to do is pick up today's newspaper or your favorite magazine and see the variety of subjects and approaches that are a part of feature article writing.

One professional writer defines feature writing as *creative, subjective* article writing that is designed to *inform* and *entertain* readers. Daniel Williamson's (1975) interpretation emphasizes the four words that have been italicized. These points help to show features are different from "straight" news or information writing.

First, features do contain more creative energy. Writers and editors take a bit more freedom in their writing style or approaches, selection of sources, and packaging of articles. Second, these articles are often less objective than conventional news writing, offering a particular point of view or the author's personal impressions, perceptions, and opinions (in addition to those of sources). Third, the articles remain informative even if they are more creative and are personalized by the writer. The level of reader utility of a story often determines its success with readers. Fourth, the article must entertain the reader while accomplishing all three other goals. The article makes readers happy they chose to spend five minutes or even an hour reading the article instead of doing some other activity. Williamson notes one other characteristic: a feature is *less perishable* than conventional nonfiction or news writing. Stories often are held for appropriate seasons or for slow news periods at newspapers. And simply because of their less frequent publication schedules, magazines often hold stories for considerable lengths of time prior to publication.

JAMES J. KILPATRICK ON THE ART OF WRITING

[T]he crafts of writing and carpentry are deceptively simple. The carpenter has to begin with a plan; the writer must begin with a thought. There must be at least the germ of an idea. Before the first board is nailed to the second board, or the first word connected to the second word, there has to be some clear notion of where we expect to be when we have finished nailing or writing.

—Red Smith lecture in Journalism, University of Notre Dame, 1985 (from Kilpatrick, 1985, p. 2).

Other professionals compare feature writing to writing fiction such as short stories. The major difference, of course, is that feature writers deal with reality. Benton Rain Patterson (1986), who has written for newspapers and magazines across the United States, says:

A feature writer deliberately puts people (characters) into what he writes. He describes them and shows them (description) doing and saying (action, expressed through narrative and quotes) whatever it is that makes the characters worth writing—and reading—about. When he puts those elements into his piece, a writer is *ipso facto* featurizing his subject, handling his material and writing his piece as a feature (p. 21).

Patterson's three basic rules for features are straight forward:

1. Put people into the story.
2. Tell a story.
3. Let the reader see and hear for himself or herself.

Just about all feature stories have these elements in common and often in large quantity. Good features use people in the story, quoted often about what they do that is so interesting.

Feature stories are *not* written like meeting minutes. Features are *not* dreary research reports. They are *not* lifeless summaries of big events. They *are* often factual short stories written in *active voice*. They have a plot. There is a story line. There are characters. There is a beginning, a middle, and an end. Many writers will say that feature articles fall somewhere between news writing and short stories.

You will see the major types of magazine and newspaper feature articles as you read further. You can focus on such story forms as color stories that emphasize descriptive writing, human interest stories, personality sketches and profiles, seasonal feature stories, reviews and critical feature writing, aftermath and follow-up feature stories, the feature series, travel article writing, personal experience stories, how-to-do-it articles, humor writing, and technical and specialized features.

There will be discussion of the tools you need as a feature writer. You will learn how to find a good feature idea and how to mold it into a story, how to research story ideas, how to write and edit feature articles, and how to successfully free-lance feature articles for publication. You will also learn professional and ethical standards of professional feature writers.

You will see these types of stories applied in their major forms: weekly and daily newspapers and general and specialized magazines. The writing strategies and information-gathering approaches for feature writing will be discussed in broad terms, but often with particular application to the print media.

NEWSPAPERS AND MAGAZINES TODAY

There were 1,645 morning and evening daily newspapers with an average circulation of 38,192 copies in the United States in 1987. There were 7,498 weekly newspapers with an average circulation of 6,894 copies in 1987, including paid and free circulation newspapers. There are many more magazines, a total of about 22,000 in the late 1980s. However, just 9,000 of these are sold to the general public, with the others designated for restricted trade or company markets for employees or customers. About 20% of all magazines are weekly, 6% are published twice a month, 42% appear once a month, 11% are issued each two months, and 12% are quarterlies.

For writers, the newspapers and magazines of the 1990s depend more and more on technology. Because of computers, fax machines, and other hardware, you are able to gather information in ways impossible for a generation before you. You are able to work on machines that make preparation of manuscripts much easier than ever before.

Publications are much more sophisticated in production techniques. This means feature writers on deadline can produce stories faster and closer to printing deadlines than ever before and supplement the usual news coverage of an event, whether it be for a daily newspaper or a weekly news magazine.

Trends in group ownership of newspapers and magazines have changed the nature of the business over the past two decades. The largest groups, such as Gannett and Knight-Ridder, have purchased major dailies. Other companies have gathered up available small dailies and weeklies. Magazines have experienced the same phenomenon. Companies have bought up independently owned magazines to form new or larger groups.

The effect has been less independent management of publications. At times, staff positions have been eliminated to create more profitable operating costs. It has meant a harder time to make a living for feature writers in some markets and some specializations. It has also meant greater resources and new ideas. It has meant some publications near failure got a second chance. And this has helped writers.

Newspapers are changing today. They are using feature material in larger quantities. Because of this, they seek better quality from writers to keep the demand for their editions high. Reacting to television and other electronic media vying for growing entertainment and leisure time of Americans, newspapers are offering material such as longer, in-depth profiles or analyses once found only in magazines. Stanford University Professor William Rivers and free-lance writer-editor Alison Work call this phenomenon the "magazining of newspapers" (1986, p. 4). Recently, some newspaper feature sections have shown interest in shorter, tightly written pieces with the same "television story" flair of *USA Today*.

Magazines have changed as well in the past three decades. Television, film, and other influences changed them in the 1960s and 1970s. General interest consumer magazines closed when operations costs became greater than circulation and advertising revenues. More specialized magazines evolved in the 1960s and 1970s to replace the general interest publication. And, suddenly, readers interested in health and medicine did not have to depend on news magazines or the coffee-table magazines of another era. They instead subscribed to *Prevention* or other similar magazines.

City and regional magazines became the rage of the 1960s and remain significant today in metropolitan areas. Entertainment and personality–celebrity publications were created and have grown.

John Mack Carter, editor-in-chief of *Good Housekeeping* and director of New Magazine Development for Hearst Corp., says the magazine industry is strong today. "And, if my thesis proves correct, we will be doing even better in the future" (1986, p. 7). Carter points to a decline in television viewing because of dissatisfaction with network television and cable television programming, and use of VCRs and personal computers.

Sandra Kresch, director of Strategic Planning for Time Inc., agrees that print media are strong and vital. "All of the technological and social change of the last few decades has had very little effect on the magazine industry in recent years. Print is healthy and vital—and shows every sign of continuing to be so in the future" (Kresch, 1986, p. 14). Kresch notes that magazines have experienced circulation growth and healthy advertising since 1979.

"Both magazines and newspapers are responding to external forces that are beyond their control. Yet they are surviving through a long process of adaptation that is changing both their appearance and content," Rivers and Work (1986) observed.

NATURE OF NEWSPAPER FEATURE WRITING

What makes a newspaper feature different from a magazine feature? Newspaper features are used throughout the newspaper, but some sections use features more often and very differently from others.

The front section, generally containing the spot news of the day from state, national, and international sources, will use features for balance. Features in these sections offer insight into the day's newsmakers and major events. Features are used as "sidebars" to supplement straight news reporting. For example, a story about a truck–van traffic accident that killed nine people might be boosted by a feature sidebar focusing on the one surviving child. The announcement of a nomination of a Supreme Court justice will often be supplemented by a feature profile of the career of the person seeking the position.

The local section of most daily newspapers will often run features on unusual individuals or events of community interest. Certainly local sidebar features are also used as described earlier. However, newspapers that have segmented their local news coverage into neighborhood sections will frequently fill these sections with features about people, school, religion, arts and crafts, parks and recreation, and small businesses.

In lifestyle and living sections, editors will devote most of the day's space to a wide variety of feature material. These stories focus on home how-to-do-it subjects, consumer and shopping ideas, profiles, health and medicine suggestions, child-care news, gardening, cooking and food ideas, and even more.

In some newspapers, entertainment news is part of lifestyle coverage, but this category of news creates a different set of feature needs for newspapers. Writers specializing in entertainment provide features on individuals, reviews of their performances, and insight into their creative activities.

Sports sections provide feature content to break the routine of daily results stories. Regular readers look for features such as profiles on coaches and players, descriptions of facilities, and depth analysis of outstanding strategies and performances. Sports features today are less focused on professionals and outstanding amateurs than they were a decade ago. Editors have found that readers want to read features about participation sports, such as jogging and swimming, in addition to articles on the National Football League or Major League Baseball. Editors have also learned that readers would like increased feature coverage of "minor" sports such as soccer, giving writers more opportunities and broader scope for features than in past decades.

Business sections have experienced growth in many daily newspapers in recent years. Even newspapers that do not have separate business sections, such as special tabloids on Mondays, still devote considerable space to business news and features today. For writers interested in business, this is an upbeat and opportune time for you. These section editors demand regular features describing new companies, new products, consumerism, successful executives, and trends in the marketplace.

Feature material occasionally is found on the opinion or editorial pages, also. Much of the time, it is in the form of a column, but the same general principles of feature writing have been used to write the feature column. These creative columnists use satire for humor, or write a profile of an individual, or give how-to-do-it advice on a subject.

Even newspapers have outlets for magazine-style writing. The Sunday magazine supplements of major newspapers depend a great deal on solid feature essay writing of traditional magazine length each week to build regular readership. Feature subjects are wide-ranging in nature. From humor columns to portraits of individuals to accounts of historical events to chronologies of conflicts, these articles are the foundations of Sunday magazines. Sunday magazines also include shorter, departmentalized features such as listings of events, reviews of new restaurants, and summaries of new products on the market.

Newspaper magazines are even running more feature *fiction* than they once did. Jay Schaefer (1987), founder and editor of Fiction Network in San Francisco, says fiction in newspapers is not a new idea. What is different now, he says, is that in the late 1980s fiction is making a comeback. Most magazine feature-fiction contains a local setting or local angle such as a local author, Schaefer maintains, and this leads to a strong reader response.

Newspaper features are usually much shorter in length than magazine features, but this tendency does not hold as firmly as it once did. It is not unusual to find a 5,000-word feature story in a newspaper today. And, of course, magazines often run short feature items, also. But the majority of newspaper features are short and to the point—500 to 1,000 words. Space does not often provide the chance for depth and development of "characters" in the article. Frequency of publication does, however, provide the opportunity for newspaper features to be more timely than magazines features.

Newspapers depend less on outside material than do magazines, as you will see in later chapters. Because most newspapers have staffs of writers and reporters available, most sections do not buy much free-lance material. Sunday travel sections or pages, however, are an exception, because very few newspapers employ more full-time travel writers other than a travel editor.

And, certainly, newspaper feature articles are produced in a shorter deadline framework. There are not too many newspaper feature writers who have not had to research, write, and turn in a complete feature within a few hours. Although this also occurs in magazine feature writing, it is not as likely to happen with monthly or weekly deadlines.

NATURE OF MAGAZINE FEATURE WRITING

Magazine features are quite different from newspaper features in a number of ways. First, these articles are often written free-lance by nonstaff members of a magazine. Many writers are attracted to the freedom of free-lance writing and are able to make good supplemental income as free-lance writers. However, it is worth repeating: It is quite difficult to make a substantial career and a living from free-lance writing. But many individuals do well selling their work to magazines while working another career both in and out of the mass media. You will learn much more about free-lance writing in the final chapter of this book.

There are many opportunities for magazine-oriented, nonfiction writers. You can select the subject, the market, and the magazine you wish to write for. You can specialize if you desire to do so, or you can be a generalist who writes on whatever subject is appealing for whatever reasons. You can certainly set your own work schedule for writing and researching articles. A staff writer for a newspaper or a magazine staffer cannot enjoy this luxury most of the time. You can set up an office at home or elsewhere, but you are responsible for whatever costs you incur—the expenses for such things as equipment, furniture, and supplies have to come out of your writer's fees. And, it follows, you are able to live wherever you want as an independent writer.

You do have a chance as an unknown writer to be published by a successful major magazine. But you have to work hard on good ideas at the right time.

Magazine feature writing is a field with tremendous opportunity. With hundreds of major magazines and thousands more of specialized business publications, you can do much as a magazine feature writer—if you have the drive.

Magazines, like newspapers, have their own styles or personalities. Part of this is the look, or graphics, of the magazine, but the other major part is the *writing* style. Magazine writing generally is in essay form with longer, more fully developed paragraphs. Usage is more formalized, also. This subject will get more attention in later chapters.

You will also find that magazine writing tends to be more descriptive and detailed than newspaper writing, but this is partly due to the additional space given to major features in magazines. And as noted earlier, these articles are a bit more subjective because writers offer their perspectives on the subject.

Just remember that, regardless of the writing approach and topic, you will find the magazine industry to be quite different from what it once was. Individuals beginning careers as magazine writers in the 1940s and 1950s found general-interest magazines flourishing. But because of television and other mass media influences on society, leisure time demands are different. To meet this challenge, magazines began to specialize. Your writing challenge will be to handle specialized subjects with the authority of experts. This, you will find, is still another reason magazine feature writing differs so much from newspaper feature writing.

THE JOB OF THE NEWSPAPER FEATURE WRITER

Newspaper feature writers also come in two varieties. The most common is the staff writer, an individual who works full time or steady part time for a single publication. Free-lance newspaper feature writers often work for local newspapers, but most newspapers do not use their work as often as they use staff-written feature material.

Most newspaper staff members work regular schedules. Most work 40 hours, but some who work on a salary find their schedule and demands of the job require more than the conventional week. The work of newspaper feature writers is not limited to a 9-to-5, Monday through Friday schedule. Nor is the work limited to "scheduled" times. Most top newspaper feature writers, even on a regular work schedule, find they never really stop working even when off duty. If you want to succeed, you must take advantage of the opportunity whenever a good article prospect presents itself.

Whether you work general assignment or a beat, the intense nature of newspaper feature writing dictates that you be prepared at all times. With daily, two or three times a week, or even weekly deadlines, much feature production is expected. You must have an endless stream of strong ideas to develop into stories. You cannot "switch off" your alertness as a feature writer.

There is challenge and reward working in this environment. The challenge of the newspaper feature writer is to know a great deal about a wide range of subjects in a given community. For specialists on beats at newspapers, the challenge is to know a great deal about a restricted range of subjects, but you carry the burden of responsibility for your entire publication.

As a newspaper writer, you will take advantage of public familiarity with your newspaper. Few communities have more than one newspaper today. If you work for that newspaper or your community weekly, readers and sources will recognize it immediately. This means you will have stories come to you, and you might find a higher level of cooperation from sources.

You will eventually also enjoy the advantage of being known by your readers. Your name will become known to the community you serve as a feature writer. If you are good, this can become a major asset in your work as a feature writer. If you are not professional in your work, it becomes the opposite—a liability.

THE JOB OF THE MAGAZINE FEATURE WRITER

Magazine feature writers are most often free-lance writers. Most magazines maintain very small full-time staffs responsible for editing and production, rather than original writing and reporting. Therefore, these publications depend a great deal on free-lance writers to submit their work as well as on solicited work by known free-lance writers.

The traditional staff feature-writer position at a magazine will vary, depending on the type of magazine. At a news magazine, for example, the difference between writers and reporters remains great. The functions of writer and information-gatherer differ widely for large news organizations such as *Time* or *Newsweek*. Although more and more reporter-originated material is being published, reporters in bureaus around the world still produce information, much of it in memo form, for writers in the main offices in New York to organize and perfect through re-writing.

At other types of magazines, the work of reporter and writer is less specialized. Most staffers, especially those at specialized consumer magazines, write *and* report. At some smaller magazines, writers may also double as editors to help handle material that comes from experts and free-lance writers.

The routines at magazines, although deadlines are less frequent, are still similar to those at newspapers for editors and staff writers. The pressure as deadline approaches is intense. Expectations are high. Performance can be no less than top level. Hours are often not within the standard Monday through Friday, 9-to-5 week that beginners might expect from the corporate publishing world.

Because some magazines today are organized into groups under single ownership, often with single publishers and editors, there could be a growing emphasis on staff writers and shrinking emphasis on free-lancers. In fact, some publications have completely eliminated the need for free-lancers by hiring full-time staffs of writers, correspondents, editors, and others with bureaus around the world or across the country. McGraw-Hill's *BusinessWeek* illustrates this point.

In fact, Time Inc.'s Sandra Kresch (1986) says this trend toward concentration of ownership will continue as competition within the industry increases and costs of launching a large magazine escalate. She also sees more specialized publications focusing on individual topics for consumers. "If consumers are looking for more specificity in the information available to them, in the next fifty years the industry may change significantly, resulting in an environment where a few, large, general interest magazines are supplemented by thousands of small ones focused on the needs of well-defined market segments" (p. 18).

If you do not become a magazine staff writer, your life as a writer for a magazine will be different. You are your own boss until you commit to work for a publication on an assignment. Your work will require that you interact with many editors throughout a year. And you will likely be an employee of several bosses at one time.

Small magazines offer the best chance for regular work for beginning feature writers. It is also a different working environment. Writers are less specialized within the scope of the magazine and are asked to produce a greater variety of writing, reporting, and editing/production work. Staffs may be closer at smaller publications because of the need to interact more often. Writers and editors work together more frequently and often exchange duties. Writers become editors. Editors become writers. Publishers become editors and writers. A beginner can learn a variety of feature writing tasks and skills.

THE MARKET TODAY FOR WRITERS

The market for feature article writers today offers many opportunities for good free-lancers. Magazines are increasing in number and so are the markets for your work. Though there are fewer dailies than in years past, newspapers emphasize their feature material even more to compete as an information and entertainment source with other soft news sources such as television, radio, and magazines.

Although you might not think much about it, smaller newspapers are the best chance for a beginning writer to find markets for feature articles. Small dailies that do not have large staffs are more often responsive to queries or completed manuscripts for timely features. Weekly newspapers, with even smaller staffs, often seek assistance when it does not come to the editor. It is likely that your own journalism school receives telephone calls from time to time from weekly editors seeking part-time or free-lance help in covering their neighborhood or community.

Magazines follow the same model of opportunity for writers. Although most magazines seek good writers outside their staffs, many small and specialized publications need quality free-lance assistance year-round. This demands that you know about what you write for a specialized magazine, and you can still become a valuable part of a publication if you do.

A beginning feature writer need only look at the latest edition of the *Editor & Publisher International Yearbook* to find out which newspapers are published in the region or area. Similarly, the annual edition of *Writer's Market* each fall gives a complete look at the magazine market that buys free-lance feature work.

And, of course, it goes without lengthy explanation that you can simply pull out the local telephone directory Yellow Pages, especially if you reside in a metropolitan area, to see which publishers maintain offices in your community. In Chicago, for example, a recent directory listed over four pages of publishers, including almost three pages of periodical publishers. Even in Lexington, Kentucky, a market of just a quarter-million residents, there were sixteen periodical publishers listed in a recent directory.

Various specialized subjects have increased visibility in the past decade. The growing number of separate and larger business sections in newspapers and business magazines means new and more writing opportunities as well. As the Business Press Educational Foundation says, today's business stories focus on supercomputers, genetic engineering, manufacturing in space, and other unlikely business topics because these activities are financed by businesses and are the work of privately funded laboratories of corporations, not the federal, state, or local governments. "The results [of these stories in the business press], moreover, promise to have major impact on existing industries and, perhaps, bring entire new industries into existence. It explains why these developments are getting even more diligent attention from the business/industry press than from the mass media" (p. 1), the foundation has stated. You will find there are more than 3,000 business publications in the United States alone, presenting a growing market for writers.

There are other examples. You could make many points about the growth in sports publications, computer publications, and even a rebirth of some general-interest publications such as *Life* in the past decade. These changes, of course, mean better opportunities for feature writers at present and in the future. And for the beginning feature writer, these publications are probably more accessible than established consumer magazines or daily newspapers.

WAYS TO BROADEN NEWSPAPER FEATURES

There are many excellent approaches to feature writing today that you will discover. Certain specific features and subjects that are getting inadequate attention or no attention might draw greater readership. A recent study by the Changing Newspapers Committee of the Associated Press Managing Editors, chaired by *Dallas Morning News* editor Ralph Langer, suggests 20 such ideas. The list, compiled by committee member Debra Austin of the *Santa Monica, California, Outlook*, named these items:

1. Add more television grids (listings) about local area programming such as cable television programs.
2. Add fitness coverage as a regular weekly feature or consider a fitness section.

3. Increase home video features as part of consumer and entertainment feature packages.
4. Consider additional science, technical/medical features on a regular basis.
5. Get more reader involvement in science and technical stories such as why hair turns grey or how freckles are formed.
6. Increase use of calendars and lists of events and community projects.
7. Strengthen travel sections by adding consumer articles on problems encountered while traveling.
8. Review the content of comics pages with regularity.
9. Add or expand outdoors and recreation coverage.
10. Expand feature content aimed at young adults.
11. Add more music and entertainment coverage that is youth oriented.
12. Start a weekly page on the electronic home that focuses on computers, stereo systems, video equipment, and so on.
13. Begin regular use of *neighborhood* features.
14. Produce a regular "Student Express" page or section that is written and edited by area school students.
15. Use more people and entertainment short items in combination with advice columns and humor in a special page or portion of a page.
16. Write more *local* features about food, nutrition, and diet.
17. List students who graduate and provide more features on general graduation events.
18. Assign regular school features.
19. Establish a regular section to honor local individuals in features.
20. Vary feature columns to explore new topics of current local interest such as retirement, investments, parenting, and social security.

A CAREER AS A FEATURE WRITER FOR YOU?

Jack Hunter, who is a free-lance writer and writing coach of the Jacksonville *Florida Times-Union* and *St. Augustine Record,* says good writing is a combination of good journalism, good business, and art. And, at the same time, he says it is good for you. This motivation to excel, combined with the satisfaction excellence can generate, may help you decide if you are destined for a career in feature writing (Hunter, 1983).

Ask the question many editors have asked over the years: Do you have what it takes to be a writer? It will not be glamorous or easy. *Writer's Digest* columnist Art Spikol (1986) has rated the characteristics of good writers and polled editors for their priorities for favorite writers. Take his test of "writeability" by ranking from 1 to 11 (with 1 being most important) the following items:

_____ Ability to work with others

_____ Appearance

_____ Integrity

_____ Love of writing

_____ Professionalism

_____ Quality of writing

_____ Self-assuredness

_____ Self-motivation

_____ Talent

_____ Writing style

_____ Vocabulary, grammar, and so on

Spikol's priorities are a bit different from the list created by asking several dozen editors of nationally distributed magazines. Here's what he found:

Editors		Spikol
1	Quality of writing	2
2	Writing style	4
3	Professionalism	1
4	Talent	6
5	Integrity	3
6	Vocabulary, grammar, and so on	10
7	Self-motivation	7
8	Ability to work with others	8
9	Self-assuredness	9
10	Love of writing	5
11	Appearance	11

How did your ranking compare to those of the professionals? If you were similar in your strengths to the priorities of these professionals, you might just have the characteristics and attitudes needed to succeed as a professional writer. If you don't, perhaps you should reassess your career direction or at least ask why there are big differences in your personal list and the editors'. As Spikol concluded, "If you're not delivering the most important parts of it [the list], you're probably not selling" (1986, p. 22).

Free-lance writers Clay Schoenfeld and Karen Diegmueller reduce the list of characteristics of good feature writers to four main categories: curiosity, integrity, ability, and confidence.

Successful newspaper and magazine feature article writers have a full tool chest ready to use.

What tools do they have? Take a look:

1. Writing ability.
2. Curiosity.
3. Attention to detail.
4. Listening skills.
5. Responsibility.
6. Observational skills.
7. Research ability.
8. Confidence.

Schoenfeld and Diegmueller (1982) have composed another self-analysis of writing potential. Answer these questions as honestly as possible for another indicator of whether you have what it takes to write features:

1. *Do you have talent?* This means an urge to write that creates a capacity to produce good writing.
2. *Do you really want to write?* Can you accept failure as a writer? Success requires a devotion to long hours of hard labor.
3. *Will you work hard yet imaginatively at writing for your readers?* This means concentration on hitting the reader target every time. Do you know your readers?
4. *Can you take advice?* Rejection and evaluation of work should help you improve what you do.
5. *Will you rest on initial laurels?* A one-shot writer will not get far. You cannot expect a publication or sale because the last article was published or bought.
6. *Will you always write your very best?* Writing your best for all publications is required.
7. *Do you start with a knack for narrating interesting experiences, telling colorful stories, or stating clear-cut opinions?* You should say yes. You must be able to document these stories and accurately. Readers must react positively.
8. *Do you start with keen powers of observation, analysis, and reporting?* You must learn how to enliven your facts and get reader identification with what you are writing (Schoenfeld & Diegmueller, 1982, pp. 13–14).

Barrie J. Atkin, director of Corporate Planning for Rodale Press, says magazines attract people who are like the publications they produce. "[Magazine publishing] attracts dynamic, lively people—idea-oriented people who want to present fresh concepts, new insights and exciting information to the public" (1986, p. 29), Atkin says. So why do magazine publishing people select their careers? Atkin lists many reasons: "The excitement of working on an ever-changing product; the pleasure of being around talented and articulate people; the psychological satisfaction of being associated with an idea leader" (pp. 29–30).

Whatever the qualifications necessary and the motivations for the choice, you are now more conscious of your own starting point for a career in professional feature writing. Some of you will start closer to the goal than others. Some will have to work harder. Some will have to invest more to succeed.

As you move on, you will find many useful ideas in the following chapters. Here's a brief look at what's in store if you read on:

Chapter 2 focuses on finding a good story idea. Chapter 3 offers approaches you need for research for idea development into a story.

After you generate and research an idea, Chapter 4 will equip you with proper writing and editing tools when you are ready to write the story.

The next 11 chapters take close-up looks at specialized feature writing approaches. Chapter 5 starts the odyssey with descriptive writing and color stories. Chapter 6 emphasizes people with the human interest story. Chapter 7 looks further at people by describing personality sketches and profiles. Chapter 8 will tell the secrets for success in seasonal feature writing. Chapter 9, venturing into subjective writing in any depth for the first time in the book, should strengthen your understanding of reviewing and critical writing.

Chapter 10 looks at a specialized type of feature used to enhance news coverage: aftermath stories, follow-up stories, and series approaches to subjects.

You will get a thorough understanding of travel writing from chapter 11. Chapter 12 focuses on personal experience stories from the perspective of the writer and from the source through the writer.

Chapter 13 outlines the steps to successful service features such as how-to-do-it articles and listings. You will find humor the central focus of chapter 14 and a review of technical and specialized writing in chapter 15.

And to conclude, chapter 16 tells you the ins-and-outs of free-lance writing.

The book is peppered with examples to illustrate points about good writing and information gathering. Both future newspaper feature writers and magazine feature writers are used to show the similarities and distinctions of the two approaches of professional feature writing.

Welcome!

Professional's Point of View

By Lucille S. deView
Orange County Register

The feature writer is like the dancer grounded in ballet who can switch to tap, jazz, or modern dance—and enjoy performing all of them.

The grounding comes from solid reporting skills honed through writing obituaries, doing the police beat, covering sports, any and all tasks that bear down hard on the who, what, where, when, and why.

The joy comes from leaping beyond these vaunted five w's, to write with style and grace. The skilled feature writer borrows techniques from literary masters to infuse stories with a lyrical quality.

Within a short span of time, the feature writer may twirl from a scientific breakthrough to the newest discovery in fashions; from explaining the stock market to a how-to piece on cultivating roses.

The rewards are great, especially for the writer open to new ideas but blessed with common sense. Some suggestions:

• Do not mistake celebrity or education as the only sources of intelligent discussion, wit, or sagacity. People whose occupations are humble and names unknown may provide the deepest insights and most compelling quotes.

Factory workers go to the symphony; a housemaid becomes an opera star; stevedores publish poetry; homemakers become bank presidents, and more.

• Be unbiased in your writing. Sexism and racism often take subtle forms and ethnic stereotypes persist unless we are careful to avoid them. Since a majority of women are in the workplace, a writer's vocabulary must keep pace. Use the word "executives," not "businessmen"; "firefighters" instead of "firemen"; and do not write "woman doctor," just say "doctor."

Don't make racial exceptions. If you say "the articulate black professor," you imply most are inarticulate. Don't indicate race unless it is relevant to the story. Why mention "the Hispanic bookkeeper" when you would not say "the German bookkeeper"?

Use the word disabled, not handicapped. People "use" wheelchairs; they are not "confined" to wheelchairs. Use appropriate terminology for specific disabilities. Is the person "hearing impaired" or "deaf"? For guidelines, write the Media Project, Research and Training Center on Independent Living, BCR/3111 Haworth, University of Kansas, Lawrence, KS 66045.

In general, don't call older people senior citizens; they prefer being called older persons. When so many are active and healthy, it is not appropriate to say a person is "80 (or 90, or more) and still going strong."

Don't portray younger people as always troubled. See the individual, not the group.

• Practice problem-solving journalism. Explaining the dimensions of a dilemma is helpful to your readers; finding an answer is curative. Seek the solution, test it, pass it along if it has merit.

• Do interviews in person, not on the telephone. Not seeing the person's raised eyebrows or scowl is a risk—and a lost opportunity for colorful writing.

• Make each assignment a learning experience. See it as an opportunity to enrich your writing and your life. (deView, personal communication, 1988)

* * *

Lucille S. deView is Writing Coach for the *Orange County Register* in Santa Ana, California. She has been writing coach and columnist for *Florida Today* and a free-lance poet and short story writer. She has also conducted a writing program for the *Christian Science Monitor* and she was a staff writer for the *Detroit News*.

2

Finding a Good Feature Article Idea

Do you notice things around you? When you drive to work or to school do you take the little extra effort to notice people or places or what is happening on that routine trip?

Do you take time to look around when you go some place new? What do you see? Is it interesting to you? Wouldn't it be interesting to others? It might be a good feature article idea.

Have you met anyone new today? What does the person do for a living? Has your regular network of friends and acquaintances brought anything unique or different into your life in the past week?

What did you do out of the ordinary this week? Was it fun? Significant? Did you learn anything from the experience?

Chances are high that any of these questions, if answered in the affirmative, might lead you to a good feature story. Finding story ideas can be easy. Some subjects practically announce their potential as a story to an alert writer. Others need the experienced eye and ear of a feature writer to work them into readable and salable articles.

If you are like most people, you have to be willing to get out of your ordinary habits and routines to find good feature stories.

You have to notice details of things around you. If you drive the same road to work or school everyday, try to vary the route. Look at the scenery with an eye for story possibilities. For example, if you drive past the same house every day, look in the driveway. The old cars that the owner of the house is working on might be more than they seem to be. Is there a chance this person restores valuable older cars? Isn't this a story prospect? Why not stop and ask a few questions?

If you do go somewhere new, think about what possibilities for stories exist even before you leave home. If you like the destination, why? Would others like it also? If that new boutique has unusual designs, tell others about it in a story.

Meeting someone new and different can be exciting for all of us. But think about the new acquaintance from another point of view. Is this person worthy of a story? What makes him or her interesting? Perhaps the person is in town for just a few days and really lives in a foreign country—perhaps a relatively unknown small country like Belize in Central America. Wouldn't this be a chance to write about the person, the country, and all the unusual aspects of life in a country that many Americans do not know much about?

And if you did something unusual, even something as simple as taking the bus to work or school instead of driving, this might make a good story. Most Americans drive to and from work and school. But using mass transportation might just make a good story if you select the right angle. Like what? *The Milwaukee Journal*'s Anne Curley (1977) once wrote about riding the bus for a week to show people in Milwaukee can get from point A to point B without too much difficulty without a car. Or perhaps a story on bus drivers would be a winner if your driver shows some personality and particular helpfulness to riders. In other words, let your imagination and your creativity take off when new situations present themselves. A story might result from it!

This chapter gives you some basic rules and some professional tips to help you generate story ideas for features for both newspapers and magazines. In fact, as you will see, the process is much the same for both types of publications.

IDENTIFYING FEATURE STORY MATERIAL

Just about everything around you is possible feature material. Use your senses. Look around. Your job is to take these undeveloped ideas and turn them into something interesting for readers.

Writer and professor Daniel Williamson (1975) says finding a feature story is easy. "A great advantage in being a reporter is that you have a 'license' to find out about all those things you've always been curious about" (p. 70), he says. The key here is *curiosity*. Once you notice things, once you meet someone, once you discover something interesting to you, let your journalistic curiosity take over. Satisfy your inquisitiveness by finding out about the subject. How? If you always wanted to learn about sailing, go to interview a local sailor or take lessons at a nearby lake. Or go to a nearby sailing club meeting.

Finding the right story idea is also dependent on the publication you will write the story for. You need to know what the publication publishes and rejects.

This is more easily done if you work for the publication, but it can be relatively easy by taking time to research the publication and its market if you free-lance.

You also need to know the basic characteristics of features. What are they? Traditionally, good features have eight basic elements, according to authors Clay Schoenfeld and Karen Diegmueller (1982). Those elements are:

1. *Appeal to people.* The story has to meet a need of the reader.
2. *Facts.* A feature that works will contain certain information, or facts, about that subject that will be beneficial to readers in some way.
3. *Personalities.* Facts are enhanced with personality. A story that can offer some unusual person or personality with facts and appeal will be much stronger.
4. *Angle.* The right "slant" or theme makes the subject tie together better.
5. *Action.* Can you make the story come alive? It will if you have some activity in the story. It is relatively simple—people should do something in your story.
6. *Uniqueness and universality.* The topic should be different and should have broad appeal at the same time.
7. *Significance.* Timeliness, proximity, prominence, and relevance create significance in a story.
8. *Energy increment.* The story should stir your readers just as the idea stirred you to write the story. You should show your enthusiasm and sincerity.

Finally let's think about the necessity that all feature ideas remain fresh. Just like bread, a feature idea has a certain shelf life and it is up to you as a writer to make certain the idea is developed and published in story form while it is still fresh. The best idea won't work with editors or with readers if it is stale.

STEPS TO IDEA SUCCESS

Free-lance writer Lorene Hanley Duquin (1987) has a four-step plan of attack for shaping story ideas before actually writing the article. She says these four steps require "simple brainstorming" by asking yourself the questions and writing down the answers. "It's that information that I mold and shape into a proposal that captures an editor's interest and imagination" (p. 38). Her four steps:

1. *Capture the idea.* Build an idea file, since writers cannot always use ideas when they come along. You can do this with notebooks, file cards, and even your word processor. At times, ideas have to wait until a market prospect presents itself too.

2. *Develop the idea.* Do some research to develop that idea into a proposal. Not all ideas are easy to develop, of course, so be prepared to do some work. Think about the idea. Is it too broad or too narrow? Does it have universal appeal? There will be more on this later in this chapter.

3. *Tailor the idea.* Shaping the idea to the readers you wish to reach is very important to a successful feature story. Ask yourself questions: What readers will be interested in your article? What has already been done on the subject? What publication will want to publish the article?

4. *Test the idea.* You will also read more about this later in the chapter. Duquin says you should be able to answer these questions: Do you really want to write the article? Are you capable of doing the article? How much will the article cost you (in money and time)? What else can you do with the material if an editor does not want it? Are there markets for reprints? Can you do spin-off articles?

Wisconsin author Marshall Cook (1986) suggests seven steps to make an idea work:

1. *Feed the mind.* Try new experiences. Relive old ones through journals and diaries. Read extensively. Talk to people. Do stimulating things.

2. *Nurture the idea.* Ideas come with a flash of lightning or with the gradual speed of a sunrise. Be ready for an idea to come to you and give it your attention by examining it from all angles.

3. *Ignore the idea.* After pampering the idea, forget about it for a while. This incubation period helps divert you from pressure of creation on demand. Decide to come back to the idea at an appointed date and time a few days later.

4. *Welcome the idea back.* When you return to the idea at the appointed hour, be fresh and alert. Be at your most productive period of the day. Write in your regular, yet special, writing place. Be comfortable.

5. *Create!* Concentrate on your idea, organize, and get going. Let the ideas flow and worry about style and clarity later. Get something on paper now.

6. *Sustain the flow.* Regular writing momentum makes a big difference to the work on your idea here. Developing your idea into an article will depend on continuation of the work.

7. *Revise.* This involves polishing the original draft into a final product. There will be more on this in chapter 4.

LOOKING AT THE WORLD AROUND YOU

You can do stories on an endless list of topics. Start by thinking about your own personal experiences. You might not realize it, but you are an expert on subjects and can write about them. Do you like to jog? If you do, you know much more about jogging than those who don't jog. You're experienced shopping for running clothes, conditioning, selection of foods, and the choice of best places to run. Another example of this personal approach comes from Joseph M. Queenan (1987), a free-lance writer in New York state. He used the painful experiences of growing up with an alcoholic father to produce an emotional personal experience piece for *Newsweek*. Like Queenan, you have to take advantage of your experiences—good or bad—and use them as a base to start your work.

Professional and personal contacts can be useful, too. Do you belong to a club or business group? Sometimes these organizations provide numerous professional and personal contacts that can be used as sources for story ideas or for stories themselves. For example, that neighborhood garden club you belong to becomes a source spot for stories. You can write how-to-do-it stories, for example, from what you learn about the flowers and other plants of your region.

Certainly meetings of groups will often host programs with instructional and educational value. Speeches and discussions can produce dozens of potential stories, ranging from child care to income tax preparation.

Conventions are another area that might suggest stories for writers. National and regional meetings always attract the most active and authoritative persons. If you are in a metropolitan area or resort region where conventions are frequently held, this source can be very valuable. To keep up with the schedule of conventions, simply make regular contact with your local convention and visitors office or major convention hotels nearby.

Every community has a public library. A few minutes browsing in the library will show you the latest books and periodicals on subjects that interest you. Larger libraries often offer exhibitions and programs with speakers and other experts providing material for potential stories.

If your community has a museum, the exhibits and specialists assembled will be useful for stories. Both permanent and temporary exhibits offer possibilities for stories, of course, even if stories are limited to just the fact that these events are occurring. Often, though, you can go beyond the exhibit itself to generate stories about the artist or event being highlighted.

In most areas, local history makes good story material. This can be a subject area to cultivate for stories, especially if you can find a local historian who is also a good storyteller. Many of your readers will be interested in their community history, especially if you can explain how and why events, buildings or other landmarks, and people wound up as they did. Former *Miami News* executive editor Howard Kleinberg, newsroom administrator of the newspaper before it closed in 1988, still found time to research and write a weekly local history column called "Miami: The Way We Were" that was one of the most popular features in his newspaper's Saturday edition for seven years.

Because house and home are important to just about everyone, writing about these topics is a natural. Numerous "shelter" magazines exist on the subject, and many major newspapers publish home and garden sections on Sundays or at certain seasons of the year.

Just roaming around can generate stories, too. When was the last time you drove through a neighborhood in your community that you haven't seen for a few months? Or maybe there are parts of your community that you have *never* visited. The curiosity and inquisitiveness a good feature writer needs should eventually motivate you to take a look at different places and people. In other words, explore and look around you.

YOUR SCHOOL AS A SOURCE FOR STORY IDEAS

Where do we get a good feature idea? Everywhere. Well, it seems like it.

For starters, your local colleges can be good sources. If you are a student, think about the story prospects in your own classes. What interesting research is going on in the sciences at your school? What work are your professors doing? Have you ever thought to ask? Many are working on serious and important projects that are often worthy of a story. This is particularly true if your school has a medical school or other health-education programs in which human health and human life may be affected by the work that is being done.

Even if you are no longer a student, these schools can be rich with story possibilities. You just have to know where to go to start.

Many universities and colleges have public affairs or public relations offices with individuals who can suggest contacts for you on particular subjects. Or, with a phone call, these persons can suggest story ideas to you based on their knowledge of the current research and service projects on their campus.

Some schools publish experts directories that are excellent sources for reporters and writers. Organized by topic, these directories will quickly tell you what experts exist in your own backyard.

Marshall Swanson (1979), a free-lance writer based in Columbia, SC, uses the University of South Carolina campus as a base for many of his feature articles. He suggests these five steps in tracking story ideas:

1. *Get to know how things run on campus.* Use the public relations people. Get maps and student-staff-faculty phone directories of large campuses.

2. *Subscribe to the student newspaper on campus.* Often these publications will tell you a great deal about campus goings-on. You can extend this suggestion by reading the campus magazines and faculty-staff publications, also.

3. *Get to know the director of the student center.* There are many campus events which are coordinated through this office.

4. *Establish contact with various deans and chairmen of departments.* Do this in person if possible.

5. *Stop off for a visit at the campus research office.* Many universities have offices for funded research programs, a campus clearinghouse for funded research.

There is often a list produced of this work, or of grants received, that might propose interesting ideas before anyone else gets them.

Swanson also suggests people on campuses are good prospects for profiles. Both faculty and students can become story ideas if you ask around to find out who is doing what. Columnist Dennis Hensley (1979) also suggests this, saying, "Colleges are the homes of the greatest minds we have in this country and the free-lance writer who doesn't tap this source of free information is literally missing the buck—the royalty buck, that is" (p. 34).

Off campus, there are numerous other places to find story ideas. The next sections of this chapter outline them for you.

LISTENING TO IDEAS FROM YOUR READERS

Many times, readers will suggest stories. You know you have become established as a writer when readers contact you to pass along their ideas for stories. Some ideas will not be worthy of a story, but others will be, and you should follow up on the suggestions.

One thing is certain: *Never* ignore tips from readers. While one tip just will not work, the next might. You cannot afford to forget about these suggestions. And you must take the time to check each one out.

Most reader ideas come in the form of casual conversations. Someone will find out you are a writer and want to pass along the idea. Or they will call. And there will be times when someone tries to be a public relations person for a friend or relative and write some sort of announcement or article to start you on your way.

If you get a call, or a letter, or someone pulls you aside in an office, listen to the idea even if you are busy and cannot do anything about it right away. And write that idea down for action later. Writer Marshall Cook (1986) says, "You [should] scramble for paper and pencil to capture this. . . . You know better than to wait. Write it down now or risk remembering later only that you had a great idea but not what that great idea was" (p. 26).

Tips and other ideas for stories from readers will need to be checked out. Occasionally, someone will present an idea to you that seems good, but it might be false, exaggerated, or otherwise problematic. You have to take the time, at the outset, to confirm and verify information before you dig in to begin work.

READING THE WORK OF OTHER WRITERS

There's absolutely nothing wrong with looking at what other writers and publications are doing for ideas. An idea that you see in a West Coast publication might not work in an East Coast market, but then again, it might.

Start by reading all of your local newspapers and magazines. If you live in a metropolitan area, this might be a chore, but you have to know what is happening locally. This keeps you informed about the potential for publishing in these publications when you have an idea, but it also gives you ideas that you can market elsewhere.

Certainly, you should try to read as many out-of-town magazines and newspapers as you can. This is especially true to help you learn markets where you might sell your work, but it also gives you new ideas. If your budget is tight and you cannot always buy subscriptions to newspapers and magazines, then head to your college or public library where you will find many major publications that arrive regularly.

Specialized publications take this concept one step further, and these story sources are discussed in the next section.

USING SPECIALIZED PUBLICATIONS, PROGRAMS

Specialized magazines and journals are an excellent source for feature ideas. If you write about a particular subject, whether it be the airline industry, computers, or food, you need to be in touch with the industries that you write about. The best way is to read about the concerns, news and developments, problems, opinions, services, lifestyles, and major issues in these publications designed to be read by the professionals, the artists, and other experts.

These publications can help you understand the language of these specialists, as well. For example, if you want to write about airline safety and take the time to read articles in *Air Line Pilot,* published by the Air Line Pilots Association for flight deck crews, you will learn about deregulation effects, airline safety, salaries and other compensation issues, aviation history, new equipment, and other matters from the pilots' point of view.

Have you ever heard the term "runway incursion"? It is a term that refers to an airplane or other vehicle which affects the takeoff or landing of another airplane. Reading articles such as the magazine's news editor, Robert Moorman, wrote in *Air Line Pilot,* you would understand this term and dozens of others like it.

Still other publications for flight attendants, engineers, mechanics, and even management will give you other points of view on an important subject such as airline safety.

Although these magazines are generally available to members of organizations such as ALPA, nonmembers can often obtain subscriptions or single copies. Or, of course, these can usually be obtained from members. But if you are serious about developing story ideas in a specialized area, then you have to have access to these publications while they are current.

Research journals are also good regular reading for story ideas. One of the most widely read is the *Journal of the American Medical Association,* which regularly publishes new medical research findings. The journal is a mainstay for health and medicine writers, but provides ideas for many general assignment reporters and free-lance writers as well.

Most journals are published quarterly, but some are monthly and even more frequent. You simply need to familiarize yourself with the existence of these publications by heading to a library or by asking sources you respect for the publications they regularly read.

Bulletins and newsletters from organizations are equally valuable. While these publications often do not offer the depth that a magazine or journal might offer, they still present issues that should suggest stories for you. Regular reading of these topics will make a difference in how you cover your subject.

Specialized television and radio programs are becoming a more useful source for story ideas also. With cable television and 24-hour broadcasting in many markets, programs of narrow and specialized nature are getting opportunities to be aired. Shows devoted to local issues or specific concerns such as business or the economy are available and often become good sources for development of stories. Furthermore, public access channels of cable systems permit relatively obscure concerns time to broadcast. The convenience, for example, of tuning to your local school board meeting or local county government meeting on a cable channel saves time and still allows you to pick up concerns of the community.

WORKING WITH EDITORS' IDEAS

Editors know their markets well. Regardless of whether they are newspaper or magazine editors, these persons are in contact with their readers and other writers, and they probably have had access to research about their publication's readership and reader demographics. You need to know as much as you can about a given publication if you want to free-lance for it, and, of course, you need to know who your readers are and what they want to read if you are a staff member.

You will have countless opportunities to work with your editor on story ideas. Beginning general assignment staff writers at newspapers will often start this way and gradually begin to initiate stories on their own as they gain confidence on the job. Magazine staffers can expect much the same, but because magazines depend more on free-lance material, editors will usually only request articles or pass along ideas for articles to experienced writers whom they already know and trust.

Editors work from idea lists, just as you should. When something interests an editor, he or she usually puts it in some sort of holding spot until planning for a new edition or issue takes place. These idea lists, when stories are assigned or when they are finished, are often called "budgets."

Like your own ideas, editors' article ideas come from a wide range of possible sources. They read extensively. They talk to people. Tips come in.

Your part of the system is to do the legwork. You research and write. But you should not limit yourself to this role when working with an editor on a story idea. You bring into the situation different perspectives, experiences, and orientations. You should always share these with your editor and offer to modify his or her suggestions if you have an angle that will make a good idea a better one. And your editor should be willing to listen.

On occasions, you will find a group brainstorming session can generate workable story ideas. You can do this with your supervising editors and with other writers. Simple conversations around the office, during a break, or even after work might do the trick. And for free-lancers not working in a regular media environment, writers' clubs and other similar professional organizations can offer the same support.

INFORMATION LINES, BULLETIN BOARDS, AND COMMUNICATION CENTERS

You can generate ideas by exploring the communication networks of your community. Many institutions and organizations today provide local telephone numbers or toll-free long distance telephone numbers to information lines. These lines are regularly updated reports designed either for the public in general or the news media. When you know you have a subject to write, and you know some of the source organizations and institutions you will use, you should find out if these services exist.

Community bulletin boards exist just about any place where people regularly congregate. Shopping centers, for example, often have community bulletin boards for wide varieties of goods, services, and other items. You will often find these at larger grocery stores, too. Churches, senior citizen centers, park centers, and other community "living rooms" will be good places to find story ideas.

For example, go to the recreation center of a park near you. Dance classes, exercise programs, arts and crafts groups, and other organized activities will be promoted in a variety of ways. And you probably see the story possibilities already.

At universities, colleges, and even high schools, campus student centers will have a lot going on. Message centers will often tell you about lectures, meetings, organizations, programs, and so on.

Today, these information centers are not limited to buildings. Electronic bulletin boards often find their way into your home on cable television channels. Community access channels often run listings of activities that can lead to stories.

Computers are now a part of the article idea search process, also. A computer BBS—short for bulletin board service—can list useful information for you if you know the telephone number, access information, and operating hours. Both public and private organizations use these services to distribute information about their activities.

The important key here is to regularly and routinely check these sources of information. Consistent use of the sources will eventually pay off with a unique and salable story idea.

CALENDARS AND DATEBOOKS

A well-organized writer will keep a calendar or datebook to plan ahead. Without it, your life as a writer will be filled with scheduling chaos.

These books can be quite sophisticated, such as Borland International's *Traveling Sidekick*, a computer program package that allows you to put all your appointments and events into an electronic calendar and all your names and addresses in an electronic address book (and you can print them out for your binder that comes with it). Or, calendar and date books can be quite simple, such as the pocket-size calendars that are often given away each semester at school bookstores. In short, you have many ways to keep track of upcoming events and activities that might lead to article prospects. Office supply houses, bookstores, and even variety stores sell these tools for your work.

Regardless of what form they take and where you get them, calendars and datebooks are among the basics of the well-organized writer. You might consider a hybrid form of a calendar-idea list. Some writers like to use file folders, one for each month of the year. Others will keep desk books and clip ideas into each appropriate day or week. Some professional writers, using their publication's office or their home work space, will use a large wall calendar for a big picture of upcoming article prospects and deadlines.

Find a system that works for you. Try different approaches until something that fits your personal style is found. You will find that if you are organized, you will be more efficient and productive in your work.

And don't forget the seasonal nature of feature writing. Although we will discuss this further in a later chapter, it's worth mentioning here, also. For example, *Writer's Digest* contributing editor Frank Dickson (1980) wrote two articles for his magazine several years ago that propose rather timeless story ideas based on the fall and winter seasons. His point, in addition to listing more than 70 ideas in the articles, is that you must plan ahead as much as 6 months for some stories if you want to sell your work.

FINDING FEATURES ON A BEAT

Staff writers for newspapers and magazines often find themselves on a beat assignment. Although there is considerable freedom being a general assignment staff member who takes just about any story assignment that comes along, the opportunity to specialize on a beat appeals to many writers. Whereas a newspaper beat can be defined as just about anything such as health and medicine, transportation, the public zoo, education and the schools, or parks and recreation, magazine beats are often even more specific and specialized because of the narrow scope of the publication. Generating beat ideas under both circumstances will be discussed here.

YOUR BEST SOURCES FOR STORY IDEAS

Your personal experiences
Personal and professional contacts
College and university campuses
Meetings and conventions
House and home
Libraries, museums
Historians
Other publications (newspapers and magazines)
Television programs
Your readers
Your editors and fellow writers
Telephone information lines
Community bulletin boards and communication centers
Calendars and datebooks

For some newspaper and magazine beat writers, feature stories can be the exception rather than the rule. Many times, beat reporters are bound by the demands of spot news reporting and find little time for features. However, a good feature can serve several purposes for beat writers. First, they give you a needed diversion from the daily deadline writing. Second, they can build bridges with sources, since these stories, if accurate and fair, seldom ruffle feathers. Third, they offer readers a new perspective on a source.

A writer covering the police department on a regular basis will have plenty of stories for his editors without writing features. Yet some of the most interesting stories will take readers behind the scenes, profile officers, highlight special programs, or offer depth and insight into an unusual event such as a crime that has recently occurred. A writer covering education will do many features about schools, students, programs, teachers, and successes and failures of the school system. One of the most widely read feature stories in *The Miami Herald*'s Neighbors section in 1986 was Candace M. Turtle's lengthy cover feature, "System Keeps Tabs on Teachers," that focused on incompetent teachers and how the public schools dealt with the problem.

Professor Daniel Williamson (1975) says beat reporters generate most newspaper features. He says, "Regardless of the reporting specialty you may inherit, feature stories will present an ever-present opportunity to win news sources, educate and inform your readers, and impress your editors with steady, high production" (p. 75).

Magazines, on the other hand, also depend on beat writers, but these specialists are not always on staff. As we have already noted, many magazines depend on free-lance writers to be their specialists for articles. Or, if you are a specialist on a magazine *staff*, remember that either way it is likely you are a specialist for a publication highly specialized in its scope. There are few general interest magazines today. Unless you work for a news magazine or one of the few other general interest publications, you will be covering a specialized area for readers who have a high level of interest in the subject and, it is also quite likely, a high level of knowledge as well.

This simply means the demands on you to find features that are educational and informative, as Williamson says, will be tougher. If you are a writer for a food and entertainment magazine such as *Bon Appetit*, feature articles about simple fare such as homemade cookies must have something new to offer before America's cooks will bother to read your work. But Los Angeles food writer Selma Brown Morrow succeeded with a recent article in that magazine that told readers how to make big cookies with big taste. Similarly, a writer regularly contributing to *Flowers&* magazine, a floral-design industry publication, has to be well versed in trade news to succeed. Readers of specialized industrial publications want beat writers who can tell them about new developments and ideas to make their businesses stronger and more successful. Melissa Dodd Eskilson, a regular contributor to the publication, found a new angle on chrysanthemums in her 1987 article, "Chrysanthemums, a Centuries-Old Favorite, Make a Comeback." She not only tells readers about a new trend, but also gives practical advice on selecting and handling both cut and potted versions of the flowers.

Being a beat feature writer has its advantages. You can carve out a niche and learn much about the topic. You become authoritative. And this, of course, makes your work even more sought after.

CHOOSING THE RIGHT ANGLE

All feature articles have a particular approach to them. It really doesn't matter whether your story is written for a magazine or a newspaper. It has to have some sort of angle, some major thrust within the subject you have selected. But it should also limit itself to one angle or it will have too much direction to it.

Make a list of all the possible angles of the subject you can think about. By exploring your options, you will begin to get the overall picture and approach. Then organize the list. Reorder it. Rank the items on the list according to which are the most appealing to readers. This should help you eliminate some of the less-desired approaches. With a practical point of view, determine what angles are within your resources. Are sources available? Can you afford the approach within your operating budget? What topics interest *you* the most? And make second and third choices for the story in case your top choice does not work out. Always have a backup idea.

Now, let's suppose you want to write an article for your local city/regional magazine on bicycling. The process of finding an angle is similar to a narrowing-down process. What do you want to write about bicycling? Since it is a city/regional magazine, do you write about urban bicycling? Touring? Buying a bicycle? Other equipment? Clothing? Training? Competition? You make this decision many times in conjunction with an editor. As a free-lancer, it is a good idea to have this angle set before you pitch the story in a query letter or prospectus.

To continue the example about bicycling, you decide you want to write about the bicycle routes or paths in your metropolitan area. But you have to go further to determine your angle. Will you do a "review" of these trails? Or will you simply do a descriptive piece that tells readers where they can be found?

The purpose here is to keep things specific and focused in your story. Without it, your article will drift without any real beginning, middle, or end.

Professor Benton Rain Patterson (1986) calls an angle "a frame that contains all the pertinent material. Material not pertinent to the angle is left out of the piece. The angle is also like a clothesline from which the piece's bits of information are hung . . ." (p. 59). He adds that a feature article's angle helps structure information around a central idea that gives the reader's mind a clear place to rest.

TRYING OUT IDEAS BEFORE YOU WRITE

To be fair to yourself and to your potential readers, you must try out the idea before you devote time and resources to it. As noted earlier, free-lance writer Lorene Hanley Duquin (1987) offers a strategy for polishing your story ideas before sitting down to write. She says the approach requires asking yourself questions and writing down the answers. Let's take a much closer look at those questions posed at the beginning of the chapter:

1. *Do you really want to write the article?* You have to consider your motivation level. If it is interesting to you and a worthy subject, you should do it. But if you cannot seem to get excited about it, how can you expect your article to show that excitement? How can you expect your readers to be stimulated by what you have written?

2. *Are you capable of doing the article?* Some topics are simply beyond a writer's abilities to complete. Because of their technical complexity, or the time involved, or the expenses, it might not be workable. Some great article ideas are just out of reach for average writers. Sometimes a subject requires the sensitivity

or personal experience that you might not have. A mature writer will recognize this and hold the idea until later or give it up completely.

3. *How much will the article cost you?* For both staff writers and free-lancers, you have to consider the resources needed to do a story. For staff writers, you might have a media organization behind you, but its budget has limitations and priorities that may prevent you from traveling, calling, or otherwise gathering the information you need. Furthermore, this is a serious problem for free-lancers when you are not sure if a publication will pay your expenses. Can you afford to take the chance? Some ideas will be worth the risk; others will not be. Finally, there is the consideration of time. If you have the resource-backing you need, does this idea merit the time it will require to do it right? Some long magazine pieces require a month or two of full-time research and writing. Others features can be done in a few hours.

4. *What else can you do with the material?* What happens to your idea and its development if a particular targeted publication does not want it? Do you have other publication options? Can this idea become part of another writing project? If you are a staff member, does your publication permit you to market your work to other outlets?

5. *Are there markets for reprints?* For free-lance writers, this is a concern that may not be so important to staff writers. If you write your article from this idea, can you find second and third outlets for the story in the form of reprints? Magazines such as *Review,* Eastern Air Lines' inflight passenger magazine, is an example of a publication that regularly reprints major feature articles. Staff writers might not concern themselves with this, since they have less control over distribution of their work. However, some newspaper and magazine groups often exchange the best of their editions through news services and syndicates.

6. *Can you do spin-off articles?* For the free-lance writer, this is a critical point. To make your work pay off at a level that can sustain you, ideas must generate more than one possible story. Can you take the idea and move into several markets with it? For a staff writer on a regular income, this is a little less important. Yet, from a similar perspective, even a staff writer might consider if the idea will have potential for a series approach or other stories for later issues or editions.

A LOOK AT FOLLOWUP FILE

Each week, Editorial Services in Hastings-on-Hudson, NY, produces another edition of a newsletter called *Followup File.* A commercial subscription service, it is ideal for beginning writers who need good ideas for stories that can easily be localized and marketed.

The newsletters are mailed about five days before the story ideas are available to handle. Listings cover the waterfront, but most importantly, Editorial Services provides seed sources for the writers—people involved in the trend or issue at the national level.

The newsletter also includes ideas for commentaries and editorials, or opinion materials. Users also find a "Datebook" section which lists upcoming anniversaries and other important dates that might be a good reason for a story for a newspaper or magazine.

Stories include national issues, problems, trends, updates, new developments, and so on. Lists report government toll-free telephone numbers, too.

Some of the topics listed in recent issues of the *Followup File* newsletter include:
Cash machine crime
Pet deaths
Risk in sharing cosmetics
Corporal punishment in schools
Household trash problems
College tuition inflation
Non-prescription reading glasses: risky?
New poverty in the United States
Graphic scenes and violence in "Snow White"
Testing for cocaine for life insurance
Computer automated homes
Saving pennies and other coins
Trip insurance
Plastic recycling
Car ignition interlock systems for drinking drivers
Abused parents
Bank fees for automated teller machines
Counterfeit sporting goods and clothing
Rip-offs by financial planners
Reverse mortgages
Service organizations and female membership update
Hotel health codes
Rural hospitals
Sunbathing and skin infections
Disposal of school lab chemicals
Microwave popcorn mania
Ice cream clones (gourmet brands)
Hospices for children

DEVELOPING THE IDEA INTO AN ARTICLE

Two steps in developing your idea into a finished manuscript are giving the idea an angle and testing the idea for its soundness.

Once you have satisfied yourself these steps are taken, then the pre-writing and editing process continues with your first efforts to gather and organize materials for your article. These steps should include:

1. *List research sources you will need.* This subject is covered in depth in chapter 3, but in developing an article idea before the writing stage, you now should consider what research will be necessary. Where do you go?

2. *Make a rough outline of the idea/article.* This will be discussed in more depth in chapter 4, but you should have some idea of the thrust or angle of the story by now and can begin to list major sections of the article on paper. This will help you understand what needs to be done next.

3. *List possible interviews you will need.* What persons will be a part of the article? What areas of expertise will they represent?

A Professional's Point of View

By Pat Clinton
Chicago magazine

To come up with good ideas, start by coming up with bad ones. Don't try to censor yourself. Write them all down: bad ones incredibly bad ones, badly stolen ones, embarrassing ones. Don't stop the flow by trying to judge them—first go for volume.

Build new ideas by doing variations on old ones. Extrapolate. Look for common

threads, related topics, parallels in different fields. One writer I know calls it the Beverly Hillbillies/Green Acres strategy. If you read a story about country folk who come to the city, you look for one about city folk who go to the country.

That's what you do with your bad ideas. Say you've read a news story about a particularly bloody divorce, but it's been covered so much you don't think anyone would buy a story on it. What are the variations? You could try to find another bloody divorce. A divorce lawyer. A lot of divorce lawyers. Expert witnesses in divorce cases. New ideas about financial support. Child support cheating. People who track down child-support cheats. Children who live in poverty while their half-siblings are affluent. Alimony for men. For a specific man. Don't stop.

Detectives who do divorce work. Your city's most notorious local detective who does divorce work. Detectives who get in trouble with the law over their divorce work. The multiple ex-spouses of some locally famous divorced person. Ways people have of not getting divorced. People who remarry. Other kinds of partnerships that dissolve: law firms that split, for instance. How about a bitter lawsuit over dissolving a family-held corporation. Or a bloody bankruptcy. Bankruptcy lawyers. And on and on and on.

Most of the ideas will be terrible; many of them will need to be filled out by calls to sources of one sort or another—experts, associations, participants, and so on. (These sources in turn will be sources of still more ideas.) But at least you're thinking along new lines.

Don't stop. Make a list of every category, every story genre you can think of. Subdivide them: don't just put down "profile," put down "*New Yorker* profile, *Vanity Fair* profile, celebrity profile, obit, oral history"—draw as many distinctions as you can. Make lists of kinds of people—old, young, living, dead, black, white, starting out, retired, entertainer, sports figure, politician, teacher, lawyer. Combine your categories and see what you get: retired black entertainers, female lawyers starting out in their careers, very young athletes. Think of some specific story ideas that arise from these kinds of people. Do variations on them. Make some calls. Don't stop.

Look at the ideas on your list. Think of them in terms of real pieces of stories. Mentally sketch a lead, a scene, a headline, a potential interview. Think about what you've sketched: Does it suggest other story ideas? Are you slowing down? Think of some deliberately bad ideas—cliched, overdone, boring, stupid. Write them down. Work with them.

By now you should have a fair-sized list. Read it over. Some of the ideas you'll like. Why? What is it that draws you to a story? Personalities? Conflict? Complex processes that need to be explained? New solutions to old problems? Look for themes in what you like and try to turn them into still more ideas. Try to anticipate sources for the kinds of stories you seem to like. (One writer I work with discovered that the state licensing office's disciplinary file was filled with stories he liked. He reads it every week now, and he's probably the only journalist in town who does.)

Make up your own rules. Remember, if you write down enough ideas, eventually you'll come up with some good ones. Don't stop. (Clinton, personal communication, 1988)

* * *

Pat Clinton is a senior editor for *Chicago* magazine. He says, "in our scheme of things, [senior editor] means I edit and develop stories and badger and cajole writers." Prior to joining *Chicago*, he was managing editor of *Chicago Reader*. He also was on the staff of *Building Design & Construction*. He studied medieval English literature at the doctoral level at Northwestern University as well.

3

Researching Feature Article Ideas

Got an idea? Need to find information about it? That's what you will learn how to do in this chapter. Research is such an important step, all writers take time to do it. Yet because you must do research for your articles, you often take it for granted.

So what sources can you call upon? There are interview resources and written resources. We'll devote our attention to both since you should employ both in working on a feature article. And expect to do some *work*. Authors Clay Schoenfeld and Karen Diegmueller, who have written both books and articles, say you should expect to spend ten hours of research for every one hour you spend at your typewriter when working on a feature article (Schoenfeld & Diegmueller, 1982).

You will find there are two categories of written sources for research: (a) those open and available to you, and (b) those which are not generally available to the public. While we will spend most of our time discussing public sources, we will also give you some ideas about how to contend with limitations of restricted information that you might need for a story.

MEDIA LIBRARIES

Most news organizations will have good libraries for you to use. A larger newspaper or magazine will have librarians and computers to assist you in your work. Smaller newspapers and magazines, as well as bureaus of larger news organizations, usually are not as well equipped, forcing you to be more resourceful in finding information.

If you are fortunate enough to have a library or "morgue" at your office, information is usually filed two ways: by newsmaker's name and by subject matter, and there are usually two categories: clips and photographs.

All libraries will have a standard set of atlases, abstracts, directories, handbooks, encyclopedias, almanacs, and other general reference books. Libraries should update their holdings as often as new editions are published.

The standard tools for finding information in these sources are card and on-line catalogs as well as book and automated indexes.

PUBLIC AND OTHER PRIVATE LIBRARIES

Public and private libraries will be you next options in conducting research for your article. If you cannot find what you seek at your own office's library, then go to you local public library. In most communities, there will also be university and college libraries, but these are sometimes restricted. Many state university and college libraries are open to the public, but some private schools limit access to faculty, students, staff, and alumni. If you need to use a private library, contact the director of the library for permission to use it.

Public libraries often contain excellent sources, particularly for local and regional subjects. If you reside in a metropolitan area, then the wealth of library resources should be great. The only restrictions for public libraries will be hours of operation and demand on resources. Some special collections will be accessible only by advance arrangement, but the reference materials you need most likely will be available for your use.

Besides your office library, public libraries, and academic facilities, there are three types of special libraries to remember. First, you can often use area historical society libraries. Most communities have these, and in state capitals there may be several that are usually open to the public. Second, there are museum libraries. Presidential libraries and museums are an example of this type of facility. Third, there are company and corporate libraries. Large corporations, such as those on the Fortune 500 list, maintain libraries for employees, but facilities may be available for your use if you request permission. If you are not permitted on site, it is possible that through the public relations or public affairs department of the company you may reach these specialists with your information request.

Most libraries have open stacks. That is, the shelves are open for you to browse and to find your own materials. However, some libraries do not open their stacks because of theft and other loss of materials. Closed stacks are a hardship for you because you must list the books you want and request a clerk to get them for you. Needless to say, this takes time. You might want to talk to the director of the library for permission to use the stacks if your research project is complex.

Your ability to take advantage of whatever library you use will depend on you and one other person: an experienced reference librarian who specializes in the subject you are writing about. Subject specialists are on staff to assist you, so call on them as you need assistance.

Another service to remember is the networking that libraries use to multiply their resources. Many libraries link together in national, state, or regional networks to loan and exchange materials needed by borrowers. These inter-library loan services may be fee-based and may take time to use, but they can save you a lot of travel expense to find materials not locally available.

Finally, check the facility's hours of operation before you leave home. Hours can change and a call may save you valuable time.

REFERENCE BOOKS

Need to know the length of the St. Lawrence and Great Lakes Waterway in miles? The depth of its channel? Go to a reference book. (The answers are 2,342 miles and 27 feet, according to *The World Almanac and Book of Facts, 1987*). Even a rather common reference book such as this, available at just about any neighborhood drug store, can be a boon when you are researching a fact for an article.

And if you take a step farther, you will find your local library's reference section to be one of the most useful sections of any library for a writer. You'll find many types and sources of books and periodicals. We will try to discuss a few of the major reference books that will be helpful to writers in this chapter.

For starters, directories are specialized books that list wide ranging content, such as membership lists and statistics. One example, of particular interest to you as a writer, is city directories. These can be extremely helpful for finding names, addresses, telephone numbers, and building occupants. Writers for newspapers and news magazines find them particularly helpful in locating sources. There are directories for several thousand cities in the United States which are published annually by private companies such as Detroit's R. L. Polk.

These books (each is different depending on the company that produced it) contain traditional white pages (alphabetic listings by last name), but also color pages that list (a) address listings in alphanumeric order, (b) telephone listings in numeric order (often called reverse phone listing), and (c) directories of major buildings and occupants. Some even include directories of government officials, addresses, and telephone numbers.

There are also almanacs. As mentioned previously, many of these basic references are inexpensive and easy to buy. These books, often sponsored by news organizations such as Associated Press or *Time*, are published annually and list facts and figures on many items. But there are other types of almanacs, too, some of which focus on only one subject, such as politics or business, or a state. The *Wisconsin Blue Book* is just one example.

Atlases and gazetteers are useful, and they include a great deal more than just geography. For starters, though you can learn a great deal by simply studying a map of an area. When geography is the subject you need to study, atlases and gazetteers will likely contain the answers. You can use them to check locations, distances, spellings, population, trade, industry, available natural resources, economic development politics, and distribution systems.

Encyclopedias should not be overlooked either, since these books can often give you an authoritative introduction to a subject. Encyclopedias are often thought of as general sets of books that are updated every one to three years and have a universal application. However, these books are often much more useful as specialized volumes devoted to limited information on subjects such as world history, physical science and music. Yearbooks are usually supplements that update existing editions of books or series of books such as encyclopedias.

Abstracts are valuable because these books take sets of statistics and other data and condense the data into useful form for the user. Abstracts can also list bibliographic information and offer annotations or summaries of books, articles, theses, or dissertations (such as *Dissertation Abstracts* or *Psychological Abstracts*).

Chronologies are reference books that list events in chronological order over a period of time. Many of these are limited to certain periods of time, such as a decade or century, or are limited to the duration of an historic event such as World War II or the Depression.

Dictionaries are critical to research and writing. Many general dictionaries are available, some in very inexpensive price ranges. And there are many dictionaries within particular disciplines, such as law or the physical sciences, that can help you when working with technical subjects that require explanation in your article for your readers.

Biographical dictionaries are extremely helpful in researching well-known persons. There are different types of biographical dictionaries, many focused on specific disciplines, so you need to know where to go to find information about the person you are researching. Good examples here are *Current Biography* or *Who's Who*. There are biographical master indexes to these reference books that are kept in most major libraries.

Books of quotations are another category of reference books that are a valued source to writers. When you need an authoritative quote or a familiar quote to make your point, these books are the source to use. The leading example is *Bartlett's Familiar Quotations*.

GOVERNMENT PUBLICATIONS

Thousands of federal, state, and local government publications can help you research an article. As has been often said about Washington, most of the time the information you need is there, you just have to know how to find it. This applies to government publications. All branches of government produce publications. These are mostly public documents, but a few are classified and unavailable to the public.

To help find the information you want, there are indexes—especially at the federal level. General indexes, such as the *Monthly Catalog of U. S. Government Publications*, can help. This contains a subject index of new materials that are issued.

Congressional sources provide us with hearings documents on specialized topics such as medical care, agriculture, and even the routine daily activities of Congress. These documents are available at local libraries that are designated U. S. Government document depository libraries or from the bookstores of the U. S. Government Printing Office.

Executive-branch sources cover subjects as broad as the various departments that help the White House carry out the laws of the land. *The Federal Register* and *Code of Federal Regulations* are both good sources for orders, proclamations, and regulations that are announced by the White House. A writer interested in the words of the president may check the *Weekly Compilation of Presidential Documents*.

Want to know how U. S. population trends are changing or how many appliances are in a state or county? Use census data. There are both lengthy census reports and shorter, more accessible abstracts of census data. The most popular one is the *Statistical Abstract of the United States*, which is published annually. However, there are several other statistical abstract publications produced either annually or at other regular intervals such as the *City and County Data Book*, produced every 5 years.

For the judicial branch and for other legal sources, two good sources are *Black's Law Dictionary* and the *Martindale–Hubbell Law Directory*. The *Index to Legal Periodicals* is also a good stating point. For court decisions, the West Publishing Co. of St. Paul privately publishes reports from many federal courts, all state appellate courts, and some state courts in its National Reporter System. This is often found in county and city libraries, law school libraries, and in some law offices.

You can also find reports by the Federal Bureau of Investigation (such as the Uniform Crime Report issued annually), by the Food and Drug Administration, and by the Federal Communications Commission in libraries or from the agencies directly.

At the state level, there are almost as many good publications. Look for handbooks, directories, guidebooks, and other volumes produced by official and private sources. One good example of the official reference book is the *Blue Book* produced by the state of Wisconsin each year.

Other general reference books include works produced state by state. These books can be excellent regional sources and are published by both public and private sources. These books, such as the *Texas Almanac* or *Florida Almanac*, are published annually or biannually. There are also general indexes of state publications. One such book is the *Monthly Checklist of State Publications*, which is produced by the Library of Congress. Some states, such as Virginia and Kentucky, produce their own similar lists. For most state documents, start with the secretary of state's office. This person is the state's official record keeper.

Local government publications vary in quantity and quality. Most metropolitan areas will produce a substantial number of publications and local reference materials. But small cities and towns will not always have the resources to do so. In this case, go to the county or parish as your main regional source. Some private sources can be helpful. For example, the International City Management Association produces the *Municipal Year Book*.

COMPUTER-BASED LITERATURE SEARCHING

For those who have toiled long hours in libraries searching for literature on a subject, the computer is the best thing that has come along since movable type. Computer-based data bases have been available for public use for more than a decade now and promise to be the way to do your research work in the future. Of course, this assumes you can use a computer. There are other problems, too, such as cost and time-sharing access restrictions.

One of the growing ways of using these data bases is through a personal computer from the office or home. In the early days of computer data-base searching, the effort had to be made from a library or other special facility. But with a modem (a device that allows one computer to communicate with another by telephone line), just about any computer and, therefore, any location, can use a computer data base.

Almost all computer data bases are "read-only" files that allow you to look at information but not modify it in any way. Almost all also require a search fee based on time or some other unit charge. These fees are not inexpensive. Some run as little as $10 per hour during off hours to as high as $100 or more per hour for more exclusive systems at corporate, prime usage time rates. Most searches cost $15 to $20, however, and may be well worth the investment in terms of time saved. Two popular examples are CompuServe and Nexis/Lexis. These are national commercial services and you pay for the time you are "logged on."

But don't despair. Most colleges and universities have libraries with access to these and other data bases at a completely subsidized or at least a reduced rate for students. You should ask about this by checking with your professors or reference librarians.

Most of the searches that your library can do for you are through a central computer somewhere else. Your library simply links its computer to the larger, "mainframe" computer and requests a particular data base for you. The data base you request will, of course, depend on the subject of your article.

Most current data bases used for literature searches are electronic versions of indexes that have traditionally been published in hardbound form. The convenience is obvious, if you are willing to pay for the time to do a broad search.

The hardest work in computer searching is to narrow down the "key word" which the computer uses to make its search. A key word or series of key words will define what the computer searches for in the data base. Because most data bases are bibliographic—that is, they contain authors, titles, and subjects—you have to have an idea who the authors are or what correct words might appear in titles. A search of animals, for example, would work if you wanted to find articles on domestic house cats, but it would be even better to request pets or cats.

Many larger libraries are also beginning to computerize their card catalogs for easy searching. But the scope of the data bases is often limited to the last 5 or 10 years, primarily because of the high cost of entering older acquisitions. Yet these data bases are helpful in finding the most recent editions of books, or at least the most recent acquisitions by libraries. These searches work on the same principle as the data-base searches: you search for the author, the title, or a subject as key words. Terminals set up in the card catalog room or elsewhere make the work convenient. If you can get the access codes and telephone number from the library, you can search the catalog of your local or university library through you personal computer from your office or home. Some libraries, to encourage use of such resources, will provide this information to qualified individuals such as students.

Many newspapers and magazines are also getting into the act. Through computers you can access the articles of most major daily newspapers published since the mid-1980s. Some larger magazines and magazine groups are following suit. In the near future, it will be easy to find an article through a service such as Knight-Ridder's Vu/Text that allows access to many of the corporation's newspapers (e.g., *Philadelphia Inquirer*, *Detroit Free-Press*, *Miami Herald*) as well as other major dailies such as *The Washington Post*. The first screen to greet you when you sign on to a portion of Vu/Text's computer system is the log-on screen and instructions.

A computer data base of periodicals called *Info Trac* is now available in many libraries. It includes newspapers and magazines and is comprehensive in scope. The service includes recent reviews and uses the Library of Congress subject headings. The service is provided by Information Access Company and encompasses its *Magazine Index*.

A WRITER'S REFERENCE BOOKSHELF

Here is a list of commonly used reference books in newspaper and magazine offices. These are the traditional favorites of reporters, copy editors, editors, and freelance writers. This is not a comprehensive list, but it can be used in building a personal library.

Encyclopedias

An Encyclopedia of World History, 5th ed., William L. Langer, ed., Houghton Mifflin, Boston, 1972.

Encyclopedia Americana, international ed., 30 vol. Americana, Danbury, CT, 1983.

The New Columbia Encyclopedia, 4th ed., Columbia University Press, New York, 1975.

World Book Encyclopedia, 22 vol., World Book, Field Enterprises Educational Corp., Chicago, annual.

Encyclopedia of Associations, 4 vol. plus supplements, Margaret Fisk, ed., Gale Research Co., Detroit, annual.

Atlases

National Geographic Atlas of the World, 5th ed., National Geographic Society, Washington, D.C., 1981.

Shepherd's Historical Altas, 9th ed., revised and updated, William R. Shepherd, ed., Barnes and Noble, Totowa, N.J., 1964 (reprinted 1980).

Commercial Atlas and Marketing Guide, Rand McNally, Chicago, 1876 to date, annual.

Dictionaries

The American Heritage Dictionary of the English Language, William Morris, ed., Houghton Mifflin, Boston, 1980 (New College Edition, 1980).

Webster's Ninth New Collegiate Dictionary, 8th ed., Merriam-Webster, Springfield, MA, 1985.

Webster's New World Dictionary of the American Language, David B. Guralnik, ed., 2nd college ed., Simon & Schuster, New York, 1984.

Webster's Third New International Dictionary, unabridged, Merriam–Webster, Springfield, MA, 1976.

Directories

Congressional Directory, new edition each Congress, U.S. Government Printing Office, Washington, D.C. (Hint: many congressman and senators will send you a copy free upon written request).

Congressional Staff Directory, Congressional Staff Directory, Mount Vernon, VA, annual.

Washington Information Directory, Congressional Quarterly Publications, Quadrangle Books, annual.

Names and Numbers: A Journalist's Guide to Most Needed Information Sources and Contacts, Rod Nordland, Wiley, New York, 1978.

City and country directories, R. L. Polk, Bresser, and Cole are among companies who annually produce these directories.

Abstracts

Statistical Abstract of the United States, U.S. Government Printing Office, Washington, D.C., annual.

Various state statistical abstracts are published by public and private publishers.

Handbooks

The Official Associated Press Almanac, Associated Press, Almanac Publishing Co., annual.

Guinness Book of World Records, Norris McWhirter, ed., Sterling Publications, New York, annual.

World Almanac and Book of Facts, Grossett and Dunlap, New York, annual.

Various state almanacs are published by public and private publishers.

BASIC SOURCES FOR FEATURE WRITERS

1. *Editorial Research Reports*, Congressional Quarterly, Inc., Washington, D.C., weekly.

2. *Europa Year Book*, 2 vol. Europa Publications, London, annual.

3. *Facts on File*, Facts on File, New York, annual cumulation and regular updates.

4. *Editorials on File*, Facts on File, New York, annual cumulation and regular updates.

5. *Followup File*, P.O. Box 330, Hastings-on-Hudson, NY, 10706, paid subscription service, weekly newsletter with up-to-date story suggestion lists.

6. *McGraw-Hill Concise Encyclopedia of Science & Technology*, Sybil P. Parker, ed., 15 vol., McGraw–Hill, New York, 1984.

7. *New York Times Cumulative Subject & Personal Name Index*, Edward A. Reno, series ed., Microfilming Corp., of America, Glen Rock, NJ, annual. Covers 1913–present.

8. *Guide to Reference Books*, Eugene P. Sheehy, 10th ed., American Library Association, Chicago, 1986.

9. *Wall Street Journal Index*, Dow Jones, New York, annual. Covers 1958–present.

10. *World of Learning*, Europa Publications, Ltd., London, 2 vol. annual. Issued since 1947.

11. *Access, The Supplementary Index to Periodicals*, John Gordon Burke Publishers, Inc., Evanston, IL, annual. Covers 1979–present.

12. *NewsBank Index*, NewsBank, Inc., New Canaan, CT, updated monthly. Covers 1982–present.

13. *The Magazine Index: Hot Topics*, Information Access, Los Altos, CA, updated monthly.

14. *Associated Press Stylebook and Libel Manual*, Christopher French, ed., Associated Press, New York, 1986.

FAVORITE REFERENCE BOOKS OF SUCCESSFUL WRITERS

Writer's Digest magazine once asked leading writers what they kept on their reference book shelf. Here are some of the suggestions from the list:

Associated Press Stylebook and Libel Manual, suggested by Winfred Van Atta

Brewer's Dictionary of Phrase & Fable, suggested by Harlan Ellison

Cambridge Encyclopedia of Astronomy, suggested by Isaac Asimov

Familiar Quotations, suggested by Art Spikol

Guinness Book of World Records, suggested by Isaac Asimov

Lange's Encyclopedia of World History, suggested by Isaac Asimov

National Geographic magazine, suggested by Winfred Van Atta

The Complete New York Times Film Reviews, suggested by Rex Reed

The Filmgoer's Companion, suggested by Rex Reed

The International Directory of Little Magazines & Small Presses, suggested by Lee Pennington

The New York Times Manual of Style and Usage, suggested by Arthur Hailey

The Shorter Oxford English Dictionary, suggested by Art Spikol

The Synonym Finder, suggested by Arthur Hailey

Webster's Biographical Dictionary, suggested by Isaac Asimov

Webster's Geographical Dictionary, suggested by Isaac Asimov

World Almanac and Book of Facts, suggested by Harlan Ellison

Writer's Market, suggested by Lee Pennington

AN INDEX OF PERIODICAL INDEXES FOR WRITERS

Free-lance writer and librarian Lois Horowitz has compiled this list of indexes for *Writer's Digest* that is particularly useful for writers:

Abstracts of Popular Culture

Access

Applied Science & Technology Index

Art Index

Biological and Agricultural Index

Business Periodicals Index

Catholic Periodical and Literature Index

Chicorel's Index to Abstracting and Indexing Services in the Humanities and Social Sciences

Consumer Index to Product Evaluations and Information Services

Education Index

Film Literature Index

Humanities Index

Index to Free Periodicals

Index to How-to-Do-It Information

Index to Jewish Periodicals

Index to New England Periodicals

Index to Periodicals By and About Blacks

Magazine Index

Music Index
New Periodicals Index
Physical Education/Sports Index
Physical Education Index
Pool's Index to Periodicals
Popular Music Index
Popular Periodicals Index
Psychological Abstracts
Reader's Guide to Periodical Literature
Runner's Index
Social Sciences Index
Sociological Abstracts
Subject Index to Children's Magazines
Ulrich's International Periodicals Directory

INTERVIEWING RESEARCH PREPARATION

Certainly an important step in preparing an article is interviewing. After you have done your homework on the subject and learned what you can about it, you still have to consider the special demands of interviews. Each interview, if done well, should have its own preparation effort, customized for the source.

Columnist Art Spikol (1987a) tells *Writer's Digest* readers the two words all writers need to remember are "be prepared." He argues ". . . there's no excuse for sounding ill-prepared" (p. 10). And California State University-Sacramento Professor Shirley Biagi (1986) says there are four basic questions a writer needs to answer when conducting research for an interview:

1. What information do you want to know?
2. Why do you want to know that information?
3. How will you use the information?
4. How much time do you have to do your research?

Without the right preparation or focus, an interview may waste both your time and your source's time. Biagi (1986) writes. "Well-documented research gives you the background you need to ask good questions, to match your interviewee's answers with what your research tells you. To be a truly good researcher, you can't be satisfied with just *an* answer. You must always look until you find *the best* answer" (p. 44).

When you get the best answer, you can then set up the interview. Most of the time, your research will tell you what direction to take. You should write down or type your questions in advance, each one based on the research you have done. These question lists can serve as a crutch during the interview. They show the sources that you took the time to prepare for the time you have with them. But you must remain flexible during the interview to get into other subjects and concerns beyond what your research told you. There are times when your well-researched questions will wind up only as a jumping off point for an interview.

In most cases, the article you are writing will require that you do some detective work to get the information you need to do the article right. A few subjects will give you the luxury of getting by without significant research. Your best bet, regardless, is to know where to go to get the answers when you need to get them *before* you go into an interview.

CONDUCTING INTERVIEWS

Too many good books are written about journalistic interviewing to attempt to tell you everything here. This discussion focuses on interviewing as a research tool and offers advice on how you can use interviews to gather information.

After you have done your pre-interview homework, the time arrives to go to the telephone or into the field. Assuming you have found the right authoritative sources for your story, your next step is to set up the meeting to talk.

Your interpersonal communication skills are put to test during an interview. You should try to relax the person you are talking to and make the experience seem less like an interview and more like a conversation between two people who just met.

How is this done? If you can, start by chatting about something neutral. Take a moment to get to know the person. Tell the person about yourself. Let them get to know you and become more comfortable with you. But you have to judge how much casual conversation is enough. It is obvious that a busy banker is less interested in casual conversation than a relaxed, grandfatherly craftsman might be.

Remember, you will have different experiences, depending on whether the interview is conducted in person or on the telephone. Although the telephone saves time, you lose the familiarity of being there with the source.

Treat your source as you would like to be treated. Dress professionally. Be polite and considerate. Identify yourself. Explain your purpose and how much time you want.

Because getting information is your goal, always be certain of the information you are getting during your interview, regardless of whether it is in person or on the telephone. Verify spellings and the meaning of technical terms. Ask a second time if necessary. Follow up the responses with questions designed to clarify, such as "Why?" Don't be afraid to show you don't know something.

Because many interviews in the course of the research process are vital to the story you do, it is often wise to take a tape recorder with you. In fact, some professional writers use two recorders to guard against failure of one of the machines. But be sure your source knows you are taping the interview. At the same time you record, you should continue to take notes as you would normally because your notes will help you in finding quotes on the tape later during the writing process.

Shirley Biagi recommends that during the interview you should relax and let your source do the talking . . . simply bite your tongue if you are inclined to talk too much or interrupt before someone finishes answering your question. Biagi also says you should display empathy and concentrate on what your source is saying. It makes a difference if you note gestures and expressions by your source, as well as his or her physical characteristics. It is helpful, of course, during in-person interviews to look around the room when you get the chance—to learn more about the person. Biagi also cautions beginning writers to watch for sudden shifts in direction of the interview. And, she says, be prepared to get away from the questions you developed if something more interesting arises.

And here's a final tip: When you are winding up the interview, make certain you know how to find the person later if you need to conduct a second interview. Get a telephone number. It may not always be in the same place as the first interview. And double check critical information before you go.

Remember, this is how just one interview goes. Most stories require that you repeat this process in researching a story. Seldom can you get a complete picture of a situation depending on one interview. And, unfortunately, this is the error of many beginning writers. There is always more than one point of view and one side to a feature story. It is your job to find the others.

OBSERVATIONAL RESEARCH TECHNIQUES

There are times when an article can be researched simply by going to a location and looking around. You might be writing a piece on flood damage, and a tour of a flooded area can tell you much more than reading books or talking to people who had previously experienced floods.

Most of the time, however, you will be combining observation with interviewing and other research skills. You do not need to be a detective, but you cannot be oblivious to what is going on, either. If you find yourself dependent on others for detail and description, you must contend with distortions of fact. Thus, the more *you* see, the richer your article will be. Most people are simply not accustomed to noting detail like a detective, and you have to train yourself through practice to do it well.

Stanford University Professor William Rivers (1975) recommends guidelines to avoid the potential pitfalls of observing:

1. Remember the process of distortion. People tend to change what they see to become consistent with their own previous experiences. And there is also

distortion of perspective. Point of view can give you a different look at matters from someone else's point of view.

2. Recall emotional states. Your emotional response to a situation can affect what you see and later recall.

3. Concentrate on important details.

4. Seek other evidence. Consider the perspectives of others.

5. Observe unobtrusively. If people know you are intentionally watching, it may affect their normal behavior. This does not preclude observation that is known to the source, but do not interfere with what you are observing.

6. Become a participant if you can, but only if you want this special point of view. You are certain to distort behavior of those around you if your purpose is known, but often the experience is still worth it for your article.

7. Watch for nonverbal communication such as body language. What a person says is not all that the person communicates.

Author Jacqueline Briskin (1979) recommends one rather unusual technique that will lend a guiding hand to your observational talents. She recommends that when you are out looking around—touring a museum, for example, to research a story—sometimes your camera can help you with your notetaking. The pictures don't have to be publishable. Yet the approach makes good sense. The detail contained in a picture might just jog your memory or provide the image for a description needed in your article. In fact, Briskin calls her 35mm camera (or any instant camera, for that matter) her most important research tool. Just consider how a camera might help you capture the color and pageantry of a festival or block party, and you might just decide this tool will help you, also, especially if you do not plan to write your article right away. In this case, a picture might really be worth a thousand words—in your notebook.

PARTICIPANT/DO-IT-YOURSELF RESEARCH TECHNIQUES

The participant form of observing is unique because you get involved in the story personally. As a participant, you become part of the story. This can have certain advantages, such as in travel writing when you relate your personal travel experiences to the reader. Other approaches are more third person and do not thrust you as a writer into the middle of the story.

You can accomplish some research for stories by experiencing an activity yourself. Usually this is research that you simply could not find from other sources. Some serious subjects require it, especially if the article subject involves illegal activities. When confronted with tough questions about illegal activities, sources will almost always deny involvement; you get first-hand knowledge by becoming a participant and witness. However, in addition to being dangerous, these stories present ethical problems because there can be no disclosure that you are a writer. Many professionals discourage deception in researching a story, but in some cases it may be necessary. You and your editors must judge that.

On less serious stories, some excellent feature articles can result from do-it-yourself experiences. One student, when assigned to write a story based on participant observation, took a flying lesson and learned to pilot a private plane. Another took it a step further and actually jumped out of the plane! She was taking parachuting lessons, of course. Both resulted in fine feature stories that dependence on another person's descriptions would not produce.

Other stories may be supplemented by participating in one or more activities. A feature article about hospital volunteers might be strengthened if you took the time to go through a training program and actually volunteered for a few hours yourself. But the story would not necessarily stand on observation alone. To make the story more complete, you would also interview veteran volunteers, the managers of the program, hospital officials, doctors and nurses, patients, and even a beginning volunteer or two. And all this would be beyond the library research you started with when the article idea first came up.

THE ISSUES TODAY

In conclusion, you should take a brief look at some of the current issues affecting your research efforts in writing feature articles.

Certainly, there are some ethical and legal considerations. In conducting your research, you may not have access to restricted information. The reasons are many, but these restrictions come in both the public sector and the private sector. Public limitations come in the form of closed records for security reasons, personnel reasons, and other reasons in local ordinances as well as state and federal laws. Private limitations are imposed by those owning the information you wish to use. You may risk legal penalties if you use information which you have obtained without permission, although at times there is public debate about what information should and should not be classified by the government, for example.

Ethically you must consider, even when you have legally obtained information, whether or not that information is best used or best not used. A recent case involving *The Miami Herald*'s investigation of the personal activities of presidential candidate Gary Hart is an example. Although the newspaper's reporters were not violating any law in observing and interviewing sources for the story, many people, both the public and media, felt the story was an invasion of privacy of the candidate, his family, and friends.

On another level, computerization of government records has created still another research problem. Many persons who once could inspect public records freely using the actual documents can no longer do so as easily because the records are stored in electronic data bases that often require clerical assistance to access.

Storage and access to information in many public and private libraries faces the same problems as more and more libraries computerize their holdings to save precious storage space.

Remember that whatever barriers you encounter and regardless of how you hurdle them, you must remain accurate in your research in any article your write. Authors Patricia Kubis and Robert Howland (1985) advise you in this way: "If you are inaccurate in your research, and your article or book is published, you will have every specialist writing to your publisher and pointing out all your discrepancies. If you write articles, inaccuracy will not have a favorable effect on your career—because truthfulness is a major part of being a journalist. . . . [B]eing inaccurate destroys your credibility as an authority figure" (p. 145).

BEST SOURCES

Recognized authorities and experts such as professors and researchers
Reference books and periodicals
     Dictionaries
     Encyclopedias
     Biographical dictionaries
     Atlases, wall maps, and gazetteers
     Yearbooks
     Almanacs
     Books of quotations
     Abstracts
     Chronologies
     Indexes

Computer data-base searches and information retrieval systems
     Your own organization's library
     Public and private libraries
     Library telephone reference services
     Corporate and commercial public relations practitioners
     Your trained observations of others
     Your participation experiences

TWO ELECTRONIC DATA-BASE SIGN ON SCREENS

VU/TEXT * PLEASE SIGN ON:

****

PLEASE TYPE YOUR INTERNAL FILE OR PROJECT IDENTIFICATION. IF NONE, PRESS THE "RETURN" KEY.

VU/TEXT INFORMATION SERVICES, INC.
A KNIGHT-RIDDER COMPANY

```
•••••••••••••••••••••••••••••••••••••••••••••••••••
*   ENTER DATABASE YOU WISH TO SEARCH  *
*        OR PRESS ENTER OR RETURN        *
*    FOR A LIST OF AVAILABLE DATABASES   *
•••••••••••••••••••••••••••••••••••••••••••••••••••
```

THESE DATABASES ARE CURRENTLY AVAILABLE:

DATABASE NAME	ACTIVE DATES	CODE
THE MIAMI HERALD	JANUARY 1, 1989 TO CURRENT	MHP
	JANUARY 1, 1988 TO DECEMBER 31, 1988	H88
	JANUARY 1, 1987 TO DECEMBER 31, 1987	H87
	JANUARY 1, 1986 TO DECEMBER 31, 1986	H86
	JANUARY 1, 1985 TO DECEMBER 31, 1985	H85
	JANUARY 1, 1984 TO DECEMBER 31, 1984	H84
	JANUARY 1, 1983 TO DECEMBER 31, 1983	H83
EL MIAMI HERALD		
(SPANISH)	JANUARY 1, 1989 TO CURRENT	EHP
	JANUARY 1, 1986 TO DECEMBER 31, 1987	E87
	NOVEMBER 10, 1982 TO DECEMBER 31, 1987	

PLEASE TYPE DATA BASE CODE, OR PUSH RETURN OR ENTER FOR MORE INFORMATION

FOR INFORMATION ON ANY DATABASE CALL VU/TEXT AT 800-258-8080 (IN PA. 215-574-4421)

•••

Welcome to IBIS
The Integrated Bibliographic Information System
of
The University of Miami Library

IBIS includes books and other library materials cataloged from 1975 to November 2, 1988.

For information on how to use this catalog, press the key marked RETURN.

◀RETURN▶

To look for a particular subject, type FIND SUBJECT (or just F S), then the subject; for example, FIND SUBJECT REFUGEES, or F S DANCE.

To look for an author, type FIND AUTHOR (or just F A), then the author; for example, FIND AUTHOR BRUCE GRANT, or F A JOSEPH CONRAD.

To look for a title, type FIND TITLE (or just F T), then the title; for example, FIND TITLE BOAT PEOPLE, or F T HEART OF DARKNESS.

To look for an item by author and title, type FIND AUTHOR, the author, AND TITLE, then the title; for example, FIND AUTHOR GRANT AND TITLE BOAT PEOPLE.

After you have typed one of these commands, press the key marked RETURN.

For more information, just press these commands, press the key marked RETURN.

◀RETURN▶

Instructions to IBIS are called commands. Examples of commands are:

FIND SUBJECT REFUGEES
FIND AUTHOR BRUCE GRANT
FIND TITLE BOAT PEOPLE

After you have typed a command, press the key marked RETURN. IBIS will then search the catalog and report how many items it finds.

To see these items, press the RETURN key. For fuller information, type DISPLAY FULL (or just DF).

If you make a mistake in typing, press the key marked BACKSPACE to backspace over the mistake, then re-type.

Always press the key marked RETURN when you finish typing.

For more information, type HELP (or just H), then press RETURN.

A Professional's Point of View

By Jacqui Banaszynski
St. Paul Pioneer Press Dispatch

Reporting—especially the daily newspaper variety—is fabulous improvisational theater.

Each day we start with a blank paper and set out to tell the history of the world. Much of that history is fairly predictable and, thus, familiar: politics, taxes, worn-out debates about abortion and gun control, sporting events won and lost.

But often history-in-the-making catches us by surprise. Only a few of us who covered the meltdown of Three Mile Island had ever studied the innards of a nuclear power plant. Fewer still had first-hand knowledge of volcanoes when we were sent to Washington for the eruption of Mount St. Helens. AIDS remains such a mystery that we struggle to find the questions—to say nothing of the answers.

Yet we are expected to write about these subjects with accuracy and authority. Often, we are expected to do that on deadline.

So we improvise. We learn to be quick with our pens, quicker with our questions, instant with our analysis. In a few days or a few hours, we cull the pertinent wisdom from experts who have spent lifetimes studying a topic. Unless we settle into a specialized beat and nurture our own expertise, we bounce from story to story armed with little but instinct and moxie.

In-depth research is a luxury in the business. Doing your homework—most would call it backgrounding—is a necessity. However rushed the assignment, there are a few basics that will save you embarrassment and mistakes:

• Start in the newsroom library, or morgue, then expand your search to the public library. Read everything available in the popular press about your subject. Tap into your newspaper's electronic library and cull some national stories for context. But beware: You are seeking information, not attitude. Don't let background reading shape your point of view. Don't enter an interview looking for a few quotes to drop into an already-written story.

• Gather quick tips from other people. Corner an editor or veteran reporter for summaries about your subject. Ask colleagues, friends, and relatives what they want to know about the subject. Supplement your curiosity with theirs. When I did a profile of North Pole explorer Ann Bancroft, my newsroom curiosity survey revealed a question I would have overlooked: How did she go to the bathroom when it was 70-below? That question led to a wonderful anecdote that gave the story some humor, humanity, and dimension.

• If you have time, conduct a few pre-interview interviews. Written research will give you background, but it won't give you quotes or character. Glean impressions of your subject first-hand—from boosters, from detractors, and from knowledgeable, but detached, observers. Check their comments against those of your subject.

Since being awarded a Pulitzer Prize, I have been on the receiving end of reporters' notebooks—a vantage point that has underscored some basic journalistic tenets that we too-often take for granted.

When reporters interview me, I expect them to already have our Pulitzer series "AIDS in the Heartland" and a few other accessible clippings from local newspapers that would include my basic biography. The diligent ones also will have talked to one or more people about me—perhaps an editor or a colleague or one of my story subjects. If they haven't done that legwork, I find myself feeling impatient and a bit insulted. I am not willing to give my time and candor to someone who hasn't shown me courtesy to do their homework. I imagine my interview subjects feel the same way. (Banaszynski, 1988, personal communication)

* * *

Jacqui Banaszynski is a special projects reporter for the *St. Paul (Minn.) Pioneer Press Dispatch*. She has been a reporter and feature writer there since 1984, covering what she calls "the bummer beat"—stories about victims and human grief. She won the 1988 Pulitzer Prize for feature writing and a 1987 Society of Professional Journalists/Sigma Delta Chi Distinguished Service Award for her moving series, "AIDS in the Heartland." The series was published in summer 1987. Banaszynski was also a finalist in the 1986 Pulitzer Prize competition for international reporting for her "Trail of Tears," a personal story of famine in Africa. Banaszynski interned at *The Wall Street Journal* and *The Indianapolis Star*. She also worked for the *Minneapolis Star and Tribune*, *The (Eugene, Ore.) Register-Guard*, *The Duluth (Minn.) News-Tribune*, and *The Janesville (Wis.) Gazette*.

4

Writing and Editing Feature Articles

The late E. B. White has said writing rules are "somewhat a matter of individual preference, and even the established rules of grammar are open to challenge." These are the tools of your trade, the rules of your game. Good writing has a certain foundation upon which it is built and a certain polish or finish upon which it is sold to the buyer.

Yet, as White observes in the writer's little bible, *The Elements of Style* (1979), his Cornell professor, William Strunk, once said, "The best writers sometimes disregard the rules of rhetoric. When they do so, however, the reader will usually find in the sentence some compensating merit, attained at the cost of the violation. Unless he is certain of doing as well, he will probably do best to follow the rules" (p. xvi).

Good writing is difficult to achieve, but with the right desire and the right tools, you can do it. Good ideas put on paper still need good massaging—good polish, that is—to make them presentable to readers. This chapter will give you the basics of good article-writing style and organization. It will also offer time-tested suggestions for editing your own manuscript to get it ready for an editor or publisher.

You will investigate the art and craft of article writing in this chapter. After reading it, you will know the ways and means of getting an article onto paper. You will learn how experts manage their writing and how varied the approaches might be to achieve the same goal of publication. You have to, ultimately, sell your idea and yourself.

THE ELEMENTS OF GOOD WRITING

Much work goes into good writing. William Zinsser, who has written for newspapers and magazines and authored numerous books, considers good writing a disciplined, rigorous effort that comes from practice. It takes rewriting, what he calls "the essence of writing" (Zinsser, 1980 p. 4). It takes the same regular, daily schedule that a craftsman might use in making furniture or art. Zinsser also explains that writing is a solitary effort of people who do not mind being alone. Yet he also believes writing can be easy and fun.

Lawyers, for example, often write with clutter and complexity. Good writers keep it simple. Zinsser calls clutter the "disease of American writing" (p. 7). He is right. This is especially true for writers for mass publications such as newspapers and magazines. And since there's no particular reason for newspaper and magazine feature articles to be complex or difficult, you should keep it simple. This means you have to translate complicated material, such as medical or other scientific terms, for your readers. "We are a society strangling in unnecessary words, circular constructions, pompous frills and meaningless jargon" (1980, p. 7), Zinsser believes.

A good newspaper or magazine writer will keep thoughts easy to understand. This is done several ways. First, it is done through your word selection. Use the right words, but don't use too many of the right words. Be concise. Be precise in meaning. Second, keep your thoughts easy to understand by using basic subject-verb-object sentence structure. Even if you can find a way to write a sentence as verb-subject, it is likely to be hard to understand, and you have wasted your reader's time. And if you do that often enough, you lose the reader permanently. A third way to help the reader understand what you are writing is to use correct grammar. Usage helps the communication process. People are accustomed to seeing certain forms of grammar, such as subjects and verbs that are in agreement or consistent use of tense. And fourth, another way to write in simple English is to keep an eye on sentence length. The longer the sentence, the harder it is to follow. You do not want your reader going through your article and wondering to himself or herself, "What did that mean?" Am I crazy? Why can't I figure out what this means?"

Style is another consideration when you think about good writing. Every writer has a style. Every publication has a style manual. Both points will be discussed here.

Writing style is much like one's personal appearance. Your appearance reflects your own way of dressing, your mannerisms, and your physical uniqueness. Writing does much of the same thing, but it reveals a bit about our minds, our thinking, our logic, and our expression of those processes.

Most experienced writers and writing teachers will tell you that to teach writing, you have to start with basics, no matter whether it is sixth-grade theme writing or freshman composition at a Big Ten university. As Zinsser (1980) has said, "You have to strip down your writing before you can build it back up" (p. 19).

WORD USAGE AND CHANGES IN MEANING

Columbia University Professor Earnest Brennecke (Wardlow, 1985, p. 24) created the following eight sentences and eight *different* meanings by changing the location of one word. Read the sentences or say them out loud. Notice how the meaning of each sentence changes as the location of the word *only* changes. Here's a lesson—one you should not forget—about saying precisely what you mean in a sentence.

Only I hit him in the eye yesterday.
I *only* hit him in the eye yesterday.
I hit *only* him in the eye yesterday.
I hit him *only* in the eye yesterday.
I hit him in *only* the eye yesterday.
I hit him in the *only* eye yesterday.
I hit him in the eye *only* yesterday.
I hit him in the eye yesterday *only*.

After mastering cumbersome language, complete sentence structure and the like, you can begin to build your own style. The late novelist Paul Darcy Boles (1985) called style a "way of saying" and a "way of seeing." He said it is somewhat born into the owner, but it is also borrowed. Many writers become the product of other writers they admire. The process of stealing technique is a rather accepted one in the business of writing—we become a mixture of the styles of writers we read and enjoy the most while we are learning to write.

And, really, you don't have to work too hard to develop a style. It is not so much a conscious matter of writing as an unconscious matter of writing. It evolves and comes through your writing whether you want it or not. Everyone has a writing style.

On the other hand, the business of a style manual is another issue altogether. You will find most, if not all, publications have their own style manuals or have adapted the manuals of other organizations. Magazines such as *U. S. News and World Report* have their own manual. Newspapers such as *The New York Times* and *Chicago Tribune* have their own. Wire services such as Associated Press and United Press International have widely used manuals for writers and reporters. You will find some of these stylebooks are for sale to the public as well. These books are reference books containing the rules of usage for local and not-so-local matters which commonly are used. The range covers basics such as numbers and names, but also more complicated matters such as religious titles, foreign geographic names, and even medical terms.

So, even if you are an independent writer, you need to know the major usage (style) guide of the publication when you prepare a manuscript for its editor.

Another element of good writing focuses on the audience, or, in the language of communication theorists, the receiver of your message. Who is going to read your article? Do you know? Have you thought about it? How can you find out?

There is a high degree of seriousness in those questions. If you don't know the answers, can you honestly write well for that audience? No.

For some publications, it is easy to know who reads each edition. For others, it is difficult to tell without research. A specialized publication, such as an industry magazine or a legal newspaper, will have a well-defined audience. But the general circulation daily or weekly newspaper and some consumer magazines must be researched before you know anything certain about the audience.

You want to be careful to write at the level of the audience. If you write too far below it, you will turn off readers. If you write too far above it, you will lose readers. In fact, if you miss estimating the audience too much, you won't even get past first base with your editor and will never reach any readers.

Certainly you have to have a sense of timing with readers and audiences, too. The right mood, writing style, and sensitivity make an article work. Make the wrong choices and the article will work against you. Thus, you have to know when to use humor, when to be serious, when to be emotional, when to be straight. Knowing your audience will help you chart the course through these dangerous waters.

Some general points about writing mechanics have already been made. You have read about the value of grammar in this chapter already. In reality, not enough can be said to beginning feature writers about spelling, about syntax, and about punctuation. In fact, former Hartford, Connecticut, *Courant* editor and publisher Bob Eddy (1979) calls spelling the curse of the working journalist. For writers, each of these skills *is* important. If you cannot handle the basic skills such as spelling, you will eventually lose your job.

Often writing students dismiss spelling or punctuation as unimportant at the moment because, they say, "It is the idea that matters. I'll learn the rules of spelling later." If a carpenter were to say that about building a house, it would come crashing down. The same goes for your writing. It will cause your plan to fail unless you use the right tools and materials: language, words, spelling, punctuation. Use of words can be helped by regular use of a dictionary, a thesaurus, and other word reference books available at most bookstores. Your shelves should be stocked with at least one dictionary, a thesaurus, and a handful of stylebooks—at least one, but several if you work for a number of publications or use different writing styles. Several good reference books were suggested in chapter 3, you might recall.

Unity is like an anchor for good writing, Zinsser says. Some might call this concept a matter of consistency in your writing. Whatever you wind up calling it, remember it is a critical element of good writing.

Verb tense, pronoun point of view, and mood are all indicators of unity in your writing. It is best to maintain a level of consistency on each. Don't mix tense. Past and present tense in the same sentence will only confuse your reader. Pronouns that jump around from first to second to third person are equally disconcerting for readers. Mixture of mood can cause perhaps the most serious confusion for a reader who does not know whether to laugh, cry, be sad or happy, or how to respond to your message.

Each of these points about good writing requires your attention and time. If you learn to manage them, you should find great improvement in your ability to communicate to the world.

FINDING YOUR WAY TO A SATISFACTORY STYLE

William Strunk, Jr. and E.B. White, in their classic *The Elements of Style*, offer "cautionary hints" to help you find a style that works. Consider these items:
1. Place yourself in the background.
2. Write in a way that comes naturally.
3. Work from a suitable design.
4. Write with nouns and verbs.
5. Revise and rewrite.
6. Do not overwrite.
7. Do not overstate.
8. Avoid the use of qualifiers.
9. Do not affect a breezy manner.
10. Use orthodox spelling.
11. Do not explain too much.
12. Do not construct awkward adverbs.
13. Make sure the reader knows who is speaking.
14. Avoid fancy words.
15. Do not use dialect unless your ear is good.
16. Be clear.
17. Do not inject opinion.
18. Use figures of speech sparingly.
19. Do not take shortcuts at the cost of clarity.
20. Avoid foreign languages.
21. Prefer the standard to the offbeat.

GIVING AN IDEA FOCUS AND DEPTH

A large portion of chapter 2 was devoted to finding a good article idea. Some attention was given to developing the idea and giving it focus and depth; now let's return to these issues in the context of writing.

Focus comes throughout the article, but it begins with the lead. A well-chosen lead, or introduction, tells the reader what you mean to achieve in the article. It is up to you to guide the reader through the article, much like a road map, with the theme or idea you have introduced in the beginning paragraphs of your article.

For a writer, focus is the key. If you can remember this, you will do better as a writer. Your articles will be stronger.

The focus of the article must carry through the rest of the article after you have constructed the lead. It carries through the body of the article as well. Then it dominates the ending, also.

Think of the focus as the article's "angle" that you read about earlier. To write a feature article only about appliance repairs leaves so much to write that a series of books could be produced. But to write about a shop that repairs household appliances is another matter. And to center the attention on the 85-year-old owner who does all the work himself re-directs the article still again.

You must be disciplined not to fall into the temptation to drift in your writing. Examine each paragraph as a unit. Is it necessary? Does it help get to the point? Then examine each sentence within each paragraph. Does each sentence help maintain the point of the paragraph? Then, finally, examine each word within each sentence. Are all words needed? Do they help the purpose of the individual sentence?

GETTING YOUR IDEA DOWN ON PAPER

How do you get the ideas in your mind on paper? Surely, as there are many outlets for your work, there are many approaches to the physical act of writing.

Some veteran writers like to labor over a manual typewriter as they have done for years. Others have made the technological leap to electric typewriters. And other have entered the computer age and write on personal computers or dedicated word processors.

There are writers who will want to work in the early morning because they are "morning people." These people rise and jump at the chance to get their creative juices flowing while they are fresh. Others, it seems, cannot get going until finishing several cups of coffee, a newspaper, the mail, and other activities. These afternoon writers seem most comfortable at that time of day. And, as you have guessed, some writers thrive at night. When all is quiet and the day is almost done, these writers are busy at creating and work through much of the night, only to rest in the morning.

There are writers who will use a dictation machine or tape recorder to write, turning over the mundane duties of typing and preparing a manuscript to an assistant. These "idea" writers don't want to be bothered with clerical duties of typing or setting up a printer. Yet, some writers feel much closer to their work when they can do just that—control the typewriter and other effects of the writer's private work environment. Some still prefer to handwrite their manuscripts and don't deal with any machines at all, not even tape recorders.

You can find writers who want to work in absolute silence to enhance their concentration. Some like to work in a social environment where other people are present, such as an office. The interaction seems to stimulate and inspire rather than interrupt and retard. Still others like to have a stereo playing loudly, or softly, or the television tuned to a program for background noise.

Some writers will produce a manuscript in one long and exhausting effort. Others will produce it in bits and pieces. And some writers will write a manuscript as it is presented, from beginning to end. You will find others who will write the middle first, the end, and then the beginning. Some author's styles will be to research first, then write. Some professionals will simultaneously research and write. There also are writers who revise as they write, a sentence at a time, and writers who write many pages and then revise.

Some people like to write at home. Some lease office space. And others, who have full-time jobs doing something else, like to write in their regular work environment.

These styles are as different as any other personal work habits. You have to find what is right for you. Try a variety of combinations to determine what is the most productive and efficient environment for your writing. Then, as Zinsser has said, stick to it. The habit of writing counts. It isn't so important what constitutes the habit, as you will see in the next sections.

ORGANIZING YOUR INFORMATION

You have several concerns when organizing the information you have collected for your article. Remember, the organizational approaches will vary depending on the style of writing and the medium, but there are several standard ways of organizing yourself before you even start writing. You will find discussion of common newspaper and magazine organizational strategies in the sections that follow.

Different organizational approaches represent the personality of the writer as much as do the space where you work, your typewriter (or computer), and work habits.

Probably the most common way to get the mass of information you have collected together is to use an *outline* to get started. Writers who use outlines have different styles of outlining as well. Some write formal sentence outlines and others use simple topical outlines. Others will sketch an outline of an article on their computer screen or on paper in their typewriter and begin to fill in the gaps as they sift through the notes and interviews that have been completed. A good procedure for beginners might be the following steps:

1. Think of the main points of the article and make these topics the Roman numerals of your outline. These are also your article's main sections.

2. Next, divide each of the main sections into subsections. What are the major characteristics, or concerns, of each Roman numeral section? There might be just one characteristic or several dozen. *List each* so you will not forget to

include these as you begin to write portions of the manuscript. You should letter each of these A, B, and so on.

3. If the article is going to be lengthy, you might want to go beyond the alphabetic listings. If you do extend the outline, these will be details of each subsection and they can be numbered 1, 2, and so forth.

4. On longer articles, or articles with sidebars and boxed inserts such as many magazines use, you should use a separate outline for the sidebar. Often, after writing the main article, you will spot a portion of the main article outline that will lend itself to a "take out" or "sidebar."

These steps will help you to write and organize, especially, longer manuscripts. Shorter (under 1,000 words) articles common in newspapers might not need this sort of rigorous organizational plan, but even shorter pieces will benefit if you find yourself confused about what you have before the writing stage.

One of the conveniences of personal computers and word processors is the ease of moving things around. If you use a computer to write, take advantage of the flexibility and ease of organizing and re-organizing your facts even at the outline stage.

Paper outlines and computers are one approach, but there are others. Some experienced writers prefer using standard file cards in 3 x 5 or 5 x 7 format. This approach works well for shuffling and re-ordering the information once it is listed on cards. The approach, again, is pretty straight forward:

1. List each important point on an individual card.
2. Place cards with related information in the same pile as you begin to sort through the deck.
3. Order the piles according to the direction you want the information to flow in the article.
4. Then sort each individual pile to logically support the general point that the pile or cards represents.

Still another approach is to use a notebook. Divide it into sections and place relevant information about each section into the binder. Then you can move material around as necessary, page by page, or section by section, until you get it into a form that you want to use to write.

Finally, a technique some writers use helps them to get "the big picture" of the organizational plan of their article. This approach requires these steps:

1. Write a very rough draft of as much of your manuscript as you can.
2. Take scissors and cut it up, a paragraph at a time.
3. Tape the pieces or tack them to a wall or bulletin board.

4. Study the pieces on the wall. Move the pieces as needed to improve the flow and direction of your article.

You have other basic decisions to make when contemplating the organizational plan of your article. Consider these as you move into the next sections that discuss the particulars of newspaper and magazine organization and structure. The American Press Institute (1985, Wardlow) says these are the three basic questions in organizing your information:

1. What type of lead?
2. What manner of telling?
3. Third person, or first?

BASIC NEWSPAPER FEATURE ORGANIZATION, STRUCTURE

Newspaper features employ a variety of leads and organizational plans. You want your article to start well and retain readership for the rest of the article. Thus, the lead is quite important. It can help determine the mood of the article. It should persuade the reader to stay with the article. Here are some of the basic newspaper leads commonly used for features:

1. *Summary lead.* This lead gives the traditional five *w's* and *h* (who, what, when, where, why, and how) in as few words as possible. Some summary leads focus on one or two of these elements of the story and save the others, that are judged less important, for later in the story.

2. *Salient feature lead.* This lead focuses on one major characteristic of the story. Instead of several points in a color story about a festival, the salient feature lead emphasizes one point about food, music, or weather, for example.

3. *Anecdotal lead.* These leads are also called case approach leads and *Wall Street Journal* feature leads. The reason is simple: these stories use a specific representative example or story to illustrate a point about a situation that is discussed in general after the lead of the story. Thus, instead of writing about the woes of unemployed oil workers in Texas, this approach would describe one person or family in the lead.

4. *Quote leads.* Some writers like to open a feature with a quotation. The quote can be from a person being profiled or an expression of sentiment common at a meeting or concert, but is must catch the gist of the article while being the exact words of a source important to the story.

5. *Delayed–suspended interest leads.* These leads deliberately hold the big news of the story from the reader to tease the reader further into the story. It is a lead that works well when there is some question of the outcome of a situation, such

as an article about a lost memento that is found or an article describing the sudden joy of a big contest prize winner.

6. *Question lead*. This sort of lead asks a question of the reader, usually in direct address. The key here, of course, is to be sure to answer the question in the story, preferably in the top half of the story while the question is still in the reader's mind.

Whatever the lead, it should be a stirring paragraph. The 1986 Pulitzer Prize-winning *Miami Herald* reporter Edna Buchanan (Knight-Ridder, 1986), says this about her lead-writing philosophy: "My idea of a successful lead is one that might cause a reader who is having breakfast with his wife to spit out his coffee, clutch his chest and say, 'My God, Martha? Did you read this?' "

Story organizational forms are also broad in scope to give you flexibility in fitting the organizational plan to the story. Here are the main time-tested story structures of newspaper features:

1. *Inverted pyramid*. This approach might work for some features, but it is best used in straight news writing. This story is less appropriate for feature material because it is structured by most important to least important priorities. It usually requires a summary lead.
2. *Chronological*. This follows sequencing of events. When a feature recounts events or describes a procedure, this approach might be best.
3. *Essay*. A rather standard approach to all writing, this is found in columns, analyses, reviews, and other personal opinion or subjective writing. The essay format is standardized with an introduction, a middle, and a conclusion.

There will be many occasions when a combination of these three plans will work best for your article. Certainly there will be some subjects that will best be handled by one approach or another, but be prepared to mix the best of each of these when the subject calls for it.

Although leads and organizational plans are at the top of the list for beginners to learn about feature writing, there are other concerns. First, remember that most newspapers maintain their own stylebooks, and usage in writing will vary from newspaper to newspaper. Certainly the differences will be distinct when compared to magazine usage. Two of the most popular stylebooks are those published by Associated Press and United Press International. Whichever book is used by the newspaper you write for, get a copy of it and use it as you write. You will notice the professional touch it gives your work.

Another consideration is point of view in your writing. Feature stories for newspapers are most often written in third person, but in some situations, such as personal experience articles, columns, and travel articles, the writing is often in first person. Remember that when you choose to write in first person, you become a significant part of the story. Do you want to be the focus of the article? If so, chose the first person "I." If not, write in third person or even second person.

For more than a decade, Maryln Schwartz has entertained Texas readers with her feature stories in the *Dallas Morning News*. Her stories illustrate each of the points about the basics of newspaper feature writing made so far in this chapter. Take a look at the leads in both stories. Each one draws you into the story. Your curiosity is aroused. The structure of each story is equally strong, resulting in easy reading and simplicity in the way each story progresses, regardless of whether it is the longer serious profile of Queen Noor al Hussein of Jordan (five pages) or the shorter, light piece about the late-night television game show (two pages). What is your reaction to reading the two stories?

BASIC MAGAZINE FEATURE ORGANIZATION, STRUCTURE

Writers Patricia Kubis and Robert Howland (1985) have stated that the *lead*, or opening paragraph, of a magazine article should achieve three goals:

1. Tell the reader what the article is about.
2. Provide the tone and mood of the article.
3. Catch the reader's attention and entice the reader to go further into the article.

Certainly the lead works with the title of the article and the layout of the first two pages to grab the reader. But the best package of color graphics won't keep a reader unless the author has done a big part in hooking the reader with a strong lead.

You have the same options for leads in magazine writing that you saw listed previously for newspaper writing. Popular among magazine writers are summary leads, salient feature and anecdotal leads, delayed or suspended interest leads, question leads, and even mood-setting descriptive leads.

In terms of structure, magazine leads are not bound by the rules of newspaper lead writing in that most newspaper editors prefer short leads that are supported by subsequent paragraphs. Magazine leads are more flexible and are quite long as often as they are short. Their purposes remain the same, however.

The examples by *Miami Herald Tropic Magazine* writer Madeleine Blais, winner of the 1980 Pulitzer Prize for her feature writing, show a variety of approaches. In her article on steam (Blais, 1987), she uses the summary lead to tell you what the story will be about, but also to describe a mood. In her article, "The Promise," a story about families and their summer activities, you are given a completely different approach. Her lead here is descriptive, yet it suspends the focus of the article so you don't get a full idea of what the article really says about summer. And finally, her third article uses still another approach—a statement that grabs you by being simple, to the point, yet only hints about what the story will soon reveal. Although each is different, each functions appropriately for the magazine feature.

The *body*, or middle, of a magazine article is the meat of the sandwich. Once the article gets started with a well-conceived lead, the momentum must continue with the body of the article. Linking together the pieces with transitional sentences and paragraphs, you must now bring in the material which you promised your reader in the lead.

General organizational approaches for magazine articles are in the essay form discussed earlier. This form emphasizes a strong lead or introduction and conclusion to fill around the body of the article. Where you set a theme or statement of purpose in your introduction by making a particular point, the body is where you support that point by providing the reader with your specifics.

Some magazine articles use chronological form. And you will find some which use a listing format that arranges information numerically, alphabetically, or in some other order.

Regardless of what organizational plan you use for your topic, your *conclusion* serves a completely different purpose. In the conclusion you clean up, you wrap up, and you tie everything together. In magazine feature writing more than newspaper writing, the conclusion plays a vital role. It is a chance to summarize the major points again for the reader. It is a chance to reveal the delayed or surprise "finish." Conclusions can be several pages or several sentences. Regardless of the length, the conclusion should not leave the reader hanging in mid air by what you have chosen to say. Reach some form of resolution. Close it out. But be careful of writing too much, as some beginning writers will do. Remember you do get a second chance at the conclusion, if you need it, when you rewrite.

REWRITING, REWRITING, AND MORE REWRITING

Some writing experts call rewriting an art. Writers Patricia Kubis and Robert Howland (1985) have said, "If you are a real writer, you *know* that *rewriting is the name of the game*" (p. 205).

Unless you are a particularly gifted writer, you will seldom find that a first draft is sufficient for publication. Most writers will find that to finish a manuscript is an achievement of note, but the real work comes in revision.

The best policy is to finish the first draft, then let it sit a while—overnight or longer, if possible. Then read it from top to bottom with a fresh mind and clear head.

You can be more critical and make some true improvements in the work. Each time you do this, the manuscript will get better as words are changed or cut, sentences are revised, and passages reorganized.

Your goal is to revise until what you have to say flows smoothly. Revise the work until it seems to glide as you read it. Although beginning writers might need more rewrites, you will find that as you become more experienced, you will write, revise, and polish to finish an article in three distinct stages.

Rewriting will help you make your thoughts clearer and, at the same time, more efficient. You can use this stage to add information, delete it, or clarify it. Rewriting is a necessary step. Even after that initial surge of creativity in writing the first draft, you will see rewriting makes a significant difference in the quality of your work. Thus you must make the time to rewrite. It is really a part of the writing process. Build it into the article production cycle you use. And remember one key question: If what you have written is not clear to you, how can it be clear to someone else? Rewriting is the answer.

USING DIRECT QUOTES

Most good feature articles are alive with quotes from a variety of people. People make features work and their words, through your use of direct quotes, give *life* to your story. Take a quick look at the articles by Maryln Schwartz (1984) and Madeleine Blais (1987). Each story is rich with direct quotes and dialogue. In fact, Blais' article, "Dyeing for Attention," is entirely constructed of quotes from an interview. It is, to say the least, a unique story approach.

There are some rules about quotes in magazine and newspaper features that you should remember.

First of all, in much of your article writing, you will find that quotes help to back up generalizations made about a person, place, or thing. Quotes give the article an element of reality beyond the perspective of the writer. For features, it means you can let someone else speak in the article when you use their *exact* words.

Many experienced feature writers use quotes in dialogue to re-create situations to provide for the reader the effect of being there—getting to watch history occur, for example, through the words of the persons who were present.

There are some helpful guidelines in using quotes in your writing. Consider these as you use quotes:

1. Make certain it is clear in the flow of your article just who is speaking. This is especially true if you change the person being quoted.

2. Vary your verbs of attribution. At times, you should rely on the standard verb, "said," but there are other more precise verbs. Most feature writing uses the past tense verb, "said," instead of the present tense verb, "says." Remember

each verb and verb tense has specific meaning when used, so take care in selecting just the right word. Thus, use past tense as your standard tense for attribution.

3. Vary placement of attribution verbs. It will be necessary to place them at the beginning of the sentence on some occasions; avoid using the verbs only at the end of sentences.

4. Be careful in using long quotes. If you must use a lengthy quote from a person or text from a document, make certain you have introduced it to the reader to explain what you are doing and why.

5. Dialogue quotations add a great deal. Use them. But be clear who is saying what. And break up long passages of dialogue, if they are necessary, with some description of action by the speakers.

6. Quote exact words and *do not* change the words in the quote. Even incorrect grammar will give the reader insight into the personality of the individual speaking.

WRITING ABOUT COMPLEX SUBJECTS

Writers who diversify their writing topics will find they occasionally will write about complicated and difficult subjects. Even those who write about one particular subject will find this challenge to their writing from time to time. You have to explain relationships, make comparisons, evaluate importance, or differentiate among a dozen elements in an article. If you can write in a clear manner about complicated matters, your reader wins.

The American Press Institute's Associate Director, Elwood Wardlow (1985), proposes three ways to explain a difficult subject and to develop a sense of comparatives and relationships. Here they are:

1. *Knowledge and awareness.* You have to be a generalist in many ways, learning as much as you can about a wide range of subjects.

2. *Practice.* The more you repeat something, the better you get at it. Try some exercises to develop your ability to describe people, places, or things. Take notes while watching events such as public hearings or meetings on television. If you can synthesize and reduce the information to understandable form without holes, you are on your way to success.

3. *Relating the unknown to the known.* If your reader has never been to a faraway place, can you describe it in terms of local nature? As Wardlow says, this is particularly true in science and technical writing (a point which will be covered in depth in a later chapter).

Wardlow notes that although this type of writing is common in the news magazines, it is not limited to those publications. All good writers, he says, should strive to do whatever is necessary to make this talent a strong point in their writing.

TOOLS: COMPUTERS, WORD PROCESSORS, AND PRINTERS

The text of this book was written on a personal computer. It was written using a word processor. The printer used for producing hard-copy drafts was a letter-quality daisy wheel printer. The specifics? The computer is an Epson Equity I with 640KB (kilobytes) of RAM (random access memory), a 20MB (megabytes) hard disk drive, and one 360KB floppy disk drive. The computer has a color monitor and color graphics adaptor (CGA) card and has the capability to run many different types of programs.

Most writers who use electronic systems to write prefer personal computers. Some personal computers are, however, dedicated to only one task and have permanent software for word processing. The machines can do only this task. You must find what is best for you. If you feel you might use your computer for purposes other than writing (such as data processing or communications with other computers by telephone line), then you probably should invest in a personal computer and purchase software for particular tasks as they are needed. On the other hand, if you feel you want to keep things simple, then a dedicated system for word processing might be best for you.

The text of this book was written on the Equity I, an IBM-compatible PC, with the Leading Edge Word Processor Ver. 1.5a. It is one of dozens of full-feature word processing software packages on the market. Most writers have specific needs for word processing (e.g., their writing) and you should make certain your software can handle your writing demands.

When looking at word processors, you will find the price often indicates the quality of available features. For example, the more expensive programs (about $200, but up to $500) will often offer features not found in less-expensive programs. You should search for software that offers all basic word processing functions. Technical writer and editor Richard Krajewski (1983) recently reviewed the market's offerings and listed these important features:

1. Good documentation (directions and instructions).
2. Menus and help options (when you get stuck).
3. Overtyping, inserting, and deleting capability (these are the *very* basics).
4. Cutting and pasting (moving things around).
5. Search and replacing (finding the changing things).
6. Automatic carriage return and word wrap (at the end of the line).
7. Page turning (moving from page to page).

8. Failsafe capability (writing or saving what is on the screen to disk with regularity).

9. Form letter generator or "mail merge" (permits insertion of addresses into a standardized document).

10. Pagination, line counting, word counting (determines lengths of manuscript in varying measures).

11. Text formatting (centering, indentions, underlining, and so on).

12. File handling (maintenance of files such as backups and storage).

13. Headers and footers (permits automatic page numbers, titles, and other standard information at the top or bottom of each page of the manuscript).

This book manuscript, finally, was printed on a Juki 6200 daisy wheel printer. It creates letter-quality, or final draft, copies. It does not print less-than-letter quality for drafts such as a dot matrix printer would permit (usually faster and less expensive).

Another feature of some computers, as mentioned earlier, is the ability to communicate with other computers or to be compatible with other computers. The convenience of interactive computers allows a manuscript's publisher to edit the manuscript without retyping it, to set it in type for publication without retyping it and, finally, to set it in type for publication without major retyping effort. Aside from saving production costs, it also means an article may be published faster and be in the hands of readers sooner.

You must make these choices about your own writing hardware (and software) needs. Some authors require only the basic pencil and paper. Others must not only have a PC, but the latest PC with all of the assorted peripherals.

READABILITY OF YOUR WRITING

Regardless of what you use to write your manuscript, good writing must be readable, just as it must be understandable. Readability is simply a term that describes how easy something is to read. Writing experts have been studying readability for about fifty years and have devised various rules and formulas for readability. As American Press Institute's Elwood Wardlow (p. 15) has observed, these tools for measuring readership have different ways of getting to the same points about readable articles:

1. Short is better than long.

2. Simple forms are best.

3. Personal is better than impersonal.

Well-known readability formulas include those created by Rudolph Flesch in the 1940s and Robert Gunning in the 1960s. Flesch found that there is an ideal number of words per sentence (17 to 19), an ideal number of syllables (150 per 100 words), an ideal percentage of personal interest words (such as pronouns; 6 per 100 words), and an ideal percentage of sentences that have human interest (such as direct address, questions, quotes; 12 %).

Gunning created his "fog index" for United Press International to determine the number of years of school your reader needs to understand what you have written. His formula is simple and can be used on a desk calculator:

1. Calculate the number of words per sentence by computing an *average* for several paragraphs.
2. Calculate the percentage of words having three or more syllables in the same passage.
3. Add the two figures in steps one and two, then multiply by 0.4 to determine the number of years of school your reader needs.

You can occasionally run this test on your own writing to see if you are creating readable articles for the market you seek to reach.

The late 1980s brought personal computing into writing education. As a result, there are now numerous programs available in secondary and higher education that address writing and readability. Students of writing, as well as writing teachers, now can use computer programs to calculate these readability assessments on the spot. Other forms of analysis of writing are also possible, through computers, to determine grammar, spelling, and punctuation errors that would make readability lower. Many of these programs are available at low cost through software clearinghouses or local personal computer stores.

POLISHING AND EDITING YOUR MANUSCRIPT

You can also think of rewriting as a self-editing process, but you will learn that the process is somewhat different. Rewriting means writing it over and over until it is right. Self-editing is making changes on the existing manuscript without rewriting major portions. The focus is on *self-editing* here.

There are two ways of looking at manuscript editing. First, you must consider what has to be done on your own part to improve your manuscript. This is an important stage, and it is the most significant portion of this discussion. The other, the handling that another person will give your manuscript, also remains vital to the writing process, yet it is out of your control for the most part.

But what can *you* do to improve your article? What is within your control? One editor has an answer. Phil Currie (Wardlow, 1985, p. 45), a Gannett

Company news executive, offers this checklist of the most significant problem areas to look for:

1. Dull, wooden phrasing
2. Poor grammar, spelling, and punctuation
3. Story organization
4. Errors of fact or interpretation
5. Holes in stories, completeness
6. Clutter
7. Redundancy

There are other concerns in tuning a manuscript. You must, as noted before, match a publication's stylebook. You must answer the unanswered questions. You have to check for attribution strengths and weaknesses. Finally, as any copy-desk chief will tell you, tightening is always a concern about a manuscript: Watch for wordiness.

THE STEPS IN THE PRODUCTION/EDITING PROCESS

When the manuscript is completed, as far as you are concerned, it then goes to another editor for a repeat of the polishing process. Editor Arthur Plotnik (1982), in his *The Elements of Editing*, explains there are ten distinct stages in editing and processing the manuscript. Here they are, with a reminder that a high level of energy and creativity goes with each step:

1. *Acquisition.* Securing a manuscript. For a writer, this means finishing a first draft. For an editor, it means finding a finished manuscript.
2. *Agreement.* This means reaching a contracted formal agreement for publication between an author and editor.
3. *Organization.* Collecting documents and organizing materials such as permissions, revisions, and other documents.
4. *Assignment.* Editors give manuscript to the right staff copy editor.
5. *Review.* Read and re-read every item in the manuscript file.
6. *Measurement and Typesetting Specification.* Manuscript length and choice of type and graphics.
7. *Illustration and Layout Planning.* Enhancing the manuscript is the primary goal here.
8. *Styling and Copy Editing.* This is line-by-line editing of the manuscript for clarity, economy, logic, and impact.

9. *Typesetting*. Mechanical act of production of type. This is done both in-house and by contractor.

10. *Proofreading and Layout*. Editors check the final paste-up of galleys, graphics/ illustrations, cutlines/ captions, headlines/ titles, and other elements.

HOW PROFESSIONALS WROTE IT

DATE: TUESDAY, MARCH 20, 1984
SOURCE: LIFESTYLE, MIAMI NEWS, P. 3C
AUTHOR: MARYLN SCHWARTZ, DALLAS MORNING NEWS

* * *

JORDAN'S QUEEN STILL REMAINS AN ALL-AMERICAN GIRL

Her life sounds like a fairy tale. She was a beautiful American living in a foreign country. She met and fell in love with a handsome king. They had a whirlwind courtship and he proposed.

"But my life is not a fairy tale," says Queen Noor Al Hussein, the American-born wife of King Hussein of Jordan. "Being a queen is really a lot of very hard work. I consider myself a working mother."

Queen Noor, 32, is the former Lisa Najeeb Halaby of Washington. She was in Dallas last week to address the Dallas Council on World Affairs. Later, she sat in her suite at The Mansion on Turtle Creek and described her courtship.

She and the king became fast friends in 1978. She was 26 years old, a Princeton University graduate, an architect. She was working and traveling extensively in the Middle East.

The king was 16 years her senior. He had seven children from three previous marriages. He had divorced his first and second wives; his third wife died in a helicopter crash.

"I had met his majesty several times," she says. "He asked me to help him with some structural problems he was having with his home. I agreed, but I soon realized he needed the help of an engineer. I was embarrassed that I wouldn't be able to help him. But I did give him some advice."

Then in the midst of the consultation, she says, the two struck up a friendship.

"It was very difficult for him to get close," she says. "He is a good example of the saying, 'lonely at the top.' It was wonderful that we got along so well, that we could become such good friends. And because I was supposed to be consulting with him, it remained very private. Not even my best friend knew we were having a courtship."

She didn't even tell her mother and father, who is of Syrian descent, until after she had accepted the king's proposal.

"They were very surprised," she says, "and also very concerned. My mother wasn't thinking about me being a queen. She was just thinking about me being happy. She didn't want me to rush into anything. But my mind was made up."

They were married in 1978 in a Moslem wedding ceremony. Her father was allowed to attend, but neither her mother nor her sister was present, because women traditionally are excluded from Muslim weddings.

The king renamed her "Noor," the Arabic word for "light," and he made her his queen. The latter decision surprised many Jordanians; his first two wives were given the title "princess." His third wife was a queen.

Although the Arab culture affords women less freedom than Queen Noor had enjoyed as a young American woman, the queen says she has had no problem adjusting to her new life.

"In Jordan, just like any other country, there are people working for women's rights," she says. "But 50 percent of the students now in our universities are women. That couldn't be more normal. There are two women cabinet members. Women are holding very important jobs in Jordan."

Queen Noor says she has considerable freedom in her country. She can walk into crowds, go shopping and talk with people. She and her husband even go out to dinner occasionally.

"A very good new French restaurant opened up and my husband arranged to have a birthday party for me there. We can do things on our own. We just don't have much time."

In her six years as queen, she has taken an active interest in her new country. She is involved with urban development and preservation of historic structures. She also works on many social and welfare projects.

She says her husband encourages her to do what she wants. "But he is very protective of me," she says. "I cherish that."

The king and queen have three children—four-year-old Prince Hamzah, two-year-old Prince Hashim and 11-month-old Princess Iman. Queen Noor's daughter accompanied her on the trip to Dallas.

"I believe very strongly in being with my children," she says. "All of my children have traveled with us almost from birth. My husband agreed to this immediately. His family was shocked."

Her children speak both English and Arabic, but she wants their first language to be Arabic and that is what she tries to use when speaking with them.

"They will be bilingual, but Arabic is much more difficult," she says. "I will be studying it all my life. But my oldest son seemed to sense that my language was really English. For a while he would speak to me in English and his father in Arabic. I had these visions of learning Arabic along with my children."

Despite their royal status, she says, she wants her children to have a normal upbringing. "They always have security men around them, but they are like members of an extended family," she says. "I don't talk to the children about terrorists. Perhaps when they are older. But I want them to feel secure and comfortable."

During the queen's stay at The Mansion, security officers turned one room in the sixth-floor suite into a command post. As they patrolled the halls, a nurse walked around with Princess Iman.

"I have to have nurses to help because of my busy schedule," she says. "But the children are very important to us."

She has adopted the king's three children from his third marriage, and they also live in the palace in the Jordanian capital of Amman.

But the queen says her home is not the kind of palace most people would imagine.

"Most people are shocked when they see our residence," she says. "We've already had to move out twice in order to build on more space for the family. Our bathroom is teensy, much smaller than the one here at the hotel. We also have a very teensy family dining room. Our formal dining room will seat 18—more than some families, but certainly not big enough to seat all of the people we sometimes entertain."

The queen was making her first visit to Dallas, although her family has strong ties to the city. Her father, former Pan Am Airlines president Najeeb Halaby, is a Dallas native and a graduate of Highland Park High School. Her sister, Alexa, who is the queen's look-alike, graduated from Southern Methodist University law school. Now a Washington resident, Alexa accompanied her sister on the trip.

The Dallas stop is part of the queen's speaking tour of the United States; she is hoping to strengthen relations between Jordan and the United States. The king has remained behind in Jordan, but they speak to each other by phone almost daily.

"I will get to see all of my family while I'm here," the queen says. "I visited with my mother in New York. I'll see my brother in San Francisco and my father in Washington."

She says her parents, brother and sister visit her in Jordan, and they keep in close touch. And like any parents, they like to give their daughter advice. It doesn't matter that she now is the queen of Jordan who travels with an entire entourage.

"You know how parents are," says the queen. "They still think I'm a little girl, and they still have to tell me how to do things. I just have to keep reminding them I'm all grown up."

Reprinted with the permission of the author and the *Dallas Morning News*.

●●●

DATE: SATURDAY, FEBRUARY 4, 1984
SOURCE: MIAMI NEWS, TELEVISION SECTION, P. 2
AUTHOR: MARYLN SCHWARTZ, DALLAS MORNING NEWS

* * *

COMING SOON TO LATE-NIGHT TV: 'THE GO DIRECTLY TO BED' GAME

DALLAS—Television game shows have been successful in the morning and in the early evening. A Dallas production company thinks the time has come for a late-night game format.

"But, of course, on late-night television, you've got to appeal to a different audience," said Adam Steinfeld, a producer with Productions West Communications. "This isn't the 'Family Feud' crowd. You can be more bizarre, more outrageous."

Steinfeld's show will be set in a singles bar. The producers feel they have come up with just the right name to capture this atmosphere. They are calling it "Go Directly to Bed."

"This is not as racy as it sounds," Steinfeld said. "What we're doing is a spoof of all the crazy game shows. Sure, our big prize will involve a bed of some kind: A trip or a stay in a local luxury hotel. But the contestants will be awarded separate beds in separate rooms.

"They did the same thing on the old 'Dating Game' show," Steinfeld said. "Contestants who won those big trips had to take a chaperone along. They also had separate rooms. It just wasn't as glamorous as it sounded. Even if they went to the beach, they weren't allowed to go into the water. The producers were afraid they'd get hurt and sue."

"Go Directly to Bed" is intended to be the ultimate game show, Steinfeld added—sort of "The Dating Game" meets "The Wheel of Fortune."

"But real prizes will be given," he said. "And the contestants will be real. After our six-week warmup, we will film our pilot. After that, we hope to sell the show to major TV markets."

The show's writer, Tony Dropsen, said contestants will be chosen from the crowd at the bar the night of the show. Two couples will be picked for each half-hour format. None of the contestants will be acquainted beforehand.

"Then they will compete in activities you'd expect in a singles bar," Dropsen said. "For example, the men will have to display their talent in bragging and trying to impress women."

The women, in turn, will be asked to show their knowledge of body language, or maybe guess the other contestants' astrological signs.

Winners will be allowed to roll giant dice. A gorilla will come out and run around a Monopoly-like board, stopping on spaces corresponding with the roll of the dice. "Each space will represent different prizes," Steinfeld said.

"We still have some wrinkles to iron out. That's why we are doing the six show warmups. We've got to make sure we are picking contestants that will bring the real feel of a singles bar right to our late-night viewers.

"At the end of the show we will have the cameras follow the winning couple right out of the club and into a limousine. That way, the viewers will feel they are leaving the club, too."

Reprinted with the permission of the author and the *Dallas Morning News.*

• • •

DATE: SUNDAY, AUGUST 23, 1987
SOURCE: THE MIAMI HERALD, TROPIC, P. 8
AUTHOR: MADELEINE BLAIS, HERALD STAFF WRITER

✳ ✳ ✳

STEAM: THE BOILING POINT

Steam anywhere but the tropics has no moral or allegorical value. It is plain vapor, the ordinary child of the marriage between heat and water. In its public application, it moves vehicles of majestic proportion—ships and trains. On a more homely domestic scale, it joins the whistle as the cheerful product of a kettle.

But in hot places, steam has a diabolical gift for making what is unbearable more unbearable. I remember complaining about this several years ago to a woman

I barely knew. She said that my problem was I had not gone native. Before I could ask her what that meant I told her how everything that summer seemed steamy.

It was 1980. The news was always bad. There were so many dead bodies in Dade County that summer the police took to calling such discoveries "felony littering." It was a dread time, a signal of riot and refugee, of waves of flame and waves of humanity. It never rained. What it did instead were these outbursts, these apoplectic downpours after which nothing got cooler. It was truly a negative miracle. The water from the clouds fell to the pavement, then boiled. And what followed was a ghostly mist known as steam.

My car had no air conditioning and the radiator had a leak that no one would, or could, fix. I spent days explaining that something was wrong with the car. I felt a panic in not being understood. More was wrong than just a leak in the radiator. I was hot. My blood was wool. Between the arteries and the skin floats a vapor similar to the vapor found on the roads after the rain. The woman listened to my lament, then told me how she lived in a cabin in the woods with fans but no air conditioning. She was in her early 40s, but she could have been any age. She often fastened a hibiscus blossom behind her ear. Instead of looking ridiculous or full of yearning for something long lost, she radiated style and defiance. Her clothes were loose cotton. She had a skirt that I think is called a pareo, which takes about 10 minutes to wrap properly around one's waist. On most people such a garment would look bandaged and improbable; on her it draped just so.

When I spoke of the steam, I said I could not imagine physical union of any kind under these circumstances. She laughed and said her lover often visited her in the afternoon, during what I called the worst, most strangled hour of the day: When you can hear the bugs; when you can almost hear the vegetation grow; when everything's hot, beats and pulsates.

She told me the Chinese cool off on hot days by drinking hot tea, and said that she and her lover had decided the best way to defy the heat was to make yourself even hotter. "Dance," she said, "for the enemy."

She leaned over. Her lips were fruity, full. She almost hissed: "That's steam."

Reprinted with the permission of *The Miami Herald*.

● ● ●

DATE: SUNDAY, JULY 5, 1987
SOURCE: THE MIAMI HERALD, TROPIC, P. 5
AUTHOR: MADELEINE BLAIS, HERALD STAFF WRITER

* * *

THE PROMISE

On the first day there is a sense of immortality, a feeling that one cannot run out of summer any more than the beach can run out of sand. Hope is tumultuous. It swells and billows and foams. On such a day it is easy to make rash promises.

"Of course you can walk to the casino by yourself," I tell my son, who is about to be 5, about to be a whole hand old. "But," I add, thinking this a brilliant strategy because at least I can stall for time, "you have to wait until the last day of the summer."

The suitcases had been unpacked, and the children are asleep, drugged on the thick tangy air.

"Boy," says my husband, "that was dumb."

Hours have passed since I made the promise, and yet I know exactly what he is talking about.

The promise introduced into our house a false and unwieldy enthusiasm for the end of something that had barely even begun, the end of something that should be sweetly savored. It was the worst kind of promise, the kind a person can't really keep. I had created a monster.

My husband: "You would let a 5-year-old go to a casino?"

"It's not a casino, it's The Casino." I could see from his expression he was nursing a vision of gangsters and decadence, of doomed humanity lurching about some kind of dark nighttime place filled with smoke and despair and sad souls sick with the wish for windfall.

"Remember that pretty building we passed on the way in, clean and wooden and New England pristine?" He nods. "That's the casino."

"But still. Alone? Not quite 5?"

"He wants to go with his cousin."

"An old man of 6."

"When I was a kid . . . "

"We lived in a different world."

When I was a kid, the casino at this small Connecticut resort was exactly what it is today, a beckoning force, like a second ocean, a big white building with lots of steps in front.

The large meeting room is used for kiddie dances and bingo and Western Night and the Hello, Summer cocktail party. On Friday nights there is a Disney movie from 7 to whenever for the young kids. Fridays is when the husbands arrive from Hartford or Springfield or New York. All subcultures have their own code: The movies are said to last one martini or two and sometimes even three.

For a 5-year-old, the siren call is from the Point Spa, your basic beachside luncheonette. The floor is always gritty with excess beach, and the place is permeated by the dueling odors of fried hamburgers and suntan lotion mingling with the salt air. The spa is the source of bad coffee and good doughnuts, of newspapers, pails, shovels, but especially of the delirium provided by penny candy that these days costs a dime or a quarter or even more.

The casino has every variety imaginable, jar after jar of sugar this and sugar that. It has the worst candy I have even seen. Bubble gum toothpaste.

The thrill, for a 5-year-old, is not simply visiting the casino, because that happens routinely enough. The thrill is in visiting it on one's own. Other children my son's age do wander freely here. They ride to lessons in the morning on squat colorful bikes, hang out by the Lagoon on the lookout for eels. But my 5-year-old has never routinely roamed anywhere. Our lives have too much asphalt in them to entertain, except in fantasy, that much prairie.

Yet here we are, for the summer, in a place where different rules apply. We spend all winter telling the children never to say hello to strangers, yet here the stranger is likely to be an older woman with gray hair wearing a belt with whales who happens to be circulating a petition to save St. Joseph's parsonage in Noank from being sold to developers. This resort prides itself in being a place where children are free, where they can walk alone, where bicycles are left out at night and no one steals from the beach, where at dawn one can see the same items forgotten at dusk, towels, T-shirts, fancy striped umbrellas, even sunglasses, the expensive kind. On hot days, when the children sell lemonade, the worst danger is that the ice will melt. I sometimes detect a threatening echo in the self-congratulation, the echo of all those people who said even God couldn't sink the Titanic.

"Are you sure he'll be safe?"

"Of course," I answered. "This is the land of buttered lobster. People eat scavengers. They don't behave like them."

"Mommy," comes the small plaintive voice at an ungodly hour. "Is it the last day of summer yet?"

"No. We have a long way to go. First you're going to march in the red, white and blue parade and go to the costume dance and the hat parade, and you get to go to the Friday night movies four more times, and finally when it's your birthday, on the day after that . . . "

"I can't wait. You know what I'm going to get?"

"No. What?" My voice is filled with fake early morning cheer, that kind of forced lilt that causes my larynx to produce weird sounds that careen into some falsetto netherworld.

"A grape slush puppy."

"Why don't you practice your counting?"

"OK. How high should I count? To infinity or to googooplex?"

"It doesn't matter, as long as you're quiet."

"This is how we'll handle it," I tell my husband. "He can go with his cousin, holding hands, and we'll just happen to strew the path with various relatives, aunts, nanas, mother's helpers, along every step of the way. We'll create the impression of independence with none of the reality. He'll never know the difference. Just don't say a word."

The children have an expression when they eat something they adore very quickly: They vanish it.

Well, we vanished the summer.

The swimming lessons were done. Our son had graduated from dolphin to something else; he now jumped off the dock at South Beach and called it diving. The kiddie dances had ended. There would be no more crabbing, no more crashing of mussels for bait, no more hopeful shouts about catching a biggie. No more racing up and down the beach while the mothers huddle beneath umbrellas hiding from the sun the children embrace while someone always says, "Let them run wild. They'll sleep well tonight."

It is time for the big walk, the solo, or really semi-solo, march to adulthood. An army of well-wishers is stationed at every point along the path. They set forth, brave soldiers.

Ten steps.

Twenty.

A slackening of pace, some hesitancy, a huddled discussion. They return. "Would it be all right if you drove along next to us?" says the spokesman, the cousin. My son seconds the request with the expression in his eyes, pure and solemn.

Would it be all right?

It starts out as a game to calm them down, to focus their attention during the final departure. The station wagon is loaded, groaning with a season's worth of new pails and towels and shovels. "Let's say goodbye to all our friends."

See you next year, waves.

See you next year, crabs.

See you next year, dock. And raft. And gulls. And the house where Sarah lives. Sean's and Garrett's house, too.

Don't see you next year, jellyfish.

But when we pass the casino, no ordinary valedictory will do:

"OK, casino, just remember this: Next year when I'm 6 I'm walking to you every day. Right, Mommy?"

Silence.

"Mommy, you didn't say 'right' back."

More silence.

"Mommy?"

I should have known. With children there is no reprieve, only postponement.

"We'll see. We'll see what the year brings."

It is the last day of vacation, a time of infinity loss and googooplex sorrow. Hope comes in scraps. On such a day it is wise to offer only hedged bets.

Reprinted with the permission of *The Miami Herald*.

• • •

DATE: SUNDAY, JANUARY 1cc 1987
SOURCE: THE MIAMI HERALD, TROPIC, P. 15
AUTHOR: MADELEINE BLAIS, HERALD STAFF WRITER

* * *

DYEING FOR ATTENTION

OF COURSE IT HURTS.

"People always ask that first. 'Does it hurt?' A lot of people think you have to tattoo down to the bone, but really it's just under a layer of skin.

"Of course it bleeds.

"But, you know, you put a little Vaseline on it, so it doesn't scab up, and then it heals like a sunburn. It itches when it's getting better.

"To me, it's the year of the tattoo. There was even an article about tattoos in The Wall Street Journal, and you know they don't just pick up on anything stupid.

"A lot of people might be intimidated when they find out I won the title of National Best Tattooed Female 1986, but I just try to act natural. I understand. It's like meeting a movie star, like Doris Day.

"Getting inked: that's what they call it. My tatoo, which as you can see is a work of art, really it's a canvas. It took over 100 hours, and, honey, if the artist wasn't a friend, I hate to tell you how much something like this would cost. But even if I didn't get a break on the price I would have gotten it done. It's that Taurus determination.

"I love it. It helps me stand tall and keep myself in shape. Recently I lost 30 pounds.

"I grew up in a family of four boys. I was the only girl, and, in lots of ways, I was one of the boys. Dad was a coach.

"My husband, Gary, and I run Wheeler Dealer in Fort Myers. Our front yard used to look like a used car lot, and then we had the bright idea, make it into a business. We're very honest. Our warranties say 'Guaranteed to have defects.' We don't doctor it up. If it smokes, it smokes. Sometimes I have to travel out of state on a repo. Usually I don't carry my gun.

"Gary is real supportive of my tattoo. You know, after I won the title, I sat him down and I said, 'Gary, what if this is something really big. What if it really takes off. What if I have to go to New York?' He said, fine he'll stick with me, whatever.

"He's a joker, that Gary. He always kids me: 'You know you've made it when your picture is next to the staples.' I've been approached by tons of bike magazines. I said no. In all honesty, I have dreams of a nice classy poster. I work easily. I can take directions. The camera loves me.

"Frankly I'm shooting for Vogue.

"Want to touch it?"

Reprinted with the permission of *The Miami Herald*.

Direct Quote: A Professional's Point of View

By Michelle Stacey
Mademoiselle

First drafts are for putting it all on paper, for getting over the starting-at-a-blank page stage, for thinking up a wonderful lead that you'll probably hate in the morning. They are not for publication. There's always that dangerous, heady moment when you've finally finished a draft of the piece, when the whole thing sits there in a neat (or not-so-neat) package. You're in the throes

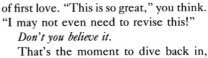

of first love. "This is so great," you think. "I may not even need to revise this!"

Don't you believe it.

That's the moment to dive back in, pencil in hand, and revise, rewrite, reorganize, rethink. But once you've gone through another draft or two and you really know it's close this time—how do you make it into a piece your editor will love, too?

When it comes to final polishing of a story, I like to think in terms of Danger Points. There are three Danger Points in every piece you write, and there are points every editor looks at and usually ends up having to revise. Save your editor the trouble on these and your stock will rise immediately.

1. *The lead.* Yes, you have already tinkered with this. You may have gone through two or three different ones. But there's a trick I've had to do as an editor so many times that it's become a basic rule: Look at the second or third paragraph. Chances are your real lead is right there. I can't count the number of times I've had to chop off the first one or two paragraphs of a story—paragraphs that, when you were writing them, made you feel comfortable, buttressed, safe, but that turn out to be completely unnecessary. Beat your editor to the chopping block.

2. *Transitions.* The most misused and underrated parts of a story, these turning points can be the weak links in the strongest of chains. There is a popular misconception that transitions consist of latching on to a stray word or concept in the last sentence of a section and using that poor stray as a rope to swing, Tarzan-like, to an entirely new section. "Speaking of cows," you write, "Mrs. O'Leary . . . ." This is the sort of lazy writing that has made many a weary editor write "weak trans." in the margin of a piece. Good transitions always have some connection to the main thrust of a piece; they are your opportunity to ask yourself: "Why am I writing this next section? How does this fit in with my overall thesis?" once you've answered those questions, you can convey the answers to the reader. Transitions remind the reader of where you've been and where you're going; they shouldn't exist in a void. Don't be afraid that you're explaining too much. "Another

aspect of municipal disasters that historians tend to ignore is the element of plain bad luck," you write. "Take, for instance, the case of Mrs. O'Leary's cows . . . ."

3. *Favorite parts.* Those luscious turns of phrase that make your heart beat a little faster every time you read them, those especially creative sentences where you've really found a new way to say something. . . be suspicious of these. They're probably the worst writing in your story. I know it seems unlikely—and painful—but trust me on this one. Those lovely phrases are more likely to be overwritten, hard to understand, high-falutin', and low in content. The best writing does not go out of its way to be cute or beautiful; it is good because it is clear, informative, and says what needs to be said in the most succinct and effective manner. *That* is elegant writing—it doesn't draw attention to itself. Go back to every favorite part you have and don't give it any breaks: Is it doing its job in the piece, or is it just serving your ego? Be ruthless.

Now you've got a piece to warm an editor's heart. Is that the last work you'll ever have to do on that story? Don't bet on it—at least if you're writing for a magazine. The nature of magazine writing, with its finely tuned attention to voice and a very specific audience, almost always requires that an author make further revisions. but if you can make your editor say, "This piece is close, really close!" when she reads your story, you've made her day. Trust me on this one. (Stacey, personal communication, 1988)

* * *

Michelle Stacey is the managing editor of *Mademoiselle* magazine.

II

TYPES OF ARTICLES

5

Descriptive Writing and Color Articles

Writing with detail by using your senses does not come automatically to the feature writer. It takes considerable effort to write well to convey color and atmosphere in a story, any story. Your goal, in short, is to make the reader of your color article or descriptive passages "see" the subject of your writing. You want to create mental images of the person, the place, the scenery. You want to present the opportunity for the reader to use his or her "mental senses"— that is, to imagine the smell, sound, feel, the emotion, the physical appearance, and even the taste of the subject.

This is what descriptive writing and color stories are all about. You will find these types of articles published often in both newspapers and magazines. This approach to writing can be applied to just about every feature subject you care to mention, yet the approach is best suited for specific subjects and types of articles. This chapter will discuss these and outline the best ways to use the technique in writing features.

You will soon learn that this type of writing requires great concentration and highly tuned observational skills on your part. An alert writer will notice the colors, odors, the noise, and other elements of a setting and put the reader in the middle of the action by describing these elements in depth. You accomplish this using precise adjectives and adverbs as well as specific nouns and verbs to convey that right image.

Writers achieve descriptive effects in their articles in a variety of ways. Some like to use adjectives, and lots of them, throughout their writing. Others work hard to find the right nouns (for example, *dirge* instead of *song*). This requires a superior command of the English language. But using a broad vocabulary will not be enough. This type of writing also requires timing—you must be able to determine when to go heavily into description and when to back away from the temptation.

The primary rule here is also a simple one. When you think description will help a story, make certain what you are writing about is *distinctive.* If you can find unique characteristics instead of the ordinary, then the additional color, or atmosphere, you add to a story through detailed descriptive writing will usually work.

Certainly, as you noted in the last chapter, the way you write also makes a difference. Choosing words and putting them together will also affect the impact description will have on your readers. Organization, or order, of the information will have a similar impact.

CREATING IMAGES IN THE MIND

A good feature article will be enhanced with good artwork, such as photographs or drawings, when the artwork and story come together as a unit on the page. Yet you have to write as if there is no art with the story; you must write to allow your readers to create images in their minds from reading your article.

It does not take much to illustrate this point. Pick up almost any magazine and you will find at least one article rich in description and detail that give a certain color or atmosphere to the article.

Clearly one goal is to provide *information* to readers through the description and color in your articles. You must also, as Stanford University's William Rivers and free-lance writer-editor Alison Work say, make the effort of reading the article a rewarding experience for your reader. Some element of satisfaction should result for your reader. "Success [of your article] pivots almost entirely on whether readers finish a descriptive [article] with the feeling that they have been through a satisfying reading experience. The most evocative descriptives—those fashioned by writers who have developed and refined a talent for using visual words—are also viewing experiences" (p. 231), Rivers and Work (1986) say.

Although they were written over two decades ago, these two short passages from Tom Wolfe's 1963 article in *Esquire* about stock cars and race driver Junior Johnson illustrate that point:

> Ten o'clock Sunday morning in the hills of North Carolina. Cars, miles of cars, in every direction, millions of cars, pastel cars, aqua green, aqua blue, aqua beige, aqua buff, aqua dawn, aqua dusk, aqua Malacca, Malacca lacquer, Cloud lavender, Assassin pink, Rake-a-Cheek raspberry, Nude Strand coral, Honest Thrill orange, and Baby Fawn Lust cream-colored cars are all going to the stock car races, and that old mothering North Carolina sun keeps exploding off the windshields.

Seventeen thousand people, me included, all of us driving out Route 421, out to the stock car races at the North Wilkesboro Speedway, 17,000 going out to a five-eighths-mile stock car track with a Coca-Cola sign out front. This is not to say there is no preaching and shouting in the South this morning. There is preaching and shouting. Any of us can turn on the old automobile transistor radio and get all we want . . . (Wolfe, 1966, pp. 105–106)

Not much later in the article, this descriptive passage by Wolfe appears:

And suddenly my car is stopped still on Sunday morning in the middle of the biggest traffic jam in the history of the world. It goes for ten miles in every direction from the North Wilkesboro Speedway. And right there it dawns on me that as far as this situation is concerned, anyway, all the conventional notions about the South are confined to . . . the Sunday radio. The South has preaching and shouting, the South has grits, the South has country songs, old mimosa traditions, clay dust, Old Bigots, New Liberals—and all of it, all of that old mental cholesterol, is confined to the Sunday radio. What I was in the middle of—well, it wasn't anything one hears about in panels about the South today. Miles and miles of eye-busting pastel cars on the expressway, which roar right up into the hills, going to the stock car races. Fifteen years of stock car racing, and baseball—and the state of North Carolina alone used to have forty-four professional baseball teams—baseball is all over within the South. We are all in the middle of a wild new thing, the Southern car world, and heading down the road on my way to see a breed such as sports never saw before, Southern stock car drivers, all lined up in these two-ton mothers that go over 175 m.p.h. . . . (p. 106)

Even if you know little about the subject, Wolfe's methodical descriptive writing makes it seem as if you are there. After reading this, ask yourself why this article creates such vivid images in your mind. Is it the unusual colors (adjectives) he describes? Is it the emphasis on an action event (driving to the races) you are able to experience? Is it the writer's enthusiasm and excitement (emotions) for the subject? In fact, it is probably a little of each of these factors that contributes to Wolfe's success.

Wolfe uses what he calls the "four techniques of realism" in his writing. In a style that has been labeled "new journalism" by the writers and scholars studying it, the "new journalists" of the 1960s and 1970s often employ these basic steps that Wolfe described:

1. *Scene-by-Scene Construction of Events*. Scene-by-scene construction is the most basic of organizational schemes and is different from narrative writing. It is a form of story telling illustrated by Wolfe's description of the drive on a Sunday morning to the stock car races.

2. *Full Record of Dialogue in the Scenes*. Magazine writers, with the luxury of more space, often can take advantage of this by using longer passages of exact dialogue from sources or between sources and the writer. In this way, however,

sources nearly become characters as this type of writing edges toward the fiction form called a short story.

3. *Third Person Point of View in Writing.* Although this is the norm in most feature writing, this type of writing exhibited by Wolfe shows less involvement by the writer than a first-person point of view would offer.

4. *Detailing of Descriptive Incidentals.* Wolfe calls this sort of writing technique a "social autopsy," the attention the writer pays to minute details of the source's life in characterizing the person.

Whenever you try to create images in your reader's mind with your article, remember you cannot drift from reality. In writing nonfiction, there must still be some information value to the article. You should always ask yourself, "What is the news hook or news peg of the story?" Its focus and current value must be clear to you and to your reader.

INTERVIEWING AND DESCRIPTIVE WRITING

There will be times when you will be assigned to conduct an interview as a basis for an article and find that the piece needs enrichment through detail. This makes your challenge as a writer even tougher, since you must not only concentrate on the interview itself by listening to your source's answers, but you must also be concerned with using your observational skills to note details before, during, and after the interview.

For example, you should be concerned with your source's body language or the source's physical responses to your questions *in addition* to what the source says. Watch for facial expressions, shifts in seating position, and other mannerisms. Listen carefully for intonations and other characteristics of speaking.

You can employ techniques of detailed and descriptive writing to set a single impression of an interview for your reader. Often, as you have probably noted, this is not necessarily objective. For magazine writers in particular this is posible. Many newspapers will permit such "writer's license" in certain types of features such as columns, analyses and interpretive articles, and Sunday magazine features. Remember, however, you still remain objective in your writing by being fair and careful about what you observe. When done well, this becomes an asset for the writer and for the article itself.

The most common interview-based feature article that employs descriptive writing in large quantities is the profile, the subject of a later chapter.

Regardless of the sort of interview-oriented story you are writing, use of description must be built on careful word selection. Remember that you will be serving as the eyes, ears, nose, and other sense organs for your readers. During your interview, take advantage of interruptions to notice things about the room you are in. What is on the desk? How is the room decorated? What objects are on the walls? How is the person you are interviewing dressed? How is his or her hair cut? What color are the eyes? Look for characteristics no matter how minute they seem. Look for subtle things such as brand names and positioning of furniture. What do they tell you about your source?

But also remember that you are *not* the brains of your readers. Leave the conclusions about what you have observed to your readers. You are better off not making judgments about what you describe. Personal conclusions and interpretations are most often not used in newspaper features and many times not desired in magazine article writing unless you are a qualified expert on a subject and can make such comments with authority.

When you take the opportunity to look around, try not to interfere with the interview. Use delays or disruptions to look around. And take notes about what you see, just as you take notes about what is being said. This is an important step, and one which beginners often overlook.

Gather as much information as you can. Be a pack rat. Collect everything you think might help you remember details later, when you sit down to write. At this point you can be selective instead of later regretting that you missed this or that item or detail critical to a finely tuned passage you have just written. But when you write, be sensitive enough about what you are writing to know when you have too much detail or not enough. Edit out the less important when you have too much. You might still be able to convey the same impression. And, similarly, add more when the image is unclear or unfinished. Therefore, when observing your source, be as thorough as possible.

New York Times feature writer and "About New York" columnist Anna Quindlen says, when covering an event for an atmosphere piece, she writes down everything she sees. "I take down quotes, names of signs and all those things. Just in case it might fit in. And I don't want to trust my memory. Sometimes you remember something red and it's really pink or blue" (Quindlen, 1984).

USING THE RIGHT ADJECTIVES, ADVERBS

You have two basic strategies to writing when it comes to word usage: writing with general, ambiguous words and writing with specific, clear words.

Adjectives and adverbs convey distinct impressions. Adjectives express qualities of the nouns they modify. Adverbs do much the same thing, except they can also modify adjectives in addition to expressing time, place, manner, degree, or cause. Writers most often use verbs to connote movement. Verbs are necessary in sentences, performing the expression of action, existence, and occurrence. Nouns describe something substantive such as things, people, places, objects. Take a look at these examples:

Adjectives and Adverbs

General and ambiguous:
"The *small* television was powered by batteries."

Specific and more clear:
"The *two-inch black-and-write portable* television was powered by batteries."

Nouns and Verbs

General and ambiguous:
"The town doesn't have any *pets* like Michi."
Specific and more clear:
"The town doesn't have any *housecats* like Michi."

The goal here is to emphasize prevailing features of the subject you write about. And, at the same time, you want to convey excitement or other emotions.

Joe Nick Patoski's portrait of the nightlife in Dallas tells us how young adults in northeast Texas spend their weekends at a mall built exclusively for saloons. One of the reasons this essay on the latest Texas trend in bar-hopping works so well is that Patoski picks up on the language of his subjects to make the story more realistic. For example, this sentence shows his understanding of the slang used by his sources that he shares with his readers through explanation: "They boogied at the Boiler Room disco, which was packed with good-looking Dallas babes ('dudes and babes' being the contemporary equivalent of 'cats and chicks')" (Patoski, 1987, p. 112). His choice of words not only helps the reader get the feel for the action of these nightlifers, but helps readers gain fuller insight into the lifestyle by capturing the language of these young adults in Dallas' fast lane.

DESCRIPTIVE LEADS

Descriptive features that convey the color of an event have the important duty of helping to balance the content of a newspaper or magazine. Of the three major types of magazine leads—descriptive, expository, and narrative—only the descriptive lead draws the reader into the article by painting pictures for the reader at the outset.

The idea of giving features special descriptive content and attention to detail and color is, of course, not a new one. Nor is giving the lead of a story a particularly heavy dose of description as a device to interest readers in the subject a new device of writers.

In fact, University of Wisconsin Professor Willard Bleyer, in his 1913 textbook on journalistic writing, said description in the lead of an article is crucial to the success of feature stories. "A vivid bit of description is sometimes used to advantage at the beginning" (p. 229), he wrote. "If, instead of merely describing and explaining a mechanical process, the writer portrays men actually performing the work involved in the process, he adds greatly to the interest of the article. The effectiveness of an explanation of a new surgical operation can be increased to a marked degree by picturing a surgeon as he performs the operation . . ." (p. 229).

Your goal is to capture the drama, the excitement, and overall emotion of an event and to share the experience of the moment with your readers.

Even with good artwork accompanying the article, a strong descriptive lead will grab the interested reader and not let go. The two elements, artwork and a strong lead, should work together to create the right feel for the article's treatment of the subject.

Professor Myrick Land (1987) says there are at least four types of magazine leads that use description and detail. Land lists the anecdote lead, the case history lead, the scene-setting lead, and the general descriptive lead as examples of types of leads that use detail and description to get an article off to a strong start. Regardless of the type of lead, she says, it should "emerge naturally from the research on your article. An effective lead can be written only if you have shown imagination in selecting a subject, have focused sharply on one aspect of that topic, have been thorough in gathering background information, and have conducted enough well-planned interviews" (p. 88). After saying this, Land offers this test for a potential lead:

1. Is it going to arouse interest of readers of the magazine you have in mind?
2. Is the lead brief?
3. Is the lead clear?
4. Does the lead focus on an important point?
5. Is the lead using the right tone for the article?
6. Even if it passes these five tests, is the lead the *best possible* lead?

GUIDELINES FOR DESCRIPTIVE WRITING

Reporter and editor Daniel Williamson (1975) suggests six guidelines for descriptive writing for newspaper features. Williamson says:

1. Remember that you are, in effect, the eyes, ears and nose of your readers. Your job is to gather an assortment of material which the readers can analyze and assimilate into an image. In this role, always be aware of any characteristic, however subtle, that would aid readers in coming up with an accurate image.

2. Don't allow your presence as a reporter to influence the subject. Try to blend with the woodwork so that you can observe the subject in a natural state. When it's necessary to conduct an interview, try to put the subject at ease so that he will act more naturally.

3. Gather an abundance of notes—much more than you can use. Then, before writing, sift through your notes to determine which observations most effectively capture the whole subject.

4. In writing, spread description throughout the story. Large "glumps" of description may get in the way of reader flow.

5. A fine line exists between the presence of too much description and the absence of too much description. That fine line is the feature writer's target. If the story is tedious with descriptive detail, chop lesser important details. If the story doesn't succeed in allowing you to "see" the subject, add more description.

6. Although a writer should, indeed, act as the ears, eyes and nose for his readers, he should never try to assume the role of their brain by inserting his personal conclusions and interpretations. Often, such conclusion is only a lazy short-cut for good descriptive writing.

In David Macdonald's (1987) article about capybaras, the giant South American rodents, in *Animal Kingdom,* the lead passes this test. His article opens with a description of a scene, the natural setting for this unusual creature. Phrases like "sun-bleached mosaic of cracks" and "this shallow pan had been a huge lagoon flush with luxuriant foliage" create very distinct images at the beginning of his article, even if you do not see his color photographs accompanying the article. Yet he does not stop with the lead, as you can see in this excerpt. Macdonald, a zoologist in addition to a writer, has peppered his article with expressions such as "deep mahogany fur" and "plate-sized turtles," leaving readers with precise impressions of this Venezuelan floodplain. As Professor Betsy Graham (1982) has expressed it, writing like Macdonald offers here is like a motion picture—in words.

Readers thrive on details such as these, especially when the writer is focusing on something unfamiliar to most readers. An article that starts with such richness in detail and imagery will win readers from the first sentence to the last. If you don't buy this, just take a look at a piece of fiction on the current best-seller list. Or read a short story by a well-known writer. Good nonfiction writers use this technique as well.

COLOR STORIES AND COLOR IN WRITING

Color stories are important feature forms. These stories are often used to provide readers with the most descriptive aspects of a news event or other activity. Newspapers use color stories as sidebars to help explain a major news story by providing atmosphere or mood—happy or sad, warm or cold, exciting or dull—for those who could not be there.

Frequently, color stories in newspapers are used with the major news of the day—tragedies such as airline crashes or car accidents or joyful moments such as a papal visit or the opening of a new public facility. Color stories are used to relate the mood of crowds at events such as football games, festivals, parties and celebrations, parades, concerts, funerals, and memorial services.

For example, at a major college football game, a color story angle might be the activities and reactions of a group of fans who followed the home team on the road several hundred miles to see a big game. It might focus on the team on the sidelines during the game. It could focus on celebrities in the press box. It might reflect the party-like atmosphere before the game in the parking lot at the tail-gate parties of alumni and fans. Or, it can focus on the reaction of a single person who might be pivotal to the major story of that day.

But rarely does a color story like this focus on the results of the game or the action of the game. That is the purpose of another story by the same reporter or, as preferred by most editors, by a second reporter.

In short, the idea behind this sort of writing is to permit the reader who did not attend to share the event with the writer and others who were there.

Color stories take advantage of certain types of sources of information. You will find color stories almost always have people, your perceptions as an observer, your observations, and a common thread, says writer and editor Daniel Williamson. These are often reaction stories, but the reaction is often that of the writer.

Professor Louis Alexander (1975) says these types of stories are usually written with a point of view or a focus that directs the article. What are you trying to say about the subject? What story line, or other literary device, are you using? How can you arrange the information you have to give the event some of the atmosphere it needs?

Alexander adds that when you successfully answer these questions, you have done your job well. He says, "Overall, because you have all the colors in it [the article] you give the reader a much stronger, more meaningful, more colorful picture—the blacks and the whites, the grays, the blues and peppermint stripes and everything else. You accomplish this by planning your story to make one major point or leave one message and by selecting a story line on which to hang or arrange your materials" (Alexander, 1975, pp. 58–59).

The story must be continuously interesting, William Rivers and Alison Work (1986) emphasize. "One sentence should grow out of another; one paragraph should grow out of another. The middle and end should be as interesting as the beginning. Although a color story has no standard structure, the 'hard news' should usually be somewhere near the beginning" (pp. 236–237), they advise.

In writing to use color as a tool in your article, you need to consider several guidelines on detailed content. Professor Benton Rain Patterson (1986) offers six rules for detailed writing to build color. Here they are:

1. Don't summarize scenes, dialogue, or action. Recreate them.
2. Be specific and avoid vagueness.
3. Show, don't tell. Let the reader see something.
4. Identify the characters/sources completely when they are introduced.
5. Describe the characters/sources in your article.
6. Include important detail to let reader see, but do not show the reader irrelevant objects or insignificant details. These mislead and provide clutter.

Patterson says: "There are . . . elements that may be added to a story to make it more interesting, more significant, more memorable: plot (or story line), suspense, conflict, change (whereby one or more characters undergoes a change in understanding, attitude, condition, etc.), and climax. When they are a part of reality, a feature writer should put them into a piece. If they are not a part of the reality, there is no way they can be included. To do so would turn fact into fiction" (p. 20).

You can often take what Patterson says about detailed content and apply it to a major event to enliven it for your readers. In covering city events for her "About New York" feature column, *The New York Times*' writer Anna Quindlen (1984) has a tested and proven strategy to portray events such as the Feast of St. Anthony on Sullivan Street in Manhattan. This sort of event, as she calls it, is a "quintessential New York event" and here's how she handles it: "In something like this, where I'm basically going to take the reader and put him on this street, on this day, on this beat, my problem more than anything else is figuring out how to organize and then pick and choose the telling details that are really going to make him feel like he was here with me."

She likens covering such an event to painting a picture—she is an artist with words.

> If you try to hold up a mirror to an event, if you paint it in broad strokes, you're going to miss on colors, you're going to miss on sights, you're going to miss on all kinds of things. I think if you're going to hold up a mirror and do the painting, the best thing to do is pointillism—a whole bunch of little points. . . . When the reader steps back and looks at it, when they're done, they're not going to see the little points, they're going to see a whole big picture. (Quindlen, 1984)

Color writing is a very personal style of writing, Quindlen explains. Each person will gain a different perspective on the same event and will probably write a different story. "Everybody faced with the same event will give you a different viewpoint, a different answer, a different set of people." And, she adds, you have to have confidence in yourself as a writer to write about your own perceptions and reactions to a given situation. "It's the self-confidence that comes from self-confidence in your personality and not so much your skills. I'm just different. I have different perceptions."

CREATING MOODS

Good color writing will set a tone for the reader. You can manipulate moods by your choice of words, organizational approach to the information you have, and of course, the subject that you are writing about.

Louis Alexander (1975) says that if you can do well writing color, that is, creating a mood for the reader, the rewards are high for both the reader and writer: "When you get your story across, when you convey the color and drama that make other people feel it, you the feature writer gain genuine satisfaction" (p. 59).

Curt Stager's (1987) sobering look at a disaster in Cameroon in West Africa creates the right mood for the type of story. His choice of words offers a degree of respect for the victims of the tragedy of a natural carbon dioxide gas cloud covering a lake village. His lead sets the mood with the very first sentence: quiet, sleepy, rural, dark, and innocent. Yet he bursts through this image with the second paragraph to impress on readers the suddenness and fatality of the night's unusual event. In doing this, you see the event through the eyes of a villager who experienced the night with his family. This personal touch makes the event seem more realistic because of the magnitude of death of people and animals.

In this chapter's final example, examine William Gruber's (1987) feature on cave artists in Europe that he wrote for the Chicago Tribune Service. This piece also accomplishes mood setting through the lead. His detailed, first-person approach brings readers into the story quickly. His personal reactions described through what he and his group did to get to the unusual art are noted in such a manner that you feel as if you are peeking over his shoulder as he walks through the underground network of passages in France. Action verbs such as "crept" instead of "walked" and "leap off the walls" instead of "move" demonstrate the point well. His use of nouns gives precision in the story. You build mental images with words such as "dripping stalactites" instead of "rock formations" and "Cro-Magnons" instead of "cave dwellers."

To keep the article interesting, Gruber does not attempt to hide his joy in discovering that these prehistoric ancestors of man were skilled artists and not limited to the "primitive-people" stereotypes of 20th century films and television. His explanation of the artistic processes used and the deterioration of some of the art work is helpful in creating the entire story of the cave art.

As you move into other specific types of feature articles in the next chapters, you will begin to get ideas for application of the techniques of descriptive and color writing in these varieties of articles. For example, you will see wide possibilities for descriptive writing on seasonal topics and on travel subjects. As you will see, some of these types of stories will be easy to write, and others will not lend themselves to descriptive writing approaches very readily. But writing with heavy emphasis on detail is a valuable tool for feature writers. Use it well.

SOURCES FOR DESCRIPTIVE AND COLOR WRITING

People and their opinions
    Quotes
    Dialogue

Your own observations
   Actions
   Environments
Your own perceptions
Your own attitudes/emotions
Your personal experiences
Personal experiences of others

COMING TO YOUR SENSES

Roy Sorrels, a correspondent for *Writer's Digest* magazine and a novelist, offers this exercise for "sensuous writing"—that is, writing with your senses. Here's what he suggests:

To make your own writing more sensuous, take a series of blind walks. Ask an understanding friend—another writer maybe—to help.

Close your eyes and let your companion guide you gently through a few environments. Down a city street, perhaps, past the busy school yard, into the park. At first, you will be a bit nervous with your vision cut off, but relax and you'll become more and more aware of all the rich input from your other four senses. Relax into the sounds, notice the surface under your feet—gritty sidewalks, cobblestones, dirt in the park, lush or scraggly grass. Smell the world—can you tell when you pass by the bakery or the fishmonger? With your friend's guidance, touch things in the park—grass, tree trunks, a worn park bench.

Of course, you can do this on your own, just closing your eyes for a few minutes sitting at a sidewalk cafe, or on a bus, or lounging under a tree.

HOW PROFESSIONALS WROTE IT

DATE: OCTOBER 1987
SOURCE: TEXAS MONTHLY MAGAZINE, PP. 112, 177–78.
AUTHOR: JOE NICK PATOSKI

* * *

EVERY BAR BUT HERSHEY'S

On a Friday night in Dallas five young dudes were looking for a good time. Three of them had just gotten off work. The other two came from out of town. Since they couldn't decide where to go, they headed for Dallas Alley, where there was something for everyone.

They boogied at the Boiler Room disco, which was packed with good-looking Dallas babes ("dudes and babes" being the contemporary equivalent of "cats and chicks"). They dug the mismatched furniture, the three pinball machines, and the low ceiling at Foggy Bottoms, a rhythm and blues club next door. They admired the high-tech gray-and-black decor of Take 5, where Extreme Heat was moving a dance crowd by exhorting, "Everybody Wang

Chung tonight!" They followed a long queue into a brightly lit bar called Alley Cats, where the boisterous preppies crowded around two piano players and sang "I Want to Hold Your Hand" with all the spirit and enthusiasm the corps puts into the "Aggie War Hymn." As happy as everyone seemed, the dudes did not wish to wait in line for half an hour to share the experience. Three of them headed back to Foggy Bottoms for barbecue, one went to a nearby food court for souvlaki and a corny dog (he never could decide), and the other one plopped down on the long brick stoop in the Alley to sip his beer and soak up the wonder of it all.

That evening the five young dudes had seen the future of nightlife. Though they passed through several clubs, each with its own music fare, ambience, and clientele, they never left the premises of Dallas Alley, a state-of-the-art fantasy world light-years beyond the corner tavern: a restaurant and seven theme bars jammed into two renovated brick factory buildings in the West End Historical District. If the five dudes hadn't gone back to the Boiler Room to admire the babes' miniskirt and moussed dos, they could have heard the Storyville Stompers play Dixieland at the Plaza Bar, grabbed a burger and shake at Bubbles' Beach Diner, rolled Skee Ball at the Tilt carnival arcade, or had a quiet tete-a-tete at the semiprivate Backstage cocktail–piano bar, all for one $5 cover charge ($3 early in the week). If they go back to the Alley this month, the dudes will be able to munch tapas while listening to Patsy Cline records in the new Santa Fe-style restaurant.

Seventeen thousand patrons looking for a good time pass beneath Dallas Alley's signature neon arches each week, five thousand on a decent weekend night. In their wake they will have left behind $10 million by Dallas Alley's first anniversary on October 18.

[The article continues beyond this excerpt.]

●●●

DATE: SEPTEMBER/OCTOBER 1987
SOURCE: ANIMAL KINGDOM MAGAZINE, PP. 24–33.
AUTHOR: DAVID MACDONALD

* * *

THE CAPYBARA: GIANT AMONG RODENTS

A SUN-BLEACHED MOSAIC of cracks sprawled across the hard-baked mud as far as the eye could see. A mirage of trees shimmered on the horizon. Only a few months earlier, this shallow pan had been a huge lagoon flush with luxuriant foliage and the province of gaping caimans and piranhas with bright orange bellies. Now, in the peak of the dry season, it was a humbling expanse of nothingness punctuated by one small muddy pool.

Yet there was life. At my feet lay the spoor of an extraordinary creature. In length, each paw print was greater than the span of a man's fist. The slender heel of the hindfoot broadened to the deeper impressions of three curved toes. One might be forgiven for imagining it was the trail of a dinosaur fossilized in a prehistoric landscape. In fact, the footprints belonged to no less uncanny a creature, for I was on the trail of the capybara—the world's largest rodent.

The capybara looks so old that for many years it confused scientists. Linaeus thought it a pig and classed it in the same genus as the wild boar. But the capybara is a rodent whose most familiar, if distant, relative is the domestic guinea pig. Both live in South America, where their ancestors were bigger than grizzly bears. The nineteenth-century explorer Alexander von Humboldt called the capybara the Orinoco hog and wrote of its massive incisors, which he claimed could rip the legs off a jaguar. Humboldt concluded that, however zoologically inappropriate, the capybara deserved the name "water pig" because its flesh was as tasty as pork.

Charles Darwin was no less impressed by the oddity of these rotund rodents. He reported that they were the prey of jaguars along the reaches of the Amazon. Indeed, the capybara is usually found in open grasslands near water, but it also frequents tropical rain forests, ranging from Panama to northeastern Argentina.

SINCE THE CAPYBARA'S "DISCOVERY" by European explorers, the passage of time has yielded little information about the species' life-style. It was the hope of unraveling the capybara's secrets that lured me to Venezuela and the llanos, or savannas, of the Orinoco floodplain.

Now, far ahead of me in the blistering hazy heat, a small group of capybaras lazed by the muddy pool. Beside them crowded the survivors of all the life that had previously populated the lagoon: caimans with saw-toothed jaws agape: plate-sized turtles basking in the sun, piled haphazardly atop one another like dirty dishes in a sink: wading birds—iridescent glossy ibises, candyfloss-pink spoonbills, and vivid scarlet ibises—all strutting hither and thither with apparently aimless longlegged busyness. What the capybaras lacked in colorfulness and grace among the waterhole menagerie, they more than compensated for with anatomical unorthodoxy.

One male, the size of a small sheep and weighing 130 pounds or more, rolled over. His deep mahogany fur, caked gray with mud, only sparsely covered his dark hide. He yawned, exposing an intimidating pair of chisellike incisors that betrayed his rodent ancestry. Then he stood up and lumbered purposefully toward the pool, leaving another line of tracks in the hardening mud. He had the distinctive oblong head of his species, round fleshy ears that quivered spasmodically, and no tail. Between and below his small eyes lay his most peculiar feature—a four inch-long naked, greasy black protuberance. What looked like a carbuncle was a spongy mass of scent-secreting cells called a morillo (Spanish for hillock), which is well developed only in mature males.

[The article continues beyond this excerpt.]

Reprinted with the permission of the author and *Animal Kingdom Magazine*.

• • •

DATE: SEPTEMBER 1987
SOURCE: NATIONAL GEOGRAPHIC MAGAZINE, PP. 404–20.
AUTHOR: CURT STAGER

✳ ✳ ✳

SILENT DEATH FROM CAMEROON'S KILLER LAKE

NIGHT FELL quietly on August 21, 1986, in a lull between the cloudbursts that drench the Cameroon highlands in the rainy season. Hadari, a Fulani cattle herder, had just fallen asleep with his family in their hillside home. Far down the grassy slope, Lake Nyos glistened in the dim light, one of more than 30 crater lakes set like jewels in a volcanic chain stretching across much of this beautiful African nation. About a mile below the lake, the village of Lower Nyos lay on the valley floor.

A loud rumbling noise awakened Hadari and his family. Rushing outside and peering into the darkness, the herdsman saw a ghostly column of vapor burst out of the lake and pour like a smoking river down into the valley. At that moment a great blast of wind roared up from the lake, gagging him with an overpowering stench of rotten eggs.

Hadari hurried his family to higher ground, where they huddled in the bushes. The rumbling stopped in an hour, but the family was too frightened to return home.

In the valley, meanwhile, a cloud of gas about 50 meters (150 feet) high engulfed Lower Nyos village, where many people had just finished a late supper after a busy market day. Families suffocated in their sleep. Others smelled the odor of rotten eggs, felt a warm sensation, and rapidly lost consciousness.

The silent cloud moved 16 kilometers (ten miles) down the valley, spreading death. Lower Nyos was wiped out; 1,200 people perished there and in nearby encampments. In neighboring villages, including Cha, Subum, and Fang, more than 500 died.

The next morning Hadari and others came down out of the hills to find cattle strewn like confetti in the tall grass. Human bodies lay in heaps in doorways, on beds, on kitchen floors beside unfinished meals.

"We see many persons just fall down," remembered Suleyman, a Fulani, at a refugee camp. He lost most of his family that night. "I feel just angry to see the dead people, my brother, my family, my mother, small pickin (children). I fell just angry for to see this thing, and that I have not any power."

It was as if a neutron bomb had struck, destroying the living but leaving buildings unharmed. Not a creature moved in Lower Nyos that morning, "not even small ants," said Suleyman. Carcasses of more than 3,000 cattle littered the area, bloating in the hot sun, untouched by flies or vultures; the scavengers were dead too.

The release of one billion cubic meters (1.2 billion cubic yards) of gas dropped the lake level by more than a meter. Lake Nyos was stained with a rusting iron compound—ferric hydroxide—carried up from the bottom by the escaping gas and precipitated into the surface water.

A water surge accompanied the gas burst, gushing as high as 80 meters to rip vegetation from the shores and deposit it on the lake. For weeks after the explosion Lake Nyos lay like a festering and angry red eye in its crater socket.

[The article continues beyond this excerpt.]

Reprinted with the permission of the *National Geographic Magazine*.

•••

DATE: SUNDAY, SEPTEMBER 13, 1987
SOURCE: THE MIAMI HERALD, P. 13j
AUTHOR: WILLIAM GRUBER, CHICAGO TRIBUNE SERVICE

* * *

SOME CAVE ARTISTS PAINTED CEILINGS LIKE MICHELANGELO

ST. GIRONS, France—We crept single-file through the narrow, winding passages of the Niaux cave. Using hand-held lamps to avoid dripping stalactites, we ducked below narrow ceilings and walked carefully on muddy floors and wet rocks.

Suddenly, about a mile into the mountainside, the cave opened into a wide cavern. There, on one wall, our dim lights revealed a highly realistic painting of a red bison under attack from arrows. Nearby were paintings of horses, reindeer, bear, bison, woolly mammoths and the outline of a human hand.

Some animals were so lifelike that they seemed to be leaping off the walls. In several instances, the cave artists created three-dimensional effects by using bulges in the rock to highlight muscles and to outline the head or back of a horse.

For years, movies have portrayed our prehistoric ancestors as apelike creatures. So it comes as a shock to realize that the artistic talents of a Michelangelo or Picasso existed 30,000 years ago, as the last Ice Age was ending in Europe.

Two hundred caves that contain cave paintings or etchings have been discovered in Europe. The most famous are in the foothills of the Pyrenees Mountains in northern Spain and south central France.

Not only do many caves have highly detailed paintings, but they also give a fascinating glimpse of how some animals looked at a time when the climate was much different from today. Horses, for example, had shaggy coats. Mammoths, an ancestor of the modern elephant, are long extinct and reindeer vanished from the area thousands of years ago.

PAINTINGS DETERIORATING

Unfortunately, some cave paintings that were discovered less than a century ago are starting to deteriorate. Tiny micro-organisms from the breath of human visitors and the artificial lighting used in some caves are causing paintings to crumble or fade under the attack of algae.

Spanish authorities this year began to limit the size of groups touring the famous Altamira caves—which contain a painted ceiling that has been compared with the Sistine Chapel—to eight people at a time. They will decide by February whether to close the caves to the public.

The equally spectacular caves of Lascaux near Montignac, in southern France, and La Pasiega, near Altamira, already are closed to all but scientists. A painstaking reproduction of the two Lascaux caverns having the most impressive artwork was built over a 10-year period and opened last year.

"That might be the answer to preserving other cave paintings," said Norman Totten, a professor of history at Bentley College of Waltham, Mass., who was our tour guide. "Or, perhaps visitors to caves in the future will have to wear face masks or oxygen helmets to prevent their breath from destroying the paintings."

EASIER VIEWING

Most caves open to the public are easier to view than Niaux. Some contain constructed walkways and steps, and they have electric lighting that highlights the stalactites and other rock formations in the caves as well as the art.

Those that have preserved much of the cave environment are the most fun to see, and they offer the best insight into the living conditions of their original inhabitants. All of the caves maintain a constant temperature of about 55 degrees, requiring sweaters and raincoats.

Using a flashlight or lamp instead of permanent electric lighting also creates shadows that often make the paintings seem to leap off the walls and give the impression that the spirits of the cave artists may still be present.

We started with a visit to the archaeology museum in Madrid, in which we saw an underground reproduction of the Altamira cave just in case we couldn't see the real thing.

Fortunately, I was among the lucky 10 members of our 20-person group who, after drawing lots, were permitted entry of Altamira, which is near Santander on the Spanish north coast. Altamira, which was discovered in 1879, was the first cave in Europe to win scientific recognition for containing paintings dating to the late Ice Age, or Magdalenian period.

A ceiling in a cavern deep inside the cave has been compared, with good reason, to the Sistine Chapel in Rome. It has a mind-boggling display of dozens of animals galloping or frolicking together. The portrayal of the running horses' legs—something which still confounds many artists—and the details of their hooves is done with a high degree of accuracy.

PREHISTORIC SCAFFOLDS

Archaeologists believe the artists lay on their backs, like Michelangelo, to paint the Altamira ceilings by the flickering light of torches or oil lamps. They mostly used rock ledges to lie on, but there also is evidence that some built wooden scaffolds. Despite the conditions they worked under, the lines of the animals are sure and firm.

The nearby Tito Bustillo cave at Ribadesella also has the painted outlines of several human left hands. They look as if a spray can had been used, but the artist is believed to have used a hollow bone to blow the paints through his fingers (iron oxide for red, manganese oxide for black).

The Gargas cave, near St. Girons, displays several hands with some fingers apparently missing or mutilated. It also has a montage of horses and other animals, some overlapping each other, that remind you of a Picasso painting.

Even more startling is the sight of a prehistoric child's footprints frozen in what must have been mud in the Pech Merle cave near Cahors, France. The toes are clearly evident in several prints.

There are few paintings to be seen of humans, however, and those that do exist are less skillfully drawn than the animals. Pech Merle has a "stick man" drawing of a man whose body is pierced by arrows or spears.

Highly stylized etchings of human figures can also be seen at the Combarellas and La Mouthe caves near Les Eyzies in the Dordogne Valley of France.

Totten says the cave artists "were people very much like ourselves biologically, if not culturally." They were Cro-Magnons, the first true homo sapiens, who replaced the more apelike Neanderthals about 60,000 years ago.

In most cases, they were nomads or lived just inside the cave entrances. The paintings, however, usually are deep in the cave passages where little or no evidence of human habitation has been found. How the artists could depict such realistic details of animals from memory, deep in the recesses of a cave and without good illumination or models to work from, is an unanswered mystery.

Reprinted with the permission of *The Chicago Tribune.*

A Professional's Point of View

By Madeleine Blais
University of Massachusetts-Amherst

Detail and color in a piece of journalism should work ideally in the same way they function in poetry or in fiction. They should function metaphorically or they should help create a mood. They should contribute to a sense of momentum, not clutter.

In the kind of journalism which is only interested in record-keeping, details and color are often used to telegraph the fact that the reporter was an actual witness. In this approach quotes are also used to prove the presence of the reporter so that often quotes are included that contain little or no information and contribute not a whit to the overall design is the last consideration, and such pieces peter out rather than build and that is why cutting from the bottom makes sense.

Journalism that attempts to be literary narrows the gap between writing that only entertains and writing that only informs. How can you train yourself to know what details to include?

First, keep up with your reading of literature. Second, when you are out on a story, use all your senses, not just your ears.

I remember once interviewing a woman who wanted more than anything else to rid herself of a bad situation. She kept saying as much, over and over, as she stood in her kitchen, but nothing she said spoke to her pain as insistently and clearly as the way in which she kept sponging and sponging an already immaculate kitchen counter.

I once wrote a story about a woman who is schizophrenic. It is one thing to say that she lives in a disordered world, another to say: "Two years after Trish's mother died, she wrote her a letter, asking for cigarettes."

Once I wrote a short piece entitled "Monica's Barrel" about a woman who had immigrated from Jamaica and who periodically sent home barrels, big cardboard cylinders with tops made of tin, to the people she had left behind. At first I was going to write that if she had stayed home she would be poor. Upon prodding from my editor I wrote: "In Jamaica Monica's brightest prospect would be a job at the bra and underwear factory making $50 a week in an economy where $5 buys a pound of rice."

Another time I wanted to convey the sense of a beach resort as the epitome of safe haven: "We spend all winter telling the children never to say hello to strangers, yet here the stranger is likely to be a woman with gray hair wearing a belt with whales who happens to be circulating a petition to save St. Joseph's parsonage from being sold to developers."

When in doubt, turn to Strunk and White's *The Elements of Style* before embarking on an important piece: read it, re-read it, memorize and then proceed. (Blais, personal comunication, 1984)

* * *

Madeleine Blais is a free-lance writer and associate professor of journalism at the University of Massachusetts at Amherst. Blais spent eight years as a staff writer for Tropic, the Sunday magazine of *The Miami Herald*. She is the winner of the 1980 Pulitzer Prize for feature writing. She has also worked for *The Boston Globe* and *The Trenton Times*. She has been a Nieman Fellow at Harvard University and she was featured on the Public Broadcasting System series, "Writers Writing."

6

Human Interest Articles

Just about everyone likes to listen to a good story. Human interest articles should always be based on good stories. These articles are the sort of stories you can curl up with on the sofa and enjoy for a few minutes. Readers react by feeling sad for those involved in tragedy. Readers feel happy because someone has beaten the odds and won a battle against a bigger foe. Readers smile because they remember an experience they have once been through. The article is a success because the story that is told is true and involves people in your own town or someone who is just like you but from a faraway place. Readers find these human interest articles a change of pace from the normal flow of news. Furthermore, as *McCall's* managing editor Don McKinney (1986) says, these stories serve readers in another way: they offer inspiration and hope for readers who might be experiencing the same troubles or frustrations.

Just what is a human interest article? This type of article has several labels. Some publications, like *McCall's,* just call it a human interest narrative. Some label it a true-life drama. McKinney says that regardless of what they are called, these articles are stories told by writers about people who have been involved in real dramas, and these emotional stories are usually told in narrative form. These articles are quite popular with readers, research shows, and some publications try to balance their editorial content with these sorts of stories appearing with regularity.

The key to telling these stories is the *human element*. And there must be plenty of emotion experienced by the primary characters/subjects in the article as well as emotion experienced by the reader: horror, amusement, excitement, joy, depression, sympathy, sadness, anger.

Your assignment as a human interest article writer is to make your readers vicarious participants in the drama. Your readers' personal involvement in the news draws them further into what you have written and into the publication generally. These articles are most often the odd and unusual stories about people.

Newspapers occasionally run human interest articles in sidebar format to accompany other articles on the same subject. Magazines like to use these articles to contrast other types of articles such as travel articles, interview articles, hard-hitting investigations, and regular departments and columns.

You will find the time element is of secondary importance in human interest articles. In fact, some human interest subjects are really timeless and could be published just about any time. Articles such as any of the four that accompany this chapter are as interesting to read today as they were when each was published. Often, the material that forms the story takes years, or even a lifetime, to evolve into the story. Only when the series of events culminates does the writer enter and begin to chronicle it for readers.

Writing human interest articles requires a unique touch on the part of the writer. Not only do you have to have the right frame of mind to find the story, you need the right strategy to handle it. Approach the usual story in a certain way and it is still only a routine news item. If you take that same story and tell it with a *human angle*, it comes alive and becomes a better overall story, a human interest story.

Natural disasters and medical problems are common sources of some of the best human interest articles. Disasters such as tornados that strike in the Midwest, earthquakes, and floods are only a few examples of events that nature brings to test human resilience. Medical problems can touch the heart like nothing else, especially those involving children. The stories of children who need transplants of organs, those who are handicapped, and those who have terminal diseases are always widely read.

WHY WRITE ABOUT PEOPLE?

Names make news—still. This is the primary explanation if you wonder, "Why write about people?" People want to read about their neighbors and neighborhood businesses, especially when unusual events occur involving them. Articles about people, not institutions or other organizations, fill publications such as weekly newspapers and newsletters in small communities. Articles about people are being used more often in larger newspapers, too, to maintain readership. Local magazines can apply the same principle, but, of course, this becomes more difficult for national and general interest magazines. However, magazines that focus on personalities and human interest, such as *People Weekly* or *Parade,* are quite successful in the marketplace.

A newspaper or magazine that is writing about people only in a personalities–celebrities page or even in the entertainment section just is not doing its job in the 1990s. Readers seek more people-oriented writing throughout their newspapers and magazines today—in all sections and departments. And, it follows, these people should be local people, not just always the meaningless names of people who live a thousand miles away.

So, what makes people so interesting? Human interest feature writing is sometimes a catch-all phrase used in newsrooms and magazine offices to describe a story about people. Whatever the subject, these stories are interesting and popular with readers because they focus on people in unusual and odd situations. Just as all features tend to emphasize the unusual and odd, these articles do so in the most human fashion. People simply want to read about other people. Readers like to see how they "measure up" to others in similar situations. People are curious about one another and enjoy the occasional "peek" at others that the human interest article gives us into other's lives. Readers enjoy reading about the difficulties and successes of our friends and neighbors. Readers enjoy seeing how others live, especially the celebrities, personalities, and leaders of our societies. And as a human interest writer, you can bring the lives of these people to your readers.

Human situations and problems are the most popular subjects of writers. Everyday occurrences translate into articles and even books partly because you, as a writer, also have that common experience. Your approaches and ideas often come from that base of experience you have had as a child and an adult, and these experiences, combined with your own values, make you a writer about people. You will see that, for example, someone's personal mannerisms or other behaviors might spark a story idea. As you begin to write human interest articles, you might have to depend on suggestions from others, but as you become more experienced as a writer, you will see these stories will be easier to identify and write.

THE ASSOCIATION–IDENTIFICATION ELEMENT

The successes of regional and city magazines and community sections of major metropolitan newspapers in recent years have been due, in part, to the fact that these publications are writing and editing their editorial products for *local* markets. The appeal to readers is broad, but one strong reason for the local appeal is the ability of readers to identify with the people, places, and things which they read about. In the late 1960s, leading daily newspapers such as the *Philadelphia Inquirer, Orlando Sentinel, Milwaukee Journal, Chicago Tribune,* and many others began to publish specially edited neighborhood sections that are "zoned" or distributed on a regional level within the larger market that the newspaper serves. These newspapers are now better able to publish stories about people in the smaller neighborhoods and communities—the cities within the cities. The space for these stories became available because smaller advertisers could now afford to purchase less costly advertising space for their shops and stores. And editors, guided by their own intuition as well as current market research, decided the best way to fill the sections was with a large amount of human interest feature material about the neighborhoods' people, churches, and schools.

The same applies to the magazine industry, but in a slightly different way. Regional and city magazines have developed to reflect a lifestyle of young adults in the metropolitan areas of the country over the past two decades. These magazines filled a void in the metropolitan market, also, giving still other outlets for human interest articles as well as other forms of reporting about urban and suburban life.

Other types of magazines also depend on human interest articles to draw readers. General interest personality magazines such as *People Weekly* focus on celebrity human interest writing. *McCall's* and other women's magazines draw heavily on this category of features. *Reader's Digest* has always used these types of features. Columns such as "Life in These United States" are just one example.

Small town daily and weekly newspapers have traditionally depended on a large amount of human interest articles in their editions.

You can make your human interest article easier for the reader to enjoy by providing lots of quotes from the people you are writing about. You can also improve the story by giving the reader detail and description, as was discussed in Chapter 5, especially when photographs are not used. Quotes capture the way the person speaks, and sometimes, how the person thinks. They enliven the human interest article because quotes allow you to tell the story in the source's own words. Description makes the person come alive in your reader's mind. How is your subject dressed? How is his or her hair styled? What is the person's occupation?

It all comes down to one point—human interest articles must be written and edited so a reader can see some of themselves in the article. You need to write in terms of people and not in terms of numbers or widgets.

Readers do not "see" themselves in an article directly, of course, but they can imagine themselves as the principals of your article. Readers can see this person could have been themselves or is somehow like themselves. The events are described in a way that readers can see them occurring in their own homes or in their workplaces. A reader should be able to say, "Wow! That could have happened to me!" All of this occurs because of the common purpose, lifestyle, ideas, values, sensations, or characteristics of the human condition between readers and the subject of your article. It is the association and identification element of a human interest article that permits readers to think, feel, and even act as they imagine the experiences of the person you write about.

THE ELEMENTS OF A HUMAN INTEREST ARTICLE

McCall's managing editor Don McKinney (1986) identifies three types of human interest stories. Here's his list:

1. *An Extraordinary Experience.* This type of story involves the natural disaster such as floods, earthquakes, blizzards, hurricanes, fires, and the like. Persons who survive these have a story to tell. There is life in jeopardy or even death. There is suffering. There is property loss, often priceless and precious possessions.

2. *A Common Problem.* Men and women who experience a relatively common human problem and succeed in battling it have a good story to tell. It may be a singular experience or a family experience. The story focuses on how this person dealt with the tension and stress in a situation that readers can easily identify with while reading the article.

3. *A National Issue.* People who suffer because of problems that are on the minds of the citizens of a nation are often heavily in demand and heavily read. Recent issues of this type include AIDS victims, the Love Canal pollution problems of New York, and so on.

THE EMOTION ELEMENT

Emotion is a powerful element in any writing. Novelists use it in their work. In nonfiction, it is used to bring closer ties between the reader and the article. With emotional elements in the right mix, you might produce one of those articles that readers just cannot put down until it is finished—regardless of the length.

Emotion, psychologists tell us, has four general levels: intensity of feeling, level of tension, degree of pleasantness or unpleasantness, and degree of complexity. Emotion is a strong feeling, either general or specific, about a subject. It is manifested in a number of physical and psychological ways. The most common emotions in human experience, of course, are joy, anger, fear, and grief.

There are also emotions that we write about that are associated with various physical experiences such as pain, disgust, and delight. Some other emotions are tied to our own appraisals of ourselves. These include feelings of success/failure, pride and shame, and guilt and remorse.

Many times, in reading a good human interest story, you can help readers experience emotions pertaining to other people. These include feelings of love and hate.

If you can find a strong emotional aspect in a possible article, it might be the unifying element you need to write a good piece. Remember that emotion can be disruptive for your readers. It can be arousing. These reactions will link your article to the reader. Because of this, emotion is often the difference between an average feature story and an award-winning feature. For example, Dan

Luzadder earned a Pulitzer Prize for the *Fort Wayne News-Sentinel* in 1983 for his description of the destroyed dreams caused by a devastating Indiana flood in spring 1982. The impact of his article comes from the emotions conveyed to readers who could identify with his description of homes, cars, businesses, and other important possessions under water. Luzadder's entire article is reproduced in Chapter 10.

Stories such as this inextricably link the reader and the story. They do so with honesty and clarity. Writers let the emotions do the job and do not have to overwrite to make a point. Stories remain simple because of the double duty that the emotion element carries.

Although journalists today will not write the type of "sob story" that was common early in this century, emotion remains the thread to tie together many human interest stories. They are stories from the heart.

Occasionally, writers will encounter stories which have to be told, and for overwhelming reasons, they cannot help but become involved in the story. This sort of reaction is quite normal, writers being people themselves, so it might become an asset if handled well. Compelling stories such as these will demand that you write first person or write third person with your own perceptions and reactions becoming a part of the article. It is hard, for example, not to react to a child dying of liver disease who needs a transplant.

Writer Madeleine Blais won the 1980 Pulitzer Prize for feature writing for a 1979 article about an old man, a World War I conscientious objector who had been given a dishonorable military discharge but who sought to upgrade it to honorable status. Blais, who wrote that article for *The Miami Herald's Tropic Magazine*, likes to get very involved with the topics of her articles and the sources themselves.

"Sometimes when I do stories, I can really tell that I've done something that's really worthwhile. I can tell it sort of lives very vividly in my mind while I'm doing it. Even afterwards, I have this level of caring about the people, almost like a kind of friendship forms because of the story," she explains. "At some point in the research something happens. Either somebody says something or there's an event that moves me in some way, that seems important to me. And then I start feeling this passion about creating through the reader the exact same psychological steps that I went through to get to the point where these people were moving to me . . . to do that for the reader as well" (Blais, 1984).

You need to remember when you do react to such a story, your own journalistic observations can become affected by the experience. If this is not desired, and in some types of feature writing it is not, Rivers and Work (1986) suggest solving this possible problem: "When an event makes a writer react emotionally, his impressions are especially vulnerable to distortion. You can often resolve this problem by recording your impressions immediately after the event to capture its details and then later, at a more tranquil time, assessing your first account to find and correct for distortion" (p. 154).

FINDING UNIQUE STORIES ABOUT PEOPLE

Author Daniel Williamson (1975) has stated that most human interest feature writers are "incurable people lovers." They have to, as he says, "relish the strange, inconsistent antics of the human race and, to a large degree, earn their livelihoods by astutely observing and reporting these antics" (p. 112). Therefore, Williamson observes that if a man bites a dog, it is not news so much as it is a human interest article.

You'll soon find, if you have not already found, that human interest stories are often about people down on their luck, people who live in the underbelly of life, people who have been dealt a losing hand.

David Nordan's (1986) article about Atlanta's Stewart Avenue demonstrates this point well. In the *Atlanta* magazine article, he describes the trials and tribulations of people like "Dave the Druggist," who delivers needed prescription drugs to people who don't have the money and have to pay him later. Or you learn about Indian immigrant Manny Patel and his Farmers Market. But you also learn about bikers, nudie bars, pornography stores, bars, shootings, punks, and illegal drugs. This story is a true people story, about change and about people enduring the changes—accomplished through a series of profiles of these characters of Stewart Avenue.

For these sorts of articles, you have to proceed with caution. Most stories that are told to you by a source are true. But, on occasion, a story will turn out to be exaggerated or untrue. Newspapers and magazines in South Florida were not too long ago contacted by a woman who was having difficulty getting public assistance for her ill child. She painted a picture of bureaucratic delays that might cost the child its life. A newspaper reporter checked the woman's story and found that most of the facts were true. Yet, because she did not reveal all the facts about the illness, there were missing pieces. The reporter found out from a physician whom he had telephoned for background that the illness was serious, but not as immediate a problem as the woman claimed. In fact, the child could expect to live a number of years before the illness turned serious or fatal. The newspaper decided not to publish the written story in light of the new information. Another newspaper, however, *did not* check the facts as closely, and did run the story.

Children make good human interest subjects regardless of their plight or the location of the story. Although it has been argued that the local human interest story is preferred, occasionally some stories are so compelling that geography matters little. *The Boston Globe*'s Philip Bennett (1987) wrote a short but sobering description of how gangs are dominating the children of Mexico City, one of the world's largest cities. He starts the article with a close-up look at one boy and his gang, punctuated with the observation that the youngster carries a revolver. He describes the case of Efrain Vargas as an illustration, yet in the article he still depicts the overall problem with staggering figures.

Similarly, *Pittsburgh Press* reporters Mary Pat Flaherty and Andrew Schneider (1985) tell a shocking story. The pair took 10 months to investigate and report about transplantation of human organs. The result was a series of articles entitled "The Challenge of a Miracle: Selling the Gift." The articles told readers about the human drama which occurred each time a family decided to donate the organs of a relative so someone else might live. The stories are also about greed, favoritism, neglect, criminality, and corruption, though—less positive elements of a human drama based on life itself. One of the series articles is presented here. The article shows the grief a family suffers during realization of the loss of a son or daughter or brother or sister. It shows what happens when someone is faced with this decision at the moment of their relative's death and the trying circumstances that exist when the decision to donate is made. By observing a number of families and talking with them, Flaherty and Schneider were able to use emotion-filled quotes to strengthen their story. The sheer number of interviews they conducted made generalizing about the process possible. And it is the quotes and individual cases that make the story come to the human level that makes it appealing to readers even now.

To find these sorts of stories, writers must keep in touch with the world around them and with people in that world. You will find the stories in many places. For starters, try the local courthouse. Criminal and civil courtrooms are filled with this type of human drama that has, for various reasons, reached the need to be resolved before a judge. Usually the best court cases that make human interest stories have a broader social issue element within them, *McCall's* managing editor Don McKinney (1986) advises.

Certainly good human interest articles come out of hospitals and other health care institutions, as the *Pittsburgh Press* series shows. Similarly, you can expect to find good stories at schools and churches. Government social services offices can often bring you in contact with good stories, too, if you can build dependable sources there. Each of these is a place where people gather and interact. You can expect to learn a lot if you take the time to talk and listen.

Established writers know these stories find their way to them. If you are new to a community, it might take some time before people seek you out to tell you their stories, but eventually they do.

Certainly neighbors and acquaintances often can lead you to stories. Listen to what they have to say. Remember people you meet and where they live and work.

Even other publications can produce good ideas for you if you take time to read the newspapers and magazines in your area carefully. Reading carefully for run-of-the-mill news stories, you might find a missing angle or perhaps the next step that was not taken. Try it and see for yourself.

In searching for that good human interest article, Madeleine Blais recommends not heading into the story right away. Give yourself time to look around even when you have a subject before you zero-in on a theme or unifying thread. "My technique . . . was listening, hanging out, absorbing—a kind of inventory. It seemed ridiculous to be standing here stockpiling every little quote or whatever because I really needed more to get impressions than facts" (Blais, 1984), she explained about her strategy on one assignment.

Blais also suggests looking for the *little* things in your prospective articles. "I love, as a writer," she says, "to take things that are not readily observable as monumental and try to find the monuments in them."

HOW ONE SMALL NEWSPAPER FOCUSES ON HUMAN INTEREST

The Danville, Ill., *Commercial-News* has a people philosophy that permeates the entire newspaper. Here's what the staff of that newspaper says about human interest articles and people:

People are our community. The *Commercial-News* is a community newspaper. Almost without fail, its columns are full of people.

People get into their *Commercial-News* in most of the expected ways—by having run-ins with police or traffic accidents, by having babies, by being admitted to or dismissed from the hospitals, by dying or being related to someone who died, by getting married, by staying married, by writing letters to the editor.

And we invite them in lots of other ways—by asking what they like about their community, by asking them for their household or kitchen tips and recipes, their holiday remembrances, their nominations for mother, father, and outstanding woman of the year, their opinions on current topics (ranging from headline news to back-burner topics of significance to them as people). . . .

People are reported in the time-tested spot news and feature ways, too—from profiles of unknowns who find themselves in the news to those who seem everyday [ordinary] until you find the hidden talents or hobbies to stories of people affected by the statistics of the headlines. . . .

By getting people into the space we can plan for and control completely and by being alert to even tiny people stories, people-conscious editors and reporters can give readers welcome relief from what would have been a tedious, depressing—and unwelcome—newspaper.

PERSONALITY–CELEBRITY COLUMNS AND ARTICLES

The international fascination with celebrities is not a new one. Newspapers and magazines have, though, placed a new emphasis on coverage of personalities and newsmakers in entertainment, sports, and other areas. You do not have to look far to find people-oriented columns and sections in your daily newspapers. Many newspapers today devote prominent portions of their news sections to personality–celebrity news. *The Chicago Tribune*, for example, runs "O'Malley and Gratteau Inc." on the back of the front section next to a full-color weather map. The column features national as well as state and local personalities each day in a gossip style.

Other newspapers simply edit wire news into personality–celebrity roundup columns featuring a half dozen or so items and pictures about well-known people. But the point here is clear—these items reflect the growing public interest in celebrities and personalities.

These features tell us the daily activities of famous people—whom they are seen with, where they are going, their latest work, their personal lives.

And, surely, there are emotional stories that can be told about the famous as well. These people may be internationally known, or even just known across their communities; others care about them and what happens to them. When a local radio announcer falls ill, or if a popular nightclub singer gets married, the event becomes human interest story material. You write about this in the same manner that you would handle any other human interest story.

The ongoing emphasis on people stories, combined with the growing attention to personality–celebrity news, is a response to the strong demand for personality human interest features today in newspapers and magazines.

WRITING STRATEGIES

You have a number of alternatives in writing a human interest article. Much of the time, the material you have collected can dictate the form of the story. But organizationally, you often choose from these approaches:

1. Suspended interest approach.
2. Story-teller's chronological approach.
3. Narrative approach.

The *suspended interest approach* is a pyramid organizational strategy. The lead is only a partial summary of what happened, saving resolution of the human drama for a later point in the article. Most of the time resolution comes at the ending. The article's body, or main section, is a description of the main events in chronological order. Finally, the article winds up with its outcome, or revelation, in the conclusion-climax. This approach has its advantages, primarily because it forces the reader to stay with your story for the big ending or "moral to the story." This plan is not unlike the plan of the novelist who unveils the murderer on the last page of his mystery.

The second major strategy for organizing human interest articles is to approach writing like you would tell a story: tell the entire story in *chronological order*. This sort of plan is simple and easy to write once you get your facts straight. The sequence of events does the work for you. But this sort of approach does not fit all human interest stories. It works well when events culminate with a major action on the part of a principal source in the article.

Kathryn Casey's (1985) article about a southeast Texas love triangle that was published in the recently closed *Houston City Magazine* illustrates this approach. The drama of this murder story pivots on love and human relationships as they are affected by highly charged emotions. Even though you do not see the entire article here, the beginning demonstrates how the article starts with a major event described in chronological order, then backtracks to the series of events, also in chronological order, that led to the fatal event she uses to open the article.

Narrative organization is also easy to use and works particularly well for beginning writers. Like the chronological form, this approach is dictated by the information you collect. Your major decision will be how to start a narrative article because you are not necessarily bound to start with the first event in any sequence. *McCall's* Don McKinney (1986) says a human interest narrative article lead should "lure the reader (and this includes the editor, who will decide whether the reader gets a chance at it or not) into your story and to capture that person's interest so that he cannot put it down until he learns how it comes out" (p. 27).

Narrative organization then just tells what happened by running from beginning to end. In this case, narrative is different from the suspended interest form because the best material is saved for the end, and different from the chronological because it does not lead with the first event or end with the last event. You have the most flexibility with narrative writing by not forcing what becomes the beginning, middle, or end through a chosen structure. You can merge elements of the story using narrative organization, pulling from two divergent tracks, or themes, if needed.

Madeleine Blais, whose articles served as some of the examples in chapter 5, uses metaphors to structure her articles when possible. Blais (1984) says: "The structure should arise from the material. The way to make it happen is to make yourself an authority, to know so much about your subject that you know almost as much about your subject as your subject knows about himself."

Blais also likes to build her human interest articles around *tension*. Without it, she says, her articles would not be worth writing. "Tension offers an element of surprise. It allows the reader to imagine many possible endings to the course of the piece. If there isn't some kind of tension, there's no story."

YOUR BEST SOURCES FOR HUMAN INTEREST STORIES

<u>People: Interviewing and Observing</u>

Neighbors
Workplace friends, acquaintances

Institutions: Interviewing and Observing

Hospitals
Social services offices
Schools
Churches, synagogues
Funeral homes
Civil courts
Criminal courts

Places: Interviewing and Observing

Parks, playgrounds
Clubhouses
Festivals and celebrations
Senior citizen centers
Missions, centers for homeless
Schools
Churches, synagogues
Halfway houses, rehabilitation centers
Courthouses
Libraries

HOW PROFESSIONALS WROTE IT

DATE: AUGUST 1986
SOURCE: ATLANTA MAGAZINE, PP. 32–35.
AUTHOR: DAVID NORDAN

* * *

THE LEGEND OF STEWART AVENUE: TO SOME IT'S SEEDY AND SUSPECT,
TO OTHERS IT'S A STREET OF DREAMS

It's a steamy summer night and J.D. and Tommy are carrying out a routine they've kept up for years as a team. Windows rolled up tightly and the air conditioner humming in J.D.'s big late-model sedan, they are puffing cigarettes and eyeing the familiar vista of strip-joint neon, fast-food outlets and monolithic, garishly decorated used-car signs that loom over the one-mile stretch of Stewart and Cleveland on the south.

But J.D., middle aged, short, and beefy, a former air traffic controller, private detective, bail bondsman and real estate agent, and Tommy, shorter, spectacled, a little younger and possessed of a clipped, almost academic manner of speaking, and likewise a jack-of-all-trades, are not working tonight. That is to say they are not haunting the clubs and bars and surveying the streets for bail jumpers and fugitives—bounty hunting, an avocation that has netted them hundreds of arrests over the past 10 years or so.

Tonight J.D.'s .357 Magnum is tucked into the glove compartment—although one is led to suspect that Tommy's baggy sport coat is concealing more than a paunch in the 90 degree heat—and the two are acting as tour guides for a pair of visitors unfamiliar with the world unto itself that is this southern stretch of Stewart, a source of Atlanta lore and legend.

Ask almost any local old-timer who spent his youth in and around Sylvan Hills, Cascade Heights, East Point, College Park or Hapeville about Stewart Avenue. They'll likely laugh and recall something outrageous that happened in one of the joints along the strip, or having their first beer at the "old barbecue place" or hours spent at the huge Funtown Amusement (Bowling) Center, now an abandoned, art deco memory surrounded by acres of buckled parking lot where tall grass grows through the cracks in the asphalt and a lonely wind whistles through the neon of its rusting 40-foot-tall sign.

Ask a more recent comer and they are likely to blink and say something like "sleazy," or "seedy," or "dangerous," or "used cars," all of which happen to be reasonably accurate, if somewhat limited descriptions. But Stewart Avenue is also, in its own way, something of an upbeat place.

It's a place where "Dave the Druggist" will home deliver a prescription, or even a box of aspirin, to an elderly patient and wait later for payment, where Indian immigrant Manny Patel and his bright-eyed 11-year-old son Vipul will chat on a first-name basis with their customers about the quality of the greens and melons in the immaculate, fresh-vegetable-smelling cool of the Stewart Avenue Farmers Market. It's the spot where 72-year-old Ed Echols and his four sons will auction off as many as 1,000 cars a week at the stadium-sized Bishop Bros. Auto Auction, which Echols has run since 1948.

It is also the home of countless "guaranteed off the lot" used-car establishments—"$400 down, $30 a week, we keep the papers, $250 repossession fee"—all with brightly bedecked buildings and billboard-size signs, each, like a racing stable, with its own color scheme, some with as many as 400 cars on the lot at a time. It's the location of the Money Market Pawnbrokers—"Atlanta's Most Unusual Pawnbrokers"—which has a gospel recording studio in the back and a gray steel funeral home casket, which manager Ray Betts is now most ingeniously trying to get rid of, in the front.

It's a place where a former pornography store then nudie bar has become a medical–dental clinic.

But Stewart Avenue is perhaps best noted as the home of numerous establishments where a conglomeration of good ol' boys from Clayton and Henry and Douglas counties and other points beyond the perimeter come to mingle with assorted shadowy figures of the night, sip on their drinks and watch mostly young women dance and take off their clothes under the lights.

J.D. and Tommy say the strip has changed a lot during the past seven years or so. Almost wistfully they note that a lot of the old-timers have been or are in prison; not a few are pushing up daisies as the result of lead poisoning. The biker gangs have at least temporarily sought other climes, and worst of all, the place has been infiltrated by what Tommy likes to call "northside punks."

"They like to stand out in the parking lot talk about what they're going to do to each other," he snorts. "We didn't have many cuss fights in the old days. If you said S.O.B. back then you'd better be talking about yourself. There used to be a lot of shooting."

Above the entrance of the Krystal Palace, a huge club situated in the center of a parking lot as big as a shopping mall, a sign warns that "semis and motorcycles must park on upper deck." The upper level is an elevated, gravel-covered field, next to the Palace's paved lot, and Tommy explained that the remaining bikers don't like to use it because "the rednecks spin off with their pickups" and fling stones at their vulnerable machines.

"The bikers are no big strain or pain right now," he explains. "There used to be as many as 80 or 100 Outlaws around here but most have moved up to Cheshire Bridge Road where they've got their old ladies working up there.

"If those northside businessmen put a $100 bill, a gram of crack, or a drive chain in their old lady's garter, well, I'm sure that's all right with them."

The joints along the strip range, according to J.D. and Tommy, from places "where you'd best shave your head before you go in to make it easier on the surgeon when he sews it up" to spots like the Gold Rush, where the omnipresence of at least four bouncers who equal in combined weight the offensive line of the Pittsburgh Steelers makes it highly unlikely that serious trouble will be encountered, at least on the premises.

One of the Gold Rush bouncers is Doug Fields, who at 285 pounds and with a slow country voice reminiscent of an 18-wheeler changing gears, explains the procedure.

"If anybody wants to be a smart aleck, we ask them to leave," he growls matter-of-factly. "Or we take them out."

"And what if they don't want to leave?"

"Then we just pick'em up like a sack of taters and throw'em out in the parking lot."

"And what if you have somebody who really doesn't want to leave and gets real violent about it?"

"We 'blige 'em," Fields says, shrugging.

The women who dance at the Gold Rush are a varied lot, but they tend to agree that they'd prefer to take off their clothes for the working class–country crowd than for those on the other side of town.

"The people down here tip better," says Nikki, a lithe, buxom, 40-year-old divorced mother of three whose 20-year-old daughter attends dancing school and performs at the Tattletale Club on Piedmont. Nikki is a licensed barber who cut hair for 15 years until she split with her second husband last November.

"I like people, I like to dance, I got divorced and I got three kids and I can't make $800 a week cutting hair," she explains coolly. "A lot of these girls in here have kids to support, and where else could they make this much money? Most of them can't do anything else."

One who can but chooses not to is Bella, a striking, 22-year-old blonde from Rockmart, Georgia, who worked her way through mortician college as a dancer and is currently a licensed mortician. She admits that she is a little "how do you say, exotic, and weird."

"Being an undertaker is fun work but it don't pay worth crap," says Bella, who drives an aging Cadillac sedan and claims she keeps a coffin and "a bunch of bones" in the living room of her apartment.

[The article continues beyond this excerpt.]

Reprinted with permission of the author and *Atlanta* magazine.

• • •

DATE: SEPTEMBER 13, 1987
SOURCE: THE MIAMI HERALD, P. 24A
AUTHOR: PHILIP BENNETT, BOSTON GLOBE STAFF

* * *

GANGS DIVIDE AND CONQUER CHILDREN OF MEXICO CITY

MEXICO CITY—Rumor had Efrain Vargas back on the street. Sure enough, there he stood near the wall of the Santa Fe explosives factory, an L.A. Rams jersey on his back and a revolver close to his heart, looking to wipe the smile off somebody's face.

"We're ready for anything," he announced, still sore from an encounter with police two days earlier. "You'll find me here, protecting my corner with my boys, fighting for freedom."

Vargas' corner of the world's most populous city extends about a block in each direction, through a labyrinth of crowded cobblestone alleys and shaded passageways. His boys belong to the Broken Shoe gang, a group of 30 young toughs that he joined four years ago, when he was 14.

The capital of Mexico is largely a city of children, and increasingly its impoverished and middle-class neighborhoods are being divided and conquered by youth gangs. Nearly 5,000 gangs are believed to be active, and their number is growing.

Estimates of their total membership now exceeds one million youths.

Few blocks in Mexico City are not colored by stylized graffiti marking the boundaries of a gang's claim to authority.

Officials and academics suggest that the country's exploding demographics and imploding economy are largely responsible for the new culture. In Mexico City, almost 40 percent of the 20 million inhabitants are under the age of 20.

Nationwide, the economy would have to support an estimated one million new jobs a year to accommodate youths entering the work force. It does not.

By some accounts, the current fascination with gangs began in Mexico City's Santa Fe district.

Today, there are about 400 gangs in Santa Fe. The Savages, the Punk Jackals, the Vikings, the Rookies, the Sex Rats, Street Machine and scores of others have laid claim to blocks sloping away from Vasco de Quiroga Avenue, the neighborhood's principal street. There are female gangs (The Cutters), homosexual gangs (The Babies), and gangs made up of grade school students.

"Look, this is a country where there's a rule for everything and nobody respects the rules," said Vargas. "We make up our own."

Reprinted with the permission of *The Boston Globe*.

• • •

DATE: NOVEMBER 8, 1985, PART 6 OF A SERIES
SOURCE: PITTSBURGH PRESS
AUTHOR: MARY PAT FLAHERTY AND ANDREW SCHNEIDER

* * *

YOU GRASP FOR TRUST

It's a sudden decision that must be made at a time when it's almost impossible to think clearly about anything.

You're gently guided away from the rest of the families anxiously waiting for information outside the surgical intensive care unit or the trauma center and taken to a tiny, private conference room.

You know you wouldn't be here if the news were good.

"There isn't any hope," says the doctor. A nurse sitting next to you grasps your hand and softly adds, "The damage from the accident is too great. It's destroyed the brain. He's dead."

Nothing makes sense.

A half hour ago, you stood by his bed, just 30 feet away. There was an incomprehensible collection of tubes, wires and electronic devices passing in and out of him but there was also life. He was breathing. His chest rose and fell. You felt his heart beat. He was warm to the touch.

"He may look like he's living but it's the machines that are making him breathe and keeping his heart beating," the nurse says. "But the tests have proven that his brain is dead."

There's a pause for tears, then: "Do you want to consider donating his organs so maybe someone else can live?" the nurse asks in a voice almost too soft to hear.

That question is gently asked of about a dozen families in this country every day. In Pittsburgh, about 80 percent answer yes, according to those who ask.

Because they say yes, strangers live.

It is their simple act of charity that is the focus of the current debate about the future of the field.

Donation begins with a nod from a grieving family who does not merely donate a heart, a kidney, lungs or eyes, but rather a son, a sister, a husband.

Just this week, throughout America, families donated. For example:

—In Pittsburgh, the family of a 25-year-old woman killed in a traffic accident in West Virginia donated her organs to these Pittsburghers: a liver to a 40-year-old man, her kidneys to a 49-year-old woman and 38-year-old man. Her heart went to a 32-year-old New York woman.

—In Memphis, the liver from a 19-year-old Wisconsin man was donated to a 43-year-old man from South Carolina.

—In Omaha, the liver of a 34-year-old man killed in a motorcycle accident was given to a 36-year-old Nebraska woman; his kidneys to a 52-year-old Omaha man and a teenage girl in Dallas.

—In Philadelphia, three people from that city were given a second chance at life with organs donated from a 13-year-old boy killed in a car crash. His liver went to a woman, 54; his kidneys to another boy, 16, and a woman, 22. His heart was flown to Pittsburgh where it went to a 12-year-old boy from New York.

—In Boston, the organs of a teenager killed in a fall were donated to three New Englanders. Her kidneys went to a 49-year-old man.

Families trying to cope with their own loss don't leap to thinking about a stranger whose life might be saved by donor organs.

"There wasn't a mark on her and she even had color in her cheeks but then they're telling me she's dead," recalls Sharon Fullerton, who donated the kidneys and corneas of her 10-year-old daughter, Michelle, two days after she was struck by a car on Pittsburgh's North Side.

The Fullertons donated the organs in July 1979. Like most donor families, it took time before their grieving passed and they were able to talk about the donation.

"On the first night the doctor told us it didn't look good and asked us to think about donating, but all we could think about was her.

"Finally, there was no hope. If we were going to donate, it had to be done then. There was nothing to base our decision on other than the trust of the doctors, nurses and Don Denny, the procurement coordinator.

"Mr. Denny sat there with the briefcase on his lap and the permission slip laying on top. I remember staring at the form wondering whether I could trust these strangers to give Michelle's organs to the people who needed them most. We weren't just talking about kidneys and corneas, we were talking about my daughter."

Michelle was the oldest of the Fullerton's six daughters. Her kidneys went into a boy and girl in their early teens and her corneas into a pair of twins, all from Pittsburgh.

As part of its 10-month investigation of kidney transplantation, 14 families permitted *The Pittsburgh Press* to sit in as they did their soul-searching over whether or not to donate organs.

In almost all cases, trust that the organs would go to the most needy recipient appeared to be the critical issue on which the decisions turned.

None of the families asked about sex, race, age or residency of the potential recipient. The single most frequently voiced concern was: "Will they go to someone who really needs them?"

Still coping with the recent death of their relatives, those 14 families did not want to publicly discuss their decisions to donate. Other families, cushioned by the passage of time, could do so.

"Our only concern was, could part of Joshua help someone else," says Chris Lamison, who donated the kidneys and corneas of his 29-month-old boy who died after his spinal cord was severed in an automobile accident in Armstrong County in January 1983.

"It didn't make any difference who got it. We trusted them (procurement people) to make the best decision. In the tragedy, the hope that Joshua's death would help another was the only bright spot we could grasp."

Lamison, a 31-year-old land surveyor from Kittanning, says both of his child's two tiny kidneys were transplanted into a 17-year-old boy from southwestern Pennsylvania.

Mary Lou Harbulak donated her husband's organs.

"At first I only said they could have my husband's kidney, then Brian Broznick (the procurement coordinator) told me that in another hospital a 30-year-old man with two kids needed a heart desperately or he'd die. I told Brian to take Paul's heart," says Mrs. Harbulak, whose 25-year-old husband died of a ruptured vessel in his brain in August 1982.

"I didn't know Brian before that night but I believed him when he said Paul's organs would save someone's life. You grasp for trust in a situation like that, without it you can't cope with anything," she says.

There are more than 550 men and women working in procurement across the country and most take their work and their word seriously.

"We put our integrity on the line every time we deal with a family," Broznick says. "It's the only thing we have on our side and if we have that grabbed away from us by anyone who abuses the gifts these people make, then we have nothing to work with.

"We're not dealing with organs. We're dealing with people. These families are allowing us to carry out their wishes. We're their link between the death that's just occurred and the generous gifts they share so someone else can live. That trust must be taken seriously. If it's violated, at all, then transplantation in this country will suffer."

Reprinted with the permission of *The Pittsburgh Press*.

• • •

DATE: SEPTEMBER 1985
SOURCE: HOUSTON CITY MAGAZINE, PP. 82–89, 124–125.
AUTHOR: KATHRYN CASEY

* * *

LOVE & DEATH IN THE PINEY WOODS: THE TRAGIC STORY
OF THE COACH, THE PRINCIPAL, AND THE SECRETARY

LAURA NUGENT knew something was wrong. She had been sitting for hours on the small porch of her parents' home 40 miles east of Houston, waiting for her lover, Bill Fleming, to drive up in his white pickup truck. He never came. He had said that he'd be there by 4:30 to have supper with her family. It was already six, but she still expected him to show up at any moment. By seven she was pacing the porch of the white clapboard house, nervously tugging the ends of her long, ink-dark hair. By eight that April evening she was driving the dark country roads near her home, searching for him.

On Saturday, she used her key to check his apartment. She found Bill's truck parked at Hull-Daisetta Junior School where he coached, but he wasn't there either.

Again she was in the car, driving slowly down deserted roads, watching for any sign of him.

By Monday night she was frantic. She lay in her bed, going over her weekend's desperate search, and the phone at his apartment that rang without answer. Bill hadn't shown up for work that morning at the school, and the district's superintendent called the police, reporting him missing. His pickup, still parked in the school lot, hadn't been moved all weekend. Now, despite her exhaustion, Laura had difficulty sleeping. When she finally drifted off she had a hazy dream: Bill was standing in the distance. She ran toward him, but just as she came close enough to touch him he turned away. He couldn't see her. Laura bolted upright in bed. "I knew it then," she whispers. "I knew then that Bill was dead."

On a quiet Monday morning a week later, Don Griffin, a retired electrician, found the body. While supervising workers who were cutting a road to his brother-in-law's land off FM 943 in southeast Polk county, Griffin saw dewberries growing on some bushes. As he popped the berries into his mouth he noticed a peculiar odor. Edging toward a clearing he saw it—the badly decomposed body of a large man lying face up. The body was dressed in shirt and jeans but had no shoes or wallet. There was a ring, however, from Stephen F. Austin State University 1973, engraved with the initials BMF.

A month later, on May 16, 1985, a Polk County grand jury indicted the principal of the Hull-Daisetta Junior School, where Billy Mac Fleming had taught. Stories of a love triangle involving the accused "black" principal, the slain white coach, and the white school secretary, Laura Nugent, spread quickly throughout the little towns. Photos of the three from school annuals were published in newspapers and national tabloids, with headlines that linked the love triangle with the death. The principal, Hurley Fontenot, with light tan skin and straight, fine brown hair, appeared on the television news turning himself in to the Liberty County Sheriff. He was charged with pumping two small-caliber bullets at close range, execution style, into the back of Bill Fleming's head.

[The article continues beyond this excerpt.]

Reprinted with the permission of Southwest Media Corporation, Dallas.

A Professional's Point of View

By Maryln Schwartz
Dallas Morning News

Sometimes writers find it hard to distinguish between a feature and a news story. This is the best way I can explain it:

We all know the biblical story of Noah and the Ark. Just before it rained for 40 days and 40 nights, Noah built an ark. He took his family and two of every kind of animal that was then living on earth. Every living creature on the ark was saved from the flood.

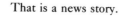

That is a news story.

If I was writing about that event, I'd want to talk to Mrs. Noah, who was probably having to clean up after all those animals for 40 days and 40 nights.

That's a feature story.

When I'm writing my newspaper column, I look for the small details that give the readers a clear view of the big picture.

For instance, when Prince Charles visited New Mexico, I wanted to give an example of what it means to be royalty. I didn't want to just write that people were bowing, because we already know that people bow to royalty. So I just watched for a little while.

Then I noticed that Prince Charles was the only person at the party who wasn't wearing a name tag. And this wasn't a "B" Party. Cary Grant was there and he wore a name tag.

This is the kind of touch that separates real royalty from mere legend. I did the same thing recently when I was watching the Miss America contestants give their predictable pre-pageant TV interviews. They were all insisting they weren't beauty queens, they had a message to give the world. They didn't want to discuss sex appeal. They wanted to talk about nuclear disarmament.

Then I would flip channels to interviews of the presidential candidates. The political analysts kept trying to talk about Michael Dukakis' charisma or George Bush's sex appeal.

I knew I had my column when I began to realize that politics and beauty pageants have somehow become confused with each other: "Would someone please tell me what's going on? Why is it that Miss Montana can't wait to discuss Manuel Noriega and George Bush only seems to want to discuss his grandchildren?"

To write a good feature story requires as much observing as it does writing. You can have a beautifully crafted story, but no one will really care unless you have something to say. Information is the most important aspect. There will always be an editor who can help you turn a better phrase. But all the editing in the world isn't going to help if your information isn't interesting.

You don't have to have been at a major news event to find a good feature story. And you just have to train yourself to see details that other people overlook.

Actress Farrah Fawcett was the most interviewed actress in the country when she was starring in the "Charlie's Angels" TV show. My editor asked me to do a story and to be sure to mention that the actress had been named one of the "10 Most Beautiful" on campus when she attended the University of Texas.

The story had been done again and again. I didn't think anyone would even want to read it. Instead, I decided to find out what had happened to the other nine most beautiful. The story went on the wire and was used in about 40 newspapers.

I got my information by phone. It took only two days. (Schwartz, personal communication, 1988)

* * *

Maryln Schwartz is a feature writer and columnist for the *Dallas Morning News*.

7

Profiles and Personality Sketches

Some profile writers will tell you that profiles are short, vivid biographies. They liken their work to that of portrait painters or sculptors. An artist paints a lifelike portrait of a person with oils or watercolors. A sculptor might use clay or marble to create a bust. As a writer, you can also create a portrait of a person using your command of some very different communication tools—words and language.

Still, personality sketches and profiles are a bit different from biographies and different from other portrait art forms. Obviously, a profile for a newspaper or a magazine will not be as long as a book-sized biography. Some newspaper and magazine profiles run thousands of words and are published in installments. And some are excerpts from book-length studies of an individual. Most, however, are much shorter and more concentrated. Writer and editor Art Spikol (1979) says article profiles require a different treatment because of their length, but also because article profiles have different *focus*. "A biography deals with the entire life of the subject, whereas in the profile . . . the focus is current. The question, *Why are we interested in this person?* is always answered, *Because he is such and such today*" (p. 8).

Daniel Williamson (1975) calls profiles in-depth stories about an individual designed to capture "the essence of his personality" (p. 151).

Profiles have been a part of the nonfiction writer's portfolio for generations. In the early part of this century, magazines in New York, particularly *The New Yorker*, began to publish personality-based stories labeled profiles.

Personality sketches and profiles are important feature articles in the overall content mix of newspapers and magazines today. Newspapers use them to introduce new newsmakers to readers on almost a daily basis. Government leaders are profiled on page one. Star athletes are highlighted in sports. Singers and musicians are subjects for the entertainment section. Some magazines regularly present profiles of industry or profession leaders and newsmakers to their readers in frequent sections devoted to highlighting individuals. *The New Yorker* has used its profiles regularly for decades. And newer magazines have recognized the value of regular profiles. *Florida Trend,* a business magazine, publishes a regular feature called "The Achievers" to focus on successful executives, managers, and owners.

These days profiles do not even have to be about people. You will find profiles of cities, companies, sports teams, management teams, committees, and on and on. These organizational and institutional profiles are popular in certain sections of newspapers such as business and sports and in similar departments of magazines as well.

The ability to produce a profile and personality sketch is a necessary skill for the versatile nonfiction writer. You will get a look at the basics of the newspaper and magazine profile and personality sketch and the different approaches to writing these stories in this chapter. Your first stop is with the basics.

BASIC PROFILE CONTENT AND STRUCTURE

Profiles do have common content and generally follow a standard format. You will find variations, of course, but most profiles include certain basic information. The result is a structure that has evolved over the years.

When profiling an individual, whether it be for a newspaper or a magazine, you should include biographical material offered in a mostly chronological order, an environment or surroundings description, anecdotes or stories by and about the subject, personal information, and family information. A combination of these categories of information about an individual should produce a full, insightful picture of the individual.

Writing the article will be easiest if as a beginner you follow the general format for profiles. After you have done a profile or two, you will probably begin to experiment with other organizational approaches as well as other means of focusing on the individual.

A standard profile can have several purposes and forms. A full profile will be a narrative article of considerable length, depending on whether the profile is for a newspaper or magazine. Many publications are publishing profiles in capsule form, called *thumbnails* by some editors. These are abstracted profiles with only the basic facts presented in a summary or listing format.

For a beginner, a profile formula has four major parts:

1. Lead.
2. Subject's current successes/accomplishments.
3. Biographical chronology.
4. Ending or conclusion.

The lead can be built by using several parts or only one component. As in other feature articles, the lead in a profile is two or three paragraphs that are interest-arousing for the reader. These can be stirring quotations, a dramatic scene description, or a telling anecdote.

The lead should melt into the current accomplishments portion through an effective transition. This portion contains the article's news peg. Now you tell your reader: This is why you should read about this person. And you, the writer, describe the subject's achievements and responsibilities.

The 1986 *Gentlemen's Quarterly* profile of journalist Carl Bernstein illustrates this point. E. Graydon Carter's look at the Watergate reporter for *The Washington Post* tells what is happening with the writer *at present*. Carter's article about the successful journalist opens with the unexpected statement: "Carl Bernstein is homeless." From there, Carter takes the reader through a series of explanations about this opening statement, tying them to Bernstein's hunt for housing in Manhattan after his apartment lease had expired. This episode dissolves into a physical description of Bernstein and then a statement to readers why Bernstein deserves this article: Bernstein's fame past and present.

With another good transition from the lead, you move to the portion of the article where you provide the personal background on the individual. This is a biographical section, told most of the time in chronological order from childhood (or beginning of professional career, perhaps) to present. This will usually demand the variety of sources necessary in a profile to give a complete picture. But beware: This section can be dull unless it is spiced up with anecdotes and quotes.

The ending is linked to the rest of the article in several ways. The most common method is to bring the reader up to present in the chronology, connecting with the points made in the "news peg" section. Another method is to link up with an anecdote told in the lead or some other observation you made near the beginning of the article.

Some publications prefer to publish profiles in a question and answer format. The Q & A has certain advantages such as brevity and the sense of realism during the interview, but it also has disadvantages such as a lack of writing creativity (editing creativity may substitute for it) and the need for precision in question-asking and in recording responses. Joshua Gilder's (1981) Q & A with Tom Wolfe in *Saturday Review* illustrates how profiles can be done well in Q & A format, focusing on Wolfe's writing. Gilder kept questions short and allowed answers to be long and revealing. *Playboy* magazine's series of interviews also effectively profile individuals, partly because of the lengthy introductions often given to the Q & A interviews, but also because of the actual depth of the interviews as well.

Art Spikol, former editor of *Philadelphia Magazine,* says there is a clear distinction between the interview story and the profile. "Even if the terms are occasionally used interchangedly by beginning writers, the fact is that the two types of writing bear little resemblance to one another" (Spikol, 1979, p. 7). Spikol says an interview is just that, a conversation with someone. He adds, "A profile is something else: It is an article whose main subject is a particular person, and it is rarely based exclusively on *an* interview or on interviews with that person. In fact, profiles are probably at their least expository—and writers at their laziest—when written with information supplied by their subjects. After all, no subject—particularly one with some sophistication dealing with the press—will supply information that might be damaging or embarrassing; the only anecdotes the writer will get will be those the subject wishes to share" (p. 7).

Profiles should not be entirely positive or laudatory. Most are neutral or balanced in presentation. In fact, some profiles will be written about a person who has been responsible for criminal activity or other socially unacceptable behavior. Your readers are likely interested in these persons as well. *Texas Monthly* once profiled Harding Lawrence, the man who built Braniff International airlines into a major company. Byron Harris' (1982) article was titled "The Man Who Killed Braniff," and it described Lawrence in depth by accounting for his rise and fall in the corporate airline world. Although Lawrence does not fare well in the profile, readers get a close look at how he succeeded and later failed.

Some profiles will seem to write themselves, up to a point. Usually you can tell your readers the news and the past about the person. It is possible, as Spikol says, to wind up without a good ending. "Profiles are like that. You have swooped down on a subject and caught him at a certain point in time; naturally, you'll have to swoop away and leave him to act out the rest of the script. About all you can do is speculate a little about the subject's future. . . ." (p. 10).

CHECKLIST OF BASIC INFORMATION FOR WRITING A PROFILE

Biographical material
  Birthdate, birthplace
  Schooling
  First job, other positions held
  Family (parents, brothers and sisters)
  Childhood friends

News peg information
  Promotions, appointments, advancements
  Awards, honors, citations
  Present situation

Environment/surroundings

Home, workplace description, decor
Former environments (for contrast)

Physical Characteristics

Physical appearance of person
Mannerisms
Clothing style
Hair style

Anecdotes/stories

Embarrassing moments
Greatest accomplishment
Memorable first times

Family

Spouse, marriage information
Previous marriages, commitments
Children, ages and names
In-laws
Pets

Personal

General lifestyle, philosophies of living
Plans for the future
Dreams and fantasies
Hobbies, interests
Favorite foods, music
Recreational activities
Religion
Military service
Volunteer work or other civic/community service
Club memberships
Major traumas and problems (current or past)

THE PROFILE SUBJECT AS A SOURCE

How do you choose the right person or organization for a profile? People and organizations are chosen for profiles because they are newsworthy. Because of what has happened to them lately, these persons are in the public eye, and people want to learn more about them. Judgments about the newsworthiness of an individual are usually based on recent developments in the person's personal or professional life.

As noted earlier, people are not the only subjects of profiles. In one example, United Press International's article on the city of Detroit points to what has happened to the major city of Michigan in the past 20 years. The article uses the same basic formula described for profiles of people—multiple sources, observations, a chronological summary of the city's recent history, and factual support for generalization (a university study, among other sources).

In choosing a human subject, you should consider that a person will be a good candidate to be profiled if the individual is well known. An individual may be popular because of his or her professional activities. Or the person may be controversial because of a position on an issue that may divide a profession, community, or even a family.

Another reason to profile someone is that the person has reached a new level in his or her career or personal life. There has been a promotion, a new accomplishment, career change/shift, or other step recently taken. When former CBS reporter Fred Graham left the network and returned to Nashville, his hometown, to work as a local affiliate manager and anchor, his career shift signaled a reason to profile him in *Knight-Ridder News,* a magazine of the corporation that owns Graham's new station.

You also want to select an individual based on a third reason—leadership. The sort of person to profile is an industry or business leader who serves as a role model.

Florida Trend's regular feature department titled "The Achievers" shows how a profile can focus on someone who is well known in his or her industry and someone who has experienced recent success and reached a new level of accomplishment. The article by free-lance writer Linda Marx (1987) tells readers about the evolution of musician Jeffrey Arthur's career—changing from rock musician to jingle writer. Marx's article uses observation and quotations from peers to establish Arthur's successes in the minds of readers.

You should try to select individuals for their talkative nature and fluency of speech. A profile is in part based on the thoughts of the person being highlighted. Someone who is not so glib or garrulous, for example, might not provide you with strong material for your story. Furthermore, it is also helpful to a successful profile for the subject to have a large circle of professional and personal acquaintances who are willing and able to discuss the subject of the article.

But you do not always have to profile someone because of fame or recent accomplishments. Sometimes, especially for feature treatment, a profile can be of someone who is not a celebrity. These "common" people, the rank-and-file, often make good stories that are appealing to readers. The idea of course, is to emphasize what makes this individual, who might otherwise be like your readers, a bit unique.

Art Spikol says profiles should be chosen depending on the answers to five questions:

1. Is the subject everything he seems to be?
2. How did the subject get that way?

3. How does the world react to, and perceive, the subject?

4. How does the subject perceive himself?

5. What can we learn about the subject by analyzing his environment—the people, places, and things with which he surrounds himself?

After deciding the person is right for your attention and effort, you need several things to fall in place. For starters, to do the profile you need cooperation. Ideally, a person to be profiled will agree to the idea and allow you to interview him or her one or more times. This is not always an easy matter because the type of person you will often profile is usually quite busy and in demand by many other people at work, home, and in the media. Some people who feel they have been treated poorly by the press will resist you also. But most people like to be profiled and would agree to it.

You need a significant block of time with your subject to get to know him or her. If possible, request interviews in several different environments. You need to talk with the person in his or her creative or work environment, but it adds a dimension to talk to the subject at his or her home in a more relaxed setting. Being in both places allows you the chance to see the subject in distinctly different (most of the time, at least) environments. If possible, find a "neutral" location as well, such as a park where your subject likes to jog or a quiet coffee shop, for conversations. The more varied the atmospheres you use, the more you will learn about the individual.

Subjects who do not want to be profiled or do not have time to talk to you can still be profiled. The job is just harder, requiring you to do more work in your research and in interviewing others who know your subject well. For example, Gay Talese's widely read profile of Frank Sinatra in *Esquire* in 1966 characterized the entertainer without directly interviewing him. Instead, Talese carefully and tediously observed Sinatra and talked to Sinatra's friends and acquaintances to gather his information for the article, "Frank Sinatra has a Cold." He watched Sinatra during filming of an NBC television program, and he watched him with his friends in a Beverly Hills bar. Talese wrote down conversations he heard for passages of dialogue in his article. He noticed what the singer ate and drank. He watched Sinatra's mood changes. And Talese incorporated all this research into his profile of a man who was, in Talese's words, "the champ."

OBSERVING YOUR SUBJECT

Take the time to watch this person do what he or she does best. *Why* are you writing about this person? Is he or she a top dress designer? Then try to watch this person designing or introducing his or her work at a show. If you are profiling a politician, watch the person interacting with constituents, on the floor of the legislature, and in a political party meeting. Each experience will tell you more about the person and help you write a more complete profile of the individual.

This will help you create a better, more complete picture of this person in your mind, and, consequently, in the minds of your readers. Note the subject's mannerisms. How does your subject deal with other people? Is his or her work behavior with others different from behavior with superiors? With family? Friends? If so, why?

You can approach this in two ways. Depending on the individual and his or her activities, you can observe him or her without the subject's knowledge you are doing so. This can be in public places, of course, when the individual is performing, speaking, or whatever. You can also, under circumstances where you might not be able to remain anonymous, watch as a known observer to the subject. This might be necessary in a small-group situation for demonstrations or less public forms of work.

OTHER NECESSARY SOURCES IN A PROFILE

As in other types of feature articles, one source is not enough to give a full picture of what you are writing for your readers. Even if that source is the subject of the story, you should not stop with just this source. You can be fooled by a good interview or series of interviews with your source into thinking you have everything you need to write.

You don't.

Good profiles are balanced in their use of sources. You should attempt to give the positive and negative elements of the individual, and you usually have to go beyond the subject for that. The profiles by UPI about Detroit and *Florida Trend* about the commercial jingle king do this effectively by using a wide variety of sources. Take another look at these two articles to check the types of sources used by the writers.

So, how many interviews are enough? Seldom do you need to interview as many as fifty people. Some writers will do this, but usually that kind of depth is only necessary for a book. Generally, you can get a good sense of the person by talking to a half dozen to a dozen sources. But this is no magic range. The real trick is variation in the type of source you use. If you use too many similar sources you will not find anything new. You need to try to find a balance of friendly and unfriendly sources, and family and professional sources, for example.

There are seven categories of human interview sources you can most often use. Here's a list:

1. Family members such as brothers and sisters, parents, spouses, and children. Former family members such as ex-spouses should be included.

2. Neighbors and former neighbors.
3. Business associates where subject works.
4. Business associates through professional organizations.
5. Competitors and rivals in the workplace.
6. Personal friends.
7. People who work where the subject shops and places where the subject goes for entertainment.

You will want to incorporate as many anecdotes as possible into your article to help generate "insight" into the subject's personality. During your interviews, encourage the subject and your other sources to tell stories that are informative, amusing, and profound.

There are two other types of research beyond interviews to use in a profile. You should also check clippings of other articles written about the person (this is particularly true of newspaper writers who have access to such libraries). Although magazine writers might not have such resources as easily available, the fact that many newspapers have computerized their libraries and now sell access to the public, research for free-lancers and magazine writers without office libraries is not as serious a problem as it was a decade ago.

The other area to research in completing the preparation of your profile is public records. You may find interesting details about a person by reviewing civil and criminal court files, police records, property records, and other public documents of similar nature. This is especially applied to profiles of individuals in public service such as appointed and elected government officials. It will also be an effective strategy for business executives, entertainers, athletes, and others widely known in your community or region whose activities are on the public record.

PROFILING CELEBRITIES

There are numerous barriers to gaining access to celebrities. These people are always in demand by writers for stories of all types. Barriers include secretaries and receptionists for business executives; bodyguards, publicists, and press agents for entertainers; public information officers and media relations liaisons for individuals in high levels of public service. Their jobs include "protecting" their employers from people who might want to interrupt or disrupt.

There is a strategy to get to your source for the interviews you need for your article. Your first step is to fully identify yourself and directly ask the celebrity's assistants for their help, explaining what work you are doing and why. Because your work is *legitimate and serious*, you might get to your subject to request the interview. You might also be asked to wait while your request is taken to your subject for a response. If you work for a publication, your reputation and your publication's reputation can be assets. Do not be afraid to use them.

If you are still denied access, then try to work your way around the barriers. One way is to find the subject as he or she leaves the workplace, or shops on weekends, or at some other *public* location where you can introduce yourself and your purpose. This direct approach will often work, even though it requires extra effort. There are occasions when a writer, stopped by a subject's staff, gets an interview because he or she went to the extra effort to ask directly. It is possible, and often is the case, that the subject never got the original request.

Still another strategy for the hard-to-get interview is offered by columnist Bob Greene. He writes letters to tough-to-reach subjects. This is the way he managed his well-known interviews with Richard Nixon, Patricia Hearst, and multiple murderer Richard Speck. These accomplishments, early in his career, helped him toward becoming a syndicated writer (Schumacher, 1983).

You can also use published or broadcast quotes from other sources you locate in your research. Of course, this means you must attribute the information to its source in your article. You can take this information from speeches, press conferences, and similar public events. And it does not harm your article to tell readers that you made attempts to reach the person, but were refused for whatever reasons.

If you are fortunate enough to get an interview with your subject, then you must, like any other interview, get yourself prepared. Larry Grobel (1978) who has interviewed celebrities for *Playboy* magazine, says it helps to have certain expectations for the "star" interview. "Know what you are getting into. Find out in advance if there is a time limit . . . . Good interviews are ones in which the subject is as interested as you are. That's difficult with celebrities, who have to hear the same questions over and over; but that's not impossible" (p. 20).

You may have other restrictions beyond time. You might be asked to conduct your interview with another writer in a small group setting. You may have a language barrier and need translation, so you actually interview the translator. You may be told that you have to conduct the interview with this busy celebrity in an unusual environment—in a car, backstage, or even at home with the kids screaming and dogs barking.

As you were advised in chapter 3, prepare your major questions in advance and write them down. You might wind up not needing them, but they serve as a crutch when awkward, slow moments occur. And tape your interview for accuracy. This also lets you participate more in the conversation.

Grobel also recommends that you work to keep control of the interview. This means you should be in charge of the direction of the conversation. Change topics if you must do so when a pause or interruption occurs.

12 TIPS ON WRITING PROFILES

Here are a dozen tips from David McDaniel (1986), business editor of the Neptune, N.J., *Asbury Park Press:*

1. One of the best ways for writers to portray character is with *anecdotes*. Get these from the subject and from people who know the person such as business associates, family, friends. One good anecdote, like a good photo, could be worth a thousand words. "What was your most frustrating experience? Why did you decide to go into business/politics?" These questions might get you a good anecdote.

2. Profile pieces should use some description of *physical* characteristics such as mannerisms, appearance, and dress, all of which can be woven into a story or dropped in with a paragraph. Don't be afraid to make obvious characterizations. Is the subject rugged looking (large build, beard, ruddy complexion)? Is he or she well dressed and attractive (well groomed, neatly pressed suit, starched white shirt, neatly combed hair)?

3. Find out as much about the person's *business or job* as you can. For a business executive, for example, what are the company's assets, annual sales, main products? How many employees, at how many locations? What is unique about the business?

4. Include all the usual *biographical material*—age, family, education, service, and so on. Much can be tacked on at the end, but it is better to weave this into your story.

5. Be sure to include the subject's *tastes and habits*. Does he or she chain-smoke? Like classical music? Have an unusual hobby?

6. Find out what the person's *goals* are. Is he or she satisfied with the present situation? Where does this person want to be in ten years—expanding the present business or sitting on someone else's board of directors?

7. Ask what *influences* made the subject a success today. Parents? Spouse? Teacher? Tragedy?

8. Try to find out the person's *shortcomings*. Use them, if necessary, to give the entire picture.

9. Get three times as many *quotes* as you need. Get them from the subject, spouse, friends, competitors, suppliers. Good quotes tell the story best.

10. Ask the subject to give *advice* to others aspiring to the same career and to make predictions about the future of the industry.

11. In preparation, *research* the subject by seeking library clips, other articles or advertisements by the person's company. Be prepared with good, thought-provoking questions and try to put your subject at ease.

12. Form your lead after the interview, but keep your eyes and ears open for the "*peg*" as you gather material.

PROFILES NEED FOCUS

You now know that a good profile has *focus*. When you are beginning to work on a profile, you need to think about what focus it will have about the subject. Most subjects that are worthy of profiles have multiple elements of their personalities and accomplishments that will force you to choose a particular direction for the profile. When you are restricted on length, particularly for traditional newspaper profiles of 750 to 1,000 words (three or four typewritten pages), you cannot afford to drift aimlessly in your description of the individual. You can probably get deeper into an individual in magazine profiles if the luxury of a longer manuscript (5,000 to 10,000 words, or 20 to 40 pages, for example) comes with the assignment. This would permit you the chance to probe several directions. But most profiles do not permit such depth and require more writing discipline through limited focus. Some profile writers also call this focus a "theme" for the article. Whatever it is called, the point is the same—give your article some direction.

The direction might become apparent in your research before you begin interviewing or writing. If it does not even after you have completed most of your research, you can still look for the focus during your interviews with the subjects and others.

The *Florida Trend* profile of the state's jingle king focuses on his business success. *USA Today* writer Monica Collins' (1987) profile of entertainer Bill Cosby was a cover story played on page one, highlighting Cosby's accomplishments as a national television commercial pitchman. Both articles have *focus*, or a story line, as some writers label it.

University of Florida professor Edward Yates (1985) suggests that, in searching for that theme, you remain flexible. "If he or she [the writer] has selected a theme from pre-interview research and a more interesting one develops during the questioning, he or she must be ready to switch directions" (p. 210). Yates says themes will often concern a subject's range or type of experience, personality or character traits, aspirations in life, personal achievements, or philosophy of life.

PERSONALITY SKETCHES

A personality sketch is not as involved as a profile. Although some personality sketches are as long as magazine profiles, sketches generally are short and to the point. The article is designed to give us a quick look at an individual and to tell us why the subject is important. These articles usually lack the depth of profiles and must not waste words with the reader.

William Rivers and Alison Work (1986) tell you that the personality sketch is a tough assignment, forcing you to "become a keen observer and recorder of significant details" (p. 242). These articles, they continue, contain imagery created by details that you find in profiles. However, there are just not as many in these shorter pieces. You must show; don't tell. You have to do this in your own sketches.

Rivers and Work also suggest that sketches are strengthened by use of anecdotes. These have tremendous value to you as a writer and offer much strength to your sketch. "They enliven articles. They need not be funny to be effective. Light or serious, anecdotes illustrate points and bring them to life. To write an effective anecdote, it is usually necessary for the writer to see the subject in action and to be able to quote him at length" (p. 245).

BEST SOURCES FOR WRITING PROFILES

People
  Subject
  Family
  Neighbors
  Workplace associates, rivals, and competitors
  Businesses where subject shops

Observations
  Subject at work
  Subject at home with family, friends
  Subject enjoying personal activities

Library Research
  Resume, press kits
  Public records
  Writings by subject, if any
  Previous newspaper, magazine article clippings
  Film and videotape, if available

CAPSULE-THUMBNAIL PROFILES

Brief or capsule profiles, often called thumbnail profiles also, are growing in popularity with newspaper and magazine editors.

These profiles are quite short, just a few hundred words, and usually follow a standard format developed by the editors of the publication or news service. These formats may even vary within the publication, with different sections or departments offering their own profiles depending on the nature of the subject being profiled.

There is also a movement toward profiles of nonhuman subjects such as institutions, corporations, sports teams, network programs, films, and so on. These follow a certain content outline and are regularly offered. A new company, a successful business, or a new investment category might be profiled by a business magazine or business section of a newspaper. At the beginning of a new sports season, standardized profiles of teams or leagues might be part of a special section or part of the regular coverage of a top game of the day or week. In entertainment, profiles of new movies, books, records, and other art forms are commonplace. Each of these serves a purpose for the reader: The capsulized profile is an information digest for a quick read. These capsule profiles can be placed within larger articles on broader subjects as a sidebar or placed beside articles of equal importance. *The Miami Herald* staff produced the profile of sailing champion W. Scott Piper in a form that exemplifies the point here. The Piper profile provides basic information on the man in four categories and finishes with a significant quote. The major categories are his sailing background, his personal or biographical highlights, his educational background, and his professional accomplishments.

Some publications ask subjects to profile themselves by obtaining answers to a short, standard list of questions. *The Dallas Morning News* runs "High Profile Self-Portraits" with its weekly feature called "High Profile." The Sunday feature is a regular in-depth look at prominent individuals in Texas and includes the brief self-portrait sidebar asking the subject to finish the following phrases:

1. When I'm nervous . . .
2. I never could . . .
3. The guests at my fantasy dinner party would be . . .
4. The person who had the most impact on my life was . . .
5. Birthdate and place . . .
6. If I've learned one thing in my life, it's . . .
7. My friends like me because . . .
8. If I could change one thing about myself, I'd be . . .
9. My mother's best advice was . . .
10. My mother's worst advice was . . .
11. Favorite all-time movie . . .
12. Favorite president . . .
13. Behind my back, they say . . .
14. My best asset is . . .
15. My worst habit is . . .
16. Favorite cliche . . .
17. The last book I read was . . .
18. I'm compulsive about . . .

By looking at the capsule example from *The Miami Herald* and *The Dallas Morning News*, you can now understand this form is an abstracted version of what you might write in a full profile, without the elaboration. These short profiles are the bare bones. There are no wasted words. And they are direct to the point.

SOME PARTING ADVICE ON PROFILES

Can you err in writing profiles? Yes. To avoid mistakes, be careful not to depend on only your subject. Use numerous sources that represent a variety of perspectives. Don't write according to chronology only. Select a strong focus for your article. Don't drift. And don't jumble your facts together. Use good transitions to connect the pieces. And above all, do not forget your "nut 'graph' " (the news peg to the story). With these things in mind, you are ready to try your first profile.

HOW PROFESSIONALS WROTE IT

DATE: SEPTEMBER 1987, PP. 31–36.
SOURCE: FLORIDA TREND MAGAZINE
AUTHOR: LINDA MARX

* * *

FROM ROCK MUSIC STAR TO A KING OF JINGLES

Jeff Arthur got an early taste for stardom. When he was only 7, he did a live performance of Everything's Coming Up Roses in his hometown of St. Petersburg. In 1971, he borrowed a guitar and won the National Collegiate Performance Award for a dazzling rendition of Light My Fire. And after that, he dropped out of the University of South Florida to tour the country as writer and lead vocalist in the rock group Arthur, Hurley & Gottlieb.

For six years the trio traveled the nation, performing with such superstars as John Lennon, Janis Ian and Van Morrison. Yet, despite the critical success of the group's two albums (*Time* magazine rated "Sun Shinin" among the top 10 albums of 1975), Arthur constantly was broke and tired of living out of a suitcase. "When the daughter of the owner of Just Pants approached me at a concert in Miami and asked me to write a jingle for the company, I laughed in her face," he recalls. "I told her I didn't do commercial schlock. Three days later I looked at the $4.12 in my pocket and called her back."

And so began Jeffrey Arthur Productions, a Clearwater-based commercial jingle company, which the 36-year-old hippie-turned-yuppie has parlayed into one of the largest custom music makers in the state. The company specializes in jingles for radio and television, audio/visual presentations, voice-overs, broadcast copy writing, film and television scores, athletic team fight songs and concept sales for broadcasters. From only $12,000 in 1978, volume of his two companies—Jeffrey

Arthur Productions and Florida Sound, a production facility—shot to $650,000 in 1986. Arthur expects sales to exceed $800,000 in 1987.

"You could say I transferred my energies for writing about love, peace and bike riding to tires, pants and football teams," Arthur says.

Arthur has written nearly 4,000 jingles to date, some of them for big-name accounts that have placed his work in markets nationwide. He has done work for the Keebler Corp., which sponsors Nancy Reagan's drug awareness program (Arthur wrote these three songs plus the famous slogan, "Just Say No"). His accounts also include the National Association of Women in Broadcasting, Tampa Bay Buccaneers, Kansas City Chiefs, Colony Shops, Caesar's Palace, Jim Walter Corp., Eastern Air Lines, Sea World and Houston Power & Light.

"He's incredibly creative, and very flexible," says Howard Skelton, owner of Howard Skelton ad agencies in Sarasota and Atlanta.

Arthur puts in 12 to 14 hours a day in his studio, but it is not uncommon for him to get the inspiration for a jingle just minutes after meeting with a client. Recently, he met with Jim Kelly, the account executive for Media Edge in Clearwater, the agency that handles promotion for 55 Wendy's restaurants. Over Sunday brunch, Kelly told Arthur that Wendy's wanted to increase business during its slow period—after lunch and before dinner—and he wanted the jingle to be unusual but not overbearing.

Arthur immediately started dreaming up clever ways to describe the desirability of dining on a combination of burger, fries and cola for $1.89 at 4 p.m. Two hours later, he was "on stage" in his recording studio, twisting and wiggling and gyrating as he belted out his latest musical creation: Let's Do the Combo Mombo . . . , an original, catchy, calypso tune with light lyrics and a tag line that simply tells people what and when to eat at Wendy's.

"Jeff was so excited he couldn't wait until Monday," says Arthur's wife of eight years, Jan, 33. "He had to call the client that very second and sing it to him."

If Arthur is easily excited by his work, it is a trait that runs deep in his family. The son of an insurance executive and a "stage mother" who always lionized her children, he constantly applauds his brother Brad, an accomplished sculptor, and his sister, Dawn, a photographer.

"My mother knew I had to be the center of attention, so she pushed me to sing on stage," Arthur says with a laugh. He attributes much of his success in business to values he learned while growing up.

"I was raised in a middle-class family and became the prototype Jewish hippie who hated money but realized what it could buy," he says. "I had a lot of trouble dealing with the realities of life. But my parents were always there emotionally. And when I started singing jingles, they helped out financially. It wasn't a lot of money. They inspired my work by feeding me when I had no food and giving me their car for a year."

Arthur is highly protective of his jingle-writing work, treating it as something of a personal domain. It wasn't until 1985 that he hired his first assistant, Cary Reich, 28, a stockbroker-turned-singer/song-writer. "Cary is the only person allowed to write, but I still do most of it myself," says Arthur, who also sings in many of the jingles.

Jerry Cachia, director of special events for 60 DeBartolo Corp. shopping malls, remembers a recording session that illustrates Arthur's hands-on working style.

"Jeff invented the word 'hyper'," Cachia says good naturedly. "His group of singers was belting out the jingle for our frequent shopper program. But something was wrong. We all knew there was a note off, but we didn't know where. Jeff kept asking the singers to do it over. He was freaking out because we couldn't find who was making the mistake. So he made us all be quiet while he tested each singer individually. When he found the bad voice, he took him out alone, told him to go home, then stepped in to sing the part himself."

Arthur's office is outfitted with two snazzy, state-of-the-art recording studios with more knobs, gadgets and colored lights than the inside of a sophisticated spaceship. Two engineers work the big boards, and Reich helps Arthur.

A typical recording session is a step-by-step process that takes several days to two weeks. If a client wants the jingle overnight, Arthur will see that he gets it, frenetically calling in singers and rhythm players. Ideally, he has a 12-to-14-day lead and can record over and over until the jingle comes out just right. Reich and the engineers say they enjoy watching Arthur perform, his smiling face sandwiched between two huge earphones. "It's really fun working for Jeff," Reich says. "It's creative and crazy most of the time. He can be demanding, but he's nice to the people who work for him. He truly cares about us. It makes us want to work harder."

The first session is for laying down Arthur's composition with a group of guitarists, drummers, piano players and other rhythm musicians. In the next session—held another day—the lead vocalist records, followed by all background singers, then violinists and horn players. Engineers work on $200,000, 24 track recorder during the final session to mix it all together.

For local clients, a syndicated package—new lyrics put to music Arthur has written for another customer outside the market—costs around $3,000 for four 60-second and four 30-second commercials plus variations. A custom package—new lyrics and new music—is $5,400. Jingle packages for national distribution can run as high as $24,500.

Arthur boasts that because he uses top musicians and is always available to talk to the head of an account, his company closes 98% of its pitches. He also says his rates are lower than those of many of his competitors. "Jeff adjusts his price to make us happy," says Cachia. "He'll do for $5,000 what a larger concern, such as Media General, does for $8,000. Jeff can get away with it because he's independent. He has no bosses."

John Saint John, owner of a jingle company in Miami, says Arthur has done some good work but goes out of his way to offer lower prices than the competition. "He always tells the client he has the best price," says Saint John. "I don't work that way. In this business you offer price, quality and speed, and the client gets two of the three. I like most of Jeff's work, but it's not all top notch. I believe people get what they pay for."

Gary Marcus, a Miami advertising creative director, says Arthur is a talented songwriter, but sometimes he can be too eager to please. Once, when he worked at Tinsley Advertising in Miami, Marcus hired Arthur to create a jingle for Miami Lakes, a residential development. He wanted the music and lyrics to project a younger image for the development. "Jeff sat there madly taking notes," Marcus recalls. "He asked a lot of questions, and before we were through explaining what we wanted, he had written the jingle and started singing it. I was worried he did it too fast to be effective, so I asked him to wait a day and call me back. He took my advice and refined it. He sang it to me the next morning, and I loved it."

Arthur won't say how much he makes personally, and he doesn't take a regular salary, preferring to pump money back into the business. He advertises in trade magazines and by direct mail, and he travels every few months giving speeches to large business groups on the marketing of music. "I love public speaking because I'm back on stage performing," he says. "I sing and write and involve the audience. And I get paid for it."

Arthur considers himself a businessman, although he concedes to doing nothing by the books. He has no business manager save for Paula Bletch, who acts as an office administrator. Rather, he uses his gut instincts to make creative and business decisions. To date, the system has worked fairly well. He demands 50% of his fee upfront, the rest on client approval. For slow payers, he gets on the phone himself and begs.

His studio walls are covered with Clio, Angel, Monitor, Addy and Golden Pyramid Awards for his myriad of jingles. Adorning his office walls are a 17th century Gregorian chant and a dozen family pictures that include his 4-year-old daughter, Lindsey, and 6-month-old son, Jake.

Arthur recently returned from a week-long family vacation in Block Island, Rhode Island. He boasts that he closed seven new accounts by phone while he was away. But his wife insists, "Jeff spent all of his time with the children, going to the beach and riding bikes through the park. He's a wonderful father, but I wish we'd see him that often at home."

That's unlikely. Even though his five-bedroom house in Feather Sound is just two minutes from the studio, Arthur has big plans that undoubtedly will keep him at work much of the time he's not traveling. He recently made a "gentleman's agreement" with the Hercules Co., a government defense contractor with excellent video facilities, that moved next door to his studio. Because half of Arthur's clients want a combined audio/visual package, he plans to capture some of that business by utilizing the Hercules visual equipment. "We'll use their video expertise and teach them about audio and retailing," Arthur says.

He also wants to make musical scores for moves and live theater. And he wants to add more national accounts to his roster.

Lately, Arthur has been so busy that he hasn't had time to wonder what life would have been like as a rock singer. "If I hadn't performed all those years, I might be frustrated today," he says. "But I have a beautiful life with a wonderful family, and I wouldn't have it any other way. When I get some time, I'll write songs for my children."

Reprinted with the permission of the author and *Florida Trend*.

• • •

DATE: AUGUST 31, 1987, PP. 1A–2A.
SOURCE: USA TODAY
AUTHOR: MONICA COLLINS, USA TODAY STAFF

* * *

COMPLICATED COSBY; TIME FLIES WHILE COSBY, 50, HAS FUN

NEW YORK—You would buy a used car from this man. In a second.

Bill Cosby is the premier pitchman of our times. Whether hawking frozen pudding or a warm, gentle message about contemporary family life in a TV comedy, Cosby has sold us. And we're sold on him.

In a career of triumphs, September will be another watershed month for Cosby. Already the most-watched star on television, he's back with his No. 1 show—tuned in by 60 million viewers weekly—a new spin-off and a new book. "The Cosby Show" begins its fourth season on Sept. 24 (8 p.m. EDT/PDT). The spinoff, "A Different World," starring Lisa Bonet and closely supervised by Cosby, premieres on NBC that same night directly after "The Cosby Show."

And with his book *Fatherhood* barely off the best-seller list, his newest volume—*Time Flies*, (Doubleday, $15.95)—already is showing up in bookstores. In it, Cosby inimitably ponders growing older.

In July, he turned 50—an age when one reflects on spent youth and contemplates mortality. "Yeah, I'm scared of dying," Cosby says. "I had a physical exam. I was fine. But they told me that my cholesterol and triglyceride levels were up. I've rectified all of that. I weigh 188 pounds and I don't want to die. But it's funny to me what this kid in high school could do."

He points to a bank of pictures on his dressing room wall. One shows Cosby, the Philadelphia kid, jumping over a high bar. The mind is willing but the body can't get over that hurdle any more. "It's not sad, it's not sad. I'm laughing."

He is a complicated man, a contradictory bundle of raw sensitivity, opinion and egocentrism who freely admits, "I have never been a saint."

Yet, when he walks onto a stage or in front of a TV camera, he puts everything in perspective. With one look—an arch of his eyebrows or pursing of his lips—Cosby reduces us to giggles.

His humor, however, does not exploit the easy punchline. Indeed, the Cosby show is built around the leanest of notions of family life.

"There are people who misread this show and feel that nobody's family is that perfect," Cosby said during a rare interview. "We're not aiming for the perfect family. We're saying that there are certain situations that come about and this is the way it was handled. And we're saying, Does anything look like you?"

"Bill holds a mirror up to us about our daily lives," says Tom Werner, the show's executive producer. "And he is able to translate all of that in a brilliant, warm and funny way."

Indeed. Cosby led the "Q ratings," television's familiarity–popularity poll, in 1986.

You might think that Cosby—who pulls in an estimated $10 million a year while he sits on a vast investment empire, who has four houses and one of the largest private art collections in the country—might want to rest here and now.

No way. He is driven to keep up with himself. Last week, while "The Cosby Show" took a short break, Cosby was performing in Las Vegas. He has filmed new commercials for E.F. Hutton and continues to be the centerpiece in Jello and Kodak ads.

He's also found time for politics. Tonight, Cosby and Roberta Flack will headline a fund-raiser for presidential hopeful Jesse Jackson at Manhattan's Apollo Theater.

Yet Cosby doesn't forget his show. Last season was not the program's finest. Despite strong ratings, many critics—and Cosby—felt the story lines had become too simplistic.

During a recent meeting with writers in his dressing room, Cosby, immersed as ever in the production, insisted to the attentive group that the bit part of a garbage collector in one episode go to a woman.

During a rehearsal, Cosby—eternal fat cigar in his mouth—gave comic timing tips to cast member Malcolm Jamal-Warner, who plays son Theo on the show. He prodded Keshia Knight-Pulliam (daughter Rudy) into remembering her lines. Occasionally, Cosby interrupts the action, asking director Jay Sandrich to change this or that.

"There's nothing worse in comedy than looking at a comedian or a movie or a TV show where you see that these people are trying to be funny," said the comedy veteran. "It makes the viewer tired and it also depresses the viewer because there's nothing worse than looking at failure."

He knows a little about failure. He knows a lot about criticism. He seems, at times, obsessed by it. "Look, I can take negative criticism. I can even take a great lie or two.

"But you read someone whose whole idea is 'I didn't like this' or 'I've got to figure out how to chop the man down,' " Cosby says. "I can play the same way."

He says critics who panned last season's final episode—which touched on subjects of black pride and academic achievement—couldn't handle the serious topics, even though the show has been chided for not facing up to racial issues.

"All of the bull—that these people write." And when the show confronts those serious subjects, he says, "They couldn't take it."

He deplores those who identify themselves by race or color or "club," as he refers to it:

"The problem with stereotyping is that it becomes rote. And your thinking becomes whatever that stereotype is. Doctor So-and-So, brilliant surgeon, male, white. Dentist, male, white. Housekeeper for black family, black, not white. Why not? Problems. Have to do racial jokes. Don't want to. Can't treat people like human beings."

Cosby says the refusal to stereotype remains the guiding principle of "The Cosby Show"—to show a family that doesn't dwell on its own particular "club."

In his personal universe, no one speaks ill of Cosby. Everyone around him is awed by him. Yes, he can be temperamental and moody. Yes, he has quirks. For instance, he says his cigars are imported from Jamaica—although one close associate insists they're Cuban.

In his chauffeured BMW sedan, he sits next to the driver. He doesn't drink alcohol. He retains the same agent and staffers that he has had for years. Around his mother, Anna, Cosby becomes the doting and approval-seeking son.

And Cosby remains devoted to his wife, Camille, 43, after 23 years of marriage and five children. He burst into the middle of an interview to proclaim: "The most important thing to know is that I love and respect my wife with all my heart."

"I'm sure that if they wanted to get me—get me—they very well could on my past experience or whatever. But the love is not enough. Love for Camille is not enough because she has all of my love. It's respect. There is no clean infidelity.

But there can be forgiveness and then a deeper, stronger love, obviously because they love each other."

The Cosbys live separate professional lives. She is involved in her own interests—photography, producing a movie about the life of Winnie Mandela, the charismatic wife of the South African resistance leader, and she's on the boards of various organizations, including Jesse Jackson's Operation PUSH.

Cosby says his wife sees the humor in things before he does. "As far as I'm concerned, women have a better sense of humor. If I'm driving a car and my wife is in the car and a wall shows up two inches from the car, I start to curse. My wife drives, the same thing happens to her, she starts to laugh."

Copyright 1987, *USA TODAY*. Reprinted with permission.

•••

DATE: THURSDAY, FEBRUARY 12, 1987, PAGE 3F
SOURCE: THE MIAMI HERALD
AUTHOR: THE MIAMI HERALD STAFF

* * *

PROFILE: W. SCOTT PIPER III

SAILING BACKGROUND: Started sailing at age 10. . . . Won North American Junior Moth Championship at age 12. . . . Won more than 200 races with Pipe Dream; has since owned Pipe Dream II and III. . . . Has finished as high as 11th overall in SORC.

PERSONAL: Born April 5, 1939, at Syracuse, N.Y. . . . Family moved to Miami in 1946. . . . Lives in Coral Gables with his wife, Gillette, daughter Michele and sons W. Scott IV and Dauphinot (Dereck).

EDUCATION: Did undergraduate work at Dartmouth College, then spent four years at the University of Miami medical school. . . . Interned at Los Angeles County General Hospital, followed by a surgery residency at St. Luke's Hospital in New York.

PROFESSIONAL: Worked five years as an Army surgeon, first in Japan, then in the United States. . . . Spent his final year in the Army as assistant chief of orthopedic surgery at West Point. . . . Returned to Miami to begin practicing in 1972.

QUOTE: "I'm very dedicated to the winning attitude. I don't think you can have as much fun if you don't go to the starting line believing you're going to be successful."

Reprinted with the permission of *The Miami Herald*.

A Professional's Point of View

By John A. Limpert
The Washingtonian magazine

Profiles are a big part of magazines like *The Washingtonian*. Here are mistakes we see profile writers make:

Thinking it's an easy payday. When writers tell me they like to write profiles, it sets off warning bells. Often they mean an easy personality piece from a quickie interview. Best-selling book author Judith Viorst was one of our best profile writers.

She would first read about the subject, then call the subject and say: "I'd like to do a story on you. I've read a lot about you. Before we talk, can you give me the names of people who know you well, both friends and enemies?" Famed trial lawyer Edward Bennett Williams said he never asked a question in court he didn't know the answer to; writers should know most of the answers before they start asking the questions of the profile subject.

Loving the subject too much. In a variation of the Stockholm Syndrome, in which hostages begin to identify with their captors, some profile writers develop too much empathy with their subjects. When it comes time to write the profile, the writer worries more about the profile subject than the reader. The writer has to make a shift in mindset after the research: When you sit down to write, your loyalty is to the reader. You owe the reader a clear-eyed, professional look at the subject, and you can't worry about pleasing or displeasing the subject.

Hating the subject too much. Again, you owe the reader a clear-eyed look even if the subject has been difficult to deal with or runs into one of your biases.

Trying to be too clever. Some writers try to cover up weak research or a dull subject with very clever writing. It's harder to fool readers than many writers think. A good editor has a sensitive BS detector and won't let you get away with it. A corollary: Write about sophisticated ideas in simple language, not the other way around.

Giving up when the subject won't cooperate. Some of our best profiles were done on people who wouldn't talk to us. It takes a lot of smart reporting to do this kind of piece, and, again, don't let the subject's feelings toward you poison your attitude, but the lack of cooperation allows you more freedom to make judgments and draw conclusions. And we've often found that uncooperative subjects become cooperative when they realize we're going to do a good reporting piece on them whether they talk or not.

Not thinking enough about how you're going to get the reader into the subject. Leads— usually a good scene or anecdote—are important, but also think about what kind of headline, art, captions, and pull quotes the story needs. Editors appreciate suggestions (but not demands). If you were the reader, what in the story would interest you the most? Suggest that these points be highlighted. Many readers graze through publications, looking for a picture or caption or headline or pull quote that interests them. Then they may read your story.

Not protecting your reputation. Some writers try to build a fast name for themselves by doing what we call "hit" pieces. It's the journalistic equivalent of an assassination. I've seen it work for some writers for brief periods of time, but media subjects are getting more sophisticated. Before they talk to you, the subjects will do some checking: How fair are you? How accurate are you? Is your main goal to leave a lot of blood on the floor? Conversely, some tough profile subjects will talk to you if you send them copies of stories you've done along with a letter explaining what a fair, thorough, knowledgeable writer you are. (Limpert, personal communication, 1988)

* * *

John A. Limpert is editor of *The Washingtonian* magazine. Limpert has worked for United Press International and has served as editor of newspapers in Warren, Michigan, and San Jose, California, and Washington. He worked in the office of Vice President Hubert H. Humphrey and was a Congressional Fellow. He joined *The Washingtonian* staff at the end of the fellowship in 1969. He is a winner of the American Political Science Association award for distinguished reporting in public affairs. He is also a member of the executive committee of the American Society of Magazine Editors.

8

Seasonal Features

Seasonal articles celebrate the regularity of life—the cycles and rhythms of nature and human life that govern our lives. Traditional seasonal stories call your readers' attention to the beginnings and ends of important segments of our lives, to special dates, and to events that demand our recognition and memory.

Seasons transcend all human life. The seasons dictate the parameters of human life: Seasons affect calendars, plant life, animal life, the world climate, Earth's natural and seemingly unnatural events, migration, hibernation, and the earth itself. British author Anthony Smith (1970) says quite succinctly that "the complex rhythm of our planet Earth, rotating upon its axis in its orbit around the sun, encircled all the while by its neighbour the moon, provides the basis for the ceaseless rhythm of life itself" (p. 16). The growing concern with man and our life rhythms emphasizes the regularity of life. The cycles of life have evolved over thousands of generations to what we know today.

In this century, modern writers have provided seasonal articles for their readers to help them prepare for changing natural seasons, for the end-of-year religious holidays such as Christmas and Chanukah, for the beginning of vacation, for the start of a new school year, for graduation, for natural and regional birthdays and anniversaries, for special days for mothers and fathers, and even for the loves of our lives.

For a beginning feature writer, perhaps one of the more basic articles to master is the seasonal feature article. These articles are necessary throughout the year and appear in just about every newspaper and magazine, and there are ample opportunities to write them.

"Seasonal articles are not particularly hard to write—in fact, I think they are easier than general articles" (p. 44), says veteran seasonal article writer Clinton Parker (1975). "They do require a certain depth of research, however, and absolute historical accuracy. That's why it is best to specialize in a particular event or field. Once you have done the basic reading for the specialty, the articles are much easier to write" (p. 44).

You will find that much of your feature work will be controlled by the calendar. Newspapers and magazines will run features to highlight special events on the calendar each year. Readers expect it.

Seasonal features are not much different from the other types of features. In fact, you will probably mix some of the different elements of feature writing when writing a seasonal article. There may be humorous seasonal stories. Or highly personalized stories. Or stories with great human interest elements. The focus here is on the *context* of the article.

One significant distinction, however, is that seasonal features should reflect the tone and the theme of the season. This is largely dictated by local customs and traditions. A seasonal feature can be ruined without the right approach. It would be, obviously, in poor taste to write an irreverent feature about the military for Veteran's Day. Then again, a newspaper reporter or magazine writer who does not try to be especially creative and tricky on April Fool's Day is completely missing the point of that special day.

It is not unusual for newspapers to run several seasonal articles at the beginning of and during a major holiday season. Some newspapers produce entire special sections in recognition of local festivals or holiday periods. Similarly, it is not unusual to find a monthly specialized magazine devoting a cover and a majority of its top articles in the issue to a seasonal theme. *Bon Appetit,* a food and entertaining magazine, recently did this with its November 1987 issue—a special holiday issue featuring new recipes, party and gift ideas, holiday getaways, and, of course, its version of the ultimate Thanksgiving feast.

Author Daniel Williamson (1975) says a seasonal feature is "an account of an annual event or an aspect of that annual event which captures its spirit" (p. 170). Take a look at R. Bruce Dold's Christmas story from *The Chicago Tribune.* Dold's article focuses on how the holiday spirit has permeated the work of an elderly man in Chicago who specializes in making holiday wreaths. Dold's story describes in detail how much this labor is viewed as a joyous activity of the season by the wreathmaker and not just as another way for a florist to make money. With good quotes, Dold tells a compelling story that is bound to give readers a touch of the same holiday spirit that fills this Chicago wreathmaker at that time of year.

WHY WRITE SEASONAL ARTICLES?

There are numerous reasons for writing seasonal articles. First, there's professional opportunity. Although editors generally have enough copy for the routine issues of their newspapers and magazines, there always seems to be a shortage of *good* seasonal material. This is a good way to crack the free-lance market and to get an editor to notice your work above and beyond others'. Even experienced writers often overlook seasonal article opportunities. These articles, geared to a special time of the year, can also open the door to you for other, nonseasonal opportunities, writer Clinton Parker says.

The importance of seasonal features extends beyond the need to entertain readers by describing the occurrence of holidays, annual events, major anniversaries, or even the changing natural weather and growing seasons. Seasonal articles are used by newspaper and magazine readers well in advance of the seasons or holidays to help prepare for the celebrations, the weather, and the special activities associated with seasonal events. There is a certain functional value to seasonal stories that extends past their pure entertainment value. A well-written seasonal story will educate readers about a religious holiday or about a national hero. It will teach our children the value of remembering an important family day such as Mother's Day or a civic activity such as voting. These stories will help readers prepare for potential weather disasters such as winter blizzards, spring tornadoes, flooding, or tropical hurricanes. The articles can teach your readers how to make, prepare for, and understand the meaning of a special meal such as a Passover Seder.

SEASONAL ARTICLE IDEAS

To begin generating seasonal article ideas, take a look at a calendar. For starters, there is a list of major holidays and seasons later in this chapter. But you should go well beyond this list because these are only the major national dates you should know. There are, of course, various other national holidays (such as those in Mexico) that are celebrated in the United States. There are also unique regional holidays and state holidays. You can probably think of one or two in your own state that are not on the list in this chapter.

Many of the *local* holidays and seasons will not appear on nationally sold calendars and appointment books, so don't depend on these sources for complete lists. Instead, check with local libraries, school systems (for their own calendars), local newspaper files, and even local museums, ethnic groups, and civic–business groups. This will help you especially if you are a newcomer to an area, or, for example, if you want to write for a publication in another region of the country that you might not live in or be familiar with in terms of its customs and history.

But a serious feature writer—regardless of whether he or she is working for a newspaper, a magazine, or is free-lancing, will get organized about writing seasonal articles. There are many ways to keep up, but the most obvious method is to keep your own calendar for the current year, and also for the next 2 years. This helps you work ahead and in the present. You might be working 1 or 2 days or 1 or 2 weeks in advance on seasonal articles for a newspaper, or several months ahead for magazines, and you need to be tuned-in to needs far ahead, not today. You will see more about this in the next section.

Another good place to check for seasonal ideas is an almanac. Most general reference books such as *The World Almanac* are quite thorough in listing public and religious dates of significance throughout the year. These books are updated annually and will often run lists of special events dates for many years beyond the current year.

Other good sources are theme appointment books. These books come ready-made for persons who wish to specialize in certain subjects such as quilting or computers. And inside these books, in addition to the regular listings, will be special dates such as anniversaries unique to that theme or subject (e.g., when the first personal computer was placed on the market, or Apple Computers' founder Steven Jobs' birthday). You might have to look a little to find these appointment books, but you can usually find them in specialty shops or advertised in specialty publications such as organizational newsletters.

The key to getting the right idea for a seasonal article is *anticipating*, being able to successfully "guess" what is going to be on your readers' minds when the season nears. You must be thinking about what people will want to know about a holiday or special event *long before* that event is on the general public's minds. You are trying to anticipate interests: What activities will be interesting? What foods will be tasty? What ceremonies are essential? You must be able to think about seasons that have not yet arrived. And you must be able to find a fresh approach to a story that has been told dozens of times before.

Successful article ideas that work must be timely. You cannot write stories about Thanksgiving meals that require a week's preparation if the article is written or published 2 days before Thanksgiving. You cannot jump the gun too much either, since even good ideas are forgotten if they come along too far ahead of the big day.

A strong idea will draw readers into your story by making them think to themselves as they read your lead: "Yes! This would be fun to do. I want to find out more about this."

Good seasonal features also have strong *visual* potential. Try to select topics that will lend themselves to strong photographs or other forms of illustration to help tell the total story. Can you suggest using color? How about proposing a schematic diagram that shows how to make an object? Or how about a boxed set of instructions that include a recipe? For both newspapers and magazines, packaging is important with seasonal features, and if you want maximum attention given the article you write, plan to propose strong graphics in addition to your well-written and reported article.

Clinton Parker (1975) recommends specializing as a seasonal feature writer. His specialization as a pastor in Plymouth, Massachusetts? The Pilgrims and Thanksgiving, of course. "Much of the trick to selling seasonal material is to stick to a certain holiday or event, mining it for neglected angles" (p. 30), he says. Simply think about the regional activities that are occurring around you, and perhaps one or more of these will develop into a specialization that can be sold nationally. He suggests looking not only at the regional calendar, but thinking also about annual local festivals and fairs for your prospects.

WRITING IN ADVANCE OF THE SEASON

There is no doubt that much of the seasonal feature article writing done today is produced in advance. This is particularly true for monthly and less frequently published magazines, but it is also true for newspapers. The major difference is that the lead time varies.

For a newspaper, work on a seasonal piece for a Sunday supplement magazine would be not much different than the deadlines you will face for a weekly to monthly magazine. Newspaper feature editors like to work as much ahead as possible while keeping their articles timely. This assists in production of graphics such as large color illustrations, posed photographs, and so on. Even for the spot seasonal feature, done a day ahead, the advantage goes to the writer who finishes early in the day to permit time for revision and collection of new information as deadline nears.

For a magazine published monthly or less frequently, you have to be particularly conscious of lead time in preparing stories with content sensitive to seasonal changes. Magazine editors work four to six months ahead of the current calendar. So, if you are reading this in December or January, you should be thinking about summer vacation, Father's Day, Fourth of July, or graduation stories already. Admittedly, this is hard to do when there is snow outside and temperatures do not easily suggest going to the beach or picnics.

The reason for this? Preparation time. Lead time is that period of time between the decision of a writer to write the article or the decision by an editor to buy it, and the appearance of the article in the publication. Preparation time includes securing rights, assigning photographers and illustrations, editing, fact verification, typesetting, paste-up, proofreading, printing, and even distribution. With all that to be done, it is no wonder that you have to finish writing your Thanksgiving cooking article in May or June to get it into the hands of readers in early November, so they can begin thinking of your ideas for their own tables at the end of November.

Jacqueline Shannon, a seasonal feature writer and former magazine editor, says the mastery of timing is critical to your success. Four months, she says, is a dependable industry average for magazines that use color.

But she warns:

If you're submitting on spec[ulation], your lead time is obviously not the same as the publication's lead time. To give your article time to be considered, you must add "reporting time" to lead time. Therefore, if the reporting time for your targeted publication is one month, you must submit a seasonal story *five* months in advance. But don't stop counting yet. There's the possibility that your story will be rejected. So you must also figure in a couple of months to market it elsewhere. That brings us up to a free-lancer's lead time of six or seven months. In other words, start circulating "Christmas Ornaments from Pine Cones" in May or June. (Shannon, 1984, p. 34)

Shannon says the same rule applies for queries on seasonal articles. In fact, she observes, many publications will provide minimum lead time for you in listings of market information. And, she advises, there is such a thing as too much lead time. Up to 1 year, she recommends, is acceptable, but only for important events such as the Olympics, an election, or a major public anniversary. So, she says, for the usual material, do not submit over 7 months in advance.

This leaves a golden window of advance work from 4 to 7 months for magazines. You become a calendar juggler, but to be an effective seasonal writer, this is part of the job. Some writers, like Shannon, keep a seasonal picture wall calendar on their desks where they write turned 6 months ahead from the present date.

All this requires a seemingly simple decision: To plan ahead when writing a seasonal article. This means developing an "editorial body clock," as Shannon calls it.

It also requires writing alertness and discipline. All the while you are working in August preparing an article for February readers, you have to keep references to "this year" and "last year" straight in your mind—or readers will be confused.

Shannon also recommends that you save a good article idea when the timing is off. As long as the subject is *timeless*, she says, it can be held a few months in the interest of timeliness and then submitted to an editor.

Authors William L. Rivers and Alison R. Work (1986) suggest seasonal feature writers should try thinking like department store managers and advertise their Christmas specials in July. "Editors also need stories that are not time-bound, stories that could be published at any time of the year without losing their newsworthy qualities" (p. 97).

FINDING FRESH ANGLES FOR THE ANNUAL ARTICLE

One thing all newspaper and magazine features editors want to avoid is the same old seasonal story each year. So, it is necessary for writers to work with their editors to come up with a creative, fresh angle for an annual seasonal article. When it is a certainty that you will need to write that St. Valentine's Day romance article, and the idea of another local couple's 60th or 70th wedding anniversary story bores you (and probably your regular readers, too), it is time to work on a new approach. Ask yourself, "What's new this coming Valentine's Day?" Check with retailers such as card shops, candy stores, and florists. Check with small companies that offer special services such as breakfast in bed or singing telegrams to find out what unique ideas they will be offering for the coming special day. You will find that these businesses will at times come to you with their ideas in hope for some advance publicity to foster business. Thus, you will find a cooperative source anxious to help you with your article.

The strategy here is to not limit yourself to the traditional story. Why stop short on a seasonal feature when you can bring your readers a better story? Why do the same old story if something stimulating is just waiting to be written?

Clinton Parker says the formula is simple for the new angle: Fresh material plus solid background equals a successful story. Like any good story idea, as you remember from the chapter on developing story ideas, a good seasonal feature must be the product of thorough looking around, extensive talking to lots of people, and careful listening. It also takes thinking and an ability to put things together. This approach will result in some solid article idea leads that could develop into that story you wanted for this year.

And, of course, there are times when a very old idea will work for a seasonal article. There are times when an idea or theme has not been used for years, or at least, it has not been used as the basis of an article. Several years ago, reporters for the *Florida Times-Union* in Jacksonville were in the office at Christmastime, a traditionally slow news period, trying to come up with a good Christmas Day feature for their readers. Reporter Jerry Teer (1973) wondered if it might not be fun to see if the true Christmas spirit still existed in Jacksonville. "Do people really believe all this Christmas stuff?" he asked. "And if they do, how deeply do they believe it?" To find this out, he asked the managing editor: "What if I wrote a story about what happens when myself [*sic*] and a pregnant woman, apparently my wife, visit inns around the city on Christmas Eve in search of a room?" (p. 24).

With his editor's okay, he asked a young female friend to join him, and the two went from motel to motel looking for a place to stay for the night. They looked a bit ragged, wearing old clothes and carrying their belongings in a duffle bag. They told innkeepers they had no money, and, with the help of a pillow, Teer's friend was dressed to appear pregnant. This modern-day version of the Biblical story of Joseph and Mary on Christmas Eve was a widely read feature in the newspaper the next day. Although he hoped to find at least one Good

Samaritan, Teer and his friend found no free rooms among the 15 "inns" they visited. This angle, far more interesting than a story about left-over Christmas trees, demonstrates what is meant by a fresh angle on an annual season or holiday assignment.

To find out what is new for the summer vacation season or what is different for Easter this spring, you have to be willing to do some digging. It takes time to find the right travel agents, hotels, or tourist commissions to get that vacation story that comes out in late May or early June—the start of vacation time for many families—when it is still the middle of winter. It might seem early, but this is the time when the decisions are, or already have been, made. The same goes for the religious holidays such as Easter. You should not only contact stores for the commercial side of the story—new candies, stuffed toys, and the like—but also should contact churches of the many denominations in your community for the celebrations that are scheduled. Depending on your deadline, you must work ahead and often press individuals for information to make your story more timely when it appears in the newspaper or magazine.

MAJOR HOLIDAY AND SEASONAL ARTICLES CALENDAR

| January: | New Year's Day (1st) |
| | Martin Luther King's birthday (15th, officially, it varies) |

February:	National Freedom Day (1st)
	Groundhog Day (2nd)
	Constitution Day (Mexico, 5th)
	Abraham Lincoln's birthday (12th)
	St. Valentine's Day (14th)
	Susan B. Anthony's birthday, also Women's Liberation Day (15th)
	George Washington's birthday (3rd Monday)
	Ash Wednesday (varies)
	Mardi Gras (varies)

March:	Baseball training season opens (varies)
	St. Patrick's Day (17th)
	First day of Spring (21st)
	Mardi Gras (varies)
	Palm Sunday (varies)
	Good Friday (varies)
	Easter Sunday (varies)

April:	April Fool's Day (1st)
	Palm Sunday (varies)
	Good Friday (varies)
	First day of Passover (varies)
	Pan American Day (14th)
	National Secretary Week (3rd week)
	Easter Sunday (varies)

Easter Monday (Canada, varies)
Arbor Day, Bird Day (last Friday)
Daylight Savings Time begins (varies)

May: May Day, also Labor Day (Mexico, 1st)
                Loyalty Day (1st)
                Mother's Day (2nd Sunday)
                Victoria Day (Canada, varies)
                End of school year
                College, high school graduation (varies)
                Armed Forces Day (3rd Saturday)
                National Maritime Day (22nd)
                Memorial Day (last Monday)
                Traditional Memorial Day (30th)

June: End of school year (varies)
                Summer vacation season begins
                College, high school graduation (varies)
                National Smile Week (varies)
                Flag Day (14th)
                Father's Day (3rd Sunday)
                First day of Summer (21st)

July: Canada Day (1st)
                Independence Day (4th)

August: Civic holiday (Canada, varies)
                Ecology Day (varies)
                National Aviation Day (19th)

September: Labor Day (U.S., Canada, 1st Monday)
                Summer vacation season ends
                Start of school year (varies)
                Football season opens (varies)
                Grandparents Day (11th)
                Independence days (Mexico, 15th-16th)
                Citizenship Day (17th)
                Rosh Hashana (varies)
                Yom Kippur (varies)
                First day of Autumn (22nd or 23rd)
                American Indian Day (4th Friday)

October: Yom Kippur (varies)
                Child Health Day (1st Monday)
                Columbus Day, Discoverer's Day, Pioneer's Day
                    (2nd Monday)
                Columbus Day (Mexico, 12th)
                World Poetry Day (15th)
                Thanksgiving Day (Canada, varies)
                United Nations Day (24th)

Daylight Savings Time ends (varies)
Halloween (31st)

November: Election Day (1st Tuesday after 1st Monday)
             Veterans' Day (11th)
             Remembrance Day (Canada, 11th)
             Sadie Hawkins Day (1st Saturday after 11th)
             Elizabeth Cady Stanton's birthday (women's rights, 12th)
             Thanksgiving Day (4th Thursday)

December: First Day of Chanukah (varies)
             Basketball season begins (varies)
             Bill of Rights Day (15th)
             Forefather's Day (21st)
             First Day of Winter (21st)
             Christmas (25th)
             Boxing Day (Canada, 26th)

USING LOCAL ANGLES FOR YOUR SEASONAL ARTICLE

The best-read seasonal material is localized. It is interesting to know what people are doing for a holiday a thousand miles away, but readers really care most about what's interesting in their own neighborhoods and communities.

The neighborhood parade for Flag Day might be just the story your newspaper needs. Or a city or regional magazine might want to begin the summer vacation season with an article on nearby vacation destinations. You cannot ignore the activities in your own areas for the highest percentage of sales to newspapers and, if the market permits, magazines.

Local angles are defined in different ways, you should note. A magazine looks at localization differently than does a newspaper. Most national magazine editors would consider too much localization a potentially serious flaw in an article. Then again, a local or regional magazine might just be looking for that localized article on coping with winter storms.

Newspapers are much the opposite. Most newspapers are edited for their specific community—a market usually defined by the name of the newspaper. Some major metropolitan newspapers serve multicounty and even statewide markets. A few others, of course, are nationally circulated. In short, know the market and write for it in an appropriate fashion for seasonal articles just as you would for any other feature article you write.

The essential nature of timely information makes the seasonal news feature by reporters Steve Goldberg and Hank Ezell work well for readers of the *Atlanta Constitution*. The beginning of the school year is usually the cause for several articles by a major newspaper, and the example from Atlanta focuses on colleges and universities around Georgia. "Localized" at the state level, the article opens with a look at how all the chaos that comes with the beginning of school affected one student facing the dreaded drop–add line at the University of Georgia. Through her experience, readers learn about the trials and tribulations of starting a new college year. At the same time this is accomplished, readers are also told the facts about the start of college—enrollment statistics, new faces, new facilities, and, of course, the long lines and traffic jams. The Goldberg-Ezell (1987) article was timely because it was done within a day. The story would not have had the impact if it were used a week later without updated information and a change of perspective from experiences of students to a fresher angle.

SEASONAL COLOR ARTICLES

Although you may have already given thought to writing color feature articles, it is important to point out that many successful seasonal articles mix in the elements of strong color and descriptive writing. Writers will use seasonal article assignments as a chance to exercise their imagination along with their descriptive writing skills.

However, use this approach with caution and skill. Authors William Rivers and Alison Work say "the worst flaw in seasonal stories is that the writer tries too hard to be overpoweringly descriptive. Instead, the writer should be content with touches of description: a few visual verbs, an unpredictable adjective or two, an adverb that is allowed to do its work because it's in a crisp sentence rather than in a sentence burdened with other adverbs" (Rivers & Work, 1986, p. 239).

Like other color articles, many times a good seasonal story with a strong dose of color will use anecdotes to open the article. This form of "storytelling" draws the reader into the article easily, Rivers and Work say.

Miami Herald reporter David Marcus' (1986) article on the end of the tourist season in South Florida illustrates this. His article opens with several examples of the point he is trying to make—May still means the traditional business closing time for some people in the region, while others go on oblivious to changing seasons.

He highlights his general point with specific people and places—ranging from "U-pick-em" berry farms to restaurants to a local Air Force base. The story is easy for readers to identify with because Marcus uses meaningful direct quotes from a wide variety of people who are involved in the change of seasons as well as those who do not let it affect their activities. Finally, an interesting three-paragraph sidebar to focus on summer's rainy season in South Florida goes with his main story.

You see many of the same elements in reporter Olga Figueroa's (1987) Valentine's Day article. She chose to tell a Valentine's Day story with a twist, and this unusual approach made the article interesting to her editors who published it in *The Miami News*. It is not enough to write about marriage and romance on this day, so Figueroa found a couple married 42 years that was getting married for the fifth time in 5 years. The story has an appropriate local angle, lots of emotional quotes, and plenty of background on the couple and on North Miami Beach's rather unusual Valentine's Day "Love-In." However, she does not limit the story to one couple. As you read on, you are introduced to the stories of other couples who will also renew their vows. And she wraps it up neatly by telling readers how they can go to the "Love-In" too.

BEST SOURCES FOR SEASONAL ARTICLES

* Published specialized or theme wall calendars.
* Topical or theme appointment books.
* General almanacs such as the *World Almanac*.
* State travel department calendars.
* City, regional chambers of commerce.
* Holiday festival committees, organizations.
* Historians and history museum curators/directors.
* Encyclopedias and annotated bibliographies.
* Newspaper or magazine files from a year before the annual event.
* Retail store sales managers and clerks.
* Product manufacturers' regional sales representatives.

HOW PROFESSIONALS WROTE IT

DATE: DECEMBER 23, 1983
SOURCE: THE CHICAGO TRIBUNE
AUTHOR: R. BRUCE DOLD

* * *

WREATHMAKER'S 15,000 'CHORES' INSTEAD ARE JOY

HIS PALMS ARE sticky and black with pitch from evergreen branches, and four chafed fingers are bandaged with silver duct tape to protect them from the green wire.

Yet, come Christmastime, the chore of binding branches around steel into wreaths is all Carl Holderrieth wants to do.

Holderrieth, 72, has been making Christmas wreaths since 1929 at C.W. Beu Floral Co., 4445 N. Pulaski Rd. He has made more than 15,000 wreaths in that time, including the wreaths that hung in City Hall in the early 1930s.

He has made wreaths as tall as 7 feet, but has cut back some in recent years. He works part time and the weight of the 4- and 5-foot-tall wreaths has prompted him to make them only for a few longtime customers.

HE HAS THOUGHT about retiring, but doesn't want to walk away from a labor of love. "I'd be lost without this," said the slight, white-haired man as he leaned over his work table, not pausing from the toil of wrapping and binding the evergreen branches to a circular wire rim.

The time of buying fresh Christmas wreaths is largely past in Chicago. Most are made on human assembly lines in northern Wisconsin and Michigan, and some smaller ones are even bound together by machines, said Harrison "Red" Kennicott, president of Kennicott Brothers Co., one of the largest wholesale florists in Chicago. Just a handful of florists still make their own wreaths, he said.

Holderrieth crafted his first wreaths in 1926, in his second year as florist apprentice in a shop three blocks from home near Heilbronn, Germany. When his three-year apprenticeship ended, he came to Chicago where his brother, Bill had moved a few years earlier.

When he went looking for a job as a florist, he didn't expect to find one that would last for more than 50 years.

"IT WAS SHORTLY before Easter, and my brother and I came into this place. They said they needed help, so they hired me. There was nothing permanent about how long I would be here," he said.

His old customers, and new ones surprised to find wreaths being made as they are sold, watch an artisan with a deceptively simple craft at work in an eight-sided wooden shed with a bell-shaped roof.

Unlike the delicacy of flower arranging, wreathmaking is heavy work. Holderrieth arranges about four branches at a time on the wire rim, wrapping green wire around the branches and rim and yanking it tight before placing the next branches in the circle. He can make a 3-foot-tall wreath in 12 minutes.

"We have customers who come year after year, and they know they're going to get a good wreath," he said. "That's what brings you joy. I know it's bragging, but I'm pretty sure people are happy with it."

Reprinted with the permission of *The Chicago Tribune*.

• • •

DATE: TUESDAY, SEPTEMBER 22, 1987
SOURCE: ATLANTA CONSTITUTION, PP. 17A–19A.
AUTHORS: STEVE GOLDBERG AND HANK EZELL, ATLANTA CONSTITUTION STAFF
        WRITERS

* * *

ENROLLMENTS LIKELY TO BREAK RECORDS AS FROSH SWELL CAMPUSES

ATHENS, Ga.—A weary Sue Volkert leaned back against the wall, closed her eyes and let her body slide to the linoleum floor.

The University of Georgia senior had waited in line for 2 1/2 hours Monday for a chance to add a badminton class to her fall quarter schedule, and by noon she'd been batted about enough.

"It was like a herd of cattle," she said. "There's a lot of unnecessary waiting . . . . The whole situation is a real hassle."

Welcome back to college.

Miss Volkert, 21, of Atlanta, was one of 3,600 students at the University of Georgia who spent part of their first day at school making last-minute adjustments to their class schedules.

That number isn't unusually large considering the size of the student body at the school this fall, said Bruce Shutt, the university's registrar. As of Monday morning, 24,487 students were enrolled in class, an increase of 667 students over the same time last year, Shutt said.

"That's somewhat surprising," he said. "We thought we might stay even or be up 150 students." Shutt said the rise was most likely a result of increases in graduate enrollment and the number of students returning to the university after summer vacation.

"The classes that entered in 1985 and 1986 were large freshman classes. They may be catching up with us, with more students staying in school," Shutt said.

Last year's freshman class of 3,536 was the largest ever, and one admissions official said this year's class could top that mark. John Albright, associate director of admissions, said a record 10,660 students applied to the University of Georgia and 7,558 of those were accepted.

Final enrollment figures won't be available until later this week, but generally about half of the students accepted show up for class, Albright said. "We don't require a deposit, so we won't know who's coming until they pay for fall quarter classes," he said.

Albright also said he expects this year's crop of freshmen to be a bit smarter than last fall's. The average score on the Scholastic Aptitude Test for University of Georgia freshmen in 1986 was 1,016 out of a possible 1,600. "This year we expect it to be at least 1,020, maybe even better," Albright said. Also, the average grade point average for freshmen is up from 3.19 last year to 3.22. Those numbers don't include students in the university's remedial programs.

Monday was also the first full day of classes since Charles Knapp took over as president of the University July 1. Knapp spent part of the morning talking with students, something he plans to do fairly often, said Knapp's spokesman, Steve Frankel.

"He plans to spend a good bit of time with the students, faculty and staff. It makes it a more tangible experience. He plans to be a visible president," Frankel said. Fred Davison, who resigned as president last year after Jan Kemp's successful suit against the university, was criticized for not being more visible to students and faculty.

Meanwhile, at Georgia State University—with the state's second largest college enrollment—the usual confusion marked the first day of classes. Since all of GSU's students are commuters, the traffic backed up into streets around the downtown Atlanta campus.

GSU officials expect another record-setting enrollment this fall. As of Monday, 21,681 students had signed up, only 198 fewer than last fall's final enrollment. Hundreds more are expected to show up before the final tally.

"This sure is a confusing place," said 18-year-old freshman Chris Galloway of Norcross. "I kind of felt my way around today, and I was late for my first class."

Ed Lemmers, another 18-year-old freshman, said he had no problems, but that all of his classes are in the same building. "I only know this side of campus," he said.

Some faculty members had to find new routes around the campus, too, as the closing of the school's Business Administration Building forced schedule changes and pushed some classes into previously underused art and music classrooms, among others.

GSU's Business Administration Building will be shut down for about two years for asbestos removal and classroom renovations. It contained 25 out of about 175 classrooms and lecture halls on the campus, a spokeswoman said.

At Kennesaw College in Marietta, officials predicted they would sign up 7,700 students, 100 more than anticipated. For the second year in a row, officials turned a grassy field into a temporary parking lot. "We don't have any dormitories, so everybody commutes," said business office director Bill Durrett.

Across the state, a total of 10 public colleges started classes Monday. All 34 will open by Wednesday.

Reprinted with the permission of *The Atlanta Journal-Constitution*.

• • •

DATE: MONDAY, MAY 19, 1986
SOURCE: THE MIAMI HERALD, P. 1B
AUTHOR: DAVID MARCUS, HERALD STAFF WRITER

* * *

'CLOSED' SIGNS MARK A CHANGE OF SEASON

Some people insist South Florida has no seasons, but those cynics probably have not spent time with National Weather Service forecasters watching summer cumulonimbus clouds marching over the Everglades. Those cynics have not banged on the locked doors at Joe's Stone Crab Restaurant or watched Gail Beane pick up her last three heaping quarts of berries at Burr's Strawberry Farm in South Dade.

"May means finishing up, taking care of your equipment, dismantling the fields, cleaning them up, fixing everything for the summer," Charlie Burr said Sunday in between bidding his favorite berry-buying customers goodbye.

The signs of the change of season are all around, from the hand-lettered "Closed until Dec. 26" notices that went up at Burr's roadside stand, to the increasingly frequent lightning in the sky. The Miami-Dade Main Library was open Sunday, the last Sunday until October. Joe's Stone Crab closed last week—and good thing, too, because the five-month ban on harvesting the critters started Thursday.

When the season changes in Florida, the pace continues unabated in one place and takes a U-turn next door. Homestead Air Force Base isn't affected by the onslaught of summer, said Capt. Rick Nelson, but the adjoining campground looks completely different. "It's empty. During the winter, all the retired folks come with their campers."

"We see very dramatic changes in the season," said Tom Fennell Jr., owner of Orchid Jungle. "Right now, everything is in bloom. It's unreal." The chocolate-brown epidendrum are out, as are the yellow and red oncidiums. Even the oak trees dropped their last batch of leaves in April and just put on their springtime finery.

Still unconvinced about the change of season? Look up. "Climatologically, the rainy season in Miami starts about the third week in May," said weather forecaster Andy Stern. From May until November, an average of seven to nine inches of rain falls each month, compared with only two or three inches in the winter.

That means slow times are ahead for retailers waiting for buyers—maybe. "Rain keeps them away," said Milton Kay, owner of Dorwin's Men's & Boy's Shop in Miami Beach.

"Rain, for us, brings out more customers. I guess it keeps people away from the beach or their boats. Thursday, during the heavy rains, we had a great day. Wednesday was sunny and it was bad," said Ed Seigel, manager of Gregg Richard's Tall & Big at the T.J. Maxx Plaza.

In the library, the last Sunday for the summer lured steady crowds of bookworms of all ages. At the information desk, Grace Rayfuse fielded questions about books on capital punishment ("most of them seem to be out; it's a popular topic for school papers") and computer competition with Japan.

At Burr's farm, the last cantaloupes, tomatoes, onions, bell peppers, cucumbers and eggplants were harvested during the past 10 days. The bushes are still laden with fat red strawberries, which will be frozen or sold to wholesalers.

Gail Beane, a strawberry lover who stops at Burr's for fill-ups several times a week, gathered her packages. She will freeze some for ice cream and turn others to preserves so she can get through the next seven months.

Under the summer-like midday sun, Charlie Burr had a chance to sum up his 26th season of strawberry farming. Hard rains in March decimated about a quarter of his crop. Low prices early in the year were discouraging, but they rose by spring. When all the bills are paid, 1986 could emerge as a berry good year.

To his wife, Mary, Sunday was a sad day. Not for Charlie. "People slow down on strawberries this time of year. They get tired of them," he said. "It's nice not to have them for a while."

SIDEBAR WITH THE MAIN STORY

* * *

THE SUMMER RAINS WILL FALL UNTIL THE FALL

If you think South Florida is thunder-struck during the summer, you're right. Twelve to 15 days during the average summer month, the National Weather Service records thunderstorms over Miami International Airport. Three times more rain falls each month in the summer than in winter months. June is the wettest, with an average of 9.15 inches dumped.

Where there's a rain there's a reason. From May until November the prevailing winds shift, so that they plow in from the southeast, bringing warm, wet air over the hot land. It condenses, creating rainstorms.

With a 40 percent chance of coastal showers this morning and thunderstorms inland this afternoon, those patterns are coming into place, with National Weather Service forecaster Frank Revitte.

•••

DATE: SATURDAY, FEBRUARY 14, 1987
SOURCE: THE MIAMI NEWS, P. 1C
AUTHOR: OLGA FIGUEROA, MIAMI NEWS CORRESPONDENT

* * *

SOME MARRY, OTHERS RENEW VOWS AT NORTH MIAMI BEACH 'LOVE-IN'

I do. I do. I do. I do. Many of them uttered those words many years ago, and today they will be uttered again.

Forty-two years ago, Betty and George Gordon promised to love, honor and respect each other. Tonight, they will repeat the vows for the fifth time, at the fifth annual North Miami Beach "Love-In."

"The highlight of reaffirming your wedding vows is the beautiful feeling you get," said Betty, a bubbly, outgoing woman whose fingernails were painted bright red, with white heart decals, to match her shirt. "Priorities sometimes go astray; we don't let that happen."

"Every year we've done it, he always goes along with it," she said, smiling and looking at her husband, who sat quietly on a park bench letting his wife do most of the talking. "There's no way he'll leave me, not after (getting married) six times."

The couple first met in Atlantic City in 1941.

"I had just graduated from high school and had convinced my parents to let me go to Atlantic City with a group of friends. George was working his way through college in the hotel where we stayed," Betty recalls. "I thought he was so handsome. I went to the lobby in my nightgown and robe to get his attention."

She got his attention. They corresponded for 18 months, until he went off to war. She thought she would never hear from him again. But their paths crossed again.

"In 1943, I went to Atlantic City again, this time with my parents. I heard a page for Mr. and Mrs. Gordon, (who) turned out to be George's parents. I was going up the stairs, when this man came up to me and introduced himself to me. It was George!"

The couple married a year later. This year they will celebrate their 43rd anniversary.

Jack and Gertrude Lipman said their nuptial vows in 1921. They will reaffirm their vows for the third time tonight, just two months from their 66th anniversary.

"The first time we heard about the Love-In we were on the way to the movies. We took a walk here (Victory Park) and saw all the decorations. They asked us how long we had been married and if we would like to get married again," Gertrude Lipman recalls. "It was only $5, that was cheaper than the movie."

Jack sits next to her, listening to her. He can't hear very well and she repeats things to him, so he will not feel left out. They met when they were in their late teens. He asked her to marry him the very same day. In 1949, the couple and their three children, moved from their native England to the United States.

"Our daughter was a GI bride, we decided to move here after she married," said the petite redhead woman, with a distinct British accent.

The Lipmans' family has grown through the years. Their three children had seven of their own. Those grandchildren have had a total of eight great-grandchildren.

Tonight one of their three daughters and her husband will be present when they say "I do" again. "It's nice to do it again, but we still remember the very first time," she said.

For many couples, the Love-In marriage will be their first.

Colette Cavanaugh and Attila Madar are both 22. They fell in love while she, a native of Scotland, was vacationing in Miami. They were planning on getting married on Valentine's Day, by a justice of the peace, until she heard about the Love-In ceremony.

"When I saw the ad in the newspaper for the Love-In, it was like an answer to my prayers," Cavanaugh said. "I wanted a church wedding, like my sisters had, but my family is all in Scotland and couldn't be here. I didn't want a church wedding with only 12 people."

The couple has not made any honeymoon plans. They are waiting for the prize drawings at the ceremony.

Helen Whitaker and Gary Packett met six years ago through their children. Both divorcees went on "friendly" dates, before things got serious.

"Our dates always included the girls. A usual date was a trip to Metrozoo," she said laughing.

They started dating two years later. Last Christmas, after dating four years, he asked her daughter if he could marry her mother.

"I was sitting next to her at the time, I couldn't believe it. My first reaction was to go up to him and feel his forehead. I thought he had a fever," Whitaker said.

The couple thought it would be fun to get married at the Love-In ceremony.

"We were both married before. Both of us had a small house wedding, we thought this would be different," Whitaker said. Tonight they and about 40 other couples will be married or have their vows reaffirmed during the ceremonies at Victory Park Auditorium, 17011 N.E. 19th Ave., North Miami Beach. Mayor Marjorie McDonald will officiate. The ceremony will have a "Roaring '20s" theme. Couples and their guests will enjoy a celebration with dancing, refreshments and wedding present give-aways.

Reprinted with the permission of *The Miami News.*

A Professional's Point of View

By Doug Jimerson
Better Homes and Gardens

Obviously timing is essential when you're free-lancing seasonal material. Every publication whether it be a newspaper or magazine has its own lead time that you must take into consideration if you want to successfully market your story ideas. At *Better Homes and Gardens,* for example, we plan our editorial calendar one year in advance of publication. This doesn't mean that we wouldn't accept a better story idea closer to deadline, but it does indicate how vital it is to be aware of your target magazine's schedule and plan accordingly.

More important, you should know the editorial content or philosophy of any publication you solicit for free-lance work. Nothing is more frustrating to an editor than to receive unsolicited manuscripts about topics that aren't even remotely related to his or her publication. For example, our magazine never publishes poetry, songs, book reviews, celebrity interviews, or first person humor stories like "How I Raised Bumper Crops of Broccoli In My Bathtub." Yet, every week we're inundated with submissions like this from misguided writers across the country, usually with a tag line on the bottom of the page asking us to send payment as soon as possible!

I realize that this all might sound pretty basic, but I can't emphasize enough the importance of research. Always take time to read and critique a few issues from the magazine or newspaper before you charge ahead with your own story ideas. It's also smart to check an up-to-date masthead and read the by-lines of all stories. You need to know the names (correct spellings please) of the appropriate editors you'll contact later. And remember, don't take notes from mastheads that are over one year old. Editors retire, die, get promoted, and move on to other publications. One of my pet peeves is that I'll often receive unsolicited manuscripts that are addressed to the garden editor who was with the magazine in the 1950s. That shows me that the writer hasn't done his or her homework about the direction or scope of our magazine in the 1980s.

In conclusion, I'd also like to suggest that you think about specializing in one or more subject areas. There's nothing wrong with being a good generalist, but if you strive to become an expert in a particular field such as: money management, electronics, parenting, architecture, food, environment, sports, or even horticulture, you'll have a leg up on the competition when a publication is looking for someone to write that "special" feature. It's also a smart marketing strategy. If you can sell yourself as a proficient writer with a strong background in a particular subject area you'll stand out from the rest of the thundering herd. (Jimerson, personal communication, 1988)

* * *

Doug Jimerson is Garden Outdoor Living editor for *Better Homes and Gardens* magazine.

9

Reviews and Criticism

Many aspiring nonfiction writers associate writing reviews and artistic criticism as a glamor career filled with opportunities to mix with the famous artists of our time. The work is attractive to beginners because reviewers and critics are often working at the cutting edge of creative work such as filmmaking, book writing, television program creation, music and dance performance, and theater.

Perhaps the lives of those who do reviewing and critical writing are filled with glitter, bright lights, and black ties for the successful *few* who are nationally known full-time reviewers or critics of the arts. But for most people who do reviewing or criticism, it is a part-time specialization and seldom offers the lifestyles of the rich and famous.

Reviewing and critical writing are still two of the most popular forms of feature writing among young writers. With the strong appeal of the performing arts to young adults in particular, it only makes sense that many beginning writers would want to develop talents as reviewers and, ultimately, as critics.

Today, however, it remains difficult for a nonfiction writer to build a career in reviewing and critical writing. Most newspapers and magazines, when they use a regular schedule of reviews and critical analyses of the arts, use feature syndication services and part-time writers for their articles. Only the largest of metropolitan area daily newspapers, newspaper wire services, and features syndicates retain full-time reviewers and critics in the arts. It is not uncommon to find as many as a half dozen to a dozen critics on a large daily newspaper's arts section staff. But small and medium daily newspapers cannot often afford full-time critics or reviewers on staff. They turn to full-time staff members who specialize in other types of reporting and writing or editing to review as additional work. Many use regular part-time writers to extend their staff coverage. Or, of course, these newspapers also turn to free-lance writers.

Magazines that publish reviews and criticism of the arts will most often use regular part-time or free-lance sources. And, like newspapers of all sizes, some magazines will depend on news services and features syndicates for their reviews and criticism. Few magazines have full-time critics on staff.

Reviewing and critical writing are quite different from other forms of professional feature writing. Generally, professional feature writers will not often cross the line from fair and objective writing into subjective writing and personal opinion, but reviewers and critics must take this bold step for their work to contain value to readers.

That's why reviewers and critics are so widely read and valuable to consumers. A good reviewer or critic will be a major asset for a publication by covering the arts as important news-based feature material. Why? There are numerous roles the reviewer and critic play in serving their readers and the region's arts community.

Rutgers University communication professor Todd Hunt (1972) points to eight major functions of reviewers in covering the arts:

1. *First, and foremost, the reviewer informs readers about the arts.* Readers learn about the existence of new works from their favorite publications.

2. *Reviewing and criticism help to raise the cultural level of the community, the region, and the nation.* By setting standards for performance, the cultural community is, in the long run, improved.

3. *Reviewers and critics impart personality to the community.* By writing lively copy, expressing well-supported opinions, and by being a little bit different, the reviewer and critic provide a unique personal dimension to their feature writing.

4. *Reviewers and critics advise readers how to best use their resources.* Reviewers and critics help readers decide what films to see, books to read, restaurants to visit, and which theaters to attend. With limited entertainment budgets, many readers depend on their local reviewers and critics to guide them in making these decisions.

5. *Reviewers and critics help artists and performers to fine-tune their works.* As an educated consumer, a qualified reviewer or critic can make suggestions that will help artists and performers to improve their efforts in later performances.

6. *Reviewers and critics identify the new.* Whenever new works are offered to the public, and at times, before these new works are presented for the first time, reviewers and critics are able to identify, interpret, and explain trends and new developments in the arts to their readers.

7. *Reviewers and critics record history*. One of the best sources of performing arts history is the review. As many nonfiction news writers do, reviewers and critics write arts history on a daily basis.

8. *Reviews and critical writing are also entertaining*. As reviewers and critics impart personality, they also entertain with timely and interesting writing.

Many consumers think of critics as snobs who influence the public, writer William Ruehlmann (1979) says. But, he adds, this is far from reality. The reviewer and critic, Ruehlmann maintains, *do not* influence readers.

Still, the reviewer and critic have an important role in the relationship of the arts and their communities. Reviewers and critics are, in many ways, in the middle with the arts on one hand and the public on the other hand.

So, who cares about the opinions expressed? Reviewers and critics have several constituencies. Consumers are in the front row. Artists and performers are also part of the group that seriously considers the work of the reviewer and critic.

And what does it take to get a job as a reviewer? Much depends on the publication. Some small newspapers and magazines without big budgets cannot afford to pay well and will offer opportunities to beginners for little or no financial rewards. Editors of these publications allow their reviewers to "learn" on the job. But most publications are more discriminating and require greater preparation of reviewers and critics. You will get a more complete discussion of the educational preparations necessary to be a reviewer or critic in the next section, but the more educated and experienced you are as a reviewer, the better chance you have finding a job.

Motivation is also a key to being a reviewer or critic. Professor Todd Hunt maintains that you must have a profound concern for perpetuation and improvement of the art form. He also says you need the roots of a newsman, that is, a sense for news on which you build your interests in the arts.

REVIEWS AND CRITICAL WRITING: THE DIFFERENCES

There is a significant distinction between a review and critical writing. Reviews are generally written by less authoritative writers and often take the perspective of the consumer of a particular work. These articles tend to summarize the work and its major features. The major distinction between reviewing and criticism is *opinion*. When a writer begins to include personal opinion and assessments of artistic performance, the line into criticism is crossed. Critical writing requires specialization and education. One of the most important differences between reviewers and critics is educational background. Most successful critics are college- or graduate-level-educated in the art form they criticize. Today, to be a critic, you must have specialized education, and perhaps even amateur or professional experience as an artist yourself. After all, what better way to criticize performers than to have been one yourself? Certainly, individuals educated in drama or film are going to be better informed critics about the correct or preferred techniques in theater or movie production than someone who is not. An English major will likely be a better book critic than someone who has not majored in English. A person who majored in food and nutrition would be better qualified to be a restaurant critic than someone who simply likes food and wants to dine out on an expense account.

The point here is rather simple: To be a critic, you must know what standards to apply in assessing professional and amateur performance. You must know what is truly excellent work and what is not. In fact, Professor Lee Dudek (1970) once suggested that because there were so many unqualified reviewers and critics in the mass media it might be best for newspapers and magazines to "seek out practitioners who can be trained as writers" (p. 31). Although this extreme might not be as necessary as it was nearly 20 years ago when Dudek made that statement, it is fair emphasis on the need for critics and possibly even reviewers to have the understanding and background to write what Dudek called clever statements and true ones, instead of one or the other.

Today it is becoming easier for beginning writers to specialize in the arts when in school. In addition to reviewing and criticism, these writers also will be covering the arts as news. Furthermore, because most newspapers and magazines cannot hire individuals solely for coverage of the arts, general feature writing or news writing and reporting skills are necessary. Universities and colleges with programs in mass communication and the arts are the best locations for academic preparation for careers as reviewers and critics. Schools that offer journalism majors in newspapers and magazines and also provide students with a chance to double-major in an art such as music, drama, or creative writing permit maximum development of those talents necessary to be a professional reviewer and critic of the next decades.

ESSAY REVIEWS

Most reviews and critical writing find their way into an essay structure. This is a simple approach that permits the maximum development of your writing. A good lead opens the essay with a statement of what you want to do. The body of the essay is a synthesis of generalizations about the work that are supported by evidence and illustration taken from the work. The conclusion summarizes and wraps up your points. And all this is done in just a few hundred to a few thousand words.

Writer William Ruehlmann recommends 10 points about the basics of what he calls judgmental features. To reach success as a critic, he says you:

1. *Make yourself an expert.* The more you know about writing books such as novels, the more authoritative you will be and the better you can handle your assignment.

2. *Don't flaunt your expertise.* Do not write over the heads of your readers. Teach, but do not assume too much about what readers know.

3. *Do not talk down.* Assume your reader is intelligent and can understand what you write.

4. *Avoid overdependence on plot summary.* Do not tell your reader everything that happened. Tell the reader how and why something happened, but not what.

5. *Explain the work in context of our lives.* In other words, he asks, is the work good entertainment? Does it help us understand ourselves or the world around us better? If so, it is art.

6. *Find a strong lead and ending.* Be specific and arresting in your lead. End with a snap.

7. *Cite specific examples to support your views.* If you say something good or bad about the work, show readers. This gives insight by providing your own reasoning behind the assessment.

8. *Write well and write cleverly.* Apply the same standards for good style and structure that you expect in the work you are reviewing to your own writing.

9. *Take your stand with conviction.* Do not be timid. Write with confidence and assurance.

10. *Have a little clarity.* Remember this in particular when you are writing about amateur artists instead of professionals. But even in dealing with seasoned professionals, take into consideration all factors when you decide you love or hate something.

Ruehlmann also says that the structure of a review is as varied as any other type of feature article. He says you must remain flexible to permit the review to take the form necessary to make your points understandable. He also emphasizes the need for readable reviews. This is done, he adds, by use of specific examples to support opinion and to enliven the critical writing.

There are two schools of thought about perspective in personal opinion-based writing. One side argues for first person writing. The other advocates third person. There is more to it than personal pronouns, however. Consider what you are saying to the reader by writing in first person. You are saying, "I am important enough to be a major part of this review." It is, of course, convention in professional journalism to write most nonfiction in third person. But the rules change in the case of personal opinion, especially reviewing and criticism, and use of first person is more acceptable. Still, many reviewers and critics today prefer to write in third person. It is really a matter of each publication's own style of writing or, perhaps, that of the individual writer.

In review writing, the philosophical approaches of reviewers and critics fall into two schools: authoritative and impressionistic. Todd Hunt defines the impressionistic approach as one that "generates an expression of the critic's . . . reaction to the work, exclusive of standards or precedents" (Hunt, 1972, p. 26). Authoritarian writing perspective tends to be third person and is highly comparative, Hunt says. "The particular work is evaluated in reference to historic models which have been previously judged worthy. The authoritarian critic must have considerable background preparation and exposure to the art form, and he necessarily accepts a set of fixed standards of rules" (p. 26).

Most of today's reviewers and critics are somewhere in the middle of the two approaches, Hunt says. Most attempt to take the best of both schools rather than fit into one or the other. "Most feel free to switch into the more comfortable personal essay style, often leading to an 'I-like-it-because' conclusion" (p. 29), Hunt says.

As in all other forms of features you may write, selection of your lead is a big decision. How do you begin? This part of your review will set the tone of the entire review and should be carefully considered before you begin. Perhaps you can open with something startlingly new about the artist. Or you have decided the work is bad and you want to warn readers at the beginning, so you choose an inverted pyramid approach by getting the "news" at the top.

Whatever you choose to say in the lead, your first several paragraphs need to establish the *context* of the review. What is being reviewed? Who is involved? When and where? And, as you move into the body of your essay, you begin to tell your readers how and why. Some beginning reviewers are so anxious to get into the opinion they forget to present the basic facts near the beginning of their essay.

You should also avoid cliches associated with reviewing and criticism or a particular art form. These worn-out statements or phrases only drag down the quality of your own writing and bore the reader. Find new and interesting ways to make your points.

Pressing deadlines may change the approach you take when writing reviews. It is one thing to dwell on a work for several days before committing your ideas to paper. But for a debuting new play, film, television program, or touring musician, you might get just one shot and only a few hours to complete your work.

For newspaper and weekly magazine reviewers and critics, a tight schedule is generally the case on all new work. For monthly magazine writers, deadlines present a different set of problems—remaining timely when you must produce your work weeks, or even months, before a movie or play debuts. The problem is so severe for some magazines that they simply do not review certain types of material unless they can get a considerable lead time through previews and advance copies. For some magazines, for example, book publishers may provide galley proofs for reading before the book has been bound and distributed.

A thorough review will offer readers comparison and contrast. Readers want to know how a new book compares to the earlier works of a favorite author or how a new album will stand against the earlier efforts of a group. What is similar and what is different? Why? Is it relevant?

Similarly, many essay reviews will compare and contrast the works of different artists on the same subject or same level in a single review. It is not unusual, for example, to find a set of summer movie reviews packaged together or one review that discusses all the new summer releases at the same time. The technique is also popular with book reviewers who might look at new books on one subject—such as the 1988 presidential election campaign—in a single review.

It is also important today to provide readers with a summary, highlight, or information box with your review. These charts of information are often "boxed" typographically by editors to run with the review. However, it is your responsibility, as the reviewer and critic, to provide these boxes. As you read about the major forms of reviews and criticism in the following sections, you will learn what specifically is needed for each art form. These inserts in your reviews focus on the basics, however, and it is essential that you present the facts in a style consistent with the style your publication uses.

WHO HAS THE RIGHT TO SAY WHAT?

Do readers really care about what you say in your reviews? Some do and some don't. Some will buy what a writer recommends because the writer recommended it. Some will ignore the comments or laugh at your carefully weighed assessments. And, it seems, some just do not get involved one way or the other.

As a reviewer or as a qualified critic, writers have been given the right to comment on the arts of their town by the editors or publishers of their publication. It is a significant role in the arts community that must be kept in perspective at all times. It is a form of public trust not unlike that of the city hall or statehouse reporters who cover—and judge—government for the public.

And to what limits are writers producing reviews and criticism? Do you as a reviewer or critic limit your work to art only? Or does it include the larger arena of entertainment? Certainly the umbrella that covers reviewing and criticism today has enlarged itself. As you will see from the subjects covered in the last half of this chapter, reviewing and criticism have extended beyond pure art to entertainment. Professor W. J. Howell (1973) argues that art is distinct from entertainment, at best overlapping with entertainment since they are not necessarily mutually exclusive concepts.

Another important consideration is the legal limitations of criticism under the First Amendment and various state constitutions. How far can a reviewer or critic go in expressing opinion before it becomes unacceptable? In terms of law, a reviewer and critic must be concerned with libel because of the potential for defamation of character of an artist. And because libel law varies from state to state, the limits of criticism will also vary according to state libel law. What a critic says might not be considered damaging by a jury in a major city as easily as it would be in a small town in the more conservative regions of the country.

Reviewers and critics are permitted to express their opinions, even defamatory, on topics that are interesting to the public. This is the privilege of fair comment, a defense that has existed since the beginning of this century. Mass media law professor Don Pember (1987) explains why: "The law allows the press valuable protection when it concerns itself with matters of importance to readers and viewers. By its very nature, an opinion is not subject to proof or test by evidence. An opinion is a subjective statement that reflects the speaker's tastes, values, or sensitivities. There is no way to prove its truth or falsity" (p. 189).

Mass media law professors Harold Nelson and Dwight Teeter (1986) add that common law and state statutes extend to "even scathing criticism of the public work of persons and institutions who offer their work for public judgment: public officials and figures; those whose performance affects public taste in such realms as music, art, literature, theater, and sports; and institutions whose activities affect the public interest . . ." (p. 186).

However, Pember says the fair comment defense against libel in a review must be based on certain requirements:

1. The comment must focus on a subject of public interest.
2. It should reflect on the public activity, not the private life, of the artist.
3. The comment should have a factual basis.

Still, Pember cautions, the difference between fact and opinion is not that clear. The courts, he says, still wrestle with the distinction. This makes life difficult for aggressive critics and reviewers and the best advice here is that you should be able to back up what you say in the public interest with evidence, and you should be concerned with context of the statement and the words themselves. This way, Pember says, the public has the ability to develop its own opinion about the performer or the work itself.

FILM AND MOVIES

The names of the best known film reviewers and critics are household words among moviegoers—Pauline Kael, David Denby, Rex Reed, Gene Siskel, Roger Ebert, Judith Crist, Andrew Sarris. You can, no doubt, add names of local and regional movie critics. The art of writing film reviews and criticism is the most visible of any type of reviewing.

Film reviews are usually written when a motion picture makes its commercial debut. When they do write an evaluation, reviewers and critics employ a number of strategies to evaluate a new film. The most common concerns are:

1. Quality of story line (plot), social relevance of the story line, or the original source material.
2. Performance of actors and actresses.
3. Performance of director.
4. Technical consistency and quality of work of technical support staff (such as special effects, cinematography, or film editing).
5. Use of conventions such as symbols or color.
6. Audience reaction and the film itself as a social event.

It is also common for film reviewers to provide background on key individuals in the film. Film scholars who focus on the director as the author of the film subscribe to the auteur theory. As Professor Todd Hunt (1972) says, a majority of film audience members are just not that interested in the film's author as a focus of a review. Most, he says, look at the importance or relevance of the film today.

Preview screenings are an important means of getting to see a film before the public does. This is essential to the success of the reviewer and critic. To gain access to previews, reviewers and critics work with studio publicists and promotion specialists as well as their own local theater managers. These individuals will contact reviewers who are associated with publications, but beginning free-lancers must find these individuals until they are known to the industry. Often, preview showings will be after hours when theaters are available (some after midnight). Showings are usually early in the same week a film is scheduled to open (such as a Tuesday for a typical Friday opening). At other times, reviewers and critics will travel to Los Angeles or New York to see special screenings set up by the studio.

Finally, the information box commonly used by newspapers and magazines for a film review usually contains some or all of the following information:

1. Name of film, local theaters screening it, their addresses, opening date.
2. Director and producer, production company.
3. Actors.
4. Writers.
5. Running time.
6. Motion Picture Association of America audience rating.
7. Quality rating by reviewer/critic.

TELEVISION, RADIO, CABLE

One of the newest types of reviewing and criticism to evolve is broadcast and cable reviewing. Newspapers, and to a limited extent magazines, are now covering and reviewing the broadcast and cable industries at levels they never have before. Beginning in the late 1950s and early 1960s, coverage was sporadic. But through the 1970s, this new type of reviewer and critic emerged. Today, these individuals focus on reviewing new, regular programs, major sportscasts, special programs, and other unusual activities of interest to local audiences.

Milwaukee Sentinel TV–radio reviewer Ron Legro (1981) says reviewers have the responsibility to reinforce experiences in common with viewers and listeners, to alert viewers and listeners to worthwhile events, to reward excellence, and to inform locally on developments with area stations.

Just as film reviewers depend on advance showings for much of their work, so do broadcast reviewers. These showings are usually available in the local stations of the community where the reviewers work. Local affiliates permit reviewers to watch previews that networks provide several days in advance of the scheduled broadcast. Occasionally reviewers will be able to watch tapes on videocassette recorders. And, of course, special opportunities are provided to preview shows in New York and Los Angeles, where many television, radio, and cable networks are headquartered.

Daily newspapers are the dominant outlets for broadcast and cable reviewing because of the timing of publication deadlines. For the same reason, most magazines do not get involved in broadcast and cable reviewing. Certain weekly magazines, such as the news magazines or *TV Guide,* are able to prepare in advance because of lead time given them by sources seeking maximum promotional value for a special program or series. Similarly, these weekly magazines will review or cover the broadcast of programs after the fact if a program has strong impact or ratings show an unusually large audience.

A review can actually serve a dual purpose because it may also serve as an advance story, alerting reviewers of the coming program. Thus, with a dual purpose, writers have to be careful not to reveal too much that would spoil viewing.

The information box (if brief enough, information sometimes runs in a trailer—a paragraph at the end) for a television, radio, or cable program advance and/or review usually contains some or all of the following information:

1. Name of program, network (if appropriate), local station(s) broadcasting it, air time(s) and date(s).
2. Major actors.
3. Content category (drama, comedy, and so on).
4. Capsule summary of content.

LIVE MUSIC AND CONCERTS

For many young arts writers, there is no more exciting assignment than to cover a live concert by a well-known band or solo artist. In fact, many reviewers and critics start out reviewing concerts or recorded music.

Newspapers and magazines, again, approach live music and concert reviews differently, mainly because of timing and deadlines.

For newspapers, there are two types of situations that concern reviewers and create different writing strategies. First, there are musicians who are on tour and may make only one appearance on one date in an area. Second, there are extended concert appearances and dates by musicians in a community.

You cannot handle each situation the same way.

For the one-night performance, a review might not be as helpful to readers from a consumer point of view. After all, they cannot use your review to decide whether to go, after the fact. A way around this is to review an earlier performance by the same musicians in a nearby community if possible.

Nevertheless, reviews of one-night concerts are still part of the coverage of the arts of a community. Certainly, persons who attended want to know how others assessed the show. And, it is important to note, those who did not go are interested in what happened from a critical perspective.

For concerts that are scheduled for more than one day in a community, you have more latitude in what you can do. A regular review will serve readers in major ways, such as helping them decide whether to attend. Naturally, it is best to publish the review as quickly as possible after the first performance. Daily newspapers usually publish the next day, or at worst, for a very late evening show, on the second day.

Most daily newspaper concert reviews stick to the basics because of their deadline constraints. But these reviews, like other print media, focus on staging, sound quality, length of performance, audience size, reaction, and involvement, names of song performed, special performers present, unusual deviations of the performed music (live versions dramatically different from recorded versions on well-known songs), and the effort of the warm-up act.

Magazines, because of their less frequent publication schedules, must take a different look at reviewing live music. Some magazines simply do not attempt it because of their infrequent publication schedule and the months of lead time they require for production. Others, such as weekly magazines, do so in a manner somewhat different from newspapers. Most magazines that attempt to write about live music do so by writing a roundup style review that incorporates several stops on the tour, nonperformance highlights, and other aspects of the events that surround a tour by a musician or group. These articles are part review and part color (or atmosphere) feature.

Your best source for information about a tour is an artist's public relations representative or the tour's road manager. Often, the management of the concert site can also provide helpful information. Press kits and other background information are provided most often by these sources if you make yourself or your publication known to them.

The information box for a concert advance or opening night review in either a newspaper or a magazine for a series of performances (not a one-time show) usually contains some or all of the following information:

1. Name of main group of artist.
2. Name of warm-up group or artist.
3. Date(s) and location.
4. Ticket price scales, locations of ticket sales points.
5. Reviewer/critic rating of the performance.

Generally, information boxes do not run with concert reviews that are written on performances that are one-time shows in a particular area.

RECORDED MUSIC

Just about all adults and most children listen to recorded music in one form (record, tape, or compact disc) or style (classical, rock, country, easy listening, and so on). Because music is so popular with the public, demand for qualified reviewers and critics is high. And because the demand for information about records has been growing since the middle 1960s (evidenced most prominently by *Rolling Stone* magazine's 20th birthday in 1987), more popular mass media than ever before devote considerable attention and space to recorded music, a turf once served only by specialized publications.

Today reviews are more popular than ever before. Because record reviews appear regularly in many newspapers and general interest and news magazines, they are written a little differently than when they were found only in specialized newspapers and magazines. There was a time when only the most devoted music listener could interpret the special language of these reviews. But because of the mass interest in records (let's use this term for convenience), reviewers have to write to be understood by more people. The review, taking on this added educational function, has helped bring up the public's level of knowledge of records and musical styles.

Preview copies help record, tape, and compact disc reviewers do their jobs in a timely fashion. Just as film and broadcast/cable reviewers preview their subjects, so do record reviewers. The record companies will mail preview copies to reviewers once you get on their promotion department mailing lists. This is done by contacting the record companies.

There are numerous approaches to writing a record review. Some writers prefer to read liner notes as they listen to the album. Some listen to the album first without taking any notes, just to get a "feel" for the album. Then they will listen a second time for technical purposes and for details to cite in their review. And some reviewers like to turn their stereo system high for full effect while others prefer a headset.

Regardless of your approach, your basic purpose is to provide a description of the content of the album. After that, you should evaluate it and provide as much background on the album content and the artist as space permits. At best, you want to be clear and practical for your readers. At worst, you will write for other record reviewers in a language only the members of the club will understand. Of course, you will want to avoid that.

Classical music and opera provide exceptional opportunities for recorded music reviewing. Much of what has been said in this section relates to popular contemporary music. Todd Hunt properly suggests that education is a most important function of reviews of classical music and opera. "Because many readers are unfamiliar with all but the best-known works of the major composers, the critic must turn teacher when evaluating performances of music by lesser-known persons" (p. 136), he says.

Hunt (1972) also emphasizes the need to analyze the technique of the artist when considering classical music and opera. This is, of course, applicable to performance of established works. A particular challenge, he says, is new works. Changes in styles, techniques, and even instrumentation are worthy of your attention.

Finally, the information box for a record review usually contains some or all of the following information:

1. Name of album and artist or group.
2. Record, tape, or disc label and catalog number.
3. List price of record, tape, disc.
4. Release date (if appropriate).
5. Reviewer/critic rating of the recording.

BOOKS

If you enjoy reading, writing book reviews should be an easy extension of that pleasure.

To get the review process underway, your first step is to get to know the book well. Look through it and then read it. Read the title page, note the publisher, read the acknowledgments, introduction, and foreword. In these sections you find out what the author says he or she is trying to do with this book. Skim the table of contents to get an idea of the scope of the book. Then turn to page one and *read the book* from front to back. It may be surprising, but there are reviewers who do not read an entire book, or even parts of it, and try to write a review or even interview the author. A review can be written without reading the book, but the quality of the review suffers, and thus, so does the service provided to the author, publisher, and the book-buying public.

Some research about the author(s) is also important to understanding the book you are reviewing. At times, the publisher will provide some of this information for you on the flyleaf or on an author page at the end of the book. Some publishers, when sending out review copies to publications in advance of an announced publication release date, will provide a press release–biography of the author. There will also be summaries of the plot on the flyleaf that can be helpful to you in deciding if you want to review it at all.

When reading a review, readers want to know about the author. A good review will integrate information about the author and the author's previous works.

It also makes sense to read as much of the previous work of an author as you can before you take on the current effort. This gives your review perspective and gives you the chance to compare and contrast within the author's own writing. Certainly, it also helps your readers if you compare and contrast the book to others like it that have previously been published.

Like record reviews, a thorough book review will summarize content in addition to educating readers about the author.

There are numerous outlets for book reviews—the leading ones are Sunday newspaper book sections and magazine book departments. Specialized publications such as business magazines often devote considerable space to reviews of books relating to the industry, so don't ignore this potential market.

Most of the time, book reviews are written by individuals who have a specialization in the subject that the book is about, not people who specialize in writing book reviews. Editors look for staff and free-lance specialists in specific subjects because of the levels of expertise necessary to evaluate a new work.

An information box accompanying a book review usually contains some or all of the following information:

1. Author and title of book.
2. Publisher and location, edition number (if applicable).
3. Book availability in hard or soft cover, prices.
4. Publisher's official release date (if appropriate, this is the date it is usually available in bookstores).
5. Length of book in pages.
6. Special features distinguishing the book from others.

DRAMA AND DANCE

Along with film, books, and television, drama is one of the traditional major subjects of reviewing and criticism in the United States. Interest in dance, such as ballet, is growing and becoming an important specialization in the arts for those writing features for the mass media.

Although the "national theater" remains centered in New York, most people who write about drama and theater *are not* in New York. These are the people in other metropolitan areas and in the hinterlands writing about regional and local theater productions at the professional and amateur levels. Theater has spread across the country like wildfire in the past thirty years, resulting in a rather sophisticated system of regional and community theaters and dramatic companies that are no longer solely focused in Manhattan. Today there are audience-supported theaters that offer drama and dance in just about every metropolitan area.

As a drama critic, you have the duty to look at all the dramatic performances in your area, good or bad. Todd Hunt says:

> The critic, who must attend *all* the plays, sees a theater that includes occasional ineptness and a great number of not-too-near misses. He knows that it is easiest to write a rave notice. . . . But more often he will have to struggle to explain a play's apparent purpose, where it failed its goal, and what rewards remain to be found. . . . What makes it worthwhile, of course, is the occasional evening in the theater when the mind is engaged, the imagination is stretched, the intellect is rewarded. (Hunt, 1972, p. 83)

Like reviewing and criticizing other art forms, you must prepare before you write a drama or dance review. Some reviewers read plays before seeing them performed—easy to do on established works but not so easy with debut material. Others do not read plays, regardless of whether they are available. What you can do, if possible, is read other material by the same playwright.

It is also important to learn as much as you can about the cast prior to the performance. Learn their names and roles, just as a sports writer learns the numbers of key players in a game before it begins. But also note the producer, director, and the other behind-the-scenes personnel who contribute to making the production work. You can get some of this background from the playbill or program, but you can also obtain it from the promotion department of the theater a few days before the performance.

Like book reviewing, drama and dance reviewing require that you are careful not to reveal too much of the story line when reviewing a dramatic performance. Telling too much spoils the experience for others.

The critical elements in a drama review must address the play's plot and its relevance, the performance of major actors singly and as a group, the direction they received, staging and sets, costuming, sound, lighting, audience reaction, and overall assessment of the night's entertainment. Any unusual developments, such as technical problems, should also be addressed if they affected the experience. And, of course, reviewers often compare and contrast a current production with earlier versions of the same work by different companies or, in some cases, the same company.

The information box for a theater advance or opening night review for a series of performances (not a one-time show) usually contains some or all of the following information:

1. Name of play, author.
2. Major actors and the touring company (if any).
3. Date(s) and location.
4. Ticket price scale, locations of ticket sales points.
5. Reviewer/critic rating of the overall performance.

Generally, these information boxes do not run with theater reviews that are written on performances that are one-time shows in a particular area.

Dance, although not nearly as popular in most areas as dramatic theater, still provides creative opportunities for reviewers and critics. Modern dance companies, many with uncertain support levels, certainly deserve the critical attention of the local media. More traditional dance groups such as ballet companies are perhaps more stable and generally receive critical review when new performances are staged.

Like classical music reviews, dance reviews must educate the public. Few readers of dance reviews thoroughly understand what they have seen enough to not want assistance in interpreting what the performance achieved or did not achieve.

What do you concern yourself with in a dance review? The focus must be on two levels: the effort of the dance group as a whole or an entity and the effort of the troupe's star dancers or directors. Since many dance groups are dominated by a single performer or director, this is an important point of view.

Todd Hunt suggests re-reviewing dance companies to measure the amount of growth and change in the company over a season. Because performances are not always the same, this is a helpful strategy if time and space permit it.

An information box for a dance performance advance or opening night review for a series of dance troupe performances usually contains some or all of the following information:

1. Name of dance troupe and the title of performance.
2. Names of the company director, lead performer, and other artists, such as musicians, if appropriate.
3. Date(s) and location.
4. Ticket price scales, locations of ticket sales points.
5. Reviewer/critic rating of the performance.

Generally, information boxes do not run with dance reviews that are written about performances that are one-time shows in a particular area.

FOOD AND RESTAURANTS

Life as a restaurant reviewer or critic is a life of diversity, and, of course, calories. Amid the menus and wine lists are certain ways of handling the job, certain liabilities, and certain deadlines.

Most food and restaurant critics are occasionally told how fortunate they are to have their jobs. *Milwaukee Magazine* reviewer William Romantini (1987) says, "Everyone tells me how lucky I am to have the job. . . . But, though eating for free can at times be a lot of fun, it involves some major liabilities" (p. 49). First, he jokes, his friends won't have him over for dinner. But more realistically, he says he must endure several bad meals for every good one.

Most restaurant critics must dine anonymously. If they are known, it is possible for a restaurant to give unusual and extraordinary attention in preparing the reviewer's meal. Some restaurants, sensitive to reviewers' power in affecting public opinion, keep pictures of reviewers on the walls of the kitchen for waiters to study. Most restaurants prefer reservations, and reviewers should make one. You might prefer to use a dining partner's name, however, to retain your anonymity. And, of course, the experience of making reservations becomes part of your assessment of the service you receive at the restaurant.

Many restaurant critics take a consumer approach to their work. They review the food not as food authorities, but as consumers. What did you get for your money? Was it worth it? Why?

Romantini says there are at least five other areas of concern of the restaurant reviewer. Those are:

1. The entrance to the restaurant and the first impressions you get as you enter.
2. The attention you receive as you are seated and the appearance of your table (settings, its preparedness, and so on).
3. The overall service and attention provided to you and your party while dining.
4. Not the least important, the taste of food served, its temperature, and timing of service.
5. Price of food, by item and not the total, and an assessment of the total value of the purchase.

In evaluating the food, be concerned with the main dishes, but do not forget the significance of soups, salads, other appetizers, breads, and desserts.

Writing the review should be easy if care is taken during the dining experience. Try to obtain a menu. Some restaurants will permit it if you ask. Others will sell you a menu. If you cannot take a menu with you, ask for an itemized check. And, of course, take some notes at the dinner table. This might give you away, but it does not have to. Many business people write notes during a meal. Do try to disguise what you are doing to keep the service and attention quality level unbiased.

Many reviewers relate their dining experience in chronological order. Romantini (1987) says writing should always be done with concern for the effect of what you say. "Keep in mind the effect your opinion will have. Can you look yourself in the eye and honestly write what you feel no matter what the consequences? Remember, it's easy to say nice things about someone, but an abundance of tact is needed if you've got to criticize" (p. 52).

The information box for a restaurant review usually contains some or all of the following information:

1. Name of restaurant, address.
2. Hours of operation.
3. Type and range of food served.
4. Reviewer/critic rating of the meal (often categorized by quality of food, price/value, service, and decor).

OTHER COMMON SUBJECTS OF REVIEWS AND CRITICISM

There is a wide variety of other reviewing and critical writing specializations that have evolved in recent years or have existed for longer periods in specialty publications. Among them are:

1. Live entertainment (ice revues, comedy shows, circuses, and so on)
2. Architecture
3. Painting
4. Sculpture
5. Photography

Live entertainment reviewing and criticism have many of the same concerns as dramatic reviews and concert reviews. As Todd Hunt says, it is hard to say anything negative about such all-American institutions as ice revues and circuses. These articles tend to be more review and less criticism. But as he observes, there is a limit to how much you can hold back. Judgment based on local standards may be your best guide here.

Architecture reviewing has become increasingly important since a Pulitzer Prize for criticism was awarded *New York Times* critic Ada Louise Huxtable. Today architecture critics such as Paul Gapp of *The Chicago Tribune* are well known in their cities and in the industry. The role of major structures in creating the personality, or face, of a community has been illustrated by the construction boom in the Sun Belt in the past two decades, and it continues. The new cities of this century have been characterized by their architecture, and the role of the critic is becoming more significant. Today, a handful of newspapers and magazines use architecture critics as their cities continue to change.

Other arts such as painting, sculpture, and photography are most often presented in galleries and museums in special exhibitions and in standing or permanent exhibitions. These exhibitions often say much about the cultural state of the community that displays them, placing a degree of importance on criticism of these exhibitions. Most written evaluations of these exhibitions are descriptive, as they should be, for persons who might want to see the exhibits.

Often, Hunt notes, painting, sculpture, and photography exhibits are housed in a facility together and a single reviewer or critic will be called upon to discuss each in a single review or perhaps in separate reviews at different times. In these reviews, attention is seldom given to a single item unless it is so dominant that it commands the attention. Showings are also often presented by artist or by group of similar style artists.

BEST SOURCES FOR BACKGROUND INFORMATION FOR REVIEWING

Films and Movies

Local theater managers
Regional or local film company publicists
National film company publicists
Distribution company publicists
Actors and actresses
Specialized industry-trade publications such as *American Cinematographer*
Producers and directors
Film credits

Television and Radio

Television and radio network publicists
Local affiliate publicists and promotion departments
Radio station publicists
Syndicated program distributor publicists
Specialized industry publications such as *Broadcasting* or *Electronic Media*
Program credits

Live Music and Concerts

Recording companies of touring musicians
Road managers
Tour publicists
Musicians
Specialized industry publications such as *Billboard, Rolling Stone,* or *Variety*
Concert site facility management

Recorded Music

Recording companies promotion departments
Regional or local record company publicists
Musicians
Specialized industry publications such as *Billboard, Record World,* or *Radio &*
    Records
Jacket information of albums/tapes/compact discs

Theater and Dance

Theater playbill night of performance
Theater managers
Actors and actresses, dancers
Specialized industry publications such as *Variety* or *Back Stage*
Directors and choreographers

Books

Book jacket or flyleaf
Introduction, foreword, and acknowledgments of book itself
Publishers promotion departments
Regional or local publishers publicists and sales representatives
Specialized industry publications such as *Book Week*
Authors

Food and Restaurants

Menus
Restaurant managers, chefs
Public relations representatives of company
Local health inspector
Specialized industry publications such as *Restaurants and Institutions*
Local and state restaurant associations

Architecture

Gallery, museum, or show curator
Architect
Contractors, builders
Specialized industry publications such as *Architecture, Progressive Architecture,* or
    Architectural Record
Financing sources
Local building inspector
Local and state architects groups

Painting and Sculpture

Artist or sculptor
Specialized industry publications such as *Art in America, Arts, Art Forum,* or *Art*
    News
Published major exhibition catalogs/books
Gallery, museum, or show curator

Photography

Photographer
Published major exhibition catalogs/books
Specialized industry publications such as *Photo Methods*, *Modern Photography*,
  Popular Photography, or *Aperture*
Gallery, museum, or show curator

Popular Live Entertainment

Specialized industry publications such as *Variety* or *Back Stage*
Theater program on the night of the performance
Theater managers
Performers
Performers' public relations representatives

ETHICS OF REVIEWING: WHO PAYS?

In 1987, *New York Times* food critic Bryan Miller spent $80,000 on restaurant meals and other expenses. That's $219 a day! Although Miller's expenses are rather extreme, more organizations are paying for what used to be provided by restaurants, theaters, or record companies. Who should pay for the entertainment you review? Should you pay for the free tickets? Records? Books? Food?

Most newspapers and magazines have two sets of rules for this important feature writing issue. For full-time staff members, most major newspapers and magazines will reject free entertainment items unless the free ticket or book is used by a legitimate reviewer or critic in the completion of an assignment. Other free books, records, and similar items are usually donated to local charities. For part-time or free-lance staff, these rules may or may not apply. At some publications, part-timers or free-lancers are left to their own decisions about who pays.

Why? Usually there are expectations associated with the gift of free tickets, records, and books. The expectation can range from simple recognition of the new work in print (news space publicity for no or little cost) to positive reviews. There has been a changing mood and set of expectations from such sources in recent years, however, as ethical standards have tightened. They expect less.

Clearly there are certain advantages to the special considerations such as good seat locations, receiving books or records in advance of release dates, and so on. It helps you do your job.

But there is a chance of abuse of these special considerations if you are not careful. The price is high, too, in terms of your credibility as a reviewer. Once you are "bought" you can never achieve the same levels of integrity in the business. It is a tough concession to make.

Finally, there is the problem of dealing with sources. At times, reviewers and critics have the opportunity to become too close to their sources. The result?

The temptation to write unwarranted favorable, or too favorable, reviews. This also diminishes your credibility.

The two things a reviewer or critic has from the beginning of his or her career are integrity and credibility. They are something worth keeping, regardless of the cost.

HOW PROFESSIONALS WROTE IT

DATE: MONDAY, DECEMBER 7, 1987
SOURCE: MIAMI NEWS, P. 3C
AUTHOR: HARPER BARNES, ST. LOUIS POST-DISPATCH

* * *

SELLECK IS AN EASYGOING CHARMER IN "THREE MEN AND A BABY"

PALM SPRINGS, Calif.—On screen and in person, Tom Selleck exudes a casual, easygoing, slightly bumbling but very masculine charm that makes you feel as if you have known and liked the guy for years.

He has been compared by co-stars to Cary Grant and Burt Reynolds. But Selleck is clearly not the next Cary Grant. You don't watch Cary Grant and think, "Gee, I'd like a go a ball game and have a few beers and hot dogs with that guy." Selleck never will have Grant's slightly intimidating, slightly British presence.

As for Reynolds, Selleck's self-deprecating comedy seems a lot less forced than Reynolds' does these days.

If you're dying to see Selleck change a diaper, his new movie, "Three Men and a Baby," has a treat in store for you: You even get to see Selleck and Steve Guttenberg change a diaper together. And a little later, Ted Danson is confronted with a similar problem. After some initial klutziness, the three stars get to be good at caring for a baby.

Somehow, Selleck is most convincing at it.

One of the American writers of this remake of a French comedy about three bachelors with a baby on their hands described Selleck's role as "the daddy of the three." Without Selleck, the movie probably would fall apart.

Apparently, this is the last season for Selleck's TV show, "Magnum P.I." He said he would finish up in late February or early March and then, after a break, probably begin work on another feature film. He said a feature film that looks into future developments in the lives of "Magnum" characters is a possibility, but there is nothing definite.

"I want to see how this movie does first," he said.

In the past, Selleck fans flocked to see such feature films as "Lassiter" and "High Road to China" right after they were released, but box-office returns soon dropped off because of the so-so quality of the movies.

Selleck said he immediately liked the idea of "Three Men and a Baby," not necessarily because of the script (which has been changed substantially, anyway) but because he saw and liked the French comedy, which was nominated for a foreign-language Oscar a couple of years ago.

"I liked the basic concept," he said. "The French movie was more of a farce, I think, and I think our movie is a little more positive about some things."

Reprinted with the permission of the *St. Louis Post-Dispatch*.

• • •

DATE: FRIDAY, SEPTEMBER 4, 1987
SOURCE: MIAMI NEWS, P. 8C
AUTHOR: DEBORAH WILKER, MIAMI NEWS REPORTER

* * *

VETERAN ROCKER SLICK DRAWS '60S FAITHFUL TO STARSHIP SHOW

The band now known simply as Starship is a third generation group that began as Jefferson Airplane in 1965, and then became Jefferson Starship during the '70s. The common link among the three is that lead vocalist Grace Slick still hits the high notes—even though she doesn't hold them as long these days.

Slick is the reason many came to the Sunrise Musical Theater last night— perhaps because interest is keen in a woman who at 48 (next month) can still rock. Her entrance was met with rousing cheers from the audience—an odd mix of '60s burnout types and clean-cut parents with their kids.

From the moment Starship appears, the attitude is "hey, we're glad you still like us enough to buy our records." Overall, this is a band that genuinely likes its work—and it shows. So what if they've gone Top 40? So what if they don't write any of their own stuff anymore? So what if they appear headed for Vegas any day now? They're having fun, and they sing their polished pop with a professional edge that comes only with experience.

Starship's 70-minute set began with "We Built this City (On Rock 'n Roll)"— a self-congratulatory ditty that revived the band from the dead when it hit No. 1 two years ago.

Next up, Slick attempted her signature number "Somebody To Love"—a tune she brought to the Airplane in 1966 from her first band, Great Society. With all this classic rock being tuned in everywhere now, the song has gotten lots of airplay lately—a good and bad thing for Slick, who can no longer replicate her radio sound. Still, she gives it a valiant, if slightly flat, try, while the band pours on the heavy metal cover-up.

Slick's partner, Mickey Thomas, is the real lead singer in this group. His soaring vocals—among the best around—carry most of the show, while Slick ably fills in behind him, taking the spotlight only intermittently. This seems to be quite all right with Slick, who wears a well-meaning, mother-hen smile while she stands in the shadows watching her boys whoop it up.

In fact, the move is a smart one. The back-up work apparently warms Slick's voice enough so that by the time she comes out front for "Babylon" and "Rock Myself to Sleep" she really cooks.

Thomas and Slick say they are both hellbent on making Starship "a completely new band," so they do almost virtually no Jefferson material. The drug anthem

"White Rabbit," is Slick's only other nod to the past—and again this is a tune she brought with her when she joined the Airplane, so she considers it hers alone.

It is during the first few chords of "White Rabbit" that Starship receives its most frenzied response. Fitting psychedelic images frame Slick in a backdrop of hot pinks and greens while she does her best belting of the night.

Thomas also has his moments—particularly during "Sara," "Nothing's Gonna Stop Us Now," "Tomorrow Doesn't Matter Tonight," and a scorching " Fooled Around and Fell in Love"—a song he made famous when he fronted the Elvin Bishop Band in the late '70s.

Guitarist Craig Chaquico, who joined Jefferson Starship in '74, sizzles alongside new bassist Bret Blumfield. Longtime drummer Donny Baldwin and newcomer Mark Morgan (synthesizers) provide competent, if at times overpowering, accompaniment.

The energetic encore, "It's Not Over 'Till It's Over," was a fitting tribute to group's longevity and featured Thomas' impish antics contrasted by Slick's regal posing.

Last night's show was to have been the first of two at Sunrise, but tonight's date was canceled when tickets didn't move. The house was only two-thirds full last night—a puzzling statement since this band has sold millions of records since 1985, and this is also rumored to be the last stateside go around for Slick.

Reprinted with the permission of *The Miami News*.

•••

DATE: THURSDAY, SEPTEMBER 24, 1987
SOURCE: MIAMI NEWS, P. 2C
AUTHOR: LARRY NAGER, SCRIPPS HOWARD NEWS SERVICE

* * *

JAGGER'S OLDER, WISER—BUT STILL A ROCKER

"Primitive Cool," Mick Jagger (Columbia)—With the Rolling Stones apparently broken up, Mick Jagger has released his second solo LP. But "Primitive Cool" doesn't try to keep the Stones' bad-boy myth alive. Instead, Jagger pretty well lays that myth to rest, adopting the role of a rock 'n' roll elder statesman.

He has even settled down with Jerry and the kids. In "Throwaway," the first of the album's 10 songs, Jagger sings "Used to play the Casanova . . . but a love like this is much too good to ever throw away."

It's a nice change from the Stones' usual bluster.

The title tune is even more surprising, as the 44-year-old Jagger looks back to the good old days. "Primitive Cool" takes the form of a dialogue between Jagger and the younger generation. "Did you walk cool in the '60s, Daddy? Did you fight in the war?" the kid asks.

"Party Doll" is another wistful tune, a folky throwback to Jagger's "Wildflowers" days. With the Irish pipes of the Chieftains' Paddy Maloney, the mood is introspective and nostalgic as Jagger sings about "the fleet, sweet bird of youth."

But he's not quite ready to trade his rock 'n' roll shoes for comfy slippers. The first single, the upbeat, uptempo "Let's Work," sets the tone, and Jagger works hard indeed.

"Shoot Off Your Mouth" is the hottest rocker, featuring the flashy guitar of Jeff Beck. "Radio Control" mixes the beat of Free's "All Right Now" with some James Brown funk. And "Peace for the Wicked" grafts the "Addicted to Love" bass line to a down-and-dirty "Harlem Shuffle" rewrite.

The album cover is a chalk portrait of Jagger with donkey ears. The production, by Jagger, Keith Diamond and Eurythmics' Dave Stewart, is just as earthy, a welcome change from the too-slick sound of "She's the Boss," Jagger's first solo LP. The result is a far more even and satisfying album.

Although Jagger seems older and wiser, he's taking more risks. No longer a self-parody, he does some of his best singing in years on the straightforward love song, "Say You Will."

On the closer, "War Baby," Mick Jagger, loving father, makes the emotional plea for peace: "Why can't we walk this road together and keep our children safe and sure?"

Given the inconsistency of the Stones in the last 10 years, Jagger solo is a good idea.

Reprinted with the permission of Scripps Howard News Service.

•••

DATE: FRIDAY, APRIL 3, 1987
SOURCE: MIAMI NEWS, P. 7C
AUTHOR: HERBERT MITGANG, NEW YORK TIMES NEWS SERVICE

* * *

EVERYONE WINS IN 'JOHNSON' EXPOSE

JOHNSON V. JOHNSON. By Barbara Goldsmith. Illustrated. 285 pages. Alfred A. Knopf. $18.95.

In Barbara Goldsmith's reconstruction of the lives and litigation of the Johnson family—the billionaire baby-powder Johnsons, that is—two real-life personalities come forward who happen not to be the main characters in the story. The case unfolded last spring in Manhattan Surrogate's Court during a four-month trial that ended in a settlement.

The one sensible person is not a blood relative—Martin Richards, a theatrical producer, who is married to Mary Lea Johnson, the oldest daughter of the late J. Seward Johnson. Mr. Johnson was heir to the Johnson & Johnson pharmaceutical fortune. When Richards speaks for his wife and the other grown-ups contesting their father's will, he sounds reasonable.

By contrast, the least pleasant person in Goldsmith's version is Nina S. Zagat, a lawyer who appeared to be in business for herself at the same time that she worked for one of those expensive New York law factories. According to the evidence that came out in court, she did things they could hardly have taught at her alma mater, Yale Law School. Zagat was personal lawyer and co-executor of the will with the widow, Barbara (Basia) Piasecka, who was hired as a chambermaid and became Johnson's third wife.

The most ironical line in the book reads: "Nina Zagat walked away with the booby prize, $1.8 million."

Instead of eventually gaining about $30 million in executor and trustee fees, Zagat, who had written herself into the will while the Johnson patriarch was dying, wound up with that measly $1.8 million. The author wisely puts a big chunk of Zagat's "evasive" testimony into the book. Most of her answers went: "I don't recall," sometimes varied as, "I really don't recall."

Johnson v. Johnson is a schizophrenic story. The first part is least appealing because the Johnson patriarch and six children, his and their marriages, divorces and bank figures eventually all run together, like those trendy magazine pieces about the terribly rich and famous. It's not just that mega-rich family scandals are all alike; rather, it's that a million here, a million there begins to read like a bank statement.

In the second part, when the case by the children against Basia reaches court, *Johnson v. Johnson* comes alive. For now the will contest becomes a contest of wills between high-powered lawyers from the most famously expensive New York law firms.

Surrogate Marie M. Lambert is very much a part of the fun and anger. The author calls her "part Portia, part Tugboat Annie." At the end, everybody wins financially, including the lawyers.

Surprisingly, the book lacks an index; without one, it is less definitive. Stylistically, Goldsmith brings herself into the story and often allows her tape recorder to show.

Nevertheless, *Johnson v. Johnson*—and lawyers v. lawyers—is a lively tale.

• • •

DATE: SUNDAY, APRIL 19, 1987
SOURCE: MIAMI HERALD, P. 2K
AUTHOR: BETH DUNLOP, MIAMI HERALD ARCHITECTURE CRITIC

* * *

BEACH PUTS TERRIFIC BUILDING IN UNFORTUNATE LOCATION

No doubt about it, Miami Beach's new police station is a dazzling building. With its gleaming white stucco and glass brick curves, it has voluptuous proportions and a dramatic contour. It is a showstopper on Miami Beach's dowdy Washington Avenue.

In a way, it is like a hothouse flower in a field where everything else grew wild; it is elegant and out of place.

It is scaled to the height of its neighboring buildings, and its curves and setbacks allude to Art Deco. But it is clearly a building of our time.

Police stations seldom look like this. Its four-story lobby, framed in glass, is rather glamorous with sunlight streaming in across its patterned terrazzo floor.

From above, police personnel have dramatic views back out through the lobby, across the Art Deco District and to the Atlantic Ocean beyond.

Of course, the glamour is deceiving in a way for it derives only from the architecture—from the glass and the stucco and the undulating walls. It contrasts with the harsh standard equipment of a police station: a lock-up, a shooting range, locker rooms, a gym for training, offices, educational quarters and lounges with kitchens. Out back is parking for both police and citizens' vehicles, consuming about half a block.

The building sits back on its site—an oversized block between Washington and Pennsylvania avenues and 11th and 12th streets—behind the old Mediterranean tower that was once Miami Beach's city hall. That building, one of the oldest and tallest in the historic district, is being renovated for court facilities and offices.

There is a canopied serpentine walkway connecting the two buildings across a plaza with concrete planters echoing the curves of the building. The plaza is the new home of a military memorial—a cannon and a monument, which was a bad idea. The memorial only emphasizes the irony of having a police facility in the midst of a neighborhood of hotels, apartments and shops.

This new headquarters was designed by a consortium of three architects—Jaime Borelli, Marc Frankel and Peter Blitstein. They had never worked together before, but since beginning on this design, they have won two more contracts from the city of Miami Beach, for the expansion of the convention center and the renovation of the Theater of the Performing Arts.

In many ways, it is a remarkable achievement. It shows off the chemistry these three architects found by joining together, and that kind of collaboration is one of the joys of any art.

This is a stunning building, but a police station simply does not contribute to the life of the neighborhood. My reservations are not about the architectural decisions that shaped it but the politics and planning that went into placing it in the heart of Miami Beach's historic Art Deco District.

This is a district of small buildings, with a rhythm that a single major structure, as this is, could never emulate. No doubt about it, a new police station was needed somewhere, but this was not the appropriate place.

As it is, the garage wall on Pennsylvania, although attractive enough for what it is, has turned a whole block into dead space. Just to underscore the contrast between big and small, this continuous block-long wall faces six separate hotel buildings.

And it should be said, again, that the city was wrong to demolish Art Deco buildings in the center of its historic district, even to build a much-needed police station. The district was compromised for this, and it should not happen again. Even though the building is an architectural success and one worth admiring, that should in no way be considered a precedent. It could lead to all sorts of dangerous conclusions.

Reprinted with the permission of *The Miami Herald*.

A Professional's Point of View

By Michael Larkin
The Boston Globe

Most people, readers and other journalists included, view critics and reviewers with bemused envy, seeing only that someone could get paid for watching movies or attending rock concerts, eating dinners or reading some hot new novel. It's hardly work, right?

Consider, though, sitting through a screening of "Rambo XI: Thin Blood" and

trying to think of something informed and entertaining to write about Sylvester Stallone's peculiar, enduring artistry. Or how about hunkering down in front of the tube for a night of the new fall season: what to say about "Hocus Focus," a new hour-long drama about magician crime solvers? Perhaps Anne Tyler's new book is out. But, then, you've already been assigned five books for the week and the book editor has given that one to someone else . . . well, maybe you'll get to it on your vacation (if you've the slightest desire to read anything more involved than the back of a Cheerios box).

It is, I think, the most difficult, underestimated, long-term assignment in journalism: Do for a living what other, normal people do for relaxation and fun. Not only that, do it on deadlines only crazed sports writers live with and do it with the understanding that everything you write will prompt a disagreement with someone—readers who know more (or often less) than you do, even probably your editors who have seen the same performance and are hideously callous in venting their opinions. Consider, too, the artists' responses. A sample: "Bigger jerks than me review books, Nathan," writes Philip Roth in *Zuckerman Unbound*. And above all, don't make a factual error; you're the expert and your performance is as public as any play or TV program.

So how does anyone do it? The critics I know love their work; almost all of them—despite crushing schedules—are trying to figure how to cover one more thing or are panting about some upcoming event. Constantly learning about their specialty, they devote their lives to studying it: reading, seeing even performances they'll never write about, speculating about an entre's ingredients at a dinner party. They thrill when someone achieves excellence or expands the definition of the form; they are mortified yet enthralled (though they may not write it that way) when they witness an all-too-public flop. Mostly, though, they deeply care about the attempts at creation. It is a caring that stems from a lifelong affection for the art; it is the key element in doing this job.

No one gets to be a respected critic simply because someone gives them the job. Usually, critics gave themselves the assignment when they were young, and

206

have spent most of their lives and education trying to figure out why some books are more moving, some films more exciting, some rock stars rockier. It is this fascination that endures. The best have it as a constant and are able to communicate it. It gives them an understanding of the past, an appreciation for the present and enthusiasm for the future, all essential elements in the confidence necessary to make judgments about the ambitions efforts of others, to review and to criticize with personal vision and voice.

Without all this, a critic might as well be going to the theater for fun. (Larkin, personal communication, 1988)

* * *

Michael Larkin is editor of the Living/Arts Section of *The Boston Globe*. He has worked for newspapers in Boston since he was a student at the University of Massachusetts. In 15 years at *The Globe* he has been a news copy editor, sports copy editor, assistant sports editor, assistant business editor, Sunday editor, and editor of *The Boston Globe Magazine*. He has been Living/Arts editor for the newspaper since 1985, overseeing much of *The Globe*'s feature writing, reviewing, and criticism. For fun, he says he likes to think about what to do next.

10

Aftermath, Follow-Up, and Depth Series Articles

When major news stories break and are in the public's eye for several days, weeks, or even months, eventually a variety of types of articles are written. New developments or anniversaries call for second or third looks at the story and these feature articles have evolved into three basic types of articles that are becoming more important to depth coverage today. Those approaches are aftermath articles, follow-up articles, and depth series articles.

These articles, although each a little different from the other, offer explanation and perspective that were not available when the story first developed. The articles use large amounts of description, extensive direct quotation, and narration to tell readers more about the story.

Accidents, fires, bad weather, natural disasters, famine, riot, war, and other events that cause high levels of human suffering usually demand additional coverage in the form of aftermath, follow-up, or depth feature articles in a series. And, on the other hand, positive events or significant changes that bring happiness and joy to a community are also the occasion for aftermath, follow-up, and series features.

By showing the human angle, the story becomes less facts and figures and more "people-ized." It should also have a *local* perspective. Typically follow-up and aftermath articles appear not on the first day, but more often on second or third days or even weeks after the event. It is also not unusual to use aftermath and follow-up articles a month or even years afterward. Some editors use these articles a year, 2 years, or more after an event as an *anniversary* article.

These articles are commonly found in daily newspapers and sometimes in weekly newspapers, but they also appear in magazines. News magazines, for example, use aftermath and follow-up articles often as a device to deal with their once-a-week publishing schedules, especially on an anniversary of an event, but also as an approach to coverage of a major event in the first issue to appear after the event. This happens each week, you might recall such coverage in news magazines for events such as the space shuttle Challenger disaster in 1986, the attack on the U.S.S. Stark in 1987, or the crash of Pan Am flight 103 in Scotland in 1988.

When something good happens to a community, such as winning a national sports championship or a major economic development such as the decision to build a new automobile assembly plant nearby, these stories also become highly read items. Although readers are naturally curious about disasters and other public traumas, people truly enjoy the success stories of our communities. Major successes command thorough coverage and part of this includes aftermath, follow-up, and series articles.

PURPOSE OF AFTERMATH FEATURE ARTICLES

Newspapers and magazines continue to tell their readers about a major event by assigning writers to write aftermath articles. These magnify the focus on a developing story and remind readers of the importance of the story in the weeks, months, and even years afterward.

Feature writer Daniel Williamson (1975) says aftermath articles are features that give new perspective "to a disaster, tragedy or profound news event that captures the impact and dimensions of the event by humanizing its effect" (p. 179).

Aftermath articles tend to contain more of a people approach than the traditional news follow-up. And although these articles often focus on disasters and tragedies, they also focus on other actions, decisions, and developments in the community.

When a river overflows in an unusual spring flood, how does it affect those involved? Readers want to know the basic facts, such as deaths, injuries, daring rescues, and damage amounts, but they also want to know the human element— the reaction to all this. How do people endure? What are their feelings? Thoughts? Emotions manifest themselves in many ways. An effective writer will try to capture those revealing displays of emotion to truly tell the story in the article.

This is what happened when a flood tore through Fort Wayne, Indiana, in March 1982. The description in writer Dan Luzadder's (1982) column, written on daily deadline for the Fort Wayne *News-Sentinel,* gave his personal reaction to the disaster. He told readers in a compelling way how this event changed the lives of residents of his community on that day and, probably, forever.

Because it is a column, it has many personal observations and feelings of the writer instead of the usual variety of nonpersonal sources. It is clear after reading Luzadder's column that he had talked to many Fort Wayne victims and had gone to the neighborhoods where the flood hit hardest. Still, his generalizations about the community's reactions capture the mood and portray the plight of the victims. There is no one named, no heroes—except the community itself—and no one directly quoted. Although it is a highly personal approach, it still achieves what an aftermath story seeks to do—and Luzadder's column earned him the Pulitzer Prize a year later for local general spot news reporting.

Long after two skywalks collapsed in the Kansas City Hyatt Regency Hotel in July 1981, newspapers and magazines have attempted to help readers remember the nation's worst building disaster by explaining the event from different perspectives. Several months after the Hyatt disaster, reporter Carole Kleiman (1981) of *The Chicago Tribune* used a two-article approach to update readers on what had happened since the accident by writing an article about a family that survived being buried for hours under the rubble in the hotel lobby and by writing a second article on a firefighter who tried to help victims on the scene moments after the skywalks fell. These articles, one on the rescued and the other on the rescuer, tried to tell the general story of those involved by looking at these two distinct points of view. Kleiman visited and interviewed a Kansas City couple and their 11-year-old son in their home and interviewed a Kansas City firefighter at a fire station with his family. The family is recuperating, readers learned, but in a slow, painful way. The firefighter still remembers victims he could not help instead of the three lives he did save. The memories of these sources, related in the articles through extensive quotes, are gripping reading.

A *New York Times* article by writer Jane Brody nearly a year after the Hyatt disaster took a different approach by analyzing the emotional scars of 1,400 survivors and the relatives of the 113 who died by interviewing psychiatrists and other doctors who treated victims. Although the mental health of disaster victims is not a new angle, it was clearly an appropriate one for this major story and focused on the need for cities to have mental health plans for such disasters.

Writer Daniel Williamson (1975) says the aftermath articles about such events as floods and building collapses use one or more of four different approaches:

1. *The epitome of the victim or the victims.* This strategy focuses on the one person or group of people who have endured the disaster such as a plane crash or a hotel fire. There may be only one real victim for the focus of the article, such as a child who becomes trapped in a well and must be rescued before the child dies. You try to focus on these individuals by finding the survivors, who become your key sources. If none is accessible, then friends or relatives may assist in telling the story to readers.

2. *The mood piece.* These articles employ many of the techniques of color articles and are dependent on description by those on the scene. These articles

are often rich in detail and help those who were not present to gain insight into the atmosphere of the site, using witnesses, survivors, photographs, and other means of recreating what happened.

3. *The hero.* In some assignments of this type, the best way to tell the story is to focus on the *individual* who saved the day. There will be times when this person is accessible and quotable. It creates a much-desired angle for the article because most people love to read about a hero and this form of the great American success story.

4. *The goat.* Occasionally, someone, or some organization, unfortunately causes a tragedy. The story becomes a strong angle if you can tell the story from that person or institution's point of view. Since most people or organizations are understandably reluctant to talk to a reporter if they have caused a death or large amounts of property loss, this is a difficult angle to pursue. Regardless, *if* it can be told this way, it is a compelling story since it is a *human* story, one of accidental or intentional human error.

You might not have a choice about which angle to chose in handling your assignment. Much of the time, the course of events will determine how you handle the story. But on some stories, you may have the choice of one or two or three approaches.

Miami Herald feature writer Bea Moss (1982) did not have much flexibility when she took on an assignment for Memorial Day. Keeping in mind the nature of the holiday, she wrote an aftermath article nearly *four decades* after a major event occurred during World War II. Taking advantage of the fact that the co-pilot of the bomber that dropped an atomic bomb on the Japanese city of Nagasaki lived in South Florida, she focused on this individual to recount the events leading up to and during the bombing and destruction of that city. Through the co-pilot's patriotism and emotional words and memories, she tells the story about an event that occurred before many of the article's readers were even born.

WRITING AFTERMATH ARTICLES

You have a number of writing decisions to make when you are working on an aftermath article. You must develop your lead, decide the article's structure, locate sources, select a writing style, and decide the article's mood. Let's look at these in a bit more depth:

1. *Aftermath lead:* The lead of the article is most important. Here you set the stage for the entire piece, and your decisions about how you plan to tell the story to readers are revealed. Aftermath leads can be anecdotal, focusing on an individual or an example of the major point of the article. This approach

makes specific points to illustrate the larger problem—the suffering of one victim can show what an entire group of survivors have experienced and how they feel.

2. *Structural plan:* Think through what you want to achieve with the aftermath article before you begin to write. How will you organize it? What are the major sections? What are the major points? In what order?

3. *Sources:* At the same time you think through the organizational plan, consider what sources are necessary for information to make your major points. Will it be victims? Their families? Official sources such as police and firefighters? Other people? Reports? Observations?

4. *Writing style and mood:* Your chosen style and mood for the particular article should reflect the type of event you are covering. In other words, for an article that describes the joy of a small town several days after it has won a state high school basketball championship, an informal, casual, and upbeat style might be appropriate. But for a natural disaster, such as a tornado striking that same small town, you should be more serious and respectful.

Author Daniel Williamson offers four more considerations for writing aftermath articles. Your approach, he says, should stir the imagination of readers by going beyond the basic facts of the event that are found elsewhere, such as other articles in the same issue or earlier issues. Here's what he suggests to strengthen your writing:

1. *Play heavily on human emotion.* Use descriptions of sorrow, fear, happiness, and other emotions to enhance your article. This comes through direct quotes and observation of what happened and it affected people and places. Can you accurately convey what people experienced? Of what remains? Exercise your vocabulary for this—accurate word choice will make all the difference.

2. *Try to help the reader identify with the victims.* Can readers think that it might have happened to them? If so, you have probably succeeded in helping them identify with the victims. Writing with detail will permit this to happen in most articles. Be alert and observant to recapture the situation.

3. *Write tersely and briefly.* A tightly written article will still get to the point and will permit more perspective to get to the reader in the same amount of space your editor has assigned to the article.

4. *Concentrate on a fast-moving, strong lead.* Good leads set the tone for the article. For aftermath articles, you must write a lead that gets the reader involved and still explains the purpose of the article.

When an earthquake struck Southern California in 1987, newspapers and magazines covered the disaster from the moment the earth began shaking. And coverage of the aftermath continued for weeks. Yet there continued to be good stories to tell about the recovery of the region weeks afterward. An article by former *Los Angeles Times* reporter Marilyn Garateix (1987) focused on citizens of the Los Angeles area who volunteered to help victims in an aid center.

Her article begins by telling readers about how a volunteer's simple act of translating for a Spanish-speaking victim made a big difference to that family. The article describes the volunteerism in several other ways, emphasizing the point through quotes from both the people seeking help and those providing it. After reading the article, it becomes clear that although the earthquake struck two weeks earlier, there were many unresolved problems and people still were helping each other get over the hurdles. It shows a very positive side to human behavior after a disaster and leaves readers with a good feeling.

Middlesex News columnist Tom Moroney's (1985) study of a swindler for *Boston Magazine* comes not days after an event, but months and years after some of the swindles had occurred. His article takes a "bigger-picture" perspective after the man, Timothy Murphy, had been arrested and pleaded guilty to grand larceny. Reading Moroney's article, you learn there were dozens of victims of this thief and nearly a million dollars were stolen. And the heartbreaking part of it—much of this money was life savings and retirement funds of elderly individuals.

Moroney, based in Framingham, Massachusetts, interviewed victims and tells their stories in his article. He talked to public officials such as police and safety officers. He checked court records. And in doing so, he learned about how the swindles took place, and he described them to readers so they can avoid being swindled. Unfortunately, the sources who did not cooperate with the writer were important ones—Murphy and the prosecuting attorney. They would not talk to Moroney.

It is important in writing aftermath stories to bring in the local angle as much as possible. This is easy enough for local events. But it might not be so obvious for events that occurred hundreds or thousands of miles away. When the U.S.S. Stark was attacked by Iraq in the Persian Gulf in 1987 and 37 sailors were killed, the story was a national tragedy. The entire nation was involved in this story as it broke. To tell the story completely, in the weeks and months following the attack and the return of the ship to the United States, aftermath articles focused not only on victims who died and were injured and their families in their home states, but also on survivors who were not hurt. Sailors who were not killed or injured became heroes and the focus of articles as well.

When an earthquake devastated Mexico City in 1985, trapping 7,000 people in the rubble of fallen buildings, aftermath stories were written that focused on medical personnel, rescue specialists, construction specialists, and other individuals who came from countless U.S. cities to help the suffering. These volunteers and their efforts became the focus of articles in many cities that told about local people involved in a disaster affecting unknown people thousands of miles away.

BEST SOURCES FOR AFTERMATH AND FOLLOW-UP ARTICLES

Participants, victims
Friends and relatives of participants, victims
Neighbors
Witnesses
First persons to arrive on the scene afterward
Public records and reports as they become available
Private sources information released to the public

WRITING FOLLOW-UP ARTICLES

Aftermath and *follow-up* are terms that are often used interchangeably. However, there is a difference. Follow-up articles are a form of aftermath articles. The follow-up article is written with a stronger news approach and is based on *new* or *updated* information, the facts and additional details that were not available in earlier coverage of the story by a newspaper or magazine. Many publications today still try to "featurize" such reporting when it is published. New developments in a story often lead to follow-up articles in newspapers and magazines.

These are commonly called second-day articles because they follow the first edition's coverage of the story. Traditionally used in newspapers. The basic approach is also used by some magazines and othe specialized publications to cover a major story.

Using the follow-up approach is routine for news magazines. With their once-a-week publication schedule, editors and writers are forced to take new angles in writing featurized follow-up articles that also serve as roundups on the event.

For example, *Newsweek* editor Terry E. Johnson and Houston bureau reporter Daniel Shapiro teamed for a 500-word follow-up 1988 article on a mass murder in Arkansas, relating the family history of the accused man and his victims—all 16 people were members of his family. Their article, quoting surviving family members and police, updates readers who may have heard about the killings that were discovered over a 2-day period but who did not get all current information in one place.

Follow-up articles have wide application. They are often used in sports as second- or third-day stories, meaning they run 2 or 3 days after a major sports event.

This is shown in an article by Robert Markus (1988), writing in the sports section of *The Chicago Tribune*. He told his Midwestern readers about the personal joys of coaches and players who won a national championship in college football 2 days after the 1988 Orange Bowl. His story about the hometown University

of Miami coach's relief after winning a major bowl game and national championship on his third try did not run on the day after the game as stories about a
sports event do in most local newspapers.

Instead, Markus filed a story for day-after-the-game editions and then wrote
his follow-up story when new information and additional background were
available. He focused on news about the winning team that was not contained
in game story coverage or *The Tribune* columnist's feature the day after the game.

Markus' article opens with a fresh angle on the Miami coach—describing
through direct quotes from the coach just how much pressure was lifted from
his shoulders by winning the game between the No. 1 (University of Oklahoma)
and No. 2 (University of Miami) teams. But this is not all the story does. It
doubles as a roundup article because it also reports on injuries which key players
suffered in the game—presenting updated medical conditions—and after-the-
game direct-quote reactions from key players that did not make the story on the
day before because of deadlines or space limitations.

DEFINING DEPTH FEATURE WRITING

There are times when routine feature coverage, whether it be aftermath, follow-
up, or other types of feature articles, just cannot do the job in a single article.
Even longer magazine articles might not be adequate for certain subjects. Major
events, such as a presidential election campaign, or public health issues, such
as AIDS, often demand more than a single article can do.

Usually this occurs because of one or more of these characteristics:

1. *Magnitude of the issue.* An issue will often affect many individuals and
communities. Public policy issues, such as taxation or care for the elderly, affect
many individuals and often command depth coverage. Showing how many
people are impacted means telling the human side of the story, illustrating it
through the eyes of the people involved.

2. *Seriousness of the problem.* It is necessary to cover certain matters in depth
because of the serious nature of the subject. For example, discovery of contamina-
tion of a major source of public water requires thorough attention. Aside from the
straight news approach, feature approaches will look at the personal effects such
a problem brings to a community by looking at individuals and at the group.

3. *Immediacy of the event or issue.* Because certain subjects are current *now*,
they cannot wait. Public concern about an issue, such as the potential risks of
AIDS or the potential dangers of nuclear power, requires attention in such a
fashion that articles serve the community's thirst for information right away.
Fear of the unknown often creates problems that compound existing troubles,
so educational-instructional articles are a public service. These articles illustrate
the situation by humanizing the problem so readers can identify with the subject

at their own level. Answering questions such as "How does this affect me?" makes a depth series successful.

4. *Broad scope of the story*. A depth feature series usually evolves when a subject is broad in scope, encompassing a number of sub-topics that must be covered in adequate depth to make sense to readers. Often, a trend is significant enough to justify thorough analysis and illustration through a series of features. The effects of the growth of Vietnamese and other Southeast Asian refugee communities on the West Coast over the past decade, for example, have been covered by a depth feature approach by various publications.

Authors William Rivers and Alison Work (1986) say that some inexperienced writers feel writing short articles is easier than writing long ones. Actually, it becomes easier to write longer material because you have more opportunity to use the information you have collected. It is also easier because of the additional dimension of organization that serialization permits.

The feature series should be a highly organized study of a subject that is neatly and cleanly divided into parts of equal significance. The pieces within each story need to be linked together with transitions. The pieces of the series should be presented in logical fashion with linkages as well. Series are often accompanied by editor's notes, sidebar boxes, or other short editorial devices to explain to readers what the purpose of the overall series might be, as well as the role of the individual story that they are reading in an issue.

Each part should be written to "stand alone." That is, the individual story should be strong enough and self-explanatory enough to be useful to readers who did not see earlier or will not see later parts. The series approach is common in both newspapers and magazines, but perhaps more frequent in daily or bi-weekly newspapers because their publication frequency is conducive to publishing in pieces over a short period of time. However, magazines also run depth feature series when a subject justifies the treatment over several issues in succession.

WRITING A FEATURE SERIES FOR NEWSPAPERS

Organization is a key for newspaper series articles. Distinct divisions of the subjects within the overall topic is necessary. A writer or editor planning such a series should outline the project first, then refine each story idea as it develops. There should be minimal overlap of the subjects, and there should be an editor's note at the beginning or end of the article informing readers that the article is part of a series and that other articles have been published and will be published on the topic. Subjects are, of course, varied but must be broad enough to permit subdivision.

One population trend experienced in many metropolitan areas in the past 20 years has been the "Latinization" of the United States. Significant growth of Hispanic populations in a number of major cities has been at such a fast rate that many population experts have predicted that Hispanics will be the largest minority group in the United States by the year 2000. This sudden growth has been experienced in California, Texas, Florida, and even New York and Illinois. Newspapers and magazines in those regions have not ignored this, devoting their resources to hundreds of news and feature articles on the subject.

To illustrate this, *The Los Angeles Times* published a series on that subject that earned the newspaper the 1984 Pulitzer Prize gold medal for meritorious public service.

In summer 1983, *The Times* published a major series of news and feature articles on Southern California's Latino community—three million Mexican–Americans and other Latin American nationals, who have moved to the large multi-county metropolitan area surrounding Los Angeles. The series was published over a 3-week period and was written, edited, and illustrated by Hispanic journalists to tell readers about the diverse and growing group. The project's purpose, stated in an editorial at the end of the series, was to open "up a community that, too often is seen as mysterious or even threatening by the rest of Los Angeles. The Latino series clearly showed that this fearful attitude, the result of Anglo indifference rather than hostility, is mistaken" (p. 132).

Features in the series were far too numerous and too lengthy to reproduce here but included articles on these subjects:

1. The cultural odyssey from Mexico to the United States.

2. The Latin dream in Orange County.

3. The actual diversity of the group tied by ethnicity.

4. San Diego as the border between Mexican–Americans and Mexican–Mexicans.

5. The American dream in the barrio in Los Angeles.

6. Two Latino political activists and their distinctly different paths.

7. Problems, pride, and promise in Boyle Heights in East Los Angeles.

8. Education of Latinos—advances and failures.

9. The new breed of wealthy Latinos.

10. Latino heroes that are few and far between.

11. Limitations of Latinos finding jobs and the limits of the jobs they do find.

12. The success stories of top Latino companies that took risks that paid off.

13. Inside the world of Latinas—five women talk about their burden of racism and sexism by discussing their experiences, family relationships, lives, and concerns.

14. The emerging generation of Chicano art.
15. The new energy of Chicano writers.
16. Latinos and their renewed bond with religion.
17. Latinos as migrant workers in the "fields of hardship."
18. Political relations between Mexico and Chicanos of Southern California.
19. The Chicano movement—a generation in search of a legacy.
20. Latinos' living on a bridge between two worlds.

This series is an impressive sociological, economic, political, and historical study of Hispanics. The subject could only be handled in a series because of the broad nature of the endeavor. Other newspapers and magazines alike should attempt to achieve such public enlightenment by publishing such depth work in news stories and in features.

WRITING A SERIES FOR MAGAZINES

It may seem unusual for a magazine to run a series, right? With all the space a magazine can give to a major article, why would it need to serialize? It is more common than you might think. Monthly magazines, especially the specialized ones, will occasionally run a feature series of two, three, or more parts.

Usually, this is done not because of a space crunch but because an editor wants to develop an ongoing readership habit. This is common for new magazines and for those which have a high proportion of newsstand sales instead of subscription sales.

Historically, it has been common for magazines to serialize. Years ago, magazines would serialize fiction, especially for readers who could not afford to buy books. With books more available and available in less expensive paperback editions in the last three decades, magazines that serialize books today tend to use parts of new nonfiction and fiction books as they are being written or soon after the manuscript is finished. A publisher might permit early publication of portions with the hope that it will tease readers enough to encourage them to read the entire book.

Newspapers also run serialized books. A number of major daily newspapers buy rights to new blockbuster books as publishers prepare to release the book. This occurred when Bob Woodward's book, *Veil: The Secret Wars of the CIA, 1981–87*, was published in late 1987. *Newsweek* ran a cover story about the book which focused on the late William Casey, director of the Central Intelligence Agency and on others high in the Reagan administration.

Personal Investor, a California-based magazine that debuted in 1985 for investment-minded readers, ran a five-part series in its first five issues about how to read a company's annual report. Each installment focused on a different part of an annual report: really reading an annual report, the income statement above the bottom line, the balance sheet, red-flags in the footnotes, and unclassified information—accessing SEC filings. Part III, for example, tells readers what to find in a corporate balance sheet and why it is important to readers. Writer Michael Geczi (1985) illustrates his points with plenty of examples to make a complex subject understandable. Using five different writers—Robert Dallos, Priscilla Meyer, Geczi, Jack Egan, and Bruce Fraser—the full series made the entire annual report easier to understand.

Texas Monthly magazine published a 1984 series by writer Paul Burka (1984) called "The Man in the Black Hat," in two parts. This series told the story of Texas oilman Clinton Manges and his empire. Readers learned how Manges achieved his success in ranching, oil, politics, and law.

Milwaukee Magazine occasionally runs a series that updates readers on Milwaukee people. "Whatever Happened To . . ." looks at well-known Milwaukeeans once in the limelight in Milwaukee. This occasional series began in 1985 and the second part was published in 1987. For readers who like to keep up with newsmakers, it is interesting reading, even though the first two parts of the series were separated by two years—showing these serialized articles do not need to be published consecutively.

Family Circle ran a 1987 series focused on mothers who seek ways to run businesses at home while caring for their children and their homes. One installment, for example, focused on how home-bound people can build careers in mail-order businesses. This part in the series, by Georganne Fiumara, looked at three women who took different routes to get to the same place—owning their own successful mail-order businesses.

Finally, the serial approach is particularly useful for specialized business/industry periodicals that must cover issues of a highly technical nature for readers with specialized knowledge. This works well for those with sophisticated levels of knowledge, but it also works for new or not widely known subjects of common interest to readers of a specialized publication.

For example, *FLOWERS&* magazine, which serves individuals interested in the business of flowers, ran a five-part series in late 1987 and early 1988 focusing on accounting. Called "The ABC's of Accounting," each monthly article focused on a different aspect of accounting. Free-lance writer Mary Frech McVicker, (1987), a small-business specialist who lives in Illinois, used part one as an overview establishing the need for sound accounting skills for those who run a florist shop. Here McVicker showed doubtful readers that accounting is an important and necessary skill by beginning her article with an anecdote/case study of one florist and his lack of concern for balance sheets, ledgers, and double-entry systems. In the first article were simple accounting basics.

Her second piece focused on more specific concerns such as trial balances, adjusting entries, and income summaries. Throughout the series, examples and illustrations made the learning process easier for those already in business.

The final installment wrapped up the series with business ratios and did it by looking at a case study shop. McVicker made the reading easier throughout this article and the rest of the series by providing re-created conversations and tables with numbers to make the points clearer. There's no doubt such a complex subject as accounting, even so focused as to limit the discussion to running flower businesses, would not have worked as well in one extremely long article. The series gave the advantage of presenting complex material in shorter, more digestible doses for those who do not have such business acumen, resulting in a 5-month short-course for *FLOWERS&* readers.

Air Line Pilot, the monthly journal of the Air Line Pilots Association, ran a timely seasonal series in December 1987 and January 1988 on winter flying. Taking a primer approach, writers Joseph F. Towers and Porter J. Jenkins wrote two articles on the hazards commercial pilots face in winter, such as the effect of icing on jet engine intakes and other problems related to cold weather. The articles, illustrated with test results graphs, diagrams and photographs, were written by an American Airlines first officer and a former NASA engineer for the thousands of pilots who must understand what ice, snow, slush, hydroplaning, frigid temperatures, cold, and clouds mean to flying an airplane. The article is scientific and purely descriptive, yet is laden with information to educate and refresh the memories of readers.

HOW PROFESSIONALS WROTE IT

DATE: MONDAY, MARCH 15, 1982
SOURCE: FORT WAYNE, INDIANA NEWS-SENTINEL
AUTHOR: DAN LUZADDER, NEWS-SENTINEL COLUMNIST

* * *

A FITFUL NIGHT FOR THOSE WHOSE DREAMS LIE UNDER THE RIVER

It is midnight Sunday, at the moment of this dispatch, and the streets are quiet. But in the heart of the city, hearts are breaking.

Homes sit under water. Cars have been swallowed up. Houses sit dark and empty of occupants as furniture floats on the floors.

The lapping, slowly rising waters make an insidious sound on clapboard walls. But otherwise, the evacuated areas are quiet. And all is calm.

This is what the eye sees, the ear hears. Yet, as the city's sandbag heroes lie down to rest tonight, only turmoil greets those made refugees of the flood of '82.

They sleep tonight on lumpy, unfamiliar cots in rooms with linoleum floors. In the church centers, this thankful and restful sleep comes only when anxiety succumbs to fatigue. And hundreds more bed down in strange houses, waiting for word of more rain.

At this hour, it is said, 3,000 have been forced from their homes. Most are of the old working class neighborhoods, which lie along the west banks of the city's three rivers.

It is mainly here that the city swallowed water and spit up refugees. Boat people. Tired Marines, firefighters, and volunteers came after them, helping the cumbersome and reluctant into small aluminum crafts, ferrying them again and again to the high ground where other transportation waited.

Now, at midnight, the evacuated parts of the central city sit in the dark, their power cut, the gas off, all semblance of normality gone.

Those who made a stand in time—fighting with sandbags and hasty earthen dikes—have only to wait for the rivers to crest. Their homes are spared, for now, and their confidence returns. They sleep in their own beds tonight. But they wonder, too, how much more water the city can take? And rain lurks in the night sky.

To the west of the rivers, the heartbreak is the hardest. The loss greatest. Where the Maumee and St. Joe only licked the levee-tops, residents climbed flood walls hourly for inspections of the water's leading edge. They looked for signs of hope. Where the levees held, they found it. Where they did not, hope drowned like a rat.

A thousand stories are being told tonight by the refugees. Things they saw and heard.

One thinks of a house on Van Buren Street, where sunlight sparkled springlike off a bright yellow picket fence. An elderly couple waits in the front yard of their little yellow house. The gentleman sits on a yellow chair on the walk, a cane across his knee. His wife, her yellow hair now white, stands watching the curious walk by. They are a Rockwell print. A yellowed photograph out of place.

A block away the water edges up the street toward them. The woman speaks only broken English. Her husband only nods. Worse flood. Ya. Worst flood. How high is it coming? A shrug. Will they have to leave? she says. Who knows?

Along the levee of the Maumee, where the river runs its widest and deepest, the whispering water rolls in the dark. Few people come and stand on the levee under the street light. It is unnecessary now. They feel safe.

In the pocketlike Lakeside neighborhood, nestled in the bend of two rivers, the waters did not win. Here there is elated relief. The sleepless anxiety of Saturday night is over. There are no cots, no anguish over flood-damaged lives. They escaped the flood. But it came so close.

Now, just after midnight, as the city slips into sleep, its 3,000 refugees housed and fed, there are still two worlds. The wet and the dry. The highlanders and the lowlanders. Two cities, separated by swollen rivers and closed bridges. Two kinds of luck. Good and bad.

Tomorrow, it is hoped, the cresting will come. The crest comes, the water recedes and the homeless return to the little sorrows of lost mementos. And to dig out once more.

But that is tomorrow. Tonight there is still that uneasy sleep of the weary; unfamiliar beds, the strange emptiness of a battle—part lost and part won. Tonight, in the heart of the city, hearts are still breaking. But the worst is over. The streets are quiet. And all is calm.

Reprinted with the permission of the *Fort Wayne News-Sentinel.*

• • •

DATE: OCTOBER 1985
SOURCE: BOSTON MAGAZINE, PP. 170–74, 218.
AUTHOR: TOM MORONEY

* * *

SWINDLED!

NO ONE SUSPECTED A THING.

Timothy Murphy was a friend, a local boy; people knew his parents.

When he became a tax accountant in his native Fitchburg, he found clients among his neighbors. But the relationships were never strictly business; when Tim did your taxes, it was almost like having one of the family pitch in to help out.

People would invite the gregarious young accountant into their homes, and over dinner they'd talk about investment deals and the best places to keep their life savings. And when Murphy offered them ways to make big profits from these savings, they trusted him.

One Lancaster couple trusted him enough to hand him $53,000 to invest. Two days later they gave him $10,000; and the next year, $7,000. Most trusting of all was a Westminster man who gave Murphy $116,000.

But the high-interest bank accounts and lucrative annuity funds Murphy peddled weren't real. They were as phony as the receipts he gave his clients.

In all, police say that between the mid 1970s and 1982 Timothy J. Murphy, now 38, walked off with at least $900,000 of his clients' money—money that only Murphy knows what happened to.

In November 1984 Murphy pleaded guilty to 125 counts of grand larceny derived from the testimony of 54 victims. He was then convicted and sent to prison.

If Murphy's trade had been murder, his victims say, they wouldn't be around to talk about it. If the man had been an arsonist, they could have collected insurance money for the houses he had burned. But he was neither. He was an artist. And what he did, his victims say, was as bad as murder or arson. He walked into people's lives and stole their futures.

Many of the people he preyed upon were elderly and retired. From them he took the savings from the last money they would ever earn. The nickels and dimes of the textile worker. The five-dollars-a-week savings of the carpenter. The money of people who intended to look out for themselves in old age. Murphy ruined, or at the very least damaged, their lives.

The police believe the money is gone. But some victims suspect that their money is in hiding, waiting for Murphy to finish a few years in prison and retire to a life of luxury.

"He told me he had a deal for me," says Donald Faulkenham, 39, of Leominster. "He said I could make 18 percent interest on my money. Was I interested? Wouldn't you be?"

"He preyed on greed, pure and simple," states Fitchburg detective David Caputi.

Murphy usually sold his clients on a way to dodge taxes or to reap sky-high interest on savings. He might have suggested an account at a Boston bank that paid 18 percent interest or a profitable Fitchburg bank annuity fund. To make his deal look official, Murphy would mail his clients receipts on the letterhead of reputable Boston banks. Police believe he simply walked into the banks during regular business hours and helped himself to their stationery.

Not all of Murphy's dealings were illegal. Dozens of his clients even made money—some as much as 25 percent interest on their investments.

"There are all kinds of people in Fitchburg—doctors, lawyers, and other people you'd be surprised to hear about—who did very well with Tim Murphy," says Gayle Guilmette, 39, of Pepperell, who once dated Murphy and later became one of his victims.

"He was a real charmer, a real Irish talker," recalls another victim, Lydia Piermarochi, 57, of Fitchburg. "If he was standing here right now, you'd love the guy."

Over the years that Murphy worked his con, some of his clients sensed occasional hints of trouble. But they say that whenever they had questions, Murphy had answers. Sometimes they even asked for their money back and he gave it to them.

But in the early 1980s things started to go sour for Murphy and his marks. Clients were being stalled. Phone messages left for Murphy were going unanswered. Now when people asked for money back, they were being told to wait.

The exact reasons for Murphy's behavior may never be fully disclosed. He refused to be interviewed, as did the assistant district attorney who prosecuted him.

[The article continues beyond this excerpt.]

Reprinted with permission of the author and *Boston* magazine.

• • •

DATE: SUNDAY, JANUARY 3, 1988
SOURCE: CHICAGO TRIBUNE, SECTION 3, PP. 1, 10.
AUTHOR: ROBERT MARKUS, STAFF WRITER

* * *

HE'S FINALLY MAIN MAN: MIAMI'S JOHNSON GAINS A CHAMPIONSHIP, RESPECT

MIAMI—They won't call Jimmy Johnson "the other guy" anymore. They won't call him the coach who can't win the big one.

Johnson's Miami Hurricanes gave him the gift of peace Friday night when they won the national championship with their 20–14 Orange Bowl victory over Oklahoma.

Never mind that the ballots aren't in yet. The Hurricanes didn't wait to have the votes counted. They finished the season as the only 12–0 team in the country and they beat the only team that was ranked ahead of them.

"We're 6–0 against bowl teams," pointed out Johnson. "We played our way into this national championship. That bunch in red we beat tonight, they're second best in the country."

That might be open to debate, especially from Florida State, which ended 11–1 and outplayed Miami in an early-season 26–25 loss. The Seminoles ended their season with a 31–28 victory over Nebraska that was not convincing enough for Bobby Bowden to demand a recount.

Indeed, so convincing was Miami against Oklahoma that the idea of a national championship playoff might be on the back burner for a while. Who is left to challenge the Hurricanes now?

Johnson was already on record as being against a playoff.

"I originally said I might favor a playoff where you take the top two teams after the bowls," he said last week. "But after thinking it over, I'm against that. I think teams would try to duck the tough teams in the bowl game."

This was the second year in a row that Johnson's team had been in the national championship game. But he had to win the big one Friday before getting the respect he deserves.

"I've sort of been like one of those pro wrestlers," Johnson was saying last week. "There's always one guy who comes in holding this big championship belt and they introduce him as a guy who hasn't lost in 15 years. Then they introduce 'the other guy.' I'm always the other guy."

Last year he was the other guy to Joe Paterno, even before Paterno's Penn State team upset the Hurricanes in the Fiesta Bowl.

This past week he took a back seat to Oklahoma's Barry Switzer—until Friday night. "Who knows," he had said wistfully, "the other guy may even win one some day." Some day finally came, and Miami had to overcome a minefield of obstacles to make it happen. They used a patched-up offensive line that protected quarterback Steve Walsh as lovingly as if he were a newborn baby.

And Walsh did what his predecessor, Vinny Testaverde, could not do: win the national title in his first year as the starting quarterback.

Walsh threw TD passes of 30 yards to Melvin Bratton and 23 to Michael Irvin as Miami beat Oklahoma for the third year in a row.

His only interception set up the Sooners' first touchdown, but the fact that it took Oklahoma 15 plays and more than six minutes to grind out 49 yards underscored the magnificence of the Miami defense.

The Hurricanes were led, ironically, by Bernard "Tiger" Clark, the middle linebacker who replaced George Mira Jr., the Miami starter who failed to pass a drug test.

Clark was voted the Hurricanes' most valuable player for his 12 solo tackles. "I wanted to make every tackle on the field," he said, and he nearly did.

Bratton tied an Orange Bowl record with his nine receptions (for 102 yards), but left the game in the fourth quarter with a knee injury. He underwent successful surgery Saturday to repair ligament damage.

Other Hurricanes also paid the price. Tight end Alfredo Roberts spent the night in Doctors Hospital after suffering a concussion early in the game. Doctors allowed him to return to action, but he complained of dizziness in the locker room.

Defensive tackle Greg Mark tore a ligament in his left thumb.

But Oklahoma was hurting even more. This was, Switzer said, his best team, and Miami destroyed it.

The Sooners made it close late in the game with a trick play, a 29-yard run by tackle Mark Hutson on the old "fumblerooski" play that Switzer borrowed for the night from Nebraska's Tom Osborne.

"Nebraska's been pulling that on them for so many years, and now they pull it on us," said Johnson, who could afford to laugh about it.

Mostly, the Hurricanes were numb—or in tears. "It's an incredible feeling," said Walsh. "I don't think it's hit me yet."

"Everyone's crying in the locker room," said Clark. "It took us three years to get those championship rings, but we got 'em."

And Johnson got that monkey off his back. He's not the other guy anymore.

Reprinted with the permission of *The Chicago Tribune*.

A Professional's Point of View

By Mike Foley
St. Petersburg Times

An aftermath story? A follow up piece? You mean, write a feature story after the news is over?

Is that journalism?

You bet. The feature story done after the big disaster, the crucial vote, the key game, or that triple axe murder is not only real journalism, but it's your time to shine.

You'll have the time, space and, probably, a lot of freedom to decide how best to handle the story. How often do you get an opportunity like that in this business?

But, it's also a real challenge. Your usual excuses—or, rather, "reasons"—for a less-than-stirring account won't work. The deadline is farther off than a few hours, or minutes. You can talk to more people. You can get the details. You will be able to sort out the confusion. Then, you can sit down and—can you believe it?—write.

So, you've got challenge, you've got opportunity. Can the possibility of massive, career-ending failure be far behind? Of course not. So, before you blow it, you might consider a few suggestions:

Relax. Take a few deep breaths, a blank piece of paper, a pen or pencil and figure out what you need to do. This preparation should include reading stuff already written on the topic, and planning other research, including public records, historical documents, books and outside experts. (You'll find later that background information is almost as important as the new reporting you'll do.)

Talk to your editor. He or she has either assigned this story, or, at least, has permitted you to pursue it. Only an expert (or fool, or maybe the publisher's kid) would ever work on a story without talking it over first with the boss.

This also will allow you to find out how much time and space you'll have. You also should at this point and throughout the gathering and writing stages, think of other material that will enhance the story—photos, maps, charts, illustrations. Your editor will thank you for any suggestions. (Editors like to look good, too, you know.)

Think about what you want to do. Sound redundant? Maybe it is. But, many writers, especially young and beginning ones, forget to set goals. They're after a "story," without thinking about what the story might be. Sure, the story will change many times as you gather information. But, it helps to start with some idea of where you could be going.

Don't forget the little things. The follow stories are the detail stories. What's the dog's name? What did the family eat for dinner? What was the dead guy wearing?

Take a look at reporter Edna Buchanan's book, *The Corpse had a Familiar Face*, if you want some examples of how to do this well.

Feel it. Attention all you aloof, neutral observers: it's time to get real. If you want to write a good story (even gather enough material to fashion a good story), you have to let loose, be a human. Don't take sides or get involved, but use your own emotions to try better to understand what the human in your story might have felt.

Tell me a story. Sure it's journalism, but let's not forget what a "story" is. It's a narrative, with a beginning, a middle and an end. Re-read your research, study your notes, shut your notebook (and maybe your eyes for a minute) and tell me a story. Step back and tell it whole.

If you have done your job, I'll even read your story, maybe all the way to the end. And that's my ultimate compliment. (Foley, personal communication, 1988)

* * *

Mike Foley is managing editor of the *St. Petersburg Times*. He has served in this position since 1984. He was a reporter and assistant city editor for the now-defunct *St. Petersburg Independent* before becoming assistant metropolitan editor for the *Times* in 1974. He was also metropolitan editor and assistant managing editor for the *Times*. He has also served as a juror for the Pulitzer Prizes. In his spare time, he is a drummer in a rock and roll band, "The Fabulous Nose-caps."

11

Travel Writing

The American public is traveling more today then ever before, creating a growing market for travel writing. Books, magazines, newspapers, and other printed material are used for guidance in making travel decisions and for getting the most out of your travel budget.

For most writers, travel stories are fun assignments. Perhaps one of the most glamorous feature writing assignments today is in faraway, exotic lands. Most daily newspapers have at least one writer or editor assigned to travel, and many larger dailies have a Sunday section filled with color photographs, stories, and information about interesting places. Small dailies usually offer a special page or pages once a week. Magazine editors depend on these types of stories to help sell their issues with articles by staff and free-lance writers. Many magazines offer readers travel departments that appear in every issue or with some other regularity. And, of course, there are numerous magazines, such as *Arizona Highways*, *National Geographic*, *National Geographic Traveler*, *Travel/Holiday*, and *Travel & Leisure*, on the market dedicated to a person's urge to wander.

These days, consumers turn to the news media for help in making decisions. A major purchase, such as a vacation package, requires the traveler to gain the expertise to make the proper decisions. Airline deregulation has made a quagmire of airline routes, service, and ticket prices. Thus, a good travel feature *can* make a difference as readers turn to their favorite newspapers and magazines for assistance. Travel writing, then, can be a form of consumer reporting. One distinction, as writing professor and former *Miami Herald* travel editor Alan Prince (1988) once said, is that the vacationer does not come home with a refrigerator or television set. The major purchase here results in photographs, souvenirs, a videotape, and memories. But not much else.

At the 1987 annual convention of the American Society of Travel Writers in Melbourne, Australia, San Diego *Tribune* editor Neil Morgan said travel writing is getting more credible with the public. Travel writing has gained this new level of respect from readers because of the "courageous and consistent" efforts of newspapers and magazines to upgrade quality. Skepticism about travel writing brought about by flattering writing and free trips that existed in the 1970s has been overcome by increased reader trust, Morgan said. "Newspapers and magazines should be able to tell readers about travel as reliably and convincingly as about abortion and AIDS" (*Editor & Publisher*, 1983, p. 13), Morgan, an experienced travel writer himself, said.

Even the short-distance or regional traveler needs information to best use his or her time. Travel writing serves this purpose when done right. Business travelers need guidance on all aspects of their travel (including airlines, ground transportation, hotels/motels/inns, restaurants, and entertainment), and an entire industry catering to business travelers has evolved in this century. Included in that movement is the travel publication industry aimed at professional travelers. *Frequent Flyer* magazine is just one example.

But to simply write about your recent vacation won't get the job done. Most travel-oriented publications provide a standard fare of information for the traveler or the person thinking of traveling, or the person simply daydreaming about traveling some day. Readers of the travel page as well as the business pages of today's publications are generally erudite. These people are in the higher income brackets with the money and time to spend going places. Thus, many of them are likely to be well-traveled and informed readers of your stories. And, as some travel editors will tell you, the writing must simultaneously serve two distinct audiences: (a) people who have not been to the place you write about, and(b) people who have already been there.

Prof. Alan Prince (1988) adds:

> This [writing for those who have been to the destination and those who have not] puts travel writers in a position of having to become an instant expert about a place in which some of his readers presumably have spent more time than he . . . and presumably know the place better than he. Therefore, he cannot pull the wool over their eyes. There's no way. Most stories in a newspaper are directed to readers who do not know the news; that's why they're reading the newspaper. But in travel writing, the writer has to assume that some of his readers already know the subject . . . and he'd better be right. (personal communication, 1988)

What do you write about? You write about places to visit. You tell readers about historical places, annual festivals, national parks, cities, resorts, and inns. You tell them about places to stay, restaurants with views, and the easiest and cheapest ways to get there. You convey the richness, the color, the excitement, the fun, the moods, the atmosphere. You give important information such as admission prices and times for an attraction. But you also relate personal experiences, such as the best place to park in a busy neighborhood—Boston's North End, for example—that will make your story complete.

Thus, you find the unusual, the unique, the odd, and the entertaining. Writing professor Shirley Biagi (1981) says: "Visiting Waikiki may have been fascinating for you, but asking a travel editor to buy 6,000 words about 'gorgeous white sand beaches' is an insult. The successful travel writer chooses the offbeat, photographs the unusual, visits the out-of-the-way" (p. 24).

Have you ever taken a major trip? Have you ever gone that one step further by writing about it? What would you tell your friends about the trip? This can be the foundation of a good feature. Travel writing requires good reporting, though, since it is much more than going from point A to point B by bus. Most successful writers are experts, too, and know the details of a successful journey from planning to budgeting to itineraries and more.

With a good market today, you need to consider what works for those already in the business. Start out by reading the weekend travel section or page of your local newspaper. But also study it. What kinds of stories are published? Photographs? Where do they come from? Does the section contain more than basic "destination pieces"? If so, what else? In the stories, what sources do the writers use? What is the writing style? Is it narrative? First person? What supplementary material comes with the stories? Photographs? Locator maps? In this chapter, we plan to consider all the elements of travel writing.

REQUIREMENTS OF TRAVEL WRITING TODAY

There are four common types of travel writing:

1. *Destination articles.* Destination stories simply tell readers about places they might go on a trip.
2. *Attraction articles.* Attraction stories are more specific than destination articles. They tell readers about a particular place, such as a park.
3. *Service articles.* The service story explains about how to travel better by letting the reader understand the mechanics of traveling.
4. *Personal experience articles.* Personal experience stories may do the same as any of the three previous approaches, but you interject a personal experience perspective.

Journalism professor Betsy Graham (1982) says travel writing appeals to most readers because people like to brag about their trips as much as they like to brag about the people they meet. She says:

> The travel article will arouse a response in most readers because place-dropping is as common in conversation today as name-dropping. The people who like to talk about their travels often also enjoy reading an interesting account of an unusual trip. In addition to being descriptive as well as narrative, travel articles may also be another form of the how-to article. They may include specific directions on how to travel safely and economically . . . . Don't ignore the travel article market because you have not visited exotic places. Write about your own town or a nearby historic site or a summer or winter resort in your area. (pp. 30–31)

WRITING STYLE: WHAT'S THE BEST APPROACH?

The experienced traveler-turned-writer is the travel writer of today. Your job as travel writer is to take the reader there on destination stories, give your reader the facts for service stories, and provide opinion about current travel and tourism industry issues.

Most travel writing is narrative. It remains descriptive, however, as writers use their command of the language to paint a mental picture for the reader. Remember, not all travel stories are illustrated with color photographs or graphics, so you must use your vocabulary to convey impressions of the subject through precise adverbs and adjectives.

Travel writing is moving toward more personalized style of writing. Where most of the newspaper is written in an objective, third person style, travel writing takes several different writing style approaches, including a growing emphasis on first person, personal experience writing that was noted earlier.

The personal approach puts the author into the story as a principal source of information. It is first hand experience writing. It is friendly and casual. Use of the first person pronoun "I" is characteristic of this style. It is story telling just as if you were talking to your friends. Your own observations and reactions are important with this approach.

Re-creation of dialogue using direct quotes of brief conversation is common in this style also. Although first-person is not as common in other sections or departments, it is a trend in today's travel writing that makes the story more appealing to readers.

WRITING THE TRAVEL STORY

The single most important step in writing a good travel story is preparation. Although taking the trip and writing the story may seem important, these steps cannot be as successful without laying groundwork before leaving home. Prof. Alan Prince (1988) believes in preparation for good stories: "In practice, there isn't time to prepare as much as one would like. The accent on preparation is important because a travel writer can often spend only three or four days in a country—and he's supposed to leave it as an expert."

The biggest single reporting asset we have today in travel writing is the telephone. Use it often. It can offer the basis for a good story and save you a lot of time and trouble in the long run.

But don't forget the mail as well. When and where you need information but are not in a big hurry for it, send post cards or letters for background information, such as press kits. Get on mailing lists of public relations firms that represent the travel industry. You will soon have more information than you know what to do with.

If you plan to get into travel writing, either for a magazine or newspaper, start a set of reference files. Organize them as you see fit, but try to put information you collect in some system so it can be found quickly when needed. One easy approach is to begin an alphabetic system based on destinations and attractions. You could also begin a set of files on service-related topics, organized by subject. Keep a telephone number file, too.

Let's move on to the story itself. To get you thinking about what goes into reporting and writing a travel story, here are some suggestions for a good start:

1. *Call sources ahead of time.* When you decide you will do a story, call or write sources at the locations several weeks (if domestic) or several months in advance (if foreign) to gather the advance information you need. Call tourism offices that are usually government-operated and government-sponsored. The best possible help on foreign sources comes from the domestic offices of government travel bureaus. Many are located in New York, Chicago, Los Angeles, and Washington, D.C.

2. *Contact local business organizations.* These include chambers of commerce and convention bureaus. These organizations can provide economic reports to give you a better feel for the area. They can also give you the best information about hotels, motels, restaurants, and transportation. Often they also have information about historical sites, popular places to visit, and more.

3. *Use visitors' bureaus.* Popular vacation and resort locations will have sophisticated visitors' offices and will be anxious to help you before your trip. They can also arrange tours once you arrive.

4. *Use sources at your hotel.* Don't forget the hotel or motel where you plan to stay. Many times the management of these places will offer help in advance if you request it.

5. *Go to the library.* Check out books about the areas you will visit. Review articles from periodicals that have been recently published so you can get a better idea of what might be a "new" angle for your story.

6. *Build your own travel library*. As you go to a new place, add a book about it. Fodor's series of country and city guides, published in paperback annually by David McKay, is a good example. Frommer's guides offer a similar perspective. Don't think these two examples are the only ones; they are not. Simply visit the travel section of a good local bookstore and you will see a wide range of travel guides—most written by experienced travel guides and travel editors. There are also a growing number of travel-oriented newsletters available by subscription. They vary a great deal in their approach, focus, and price, but can be the most up-to-date sources of information available to you as a travel writer. Examples? International Railway Traveler, Offbeat, and Entree.

7. *Contact specific site sources*. Once you know where you are going and when, start to ask specific questions when you write or call. Contact the individual sites and begin to request information to give the needed background for your story. But always remember the wide range of possible sources you have at your disposal. A good travel writer, like any reporter, has multiple types of sources.

8. *Use a wide variety of sources*. Many good sources serve the travel industry. These sources are individuals working for hotels, airlines, cruise lines, automobile clubs, and the specific attractions. Many are in public service, such as city and county tourism commissions, state tourism offices and departments, and regional agencies. Many are in private service, representing businesses such as local and state chambers of commerce, tourism cooperatives, and promotional organizations. But you must exercise care in dealing with industry sources because they have a particular point of view to represent and may try to influence you toward their way of thinking.

9. *Call to confirm appointments and visit dates*. Your time is valuable, but so is the time of the person who might be your tour guide or source. To help your work, be reliable and keep promises, such as appointments.

Many offices are set up to deal with drop-in visitors such as journalists. But others are not, so consider the source and determine if the people you need to see will be able to see you at a moment's notice, or if these people need a call ahead of time. It never hurts to call ahead. Use the telephone to your advantage.

USING YOUR OBSERVATIONAL SKILLS

After your research stage is complete, after all the appointments are made, and after you arrive, your reporting work begins. Remember your own senses will be serving as the senses for your readers when the time comes to write the story. Good observational skills are critical here and are developed through discipline and practice.

A good travel writer always has an eye or ear open for new possibilities. There are stories that will develop, unexpectedly, forcing you to abandon part or all of the original plan. You cannot be so rigid as not to consider the chance this will occur.

If you are fortunate, you could encounter a new angle on a story that you planned to write. This will not only be exciting for you, but it will also excite the readers of your story. You must constantly look at the story with the idea there is something new to this approach.

A good observer will use the senses to the fullest and convey the experiences to the reader. Consider colors. Sounds. Smells. Notice textures. Tastes. All of these, if written with the right adjectives and adverbs in your story, will take the reader to that special place that you write about each time.

Finally, another word about writing travel articles. Avoid cliches. There is special temptation to use them to convey impressions. Don't use them, since cliches often turn off readers. Work a bit harder to find the words you need to describe what you saw, heard, or felt. It will pay off.

Below are checklists of major sources for newspaper and magazine travel writers. Some of these sources are important to you because of the organizations they represent. Others are going to be important to you because of the positions they hold within an important travel-oriented organization. The best advice for you is to use them often because they will be there to help you before, during, and after your trip—as well as when you are writing about it.

CHECKLIST: PUBLIC AND PRIVATE TRAVEL SOURCES

Public Sources	Private Sources
Neighborhood tourism offices	Specific attractions
City, county tourism offices	Hotel, motel offices
Multiple-area tourism boards	Development boards
State tourism departments	Airline travel desks
Parks, recreation offices	Airline public relations offices
Public relations firms under contract to local governments	Chambers of Commerce
National tourism offices	Tourism boards
	Business associations
	Local corporations
	Restaurant associations
	Hotel, motel associations

CHECKLIST: HUMAN AND WRITTEN SOURCES

Human Sources	Written Sources
Local editors, reporters	Tour books (annuals)
Tourism directors, staffs	Local authors' books
Hotel staff where you stay	Local newspapers' files
Public information officers	National, regional travel magazines

Managers of attractions
Residents of the area you visit
Tour guides
Shop merchants
Local authors
Local historians
Local museum directors
Cab, bus drivers

Attraction press kits
Telephone directories (usually a local information section)
History section at a local bookstore
Hotel, motel room guest books
Airline in-flight magazines
Auto association guide books
World atlas
U.S. atlas

CHECKLIST: COMMON TRAVEL BOOKS, PERIODICALS

Books

Hotel and Travel Index
Official Hotel and Travel Guide
Arthur Frommer's guides
Fodor's guides
Travel Research Bibliography
AAA Tour Books
Air Traveler's Handbook
Goode's World Atlas
The Travel Writer's Handbook
Steve Birnbaum's guides

Periodicals

Odyssey
ASTA Travel News
Airfare Interline
Conde Nast's Traveler
The Travel Agent
Travel Smart for Business
Southern Living
Sunset
National Geographic
Signature
Frequent Flyer
National Geographic Traveler

Periodicals (continued)

Official Airline Guide
Travel and Leisure
Endless Vacation
Departures
Family Motor Coaching
Travel/Holiday
World Traveling
The Travel Advisor
Travel Smart
Hotel & Travel Index

Newsletters

International Railway Traveler
Entree
The Update
Travel Fit
Offbeat
Traveling Golfer
The Diabetic Traveler
Winston's Travel Deluxe
Around and About Travel
Get Up and Go, the Mature Traveler
Inside Ireland

DESTINATION ARTICLES

One of the oldest, and still the most common, forms of travel writing is the destination piece. These stories are designed to focus on a place the reader might want to visit or has already visited. Generally descriptive, these stories are designed to tell your reader about the place, whether it be an exotic location, such as Honolulu or Singapore, or a more traditional vacation destination, such as Niagara Falls or the Smoky Mountains.

These stories focus on cities or specific attractions. They must be crammed with facts. The reader will be seeking the best information about these locations as possible destinations for a meeting, vacation, or other purpose. Tell the reader what he or she should see. Tell what should be avoided and why. Tell your reader about the major parks and other public facilities. List historical sites. Give details of hours of service, costs, and other necessary information. Where does the reader write for additional information? You should know this and should tell the reader.

Destination stories should be rich in detail and offer direct quotes to back up generalizations about places you have written about. Quote residents and experts. Talk to historians and visit historical sites. Talk to food critics about the best restaurants. Ask other travelers to comment about the same things you experience.

Then summarize the most important facts in a special abstracted form known as the facts box. This will help your reader by being a fast-reference list while he or she is in the car or plane.

Michael Carlton's (1988) article about birding in Great Britain is a good example of the complete destination article. Written from the destination, Kinbrace, Scotland, and Borrobol Lodge, Carlton provides a detailed and descriptive look at this unusual out-of-the-way heaven for birdwatchers in north Scotland. His article comes alive with the peculiar names of the birds, through quotes from the "birders," and through the excitement he felt that permeates the article. He makes readers feel the environment, see the birds, and almost taste the food in the lodge. And he even tells readers that if this place seems interesting but birding isn't that appealing, it is still an intriguing destination for a trip, for there is much more to do than birdwatching.

Carlton's article comes with two boxes of information. First, he provides listings of information sources for readers who want to learn more about Scotland, Borrobol, and the costs of the trip. Second, he lists for readers how to arrange the trip to Kinbrace from the United States. This is helpful for anyone serious about going to Borrobol.

ADDING THE DESTINATION "FACTS BOX"

A popular approach to writing destination features today is to publish a sidebar "facts box" with the story, as you saw in Michael Carlton's article on birdwatching in Scotland. This information goes beyond what is contained in the main article by supplementing the article with an abstract of key information for your reader who skims the section or who is interested in clipping only the most basic information about this destination.

What do you include? Here is a list of the ten most common categories of information for the box:

1. *Directions:* How do you get there? What is the address? How do local visitors get there by car, by train, boat, bus, or other forms of transportation?

2. *Parking:* Where do you park? What is the cost? When does the lot open and close?

3. *Days and hours of operation:* When are the attraction and accompanying facilities open?

4. *General information:* Whom does a visitor contact for general information, such as advance tickets and brochures?

5. *Contact:* What is the contact telephone number and address?

6. *Lodging:* Where can readers stay? Price ranges?

7. *Food and other facilities:* Can you buy food? Restaurants? Price ranges? What other facilities (or the unusual lack of them) are worth mentioning to your reader?

8. *Souvenirs:* Can you buy anything? Is taking anything (e.g., at a national or state park) illegal?

9. *Tours:* Are there organized, regular tours? How do you sign up or reserve space?

10. *Special upcoming events:* What's in store for the current or next season?

SERVICE ARTICLES

One of the most useful types of travel features is the service article. These pieces provide practical and important information to help readers make decisions about an upcoming trip or what to do with their time while on the trip. Service stories also provide another important function because these stories, short or long, offer tips and ideas for simplifying the trip and the means for making the trip.

For example, a travel service story will help your readers negotiate a major international airport, such as Atlanta's Hartsfield, Chicago's O'Hare, or New York's Kennedy, by offering descriptions of the terminal, concourses, parking, other fees, luggage storage, and security policies. These stories will tell your readers when and how to book reservations on cruises or at that popular area resort by providing information such as names and addresses, deposit amounts, and deadlines. Service stories also give tips on getting good camera angles when photographing sites such as national parks or historic neighborhoods or buildings.

To tell someone how to negotiate an airport or public transportation in a foreign country, you have to know the place inside and out. These stories are strongest when they draw upon the experience of the travel writer who has been there. This means you must get out on the road as often as possible to write these articles.

It is not impossible, however, for you to write good service articles from where you work. Many times a story, such as the examples about reservations for a busy vacation spot, can be done by telephone to the right source. Or, if you are writing for a market outside of the region where you live, a local story might be appropriate for that market, and the story would not necessarily require you to leave the office to do it well.

The service article requires good timing to be valuable to your reader. If you want to write the type of story readers will clip and save—sometimes these are called "refrigerator stories" because people clip them to their refrigerators or put them on office bulletin boards—you have to produce the story with sufficient advance timing to get it to the reader when it is needed. Usually this requires months for magazines and weeks for newspapers.

Philadelphia Inquirer travel editor Mike Shoup's (1987) service article on bicycle touring is filled with good ideas for travelers who want to take an unusual vacation—on two wheels. Shoup does not describe scenery or go into detail about the trips he has taken in his first-person perspective on long distance touring by bicycle. Instead, you can see his point of view is to convince readers that bicycle touring is a good travel and vacation idea, and then he proceeds to tell readers how to do it right, step by step.

Shoup offers advice as an experienced bicycle tourist and has no need to go to other authorities for the basics of the article. The article also has a strong consumer perspective, offering prices and advice on equipment needs. For someone who has considered taking a long trip by bicycle, or even someone who has thought about longer local trips in his or her community, this article has real value.

Whereas Shoup's style and voice are highly personal, other service articles do not always follow this more conventional approach. A successful service article in a newspaper or magazine does not even have to be in traditional story form. The 1990s travel sections and departments will continue to provide important travel information in tables, charts, and boxes that stand alone (without a story). These are called informational graphics and are a specialization in the news media today. Yet it will still be the responsibility of the travel writer to gather the information for the graphics artists who compile it with their mastery of art and the computer.

For an effective service article, you must know your traveling readers' information needs. This takes research and a thorough knowledge of the traveler and the reader of your particular market. A writer who does not know the market won't have his or her stories read if they are published, and a free-lance travel writer won't get the stories published very often.

Finally, service articles most frequently take the form of one-shot feature articles. These stories are designed to stand alone. But there are other forms. Some travel editors and writers produce columns that are functional, with service-type information to help consumers make those big decisions about vacations and business trips. And there is the opportunity on certain service subjects to develop a series. Ideas? How about highway safety and auto maintenance in preparing the family car before a long trip?

SPECIAL NEEDS OF MAGAZINES

In the late 1980s, there has been a surge in the number of travel magazines in the United States. There has been a boom in the national and regional travel magazine market. *Traveler* was founded by Conde Nast Publications, its first such publication, in 1987. The period also saw renovations of existing travel magazines such as *Southern Travel* by the New York Times Company and *Travel/ Holiday* by Reader's Digest.

Take a look at any free-lance writing market book (such as *Writer's Digest's* annual volume entitled *Writer's Market*) and you will get a good idea of what magazines want from free-lance travel writers. Most magazines maintain very small in-house staffs of full-time writers. These publications require the services of free-lance writers to fill their space.

What do they want from the free-lancer? Wisconsin's *Odyssey* magazine wants material well in advance, as outlined in a recent edition of *Writer's Market* (Neff, 1988):

> We like short, off-beat articles with some astronomy or space-science tie-in. A recent example: an article about a baseball game that ended with an explosion of a meteorite over the field. Study the styles of the monthly columnists. No general overview articles; for example, a general article on the Space Shuttle, or a general article on Stars. We do not want science fiction articles (pp. 376–377).

Travel & Leisure, a dominant travel magazine produced by American Express Company, depends on free-lance writers for material on travel and vacation places, food, wine, shopping, and sports. Nearly all of the articles for this magazine, however, are assigned to experienced and proven writers. *Travel/ Holiday*, another major travel magazine, seeks destination manuscripts. In *1989 Writer's Market* (Neff, 1988), the magazine editors say:

> Don't ask if we would like to see any articles of San Francisco, France or China. Develop a specific story idea and explain why the destination is so special that we should devote space to it. Are there interesting museums, superb restaurants, spectacular vistas, etc.? Tell us how you plan to handle the piece—convey to us the mood of the city, the charm of the area, the uniqueness of the museums, etc. (p. 619)

You must know the market. As mentioned in earlier chapters, study the magazines before you begin to write for them. Know their particular style of writing and presentation. Know the approaches. Magazines are a tough market, but if you can meet the orders of your editors, you will have a widely presented and widely read article.

TRAVEL COLUMNS

Travel columns are permanent fixtures in most newspapers and many travel-oriented magazines. These columns are given a wide variety of titles, such as "Going Places" in *The Miami News*, "Travel Notes" in the *Akron Beacon Journal* and *Philadelphia Inquirer*, "Q & A For The Traveler" in *The Milwaukee Journal*, or "Travel Questions & Answers" offered by the New York Times News Service. There is also a wide variety of byline formats, such as single author, multiple-author, or just staff credit. Some publications list no credited author.

Smaller publications often depend on syndicated material and wire services for their travel columns or other material that make up an edited travel column. Magazines will depend on free-lance writers to provide material on a regular basis, and editors pay by the item. Syndicated travel columnists cover a variety of subjects. For example, airline industry attorney Donald Pevsner (1988) writes a column, "Travel Wise." Stephen Birnbaum has turned his *Chicago Tribune* column, "Good Questions," into one of the most widely published in the world, syndicated by Tribune Media Services. Michael Carlton's travel writing appears in many daily newspapers nationwide through the Cox News Service.

Travel columns can be used as a collecting point for shorter items that come to your attention but might not make a publishable story on their own merit. Calendar information, such as upcoming events, hours of operation, and free information by mail, fit neatly into a column.

Put together, rewritten into tight form with minimal promotion of the source (such as a commercial enterprise), the information can be practical and go well with the longer features in the section or department. *The Milwaukee Journal*'s "Brief Cases: A Traveler's Advisory" each Sunday is an excellent example of this approach.

The column is also a feature in its own right, with the author taking advantage of the regular space and appearance date (weekly or monthly, for example). In this format, writers such as editors of sections will present their personal perspectives on subjects. Travel editor Mike Shoup of *The Philadelphia Inquirer* handles his column this way.

Many columnists choose this personal approach because of their extensive backgrounds. Whereas this sort of commentary might be inappropriate in other sections or other articles in the travel section, in a column you can express opinions, reactions, interpretations, and generally comment of current travel industry developments.

Donald Pevsner's travel column demonstrates what a functional travel column can accomplish. Each week the consumer advocate–lawyer writes about the most current issues and events in the travel industry. He will write about bargain fares and how to take advantage of ticket pricing policies. Or he will write about the need for automobile rental car insurance. But the consumer approach in his column is sprinkled with his opinions to guide the reader through the maze of travel decisions that must be made in planning an out-of-town business trip or a vacation.

Pevsner's column on new year travel bargains helps readers find the best use of their travel dollars. He focuses on advantages for frequent senior citizen travelers by clearly explaining how the airlines' programs work. He also tells readers about a special deal on the Concorde, the dream trip of many frequent flyers today. His explaining how a trip on Concorde can be made at substantial savings allows readers to benefit from his advice and take a truly memorable air trip.

Travel columns can also be on special topics. *The Milwaukee Journal* often publishes a travel photography column written by D. J. Herda called "In and Out of Focus."

TRAVEL ISSUES TODAY

Travel and recreation have emerged in recent years to become major subjects for coverage by magazines and newspapers. Sections and departments have enlarged beyond simple articles on destinations. Serious articles discussing public and private travel and recreation issues are found today in addition to the more traditional destination piece.

American society is moving in two distinct directions. First, there are individuals who are working more and more hours per week. The percentage of persons working long hours has risen. But second, and even more important, the percentage of unemployed and underemployed has also increased. Researcher Thomas Kando (1980) has written:

"The point is that those persons who have increasing free time on their hands are involuntarily retired, poor, unskilled, chronically unemployed. Thus, there is a growing category of people *condemned to leisure*, as well as a growing minority of persons who, of their own volition, work increasingly hard" (p. 13). Thus, travel and recreation writing should become more and more important content of newspapers and magazines in the years ahead.

National public opinion expert Daniel Yankelovich (1981) has identified what he calls the declining value of work. He says it is apparent there is a significant shift in the attitudes of Americans toward work and success in a relatively short period of time. Other research tells us people do certain things with their leisure time, including travel, and these studies raise certain issues travel writers need to investigate for their readers. Here are six general trends relating to travel and leisure time issues you should consider in your writing:

1. *The idea:* What is the general idea of leisure? What constitutes travel and vacationing patterns in your region?

2. *Types of leisure:* What are the prevailing community types of leisure activities? Vacations? What seem to be the different philosophies about leisure time usage in your area?

3. *Priorities:* How do your readers spend their personal funds on travel and leisure? How do they spend their time? Is it local? On the road? Simply, what do people think, feel, and do about their nonwork time?

4. *Development of attitudes:* You will not only want to know the characteristics of leisure, but you might benefit from understanding how priorities have developed. What are the conditions leading to decisions? What does government policy toward travel and recreation/leisure have to do with it? What are the influences of the private sector?

5. *Social problems:* For a reporter using this approach, you can ask: "What are the different leisure/travel needs of different sectors of the community/market I serve?"

6. *Promotion:* What are the best ways a community can promote its travel and tourism? What are the roles of government and the private sector?

Economics alone cannot explain leisure and travel activities. It is difficult, if not impossible, to split the economic from the social, political, and technical, according to sociologist Max Kaplan (1975).

HOW PROFESSIONALS WROTE IT

DATE: SATURDAY, JANUARY 9, 1988
SOURCE: MIAMI NEWS, P. 3C
AUTHOR: MICHAEL CARLTON, COX NEWS SERVICE

* * *

SCOTLAND'S BORROBOL LODGE A BIRDWATCHER'S FLIGHT OF FANCY

KINBRACE, Scotland—It is 10:30 p.m. in the wild Scottish Highlands, the graying of the evening. Walking on a pebbled drive wet with the evening rain, the traveler can hear the river, and the throaty mutterings of two English setters settling down for the night, and the creak of a single gate as the gamekeeper opens it into the night.

It is the end of a long day in the field, a day of harriers and golden plovers and the evocative calls of curlews. A birder's day.

Here at Borrobol Lodge, at the top of Scotland, on a wild moor closer to the Arctic Circle than to London, the birders are snug in their beds, dreaming of kittiwakes and gannets, wheatears and pied wagtails.

The traveler is on his first birding expedition, and is confused—and amused—by the passion of the three couples who have spent thousands of dollars to come to this wild and remote place at the north end of Great Britain. They have come from

Jacksonville, Fla., and Philadelphia and Winnetka, Ill., to spend long, wet days tramping through the heather and the Scottish broom to spot a single golden plover. "He's beautiful," shouts one. "Yes, he is a good bird, isn't he?" agrees another.

Later—post-plover—the birders push into 50 mph winds, climb the skinny neck of a rock outcropping called Strathy Point and crawl along a cliff to see a family of puffins, all black and white and orange and yellow. A comical bird; a comical group of people, at least to the traveler, who now knows where the expression "crazy as a loon" may have its genesis.

But the traveler may be a strange bird, too, for as the week goes on, he begins to become more interested. He is anxious to be the first to spot an arctic skua or a razorbill and is pleased by the group's enthusiastic "well done!" when he points out an oyster catcher on the wing. He has become a birder too, albeit an inept one.

By becoming a birder, the traveler has joined many others. A recent study completed for the U.S. Fish and Wildlife Service claimed there are at least 2 million highly committed birders in America, people who watch regularly, use a field guide, keep a life list and are able to identify 100 or more species of birds.

Another 7 million are fairly interested (able to identify at least 40 species), and 60 million—or one American in four—are at least casual birders.

More than 600,000 field guides to birds are sold each year in the United States, most notably Roger Tory Peterson's classic "Field Guide to the Birds of Eastern and Central North America," which has sold more than 3.5 million copies since its introduction in 1934. Our feathered friends are a big business, generating more than $14 billion in sales of binoculars, spotting scopes, cameras and exotic trips last year.

One of the more exotic birding trips is this seven-day journey to Scotland's Birding Brigadoon—Borrobol Lodge.

From late April through July, Borrobol hosts six birders each week, folks who travel halfway around the world to see the vast seabird colonies of this part of Scotland, to spy on cliffs on which a quarter of a million birds raise their young and spend the short summer. These great "bird cities" are among the largest concentrations of sea birds in the world.

Borrobol sits in the midst of 22,000 acres of land, all inherited by 35-year-old journalist Michael Ian Wigan, who combined his good fortune with his love of bird watching and now hosts fellow birders in his turn-of-the-century Edwardian sporting lodge.

When they are not out in the field, Wigan's guests are well looked after in the lodge, with its high-ceilinged bedrooms (three bedrooms share two upstairs baths), gracious pine-paneled formal dining room and drawing room where a fire crackles each night to draw the Scottish chill from tired bones.

Meals at Borrobol, prepared by a young Swiss chef, are splendid affairs: red grouse and venison, salmon and lamb and—for breakfast—kippers and deer sausage. Wine flows freely at dinner, and the conversation is of politics and fashion—as well as birds—for this is a well-educated group (two physicians, a lawyer and two journalists) with eclectic interests. Before the chime sounds at 8:30 for the main meal, birders sit in the drawing room and sip single malt, 103-proof whiskey, and conversations begin. All this is included in the price of the stay. And, of course, one does dress for dinner, old chap.

All is very civilized at Borrobol, from the seven-passenger Citroen that whisks birders from point to point, to the walking sticks one can borrow for a march over the moors. The only uncivil part of a Borrobol visit is the weather, which often howls fiercely and always—it seems as one tugs off soaking pants each evening—rains.

But weather doesn't daunt true birders, who ignore the wind and the mists as they search the skies and the meadows, the cliffs and the ponds, for birds. As many as 125 different species of birds have been spotted in a week at Borrobol, few of them found in North America.

That is what brings the birders here—the chance to return home with a bird list that none of one's birder friends can match.

But even non-birders will find a visit to Borrobol intriguing. There are great herds of red deer to be seen, the brutal beauty of the Highlands to enchant and salmon to be caught.

Trips can be arranged. Magnificent Dunrobin Castle, the seat of the Dukes of Sutherland, is a short drive away, and tours of the charming Laidhay Croft Museum to see how Scottish farmers lived 200 years ago are popular, as is golf at nearby Dornoch, one of the world's best courses. You can take a ferry across the pounding North Sea to the Orkney Islands to see ruins from a society 4,000 years old or stray on the mainland and visit the Cairns of Camster, burial chambers dating to 2500 B.C.

There are gatherings of fat, brown hares on the Borrobol lawn each evening, and pubs in towns such as Thurso, where you can have a first-rate drink and a second-rate meal.

There are no tourists about—or almost none—so the adventurer can meet the locals, not some guy from Indianapolis or Munich. There are no crowds, almost no traffic, and white-sand beaches are wide and empty.

This part of Scotland is seldom seen, little visited, as wild and thundering as it was a century ago before hordes of tourists descended on Great Britain from the colonies.

That is why the birds are here, and why the birders come and why a week at Borrobol Lodge is one of the most fulfilling vacations the traveler has enjoyed in his many years walking the pathways of this Earth.

Reprinted with permission of Cox News Service.

* * *

(INFORMATION FOR TRAVEL BOX WITH MAIN ARTICLE)

Information: For more information, contact Josephine Barr, the U.S. booking agent for Borrobol, at 519 Park Ave., Kenilworth, Ill. 60043 (800-323-5463). The address of Borrobol is Kinbrace, Sutherland KW11 6UB, United Kingdom. Because only six birders are accommodated at a time and the season is short (April 30–July 23 in 1988), it is advisable to book as early as possible.

For general tourism information on Scotland, contact the British Tourist Authority, 40 W. 57th St., New York, N.Y. 10019 (212-581-4708).

Rates: A week at Borrobol costs $995 per person, double occupancy. The price includes all meals, accommodations, bird expeditions and drinks. An optional two-day trip to the Orkney Islands is available for an additional $300 per person. A one-day trip with no overnight is $60.

Reprinted with permission of Cox News Service.

* * *

(INFORMATION FOR IF-YOU-GO BOX WITH MAIN ARTICLE)

If you go:

Borrobol is most easily reached by taking the train from Inverness to Kinbrace, which is only a few miles from the lodge. You are picked up at the station. The lodge is 1½ hours by car from Wick, two hours from Inverness.

British Caledonian and Delta fly between Atlanta and London's Gatwick Airport; Dan Air flies between London's Heathrow Airport and Inverness (helicopter, rail, taxi and bus transportation is available between the two airports). Fares depend on season, advance purchase and other factors; check with travel agents, or the airlines, for more information and reservations.

Reprinted with permission of Cox News Service.

•••

DATE: SUNDAY, AUGUST 30, 1987
SOURCE: THE PHILADELPHIA INQUIRER, P. R3.
AUTHOR: MIKE SHOUP

• • •

LONG-DISTANCE BICYCLING, YOU CAN IF YOU WANT TO

The two responses I hear most often when the talk turns to long-distance bicycle trips are (1) that sounds great, and (2) I could never do it. My inevitable rejoinder is (1) you're right, and (2) baloney.

For many, especially those past the age of 35, bicycling seems to carry with it some of the same mystery as skiing—it's something exciting that others do. But, if my own experience and observation are any measure, there are only two essential ingredients to a successful and enjoyable bicycle trip: a spirit of adventure and a bicycle. And that comes from somebody who never biked more than 20 miles in a day, nor skied for that matter, until well past the age of 40. Yet today, I count both sports as major, pleasurable pastimes.

You do have to be in good condition, however, and for any major long-distance bicycle riding, it's probably best to have a full physical exam and perhaps even a stress test. This is especially true if smoking, drinking or overeating are among your pleasurable pursuits.

Just as there is no great need to go out and buy all sorts of bicycle clothing and equipment, it's not necessary to join a gym and pump a lot of iron to get into condition—even if you are so wimpy that scrawny teen-agers kick sand in your face at the beach. There's no better way to condition your body than by just riding the bicycle, and you can supplement that with walking or running, or aerobic and stretching exercises at home.

Through it all, listen closely to your body; not even your doctor knows it as intimately as you do. For example, because I often ride in the heat of summer, I have learned the hard way that it is absolutely necessary to stay hydrated. I drink a lot of water, often supplementing it with orange juice or

Gatorade. Before a recent 1,000-mile trip to northwest Michigan, I was assured by a trusted doctor that this would be sufficient in the heat. Yet I know that my body was badly out of balance until I began taking buffered salt and potassium tablets a week into the trip.

Now, if you are still with me at this point, you've probably got the spirit of adventure. A few words about the bicycle:

Those who feel fairly certain that they'll just be riding occasionally, for short distances, should probably stick with a bottom-of-the-line model, which will cost somewhere between $159 and $229. This bike will be of steel components and weigh in the vicinity of 30 pounds.

If you're contemplating riding more than a dozen times a year, with even one long-distance trip, my advice is to consider stepping up to the next model line, where the price range is something like $279 to $329. This will buy a bike with alloy parts that weighs 24 pounds—you'd be surprised what the six-pound difference does—and has quick-release front and rear wheels.

A bicycle of this kind should be entirely serviceable for trips and, if treated well, will last until you either trade up or leave it to rust in the basement.

• EQUIPMENT. Friends who have fallen tell me that their last recollections before passing out in pain have been to hear the bang of the helmet on pavement. This has turned me into a believer in helmets, an absolute believer when riding in city or suburban traffic.

Beyond that, you should acquire a bike pump, a tire-repair kit and spare tube, the essential tools and a small bag to carry all this. Anybody who gets the least bit serious will want to add a lightweight luggage rack in the rear to carry things on day trips.

My own experience with both touring and racing handlebars—the latter being the ones that curve down and force you to lean forward—leads me to strongly advise racing handlebars except, perhaps, for those who are sure they'll never go beyond the novice stage. When you buy the bike, be sure that it fits you properly and you've got the seat at the right height.

As for rear-view mirrors, I've never found anyone touting them. While you're looking to see what's behind—something totally beyond your control anyway—you're going to hit glass or a rock, or run off the edge of the road and fall.

Once you begin to get serious about biking, you'll want to add toe clips to give you added pedaling power. For overnight trips, there are now front handlebar bags on the market that clip onto a simple bracket and are big enough to hold a camera, basic tools and a change of clothes. This type of bag also can be a later supplement to rear panniers, if you decide to take longer trips. Gloves are essential for longer trips; the extra padding absorbs road shock and minimizes wrist and shoulder pain. Speedometers are great fun, especially the more expensive digitals that cost between $50 and $60.

When you really get serious, you'll know it. You'll be taking junk like luggage racks, kickstands and bag brackets off the bike, or you'll start to consider a custom bike or new and better components for your old one. You'll definitely buy biking shoes. Maybe you'll even buy biking clothes.

• CLOTHES. A good many veterans absolutely swear by biking shorts, which can cost $40 a pair and more. I can only tell you this: I've used $10 nylon running shorts for years with a sheepskin seat cover and never had any problems. On a trip of more than 1,000 miles, I had only minor chafing; my companion wore bicycle shorts, and by his own account, he had a very sore rear end in half the mileage.

You need absolutely none of that colorful gear you occasionally see on the road. In fact, you may delight, as I do, in zipping by these peacocks wearing a simple T-shirt and shorts.

• COMMON FEARS. The only major ones I know are falling or getting hit by a car. Any biker will tell you that the first is inevitable if you spend enough time on the road. You have to accept the second as a possibility. Minimalize the risk by never riding at night. Ride to the side of the road, but remember that, in most states, you have equal rights with automobiles. Riding too close to the edge, or running off the road into the dirt just because some fool behind you blows the horn, is a sure prescription for a bad fall.

• FLATS AND MECHANICAL FAILURES. In thousands of riding miles, I've never had a flat. I attribute this to keeping the tires slightly underinflated from the recommended pressure; others might argue to the contrary. A bicycle is not that complicated; and there's no reason you can't make minor adjustments yourself in emergencies; any bike shop worth its salt will sell good repair handbooks.

Beyond that, the best advice is to find a good bike shop somewhere reasonably close to home, where the proprietors will take enough time to answer your questions and be receptive when you come back for repairs or additional equipment. These shops are often the best source of information about bicycle clubs, where you can find organized rides or, perhaps more important, meet a compatible companion or two to ride with at your own discretion.

Bicycle tours are offered the world over; if your travel agent is in the dark about them, try a good bookstore.

Happy biking. And hey—be careful out there, will you?

Reprinted with the permission of the author and *The Philadelphia Inquirer*.

• • •

DATE: SUNDAY, JANUARY 3, 1988
SOURCE: THE MIAMI HERALD, P. 6J
AUTHOR: DONALD PEVSNER, COLUMNIST, SPECIAL TO THE HERALD

• • •

TRAVEL WISE COLUMN
AIRLINES TOAST NEW YEAR WITH 2 OUTSTANDING BARGAINS

1988 is here, and with it, two outstanding travel bargains:

• SENIOR CITIZEN AIR PASSES: Several airlines, including Eastern and TWA, have offered annual air passes for senior citizens during the past five or so years. The passes work like this: You pay a flat annual fee, with supplements for foreign travel in most cases, and can fly for a year on the issuing airline's system. Various restrictions apply to reservations, frequency of use between two specific cities and so on.

There has always been a major psychological stumbling-block present on all air pass purchases: the buyer must seriously wonder whether he will, in fact, get his money's worth. Eastern Air Lines has just revised its air pass offering—and it is now one of the great travel buys. The Eastern "Get-Up-And-Go Passport" air pass has been reduced from $1,299 to $999 for all sales through Jan. 31, 1988, only. And, for the first time, there is a so-called "guarantee" included, which is not available from any other airline.

Here's how it works:

If, after your pass year is up, you feel that you have not really received $999 worth of air travel, you have 60 days to claim a phenomenal offer from Eastern. In exchange for a $25 processing fee, the airline will recalculate the value of the trips you flew, based on the lowest published adult air fares it offered in the market at the time you flew—whether or not these lowest fares were available on the flights you took—and will refund any difference to you.

This means that, as a worst case, your $999 air pass fee will serve as a hedge against not being able to obtain the lowest, "MaxSaver"-type fares on every Eastern domestic flight you take for a full year. All this hedge really costs you out-of-pocket is the $25 processing fee, and the interest you would have earned on the $999 sales price—say about $60.

There are a few catches, as always, on a deal this terrific. They include:

(a) You must be at least 62 years of age to buy the Eastern air pass. (For TWA's you must be 65. The TWA air pass costs $1,399 and offers no after-the-fact refund guarantee.)

(b) A companion air pass is available at $999, for a traveler of any age—but you two must travel together at all times.

(c) You may fly no more than three times a year between the same two Eastern cities—this cuts out the weekly commuting senior citizen. But there is a good ploy available to boost this number of trips. Eastern counts Miami and Fort Lauderdale airports as one city for air-pass purposes; the same goes for the New York City airports of JFK, La Guardia and Newark; and the three Washington, D.C.-area airports of National, Dulles and Baltimore-Washington.

But you can fly to a nearby airport three additional times! Use West Palm Beach, Key West, Fort Myers, Sarasota or Orlando for South Florida after you have used up your "direct" flights allotment.

(d) Reservations may be made no earlier than one week before your departure, and two weeks before your return, on any trip.

(e) Travel is limited to noon Mondays through noon Thursdays, plus all day Saturday. (A few short holiday-period blackouts apply.) And no more than one trip per week may be flown.

For $300 more, Eastern adds its 17 Caribbean destinations to the pot, if you buy by Jan. 31. And an all-first-class option costs $500 more for a full year.

The base price goes back to $1,299 on Feb. 1. For details, call Eastern at (800) 225-8300 (for a brochure) or (800) EASTERN.

• SPECIAL CONCORDE DEAL: It's no secret that the sleek, supersonic Concorde is the ultimate in air travel. But flying 1,340 miles per hour at up to 60,000 feet costs a fortune—British Airways charges $2,999 one-way from New York to London ($2,936 Miami–London; $2,759 Washington–London).

It is sometimes forgotten that Air France, too, flies the Concorde, once daily, from New York to Paris. And this carrier is repeating last year's offer: Buy a round-trip New York–Paris Concorde ticket on an American Express Card, and you'll fly for the ordinary subsonic first-class fare both ways.

The standard round-trip first-class fare from New York to Paris is $3,670 compared to the New York–London fare of $4,560. The Air France Concorde deal, at $3,760, gives you two trans-Atlantic Concorde crossings for just $1,346 more than the cheapest round-trip New York–London business-class fare. Air France also throws in a free night in the Crillon, George V or Plaza Athenee Hotel in Paris—worth $300 to $400.

This offer is good only for travel originating in the United States between Jan. 1 and Feb. 29, 1988, and all reservations must be made at least 48 hours before departure. Air France information (800) 237-2777.

Have a supersonic New Year!

Donald L. Pevsner is a Miami lawyer and consumer advocate. Though his legal clients include General Rent-A-Car and Eastern Airlines, the opinions expressed in this column are strictly his own.

Reprinted with the permission of the author and *The Miami Herald*.

A Professional's Point of View

By Mike Shoup
Philadelphia Inquirer

Travel writing by its very nature tends to be positive, but that doesn't mean it has to be puffery, and it certainly doesn't mean that normal standards of fairness and accuracy can be ignored or compromised. There is simply no substitute for good, old-fashioned reporting with pen and note book. If the facts aren't there, or they are wrong (and my finding is that this is often the case), the story will simply never get off the ground.

My wall is practically papered with the humorous errors of would-be-writers, including no less than 37 wrong spellings of my last name—Shupe, Shamp, Shout, Sharp, Shroup, Short, Schub, Shoop and Soup, to mention but a few. And my reasoning is this: If the writer can't get the editor's name right, what guarantee is there that any place or name spellings in his story are correct?

Travel writing is not simple. I receive from 50 to 100 manuscripts a week in my job and reject 99 percent of them. Some are inaccurate, some are sophomoric, but most are just plain boring, dull and lifeless. It doesn't have to be that way.

Those who are not brilliant writers (and most of us aren't) should look for the details and nuances that make one part of the globe different from another. It is these same details that breathe life into a narrative and make each story different from the next. Writers should employ concrete examples rather than hyperbole, and be sparing with the use of adjectives.

Most travel stories written for newspapers seem to occur in a vacuum that excludes humanity—there are no people in them. It doesn't hurt any to inject characters into a story, when and if they fit.

The best stories, in my opinion, accurately reflect the whole travel experience, whether good or bad. They also reflect preparation and research, and often have a historical or societal perspective. It is difficult, for example, to write a travel story about Mexico City without at least mentioning the air pollution, or the street beggars. This does not mean it is necessary to dwell on such subjects, but mentioning them in passing gives the reader the idea that he is, after all, in the real world and not in some make-believe La-La Land invented by a travel writer whose trip is paid for by the Mexican government.

My final word would be my first: There is no substitute for basic reporting and writing skills. Those intent on travel writing—or any form of writing—will find a year or two of newspaper reporting invaluable.

Meanwhile, yes, it is Soup. But with an "H," please. (Shoup, personal communication, 1988)

* * *

Mike Shoup is travel editor of *The Philadelphia Inquirer*, a position he has held for 9 years. He has also served as managing editor of *Inquirer Magazine* during his 18 years at the newspaper. He enjoys biking, hiking, running, gardening, and yes, traveling.

12

Service Articles

Miami Herald columnist and suburban features writer Jill Singer is the mother of twins. She has turned her decade of raising these children into the subject of a column called "Parenting." It appears in the newspaper's Living Today section and is based in large part on her own experiences as a suburban working mother. Each time her column appears, she tells readers how she has mastered another aspect of being a parent. Her column topics vary widely. One column recounted how she was able to apply the tricks she had learned from her own experiences and the advice of an expert on "parent survival training" with her own family. Re-creating scenes, dialogue, and reactions, she related what happened when she tried in her own home "to make some changes around here" (Singer, 1987, p. 1B).

Not far way, *Orlando Sentinel* writer Diane Hubbard Burns (1987) also used a book as an idea for a how-to feature article for her newspaper. Burns talked with the two authors of the book, *Parent Survival Training*, and based her 3-page advice-filled article on what she learned from the book and her interview. Her story outlines specific methods parents can use to deal with childhood tantrums.

Like Singer's column and Burns' feature article, many feature articles are written as a *service* to readers. These articles are not necessarily "news" in the sense that we usually talk about news. But the service feature article is an important part of any newspaper or magazine today, and readers depend on these articles as part of their total newspaper or magazine package. These articles help readers do something better; they help make life easier.

These articles are usually found in the how-to-do-it form, but also are found in the form of listings, "art of living" articles, and chronological case summaries. We will focus on "how-to articles" in this chapter.

The *how-to article* explains how something is made, built, cooked, protected, purchased, or otherwise accomplished by an expert on the subject. These articles are often found in home and garden sections, food/cooking sections, and increasingly in consumer-based sections of newspapers and in the similarly named departments of magazines.

Steve Dupler's (1987) article about modern record production in *Popular Mechanics* is an example of how a reader can learn in an article how something is done. As in the case of Dupler's in-depth cover article on the high-tech world of a recording studio, most readers will never have a chance to try to produce a recording. But most readers do enjoy recorded music—records, tapes, and compact discs. So, many readers have a natural curiosity about how the creative works of individuals such as Stevie Wonder and Quincy Jones are made and polished. Dupler's article explains it.

The how-to article is the most frequently published form of service article. It is certainly a popular story form with editors, says Prof. Louis Alexander (1975). "In this pragmatic era in a pragmatic nation, Americans look more and more to magazines to advise them and show them how to do the things that are important in their lives" (p. 213), he writes.

Listings have become more interesting in recent years in both newspapers and magazines. Sports sections of newspapers and sports-oriented magazines use lists of records and interesting trivia as regular features for readers. Business- and finance-oriented publications frequently run lists of top businesses, top salaries of executives, real estate transactions, and so on. Feature sections of newspapers and city and regional magazines have for many years listed in calendar form the major events of an upcoming weekend or month and have listed top restaurants and theaters in their circulation areas.

Art-of-living articles teach us how to get more out of life. These are inspirational articles many times, with readers feeling uplifted after reading about someone else's skill at making his or her life better. Sometimes these articles (and books) are called self-help articles and are often simply no more than narratives or essays that affect readers in one way or another and give them ideas about how to improve their own lives or the lives of family members or friends. These articles include subjects such as retirement, love and family relationships, and making tough decisions.

Chronological case summaries teach us about something by looking at a particular example in depth. Readers are served by the lesson learned from the case history. These can include descriptions of purchasing a house, curing a medical problem, or resolving a conflict between neighbors.

The approaches to these articles are not limited to single articles. There are entire magazines that specialize in how-to journalism, for example. One such publication is *Personal Investor*, which calls itself "the how-to magazine of investing" on the cover. This magazine began in 1985 and is based in California.

Books have been written on hundreds of subjects to help readers in the same way—everything from career choices, resume writing, and job hunting to personal finance, automobile repair, and relationships with the opposite sex.

TWO BASIC APPROACHES TO SERVICE ARTICLES

Although *service article* seems self-explanatory, there is more to it than the name indicates. The best service articles provide information, the sole reason for the reader using the article at all. By providing information, you are offering your readers the best advice you can find on the subject. This is done in a readable fashion, but at the same time in the clearest way possible because you are explaining how something works or how something is done.

The service article, like personal experience feature articles, takes two fundamental reporting and writing approaches:

1. *Writer-as-expert perspective:* Many how-to articles are written by individuals who are experts on the subject. As writers, they are able to communicate their expertise to persons who want to know about the subject. Merrill Lynch, the financial services firm, has published numerous editions of its 10-page booklet, *How to Read a Financial Report*, since it was first published in 1973. The firm's expertise adds credibility and authority to the effort.

You can often write as an expert from your own personal experiences, thus combining the best elements of a personal experience feature with a service how-to feature. John Wasik accomplished this when he wrote a "Money Matters" feature for the *San Antonio Light* in 1987 about complaining. His article, headlined "How to draft a complaint" was based on his own experiences with a troublesome automobile. Through his difficulties, he turned frustration into a sound feature article that teaches other readers the correct steps to take—the "proper channels," as he described them—when a complaint about workmanship is necessary.

2. *Someone-else-as-expert perspective:* This is the more common approach to how-to service articles. This approach requires you as a writer to find some expert on a topic and relate in detail to readers how he or she does the activity. Finding these experts is relatively easy—there are hundreds of them in your own community at colleges and universities, government offices, and in private business. In this story, your task is equal to that of the reporter-as-expert approach by which you take the approach of the expert and tell

readers how he or she does it. Many times, these articles are primarily for enjoyment and not necessarily to be used by the reader to improve his or her lifestyle. *Miami Herald* feature writer Jane Wooldridge (1984) took this approach when she wrote an article telling men how to grow a proper beard. Wooldridge contacted local experts—barbers, hair designers, and even a dermatologist–author of a book on home skin care. But the one source she could not use on this story was herself!

SUBJECTS BEST SUITED FOR SERVICE ARTICLES

Possibly because there are so many subjects and sources available for how-to, lists and other service articles, some experts feel writing how-to articles is one of the easiest ways to break into print. Feature writers Clay Schoenfeld and Karen Diegmueller (1982) make that point when discussing service features.

Subjects that readers want to learn about tend to make the best service articles. These are day-to-day "how-to-live better" subjects of a rather routine and practical nature. These include subjects on personal health care, fashion, car and home repair/care, home and office decoration, gardening, food preparation, money and finance, shopping, and a variety of arts and crafts subjects. You will find that readers often depend on their hometown newspapers and regularly read magazines for advice on living better.

You should also be concerned about your own attention span in dealing with a subject. For service articles, pick subjects you really care about and have interest in. This makes your efforts much less painful when you have to spend a large amount of time learning about the subject.

What are hot service topics? If you are a good researcher, use your skills to compile unusual idea lists. How-to articles can include a variety of topics outside home and garden usuals, such as how to hang wallpaper or how to grow a bonsai exhibit. Include timely and socially or financially important topics, such as how to survive sex in the era of the Acquired Immunodeficiency Syndrome (AIDS) or how to survive the extreme ups and downs of the stock market.

If you are not the expert in such complex stories as AIDS and securities, then you must locate authorities on the subjects to help you do the story—just like the *Orlando Sentinel*'s Diane Hubbard Burns (1987) did by interviewing child psychologists on how to survive children's tantrums. But a problem with these stories is simple enough: some experts make a living from their expert advice, and they might therefore be reluctant to share it with a newspaper or magazine writer. The result, many times, is the need to go to several local or national authorities on the same subject to put together your story.

Writer's Digest contributing editor Art Spikol (1984) says his best advice for how-to writers is to pick the right subject. "The secret of success is to identify a need that isn't being sufficiently filled, and to fill it. In other words, take on a job that nobody else wants" (p. 15). This is the case for service articles, he says. "If you weigh the time you must put into them against the money you earn from them, you have to strain to reach the poverty level. That's the bad news. It's also the good news, because that's one of the reasons that nobody else wants to do them" (p. 15).

Spikol says service articles should do leg work for readers. You become the reader's helper. If you can select subjects that do this, you will have a successful service article. He points out their importance today: "They sell magazines. They're staples, often staff-written, at many publications. Especially today, when special-interest publications abound" (p. 15).

To get assignments from your ideas, Spikol recommends querying editors with a few ideas *before* investing time and money. This way, if an editor likes an idea but wants slightly different focus or different sources, you can make the changes early in your work.

SHARING YOUR EXPERTISE
AND WRITING AUTHORITATIVELY

When you have first-hand expertise in a subject, it is easy to speak with the voice of authority. For example, a journalism graduate student at the University of Miami combined her interest in magazine writing with a specialty in South Florida wild animal life (she has a major in zoology). Some students double major in college and can use a second major with their journalism major as a speciality. Regardless of how you obtain it, your expertise should dominate the article. Without conscious effort, it might become difficult for you to write for readers who do not know the subject as well as you do.

When you know the ins-and-outs of a subject, you know the detail and precision needed for such service writing. But when you do not and you are a feature writer with no particular speciality or are just starting out, then you must be able to give your articles the sense of authoritativeness when you go to other sources for your expert information.

Leonard McGill (1984), author of how-to books such as *Stylewise: A Man's Guide to Looking Good,* says you can accomplish the same type of firsthand authoritativeness in your writing even if you go to other sources for your how-to article.

"Two traits are essential: Curiosity. And a willingness to use your inquisitive pick and shovel to unearth information that makes you sound authoritative" (p. 26), he says. "I've recently sold articles on how to order clothing from Hong Kong, how to combine various sports in an exercise program, and how to cut the cost of shaving. Before researching these subjects, I knew about as much about them as I do about building submarines. Nothing." (p. 26).

McGill recommends that you seek four types of information when doing this research:

1. Specific descriptions.
2. "Subject-bound" terminology.
3. Concrete examples.
4. Expert facts.

As McGill says, experts talk shop by using specifics. They just do not generalize. If you are writing about bicycles, for example, you just do not talk bicycles. There are racing bicycles, sport/touring bicycles, all-terrain bicycles, and women's bicycles—four basic types. And then you can begin talking about frames, gearing, brake systems, rims, tires, and hubs.

Take this specific type of description, combined with correct technical language used by the bicycle industry (terms such as freewheel, derailleur, crankset, or head tube angle), and you can write with the authority of a veteran. Current examples make these terms come to life—discussing whether or not to get a Sun Tour brand or Shimano brand front or rear derailleur on a sport/touring bicycle begins to make sense to readers when applications are made (e.g., a specific brand bicycle such as a Fuji Sagres SP or Ross Centaur). Facts, such as the number of new products on the market or prices, make the story practical and useful.

When you are writing authoritatively about something you actually know little about, you must consult as many different sources as possible. The wide variety and diversity will give you insurance against conflicting information and advice. McGill warns of two things:

1. Make certain you are not presenting opinion instead of facts. Multiple sources will help filter out opinion.

2. Present the facts and instructions as yours, not someone else's. A number of interviews with different sources will lead you to certain conclusions of your own and make this easier to do. You do become authoritative on your own in this way.

McGill advises against overuse of the pronoun "you" in how-to articles. Most editors complain about this, he says. Do not rely on it; use it in a limited fashion.

ORGANIZING SERVICE ARTICLES

The general formula for a how-to service feature takes three steps:

1. An *introduction* tells what the story will accomplish. This lead portion of the article contains a paragraph that is a statement of purpose. It helps the reader so he or she does not have to struggle with your article to figure out what will be gained from reading it.

Writer Leonard McGill recommends "letting readers know you will teach them something valuable" (p. 28). State the benefits of your advice, he says. Tell readers you are going to help them solve a problem, if that is the point of your article.

2. The *step-by-step procedures* you are providing the reader make up the main body of the article. This is detailed and leaves no guessing. You must be careful to explain all steps with the assumption that your reader does not know certain basic points about the process.

McGill says readers expect information in how-to articles in a "cadence" approach. This means writing the body of the article in a cookbook style, a style that is most effective in the instructional portions of the article. For example, you might write four quick, short sentences: Collect tools: drill, bits, ruler, pencil, dry wall mount. Measure location of picture. Drill hole. Screw mount into wall. "Readers expect to receive how-to information in such a cadence" (p. 28), he says.

3. A bit of *final advice* for your reader is offered in the conclusion. Tips might hint at trouble shooting, set-up, or maintenance, for example.

Writer Art Spikol (1984) urges that you create a chart to help keep organized when producing service articles. "List everything you want to know about whatever it is you are investigating" (p. 16), he says. "In constructing such a chart, you might begin by listing the names, addresses, and phone numbers" (p. 16) of your primary sources, along with other essential information about the sources.

In short, a key to success is being organized when gathering facts. This should also benefit you when you begin to write the article itself.

Your urge to keep the article brief might have to be quelled in the interest of clarity in service features. Additional words, used in the right places, might make the difference in a positive direction in this type of feature writing.

A good way to double-check your approach is to write a rough draft and then ask someone who knows absolutely nothing about the subject to read it to see if the article makes sense. This way you will likely spot unclear passages before you send the article to your editor. You want to be certain to eliminate ambiguous or vague content that would lead to guessing on the part of readers. Because you are often so familiar with the material, it is easy to lose sight of a detail that someone unfamiliar with the process will easily spot. On the other hand, if you are unfamiliar with the material, you might have the same problem spotting problems with details.

But even after you have checked your article, your newspaper or magazine will also give it a thorough once-over. For example, many major newspapers and magazines test new food recipes and review other how-to food articles before publication in their own kitchens or in the kitchens of experts. Editors for how-to publications such as *Popular Mechanics* check potential how-to articles by building the furniture or equipment or by testing repair hints in labs or workshops before an article is published.

USING ILLUSTRATIONS WITH YOUR ARTICLE

One way to strengthen your article by making it clearer to readers is to use analogies. This helps you look more authoritative, writer Leonard McGill says, and readers understand better.

But if you have the chance, illustrations will make things even clearer. Many how-to articles are presented with illustrations to help describe the process, a critical step, or even the final product. These charts, graphs, diagrams, photographs, or tables are used to clarify your article's content.

Charts and tables will serve as summaries of steps, outlined one at a time, or perhaps as rundowns of costs or options.

Graphs and diagrams can show pictorally how steps or stages in a procedure tie together. As an expert on the subject, you should work closely with artists to make certain such graphs are correct to every detail.

Much of the time, photographs do the trick. Photographers will pose the subject matter as an illustration, and the photograph is presented with your article. You should attempt to tie the photo in with references to it in the text of your article. Collaborating with editors and photographers makes the total package work better. The tasks of writing and preparing artwork for how-to or other service features should be team efforts if possible. Most editors appreciate the advice and assistance.

POPULARITY OF HOW-TO ARTICLES AND BOOKS

There are countless how-to books on the market today, many which have grown out of original newspaper or magazine articles.

One recent how-to book is Stafford Whiteaker's *English Garden Embroidery: 80 Original Needlepoint Designs of Flowers, Fruit and Animal*, published in 1988 by Ballantine. This book is unique because it combines usually unrelated subjects of needle art and flower gardening in one volume. Steven Jay Fogel and Mark Bruce Rosin wrote *The Yes-I-Can Guide to Mastering Real Estate*, published in 1987 by Times Books-Random House.

A look at the *1989 Writer's Market* shows a large number and wide variety of publishers involved in producing these specialty books. The 1989 edition presents an entire section of listings of both major and minor publishers who consider manuscripts on this subject.

Specifically, one hot category in recent years has been self-improvement. The *1989 Writer's Market* also contains a two-plus page section listing five publications that seek manuscripts on psychology and self-help, including

Psychology Today. The section heading describes the demand for these types of articles: "These publications focus on psychological topics, how and why readers can improve their own outlooks, and how to understand people in general. Many general interest publications also publish articles in these areas (p. 447). *Psychology Today* is the leader in this category. Editors recommend queries on subjects within psychology and other social and behavioral sciences.

How-to audio- and video-tapes are also popular today, evolving from articles and books on personal development subjects (exercise and stress management), sports subjects (golf and tennis), and personal finance (real estate and stock market investments).

COMPILING LISTS

It is not unusual to find stand-alone lists in today's newspapers and magazines. However, you can enhance your service feature by combining the best of the narrative article with a listing. The listing becomes a sidebar or remains a major portion or purpose for the article.

These approaches are often given titles such as "Ten Richest Women in the State" or "Five Steps to Losing Weight Overnight."

Newspapers such as *USA Today* have capitalized on the curiosity lists arouse in readers. Combining the *USA Today* staff talent for inviting graphics, these lists often are provided as a visual feature for readers.

To be successful at listings, you have to have a creative energy for research. Compiling lists often requires multiple sources in different locations for the most unique lists of information. At other times, information may be found in one place but is unusual enough that you have used your creativity in finding that one source.

Listings must also be current and timely. To provide the service to readers, they must be the most recent and current information available from the most authoritative sources. Therefore, your list is also the most accurate. Newspapers and magazines that publish listings are often considered authoritative sources on their own and find their published lists cited and reproduced elsewhere. For example, many morning drive-time radio program announcers pick such information out of the newspaper or news magazine to read to their audiences.

Most stand-alone lists are short and to the point. These are a top 10 or top dozen. If there is too much information, it is usually neither retained nor read in listed form. Thus, a brief list of the top 10 busiest airports might be appealing, but a top 100 becomes useless and overly thorough.

And, finally, most lists are presented in tabular form because they are quick and easy to read. Paragraphed information of the same kind is just not as easily skimmed and understood.

ART-OF-LIVING ARTICLES

Articles such as self-help or self-improvement are part of a broader category of service articles called art-of-living articles. These have been made popular by their regularity in widely read publications such as *Reader's Digest.*

Art-of-living articles can be an easy market for beginning feature writers, says *Reader's Digest* senior staff editor Philip Barry Osborne (1987). These articles include features that are inspirational narratives and essays, inspirational essays on faith and religion, and self-help articles.

Inspirational narratives and essays tell stories with a message to readers. The main difference is in approach. Narratives are chronological, whereas essays are in "essence" dealing with philosophy and "feel." These are "good" stories about people that make readers feel better after finishing them. Inspirational essays on faith and religion are not always sermons; they are, instead, articles on worship, personal revelation, prayer and meditation, and love. As Osborne points out, they can vary greatly in length as much as in topic.

Osborne offers five tips for art-of-living articles:

1. *Guard against overwriting.* Do not get too ornamental or exquisite in your writing. "Think more in terms of creating a small, delicate watercolor, rather than a giant oil painting" (p. 22), he advises.

2. *Steep yourself in what you're writing about.* Simple themes, he says, require much more than simple or superficial research.

3. *Pinpoint your lesson or message.* This is a fundamental requirement, so give the article what *Reader's Digest* editors call a "takeaway"—some theme that readers can take with them upon finishing the article.

4. *Sharpen your eye for the telling anecdote.* These articles are about people, so use anecdotes. In fact, anecdotes can become the entire basis for an article.

5. *Don't be afraid of ghosting.* Writing under someone else's name is acceptable at *Reader's Digest* because art-of-living stories are best told in first person. Thus, write for experts who cannot do it themselves, he says.

CHRONOLOGICAL CASE SUMMARIES

You can often learn easiest from example. This is where chronological case summaries/histories enter the category of service feature writing. Just as how-to articles, listings, and art-of-living articles teach readers, so do chronological case histories.

A good case history can hit home for your readers. A patient who has had heart trouble and has made it through major surgery to repair the problem has a story to tell. Other patients and their friends and families will benefit from the story.

A chronological case summary will outline the case of the patient for readers in a moment-by-moment, day-by-day approach. Many times, in fact, these articles are organized by date and time.

In telling the story of the heart patient, no detail should be spared. And in concluding it, resolution must be achieved. Tell readers whether the efforts of doctors and nurses paid off—did the problem get solved? Did the patient live? Are there breakthroughs in health care to result from this?

SOME CAUTION URGED

It is quite possible to get so enthusiastic about service articles, especially how-to articles, that you can forget potential dangers related to these articles.

Especially dangerous or potentially dangerous subjects, such as those involving poisons (in gardening) or electricity (installations) might need an extra note about safety written into them for readers. As a writer, you do not want to de-emphasize the possibility of risk in the stories you write—if it exists. On the other hand, nonhealth-threatening stories that involve other kinds of risk, such as financial investments, should be written just as carefully and thoughtfully for readers.

One particular area of concern is the subject matter itself. Although it might be interesting and entertaining reading, a now-famous article in *Progressive Magazine* about how to make a hydrogen bomb created quite a controversy when it was written. On a practical level, there is still concern about how much you tell readers, even if you personally know about or if an expert is willing to discuss certain sensitive subjects.

The ethical considerations in stories about crime such as auto theft, for example, are many. Do you write an article about how parking lot car thefts occur? How much do you tell? Is it right to have a former thief as your source—and have him describe in detail how to produce tools to break into and steal a car? Or, if your community has a problem with arson in a particular neighborhood, should you write a how-to article about how an arsonist does the job?

One 1987 newspaper feature highlighted a one-woman crime wave. This woman, the article relates, broke into countless homes of wealthy individuals by dressing the part of a well-to-do visitor—including wearing fancy clothing and driving a luxury rental car. Too much information about how this woman achieved her 300 to 500 burglaries might suggest the idea to someone else. But it can also alert residents to a potential thief in their neighborhood. Content of such articles must be governed by a fine line of judgment.

In another case, three Florida teenagers were arrested in 1988 for making an incendiary device—napalm—after reading how to do it in a book, *The Anarchist Cookbook*, written nearly 20 years earlier. They were mixing up the substance in their kitchen when they were discovered by local authorities. Even the newspaper reports of the arrest described in detail the key ingredients the boys were using. Would you write the article?

BEST SOURCES FOR SERVICE ARTICLES

There are a number of individuals who will be your best sources for service articles. Here is a list of major categories:

How-to Articles
  Craftsmen
  Mechanics
  Artists
  Technicians
  Authors of books
  Inventors
  Investors
  Builders/contractors
  Carpenters/electricians
  Gardeners/horticulturists
  Chefs and culinary experts
  Consumer advocates
  Scientists
  Decorators

Listings
  Historians
  Reference librarians
  Government studies
  Statisticians
  Museum curators
  Census data

Art-of-Living Articles
  Ministers
  Lawyers
  Psychiatrists
  Physicians
  Psychologists
  Financial advisors

Chronological Case Summaries
  Social workers
  Psychologists
  Teachers
  Sociologists
  Physicians
  Psychiatrists
  Police
  Historians

HOW PROFESSIONALS WROTE IT

DATE: WEDNESDAY, AUGUST 19, 1987
SOURCE: THE ORLANDO SENTINEL, PP. E-1, E-4
AUTHOR: DIANE HUBBARD BURNS, ORLANDO SENTINEL STAFF

* * *

AUTHORS PRESCRIBE DOSE OF DISCIPLINE IN FAMILY FORMULA

Child psychologists Marvin Silverman and David Lustig have developed what they say is a solution for that most awful of parental afflictions—the childhood tantrum.

This idea alone may make the South Florida duo's new book plenty popular with parents. *Parent Survival Training* ($10, Wilshire Book Co.) already has landed its authors on a host of radio and TV talk shows, including the CBS Morning News.

Silverman and Lustig's answer to childhood hysterics is an exercise in psychological turnabout, a bet that kids can dish it out but not on demand. Here is their plan of action:

Tape-record the child's tantrums and play them back to him. Then, make him repeat the tantrum each day, at an appointed hour, and tell him he must make each day's performance a little louder, a little longer, a little wilder. (You have the previous day's tantrum on tape for comparison.)

If the child has tantrums other than at the appointed time, tell him that he will run out of steam and not have enough histrionics left in him when his tantrum time arrives. (Most young children, Lustig said, will believe this.) If the child refuses to have tantrums at the appointed time, punish him by denying television viewing or some other privilege for a set period of time.

(This technique is recommended only for children 4 and older. Younger children should be isolated in a bedroom or bathroom until their tantrum is over, Lustig said.)

Within a week, the child will be begging for mercy and promising never to have another tantrum, the authors predict. "The longest any parent I have worked with has used the tantrum technique is 10 days," Lustig said. "I haven't had it fail anytime it is applied properly."

Unconventional? Yes, admit the authors. Too extreme? No, say Lustig and Silverman, whose tantrum technique is just one of a host of ideas in their book aimed at putting the reins of family life back in the hands of parents.

Tantrums must be dealt with because they usurp a parent's authority, Lustig said from the offices of the counseling firm where he and Silverman both work. The child either gets his way or reduces his parent to an angry, shouting maniac. Either way, the child has controlled the parent's actions.

But "as soon as the child gets the message that the parent is going to be more assertive and more stubborn than he is," he'll quit, Lustig said. What's better, once the child realizes that the parents mean to maintain their authority about this one thing, the child will take parental demands in other areas more seriously.

"Most of the techniques in *Survival Training* really involve the parent behaving properly," said Lustig, a 31-year-old licensed psychologist. "Most behavioral problems in children result from the parent not behaving properly."

Silverman, who has his doctorate in education and is a licensed school psychologist, said *Parent Survival Training* is based on established principles of behavioral psychology. The authors have attempted to translate those principles into practical, how-to techniques.

"Our goal was to have a jargon-free book that any person with a seventh- or eighth-grade education could read and understand," he said.

Their techniques have not been tested in a scientific study, but they have been tried on many youngsters and parents who have come through their counseling practice. And in many cases they have been put into practice in Silverman's home.

Silverman is 38, single and the father of two adopted sons, ages 11 and 13, from the Dominican Republic and El Salvador, respectively. A chapter on reducing conflict between siblings by not getting involved in their conflicts was played out in his home even as he wrote the book, Silverman said.

"My sons got into their biggest fight, and what I did was disconnect the TV cable box and the VCR from the television. I put both in the trunk of my car and said, 'If you have one more fight in the next 48 hours, the cable box goes back to the company and the VCR goes to the office, for kids to watch in the waiting room.' "

With adequate incentive provided, his sons learned to resolve their own conflicts, he said. But he added that if the boys had fought again, it would have been necessary to make good on his threats. Otherwise, all future threats of punishment would be empty ones, he said.

Silverman and Lustig believe the United States is "poised for a return to less permissive parenting," as Lustig puts it. They are ready to throw out the last 20 years of parenting theory, with its emphasis on communication, personal expression and individualism. Communication is fine when it doesn't involve a challenge to an adult's authority, they say.

They are in favor of making kids tow the line and letting parents decide where that line is. Their first chapter, for instance, is titled "How to teach your child to follow directions on the first request."

Lustig rejects the idea that children trained to follow orders inevitably will grow up to be automatons who can't think for themselves. What such training will create, Lustig said, is "a nation of children who grow into adults who know what the word 'limit' means, and who deal effectively with responsibility."

Reprinted with the permission of *The Orlando Sentinel*.

• • •

DATE: NOVEMBER 1987
SOURCE: POPULAR MECHANICS, PP. 79–81, 156.
AUTHOR: STEVE DUPLER

• • •

COVER STORY: AMERICAN HOT WAX

It might be one of NASA's flight-control centers. Streamlined banks of electronics equipment flash and blink their multicolored lights. Headphone-bedecked technicians peer into TV monitors as they throw switches, joggle dials and shift sliders. You can sense nervous electricity in the room, but it's not the scene of a manned space mission. A recording is in progress at Master Sound Astoria in New York City. And though musical stars routinely rocket into orbit from modern studios such as this one, something special is being launched today.

The producer and the chief engineer sit attentively at MSA's mixing board, which itself appears capable of providing navigational guidance for a moonshot. Seated beside these intense individuals is a genial-looking fellow who sets his wide-brimmed hat on the back of his head before positioning his fingers on the guitar across his chest.

He's Nile Rodgers, the musician and producer responsible for hit albums by artists such as Madonna, David Bowie and Duran Duran. Rodgers and his companions peer intently at a video monitor upon which Stevie Wonder and producer Quincy Jones appear. They are in another, similarly equipped studio in Los Angeles. This group of musicians and technicians, separated by some 3,000 miles, is about to link the two studios in the first simultaneous, remote digital recording session in history.

Utilizing digital satellite communications equipment operated by Teleport Communications in Staten Island, New York, the musical link was established across 45,000 miles of space, as shown in the accompanying illustration. Without leaving his chair at MSA in New York, Rodgers was able to record the guitar accompaniment to Wonder's antidrugs song "Stop, Don't Pass Go" at the very same moment the vocalist sang the lyrics.

In another remote digital link-up that same March day, Wonder's harmonica work traveled from Los Angeles to New York where it was overdubbed onto the soundtrack of TV's "Moonlighting" theme.

Although this was the first simultaneous "long-distance" digital recording session, quite a few others have utilized the capabilities of digital audio-storing the musical signal in a numerical computer format, and then beaming it to another location via satellite or land-based telecommunications lines. Recording industry professionals refer to the process as "The Mothership Scenario."

"What we are going to see—and not too far in the future—is a situation where musicians and producers will work in small, self-contained home studio units that are equipped with the highest-tech audio and communications gear," says Gary Helmers, executive director of the Los Angeles-based Society of Professional Audio Recording Studios.

"The work they complete in these small, self-contained digital studios will then be beamed to larger, world class recording centers, where parts of a whole come in from all over the country, or even the world, and are assembled by digital editing." These large, state-of-the-art recording facilities such as MSA are the "motherships" of the scenario.

Coincidentally, Wonder's pioneering remote–digital session comes 20 years after The Beatles recorded Sgt. Pepper's Lonely Hearts Club Band. It is considered by many to be the finest rock album ever, and certainly one of the most influential in terms of recording technology. Looking back in retrospect, it's incredible that producer George Martin was able to achieve so much with such Stone Age tools.

If Sgt. Pepper led his band into a recording studio today, he and the boys would definitely be in for some heavy shellshock.

Twenty years ago, the recording studio was a place where musicians went to record albums—period.

Today, many of the top recording facilities in the world are equipped to handle digital audio scoring-to-picture for video and film, and a host of other specialized, audio/video marriages. Many are capable of digital satellite uplink and downlink transmissions, including London's Abbey Road Studios, where The Beatles recorded Sgt. Pepper.

Special effects were pretty scarce back when Sgt. Pepper was recorded, with tricks such as fluctuating the tape's running speed by hand used to provide sound effects. Most of the more common toys in today's studio arsenal simply didn't exist. This includes things that now are taken for granted, such as stereo chorus effects, pitch doublers and harmonizers, high-tech digital reverbs and delay lines.

In 1967, when the venerable Pepper taught the band to play, the grandest repository for their learning was a 4-track open-reel recorder—occasionally linked to another to provide eight recording tracks. In today's studios, equipment for recording 24, 32 and even 48 tracks is commonplace. Interestingly, cassette-based 4-track recorder/mixer systems now available to home enthusiasts for under $1,000 perform as well or better than the machines on which the Fab Four transcribed their landmark album. In fact, rock star Bruce Springsteen used a 4-track Tascam Portastudio for the home-brew stage of his Nebraska recording.

The advent of multitrack recorders and multitrack mixing systems has opened up new avenues of creativity for recording stars and technicians.

For purposes of clarity, "channels" refers to the number of input sources (microphones, electric guitars and so on) that can be fed to a mixing console. "Tracks" describes the number of positions or paths along the tape available for those sources. the mixing console is the traffic cop between the source channels and the tape tracks. If a 56-channel console is feeding a 32-track recorder, some of those input source channels will be blended or "mixed down" at the "board" to fit the tape track format.

Eventually, the multiple tracks on that 2-inch-wide studio tape will be variously assigned and distributed between a single left and single right channel, for stereo LPs, CDs and cassettes. But all those channels and tracks do not go for nothing. They enable the artist and producer to shape the recorded performance as they see fit.

For example, though there might be only four musicians in a band, the producer might beef-up the performance by inserting background vocals or instrumentals on the extra tracks—even after the band has recorded its parts. The band itself needn't even record together. The lead singer can add his vocals after instrumentalists have "laid down" their tracks—or vice versa. In olden times, it was possible to add backgrounds by blending copies of the overdub and the original recording onto yet another tape—a process that degraded the sound. Today's digital recorders yield copies indistinguishable from the original, but thanks to the extra space available on multitrack equipment, even analog recordings suffer no loss of fidelity when overdubs are made.

Multichannel equipment makes all manner of musical manipulation possible after the actual recording. The drummer can be moved electronically to the left side of the soundstage from the right, as though that were the original physical arrangement. The recording can be rebalanced, to emphasize the sound on certain tracks over the others. This happens often in classical recordings. Because the home listener lacks visual cues someone in the concert hall might see, the conductor and engineer might pump-up the channel that contains a violin solo—in effect focusing an acoustical spotlight on the soloist.

Imagine what it would be like for the Pepper boys to enter the control room of a professional 32- or 48-track recording facility today: The first thing to strike their attention, no doubt, would be the massive mixing console around which the room is centered. It's likely to boast as many as 56 or more input channels.

Boards on this grand scale almost always are equipped with on-board computers. These allow engineers and producers to keep track of the thousands of control settings, signal routings and complicated mixing moves. All this information is stored in the memory of large-capacity, specially formatted magnetic disks. When The Beatles were making Pepper in 1967, information of this sort could be maintained only on hand-written tracks sheets, and in the producer's and engineer's heads.

In front of the mixing console they'd find the studio monitors (a.k.a. playback speakers), either placed left and right atop the console or hung from the walls on each side of the control room glass facing the engineer.

The sound monitors, and even the mixing board, would be familiar to the old-timers. But nowadays, there is usually a video monitor or two mounted between the speakers and above the control room glass. This is used to synchronize the audio and videotape during music video post-production.

Directly in back, or to either side of the mixing console, they'd see metal racks chock-full of signal-processing equipment (called outboard gear by the studio hands), as well as the multiple power amplifiers needed to make the whole thing sing. The signal-processing gear would include, among other things, Dolby tape-noise reduction units that didn't exist when Sgt. Pepper was in gestation—not to mention digital reverb systems and other "black boxes" of the studio magician's art.

Also behind the console they'd see multitrack tape recorders—either digital machines from Sony, Otari or Mitsubishi, or analog decks from Studer or Otari. There are also 2-track mastering recorders for use during mixdown, where the multitrack tape is boiled down to one left and one right channel prior to mastering for a stereo album.

One reason Sgt. Pepper was unique for The Beatles is that it was the first time they used an electronic music synthesizer, called the Mellotron.

Unlike current synthesizers, the Mellotron did not electronically create sounds of instruments such as flutes or violins. The Mellotron actually used tapes of those instruments, housed inside the large keyboard. Striking a key activated the tape of, say, 100 violins, playing a "C" note.

Today's technology has updated that concept significantly— and created some potential legal hazards.

Many studios are now equipped with instruments called digital sampling synthesizers. These keyboards are capable of recording any sound digitally, storing it in memory, then allowing the user to play back the sound over the entire musical spectrum on the keyboard.

Chances are you've probably heard one of these synthesizers. Jan Hammer, the composer/musician responsible for scoring "Miami Vice," uses a $100,000 Fairlight Computer Musical Instrument to create whole orchestral scores, as well as 12-string guitars, vibraphones, drums, horns, woodwinds, and other instruments. Not a single instrument heard on that TV show score is being played by a live musician!

And there's the rub. Musicians' unions complain that these samplers are cheating musicians out of studio work. Also, because sounds created by real musicians are being recorded or sampled for use in the Fairlight's sound library, the unions say that these musicians should be eligible for royalty payments each time their sounds (or performances, in a way) are heard.

It's a confusing issue that eventually will have to be hammered out, perhaps in a courtroom. For the meantime, samplers are here, and they're not going away.

They're just one more part of the space age technology of the modern recording studio.

A Professional's Point of View

By Joe Oldham
Popular Mechanics

If I had the opportunity to say only one thing to a young writer who was interested in making a living as a feature writer for magazines, newspapers, or any other medium for that matter, it would be this:

Write the way you speak.

Be natural. Write the words as if you were having a conversation with someone. Imagine that you're telling the reader a story or giving the reader some new information. This is specially true of service-oriented and/or how-to articles. Here, it's essential that you get the interest of the reader with the lead, then hold his interest by transmitting information in an easy, accessible style. For most of us, that means, again, writing the way you speak.

Just about everyone can speak to another person and transmit a thought. That's really all non-fiction, feature writing is. There's nothing mysterious, nothing magical about it. It's just transmitting a thought. Then another. And another. Until finally, you've written an article that transmits many thoughts in a logical sequence.

"Talking" to another person on paper should give your article a conversational tone. Unless you're writing a formal paper or treatise, you want that conversational tone in all your feature writing. That means speaking (on paper) clearly, using common language, and just being yourself.

For instance, most of us speak in contractions. We say "You're going," not "You are going." So write that way. Your sentences will flow a lot better.

Most of us speak in the vernacular. It's true that we all have several different vocabularies, and that our writing and speaking vocabularies are not the same. Still, good writers don't differ much in the way they write and the way they speak. An easy, conversational tone is always the end result—and with it, a well written article.

It always amazes me when someone I know as a regular guy writes something in a pompous, affected style that is totally unlike his natural manner and normal speech pattern. Somehow, when some people sit down at the typewriter, they feel that they have to become more formal or stodgy or achieve a so called higher tone than they usually operate in as a person.

Wrong.

Just the opposite is true.

Good writers are who they are all the time. They don't take on a different personality when they sit down to write. Instead, they extend their own personality

271

right into the words and sentences and paragraphs they're writing. They never step out of character.

Good non-fiction writers also write to one person at a time, no matter what the circulation of their publication. Each month, *Popular Mechanics* staffers write for over seven million readers—one at a time. Especially in non-fiction, service, how-to and the like, you've got to talk to that one person out there reading your stuff. When you reach him, you've reached them all. Use the word "you" a lot. Not the word "I". You should do this. You shouldn't do that. You should buy this. But don't buy that. Sometimes the "you" is implied. But it should always be there.

Be yourself. Be natural. Relax. Write the way you speak. Then you'll be a good writer. (Oldham, 1988, personal communication)

* * *

Joe Oldham is editor-in-chief of *Popular Mechanics*, a Hearst Corporation magazine in New York.

13

Personal Experience Articles

In 1988, *Texas Monthly* magazine celebrated its 15th birthday. To honor the occasion, the editors of the magazine chose to look at the highs and lows of the state over the period and how these moments affected everyday Texans. So the editors assigned articles by asking writers for stories about "what matters most to them, what dreams and longings shaped them" (p. 6), according to *Texas Monthly* Senior Editor Mimi Swartz, who edited the anniversary book. The issue that was published in February 1988 took a year to produce. It was a collection of highly personal stories about love, family, friends, health, careers, church, community, and values.

These are personal experience articles.

The unique *Texas Monthly* issue succeeded because of the extraordinarily personal nature of the stories:

> Texans have long been infatuated with the notion of ourselves as friendly and open, but most of us learned very early that personal matters are our most private property, to be hidden behind walls of silence of thickets of effusiveness. Texans view sentiment and sentimentality with suspicion; to get this issue to work, we had to convince our writers and their subjects that we weren't planning an issue that would be (a) gushy, (b) whiny, or (c) sissified. (p. 6)

This is what you try to achieve in personal experience feature writing. It allows you to do much as a writer because you can be highly involved in this type of writing. For most of this book, you have been encouraged to take yourself out of the writing as much as possible. Here is a chance to become part of a dramatic story through personal experience article writing.

Most writing students have experienced events in their lives that would make a good foundation for a personal experience feature story. One enterprising University of Miami student writer jumped out of an airplane (with a parachute) to write a feature about skydiving. Without that frightening experience, she might not have had the right mood, or the right words, for her article about skydiving.

Another University of Miami student writer grew up with an alcoholic father in a high-income suburban neighborhood. Her very personal article described her very emotional relationship with him. It was startling to some readers because this young woman who seemed to have everything really did not have what she wanted most—a normal childhood with a normal father. When you become part of your story, your sources become closer to you because they find they can identify with you. You gain detail in your writing from the close-up observation.

This type of feature story can be something as simple as spending a shift at work with someone—getting involved personally.

Personal writing is a broad-based approach to your craft. Your own point of view and your attitudes, make a difference in any story, but on these assignments, you can let them become part of the story itself.

Distinguished journalism professor and writer John Hohenberg (1987) stated this succinctly when he wrote: "It should not be imagined that the exercise of personal journalism is confined to criticism of government. Indeed, its role is far broader than that. This useful convention of journalism makes possible, first of all, a breadth of emotion and personal expression in our writing for immediate publication. . ." (p. 256).

APPROACHES TO PERSONAL EXPERIENCE ARTICLES

Generally, there are two major types of personal experience articles:

1. *Personal experiences of others that you write about.* These articles describe in detail the unusual and appealing experiences of individuals in a highly personal approach but are not written first person. These are descriptions by a writer who uses the experiences of another person for the basis of the article.

2. *Personal experiences of your own.* These are commonly called first person articles. These articles draw on your own experiences for material for the article. These articles are often stories of medical problems, trips, crimes, life or death situations, human relationships, family experiences, and similar events. You are the reporter, storyteller, and the central source—or at least one of the major sources—in the article.

Both kinds of articles can be about everyday occurrences, but the articles that receive the most attention are unusual, adventurous, frustrating, or dramatic.

For example, *Newsweek* Chicago bureau chief Frank Maier (1988) wrote a recent cover story about his "second chance to live" when he underwent a liver transplant at the Mayo Clinic in Minnesota. His detailed, chronological account of the elaborate steps taken by a team of doctors to help him enlightened readers and provided hope for others as ill.

Feature writer and teacher Nancy Kelton (1988) says personal experience articles should look at the world as honestly as possible, "seeing the truths— both the dark and the light—within our experiences so that we can share them with other people who will nod and say, 'Yes, that's how it is. I've been there, too' " (p. 24).

THE MAJOR COMPONENTS

A personal experience article must provide readers with an unusual story, an adventure, or a real-life drama that goes beyond this point. *Newsweek's* Maier achieves this in his insightful story. As Maier does, a personal experience article should also attempt to put that story in context. Usually, the context will be current trends in the community or society, such as medical care. Yet it could add the dimension of historical context as well.

There are three major components of a personal experience article, according to Nancy Kelton, a specialist in personal experience article writing:

1. *A point of view.* What is the unique way in which you can present the situation? How were you or your source involved? What perspective do you offer? An inside view will generally be preferred. Usually, Kelton says, this fares better than filling the article with descriptive details of the actions of others at the expense of personal reactions and opinions. You have to tell how it felt, what it meant, and how you grew as a person during and after the experience. This, she says, is the best way to write a personal experience article.

Andrew Kreig accomplished this in his article, "Death Wish III" for *Connecticut Magazine* in 1986. Kreig's article describes how he felt after being mugged in Hartford. After experiencing this violent event, he writes about physical safety, noise, and other aspects of a changing urban residential neighborhood life. How did it happen? Why? What did he do afterward? These questions are answered in his unique personal presentation of the situation and the events that followed.

2. *Arrival at some basic truth.* After you have made your trip, been released from the hospital, or floated to the ground after parachuting from an airplane, you should be able to reach a conclusion about what you have learned. "Something should become clear to you," Kelton says. "You should reach a new level of understanding that you convey to your readers."

Reporter Mark Winne (1983) watched an execution at Alabama's Holman Prison. His stirring story about watching a man die in the electric chair will draw reactions from most readers. Winne described everything he saw in his *Atlanta Journal-Constitution* article and then arrived at his own judgment about the experience. He says once a person watches an execution, he or she cannot forget the image:

"Small talk dies suddenly when the color test patterns flicker and there before us sits Evans, strapped in the bulky, lemon-yellow electric chair.

"That's when the change starts in you, when you cease to think of the chair as a modern, efficient way to carry out a court sentence."

Winne ends his sobering story with this sentence:

"Next day you drive an hour or so to the Florida beach and stare at the rolling surf at night while the wind blows, and you are still thinking about what you saw."

3. *Emotional involvement.* It helps readers to share your experience if you can place them in the middle of your emotional reaction to the situation. You cannot afford to hide your feelings in writing such an article. You have to offer a complete description of what you felt. Write in such a manner that you can put your reader next to you, watching the experience all over again.

Winne's execution description is filled with emotional reaction—his and that of others present. The involvement is obvious and necessary to the mood of the article. Here is just one paragraph that points out how he was reacting to the unfolding event:

"You pray. You say the same prayer over again, and the story you've dogged for two days fades. You just want someone to step across that TV picture and announce that a call has come from the governor stopping it all."

And another paragraph that describes others' reaction to what they see:

"Their (reporters) faces are blank. Many are shaken. A TV anchorwoman is helped from the room. Later, as speakers are marched to the microphones in front of her in the clamor of the press room, she sits wide-eyed, her hand over her mouth. When she leaves that night, she is still pale."

Putting these three main components to work is the key to a successful article, Nancy Kelton says. Here's how she does it:

1. *Pick an experience you care about deeply.* Some writers, Kelton relates, like to say that subjects pick writers, not vice versa. Although you do not have control over the events that you might use for an article, you can control your selection of those you feel most strongly about. These are the ones to use for your articles.

2. *Don't make publication your primary goal in writing your article.* Your primary objective should be to discover how you feel about an experience by writing about it. Then, in writing, you also will try to publish the article, and you have an added benefit. "Your initial satisfaction should come from the writing and

the discoveries you make in the process," Kelton says. Her new experiences with motherhood, which she eventually wrote about, were her reasons for thinking about and trying to understand her new emotions.

3. *Don't write a personal experience article to vent anger, indignation, or other negative emotions.* Sometimes you will experience something that makes you angry. It might be bad service at a garage or an annoying neighbor's lifestyle. Personal experience articles should not be used to vent these feelings. Instead, the anger may make it difficult or impossible for you to express your feelings.

4. *Have the courage to reveal yourself honestly.* You must convey feelings by opening yourself to others, perhaps thousands of others. That takes nerve, Kelton says, and is not for everyone. These feelings are not always positive and bright. "You must be courageous enough to reveal yourself honestly," she says.

5. *Don't tell what you went through—show it.* To show it means to dramatize it. Re-set the scene and put yourself and the reader there together. Often this means telling the story in chronological fashion. This is a simple step-by-step process that takes readers from beginning to end.

6. *Don't show everything—don't write about the mundane details of the experience.* Much of the time, too many details will drag the story down. The clutter can get in your way. Is the detail relevant to the story? If so, include it. If not, forget it.

IDENTIFYING EXPERIENCES THAT INTEREST OTHERS

What have you done that makes interesting reading for others? You are aware of successful personal experience articles already.

Much of it is good luck—or bad luck, depending on the nature of the article. A writer often finds himself or herself in a place to develop a story by sheer coincidence.

Your basic news sense will often be a guide. Knowing what makes a good feature will be even stronger if you are personally involved in a topic or event. So instead of being a routine story about the problems people have settling with insurance companies after a break-in or an automobile accident, your story takes on more meaning if you have had the misfortune to experience such an event yourself and can write about it.

Sometimes the routine at home makes good material. Many columnists, such as "Parenting" columnist Jill Singer of *The Miami Herald,* do this. Singer is not at all hesitant to discuss topics such as sex education by using her own family as the example for others. Writing in first person, she even mentions her husband and children by name to her readers when making her point in the regular feature.

Unusual adventures that most people cannot experience are the focus of many appealing personal experience articles. George Plimpton has made a career of trying unusual sports and other activities and writing magazine articles and books about the experiences. He has been an athlete as well as a jet fighter pilot. In an article prepared for *Popular Mechanics* in 1986, Plimpton wrote about his experiences flying an $18 million F-18 Hornet at Mach 2 above the Atlantic Ocean.

And, of course, more serious subjects, such as health and crime, make good personal experience stories. This is illustrated by the case of a student journalist who was once a cocaine addict. Her experiences gave a critical dimension to her story about the impact of drugs on a middle class coed that she could not have achieved as meaningfully from a source in an interview. If the student can bring herself to write about this part of her life and others learn from it, then the story has had impact.

Her story, written for the University of Miami student magazine, *Insight*, chronologically told of how her increasing dependency on drugs cost her a career, her brief marriage, and an entire lifestyle. Her article described how she managed to win the battle at a high price. From this writer's rare personal situation, we learned how a peek into someone else's life can teach us much— about a woman's highs and lows and how she put herself back on the road to a productive life as a writer today.

Ideally, these personal experience stories should relate to broader community concerns, if possible. Although it may be interesting as an isolated happening, an experience takes on more value if it is placed in a more meaningful big picture.

The final test? Can you tell this story to someone else? Would someone else want to know about what you experienced? If so, then you might have a good story idea.

FINDING YOUR AREA'S BEST STORY TELLERS

In every community there are storytellers. You might have occasion to tell your own personal experience stories from time to time, but much of your grist will be from other sources, people known as the local storytellers.

Who are they? They take many roles—minister, Boy Scout leader, historian, police officer, social worker. People who are involved with other people on a regular basis often have the best experiences to tell you about.

If you can seek one of these persons out, perhaps by word of mouth, you will find rich potential for a story.

Research, as you are often reminded, makes a difference even in personal experience storytelling. You might be aware of events that can be the basis of a good personal experience story. By searching records and newspaper clippings, you can often get the names of persons who were witnesses, victims, or were otherwise involved in the event.

They are your storytellers.

TELLING A STORY

These types of feature articles are often called factual short stories. This might help you as a way to remember a good approach to writing them—write and organize as you might handle a short story, but just be sure to keep the content factual.

Accomplishing this is easier than it seems. It helps a great deal if you use the same storytelling techniques of short story writers:

1. *Dialogue.* Use lots of quotes and reconstructed conversation between key individuals.

2. *Description.* Bring in plenty of rich descriptive words. This includes active verbs and adverbs and impression-filled adjectives.

3. *Plot.* If your story permits, try to organize it so that it has a plot or story line. Make it suspenseful if appropriate. Give the story a moral. You should introduce the plot/story line early in the article and stick with it throughout.

There can be problems that come with telling a story. One of the most serious ones is selective or failing memory. On some personal experience story assignments, you might depend on memories of events that occurred months or years ago. Your memory gets hazy. It filters out certain details over time. And if this happens to you, it will happen to your sources, too. Therefore, you must be prepared to go to extra lengths for details that might be forgotten. For example, you can use yearbooks, photo albums, and other devices to stimulate detailed recollections.

Many writers, when faced with missing information, are better off admitting to readers that they cannot recall some detail or piece of the puzzle. Don't guess. This openness and honesty are personal touches that make the article even more appealing to readers.

USING YOUR OWN LIFE FOR RESEARCH

Has anything extraordinary ever happened to you? Would it make an appealing story? Can others learn from your experiences? There will be unusual events and circumstances that will occur in your life that could generate an article. Newspaper reporters and magazine writers experience the full range of human experiences, and you should be prepared to write about the unusual that you experience. And, of course, the ordinary activities in your life might make good article material, too. Susan Burnside, editor of Northwest Neighbors (a suburban section) of *The Miami Herald,* has often written about her family in her column. As her children have grown from babies to teenagers, readers have been able to learn from the Burnside family's experiences. Sharing the band trips, the dented fenders, and other experiences in her column is not only humorous and entertaining, but also educational for other parents.

Writer Nan Robertson told a compelling story in the *New York Times Magazine* in 1982 that explained to readers her battle against toxic shock syndrome. The article, appealing because of the very personal story it tells, earned the 1983 Pulitzer Prize for Feature Writing. Robertson wrote in rich, precise detail about her experience with the rare medical problem. Structurally, she takes a chronological approach, beginning just hours before she was stricken. She takes readers through her near-fatal attack, the ride to the hospital, diagnosis, and treatment. Her article uses direct quotations of recalled dialogue during her attack and treatment. She depends on family members and friends to remember details and quotes, using a diary one friend kept for her during her hospitalization. After setting the scene—her trip to the hospital in Illinois—she tells her readers:

> This is the story of how, almost miraculously and with brilliant care, I survived and prevailed over that grisly and still mysterious disease. Almost every major organ of my body, including my heart, lungs and liver, was deeply poisoned. . . . This is also the story of how—with luck and expertise—this life-threatening disease can be avoided, detected, monitored, treated and destroyed before it reaches the acute stage. (Robertson, 1982, p. 30)

Robertson's article, autobiographical in style and written in first person, is understandable even when she discusses the medical reasons for the disease. Readers are able to share the experience of her personal fears, her suffering and her pain, and her joy in winning the battle. Yet she also incorporates into her article considerable discussion about the disease by experts from the Centers for Disease Control and other medical research centers. Woven within her own experiences, this makes the article instructional in addition to its pure entertainment value.

These two examples illustrate how a reporter with an experience that appeals to others can use his or her own life as research for personal experience articles. Where one writer chose to use her own amusing family experiences as material for a lifestyles column, the other turned a dangerous medical situation which she involuntarily experienced into a magazine-length article.

ORGANIZATIONAL APPROACHES AND NARRATIVE ARTICLES

Personal experience features require care in organizing the material. Because you or someone you are working with has experienced the subject firsthand, writing about the experience can become difficult—you or your source are so close to it.

Many features rise or fall because of their leads. A strong personal experience story will also. Because many personal experience stories are not written in inverted pyramid—with the most important facts first—a strong lead will make a difference. This lead must capture the flavor of the article by hinting at its essence without giving away the outcome or moral. The lead must arouse readers by piquing their curiosity, teasing them, and even making them raise their eyebrows in reaction to what they have read.

Newspaper reporter Mark Silva's (1983) lead to his feature on the problems he experienced during an airline strike works because he uses description, personal reaction, and surprise:

> I was weary, worn out by the last strong September sun and an afternoon of bathing in the hot confluence of a boiling spring-fed river and a cold trout-filled stream in Yellowstone National Park, when I learned that the airline that got me there had gone bankrupt.
>
> There is something seductive about imagining, for a moment, that one's vacation will never end. . . . (p. 1B)

Most personal experience articles are essays written in chronological order, simply recounting a series of events that might interest readers. Still, an essay requires basic organizational structure—a beginning/introduction, body, and ending. And chronological stories must be told in a time-based order of events— often including the times to help the reader understand the sequencing.

It is essential that you stick to the topic in your article. Because it is often a personal story you are telling, the temptation can be great to drift away from the real focus.

You must also keep the story moving. Doing this requires pacing and a skill with transitions. You can describe each single episode that contributes to the entire experience an item at a time, but you must constantly try to tie them together with good transitions that remind the reader of the links. For example, using times of the day or days of the week in a chronological piece will aid readers a great deal. Helter-skelter movement around a series of events confuses readers, and you lose them.

FIRST PERSON APPROACH

Like travel writing, personal experience features are often written in first person. When you are telling a story you have experienced yourself, it is often easier to write in first person.

Sarah Bartlett, writing for *Business Week,* used first person writing to tell readers about her experiences as a currency trader for Citicorp. Her 1988 article explained to business-oriented readers how the everyday "wheeling and dealing" of $150 billion worth of international currency trading goes. "What drives these folks [who trade], anyway? It's hard to know without being a trader yourself. Sit in a trading room and you'll do little more than drink in the atmosphere. Listen in on conversations and you'll mostly hear monosyllabic grunts that only jungle-stalking Jane Goodall would appreciate. Persuade a trader to translate, and it sometimes just gets murkier . . . " (p. 70), she wrote. "That's why when Citicorp said I could try my hand at trading, I leapt at the chance" (p. 70). Her personal point of view here makes the story worth reading because as readers we want to know her reactions, and she tells us by using first person perspective.

In editor David Hamilton's 1985 feature for *Newsday*, "The New Member of the Mid-'80s Family," he wrote about the changes his own family experienced when it got a personal computer. Rather than take a detached third person perspective, he chose to write in first person and discussed how the new machine affected mom, dad, and the children as well as how the Hamilton family adjusted. Using pronouns such as *I*, *we*, and *our*, Hamilton let the world know how his "family user group" as he called it, became high tech.

In addition to describing the individual reactions, Hamilton, an assistant managing editor, also provided a list of "useful tricks" for other families who have recently acquired, or might consider acquiring, a PC.

Here's how he used personal pronouns and his own experience to describe the decision to get the computer:

> But we are an optimistic group, ever bent on progress, and so we emerged from the decision huddle vowing that the interest and need of each family member would ensure their care and concern. Yes, we cannot always manage to put the cheese away and close the refrigerator door in a single trip to the kitchen, but no we would not neglect the instrument our 3-year-old dubbed, importantly, the "the 'puter". I'm here to testify that we've done about as well as might have been expected. (p. 3)

And this gives us a very real look at a family situation that many readers can easily identify with throughout the article.

First person is an approach so appealing to readers in Kentucky that editors of the *Louisville Courier-Journal* occasionally publish a column Features section called First Person. This column contains "personal experiences by local and wire-service writers," the newspaper tells its readers whenever it is published. It is a strong news feature package approach that is available to editors without requiring staff to provide such material when material quality may not dictate it. One recent example was a personal essay by New York Times News Service columnist Anna Quindlen on her chance encounter with actress Katharine Hepburn on an East Side Manhattan street. Quindlen described her reactions to this moment and why she decided not to meet her. The reason? She did not want to see her today, preferring to remember her in Hepburn's prime as an actress.

The key to remember when deciding whether to tell a personal experience story in first or third person is whether you believe that you, as the writer, should be a major component of the story. In David Hamilton's case, and in the case of many of the other examples we have discussed in this chapter, it was critical to the success of the feature story to write in the first person.

You should also remember that when writing a personal experience story from someone else's experience, the best writing approach is third person. Taking a first person approach is only confusing to the reader if your byline is on the article and someone else is really telling the story.

BEST SOURCES FOR IDEAS

To write about the personal experiences of others and the personal experiences of your own, here are some common sources for your articles:

Researching the Experiences of Others
  Other newspapers and magazines
  Civil and criminal courts records, files
  Radio talk shows
  Neighbors and friends
  History books
  Local museums and schools

Your Own Experiences
  Family albums
  School yearbooks
  Observation
  Notebooks, diaries, or logbooks
  Home movies and video tapes
  Conversations with family and friends

HOW PROFESSIONALS WROTE IT

DATE: JULY 1986
SOURCE: CONNECTICUT MAGAZINE, PP. 71–73, 98–99, 123.
AUTHOR: ANDREW KREIG

* * *

DEATH WISH III

In early 1985, a slightly built folksinger was trying to decide whether to move onto Mortson Street, a blue-collar neighborhood in the Frog Hollow section of Hartford. She surveyed the tree-lined street of three-story, red brick apartments. Some verged on shabbiness; others were well-kept and had neat flower gardens.

"Is this neighborhood safe?" she asked, adding that she sometimes came home late from concerts.

"I've known of some burglaries during my nine years here," I replied, "but I've never thought there was any reason for physical fear. Then again, I'm 6-foot-4."

"You tell that girl that this is the safest street in Hartford," neighbor Anthony Giguere said to me later, doubtless speaking more out of civic pride than anything else. "In 18 years living on this street," continued the retired French-Canadian carpenter, "I've never heard of a mugging."

As it happens, I was the one who would end up getting mugged. The further irony is that it stemmed directly from my affection for the neighborhood. Its history and community life have fascinated me, and encouraged me to undertake major renovations of my building.

Because my third-floor porch is on high ground and overlooks a big, grassy schoolyard, the view north is largely unobstructed. On the extreme right is the golden dome of Connecticut's state Capitol. Dominating the view straight ahead is the huge colonial-style headquarters of Aetna Life and Casualty Co. Some 300 yards to my left, the gray cement floors of a new 18-story office complex are rising up on the side of the old Underwood typewriter plant.

Nothing remains in view of the factories that once made the neighborhood a nationally important manufacturing center. Products included Sharps rifles, high-wheeled Columbia bicycles and Pope-Hartford automobiles, as well as machine tools made by Pratt & Whitney at the firm's first building, near the bicycle factory. The section's name, "Frog Hollow," comes from a marsh near the present site of Trinity College.

Park Street, the community's central commercial thoroughfare, went into a serious decline several decades ago as industry vanished and middle-class residents left for the suburbs. More recently, Frog Hollow has been revitalized by office construction on three sides for law, government and insurance workers. The post-industrial trend is best symbolized by Aetna's handsome restoration of a brick factory building at the Pope-Hartford site.

At the same time, Hartford suffers from the housing shortage typical of most cities in Connecticut.

Poor people displaced from some of the bleakest parts of the city have desperately sought housing in Frog Hollow. It's fostered tensions reputed to be unprecedented even in a neighborhood long known as the city's main melting pot. There is an ongoing struggle between the more stable residents and those "for whom self-expression is more important than self-control." (These words are from sociologist James Q. Wilson's book on city problems nationally, *Thinking About Crime.*)

My next-door neighbor Evelyn Kruk, an insurance worker of retirement age, told me she never worried about her physical safety in the fastidiously maintained building occupied by her family since 1915. Indeed, her late mother, Mary, regularly swept outside at the crack of dawn—not just on the sidewalk, but in the street. "The street-sweepers miss places," the octogenarian once explained to me.

There has, however, been a disturbing growth in street noise, such as a car honking at all hours of the day and night. The Kruk family moved to Wethersfield last summer.

"It was the noise—the unnecessary noise—that drove us out," explained Evelyn.

I've often thought of their departure when I've heard the horns. These days, many people would rather lean on a car horn than walk up to a doorbell and ring it. While some cities such as Honolulu enforce a law against it, even city-contracted school van drivers in Hartford blast away with impunity.

"It's a breach of peace violation between 10:30 p.m. and 6:30 a.m.," Hartford Police Chief Bernard Sullivan told me when I complained. "At other times, it's not against the law."

Just before 2 a.m. on Aug. 21, I heard BA-PAA, BA-PAA, BAAAAAAAAAA from the middle of the street. Then again: BA-PAA, BA, BAAAAAAAAAAAAAAAA. I threw on some clothes and walked down. Two young men and a woman were in the car. A third man stood to the side.

"Couldn't you ring the doorbell?" I said. "Everybody on the whole block has to hear that."

"What's it to you?" responded a hollow-cheeked, belligerent young passenger. He piled out of the car along with the other occupants. "I pay my taxes. It's a free country. Understand?"

I walked to the rear of their car to look at the license plate. The argument continued, but I decided it was a no-win situation. I turned to walk home. The horn-honking driver (whom I've come to know as Basilio) moved out in front of me and began talking. The others followed, with the lean-faced, loud-mouthed passenger becoming more abrasive in his comments.

Just as I reached my front porch, the lean-faced passenger following me shoved me from behind. The push sent me sprawling onto my red picket fence.

I struggled to get up. But one of my assailants kept me off-balance by holding my right foot in the air. It was easy for them to topple me onto my fence again. Pickets splintered under me, with the broken staves goring me in the stomach.

This can't really be happening.

Every time I'd half rise, I'd be pushed onto the fence again, speared either in my stomach or back. Punches cascaded into me. Finally, wrestled to the ground, I was battered by leather—repeated kicks to the face around my eyes. I wasn't able to throw a single punch in the four or five minutes. My four adversaries ran down the street and drove off in their tan '78 Chevette.

I was dazed, with my front teeth wobbling enough that I wondered whether they'd turn black or fall out. Dripping blood from the deep gouges in my face, I tottered upstairs to telephone for help. When a patrolman arrived about 25 minutes after my first call, I got the biggest surprise of the night. Even though I remembered the muggers' license plate, the police could not trace it.

"The marker number doesn't show up on the Motor Vehicles Department computer" said patrolman Serge Khuzkian. "Maybe it's a new registration. There's about a three-month clerical backlog at MVD for listing cars. We'll just have to wait and see."

There are many indignities one learns to shrug off. This assault wasn't one of them. I could have been maimed by what these people did. And if they would beat up someone my size, it seemed likely they had attacked others—and might again.

[The article continues beyond this excerpt.]

Reprinted with the permission of *Connecticut* magazine.

• • •

DATE: THURSDAY, OCTOBER 6, 1983
SOURCE: MIAMI HERALD, P. 1B
AUTHOR: MARK SILVA, HERALD STAFF WRITER

* * *

TAKE MY PLANE TICKET—PLEASE

I was weary, worn out by the last strong September sun and an afternoon of bathing in the hot confluence of a boiling spring-fed river and a cold trout-filled stream in Yellowstone National Park, when I learned the airline that got me there had gone bankrupt.

There is something seductive about imagining, for a moment, that one's vacation will never end, that all airlines will quietly fold and that western Wyoming suddenly will be in need of resident writers.

Not until a few days later, somewhere in the middle of Merle Haggard's Montana, did I begin to worry about not only Continental Airlines, but also myself. My plan had been simple: Fly from Miami to Denver, rent a car, spend two weeks exploring the Rocky Mountains and return home on a flight from Great Falls, Mont. It was working well, until Continental dropped me in the wild West and turned belly up.

I'll always remember the cheerful but apologetic voice of "Gail," a Continental "representative," the first of several faceless airline officials who answered my calls from one of the northernmost telephone booths in America: Eureka, Mont. Their explanations were varied, but their messages were the same; it was as if Thomas Wolfe were on the other end of the line, explaining: "You Can't Go Home Again."

"We're not flying in to Great Falls anymore," said Gail, who explained that the bankrupt airline was resuming flights to only some of the cities it previously served. If I were to reach Denver, I asked, could Continental get me to Miami? "We don't fly to Miami anymore."

Surely all the other airlines are rushing to the aid of stranded travelers, you say. Surely not. Northwest Orient Airlines was only the first to explain, in not so many words, that Continental's tickets are suddenly tantamount to funny money. American, Delta, Pan Am: Ditto.

The champions are few, and they deserve credit. Miami's own beleaguered Eastern Airlines is accepting Continental tickets, subject to a number of restrictions. But "Eastern" is a dirty word in parts of Montana, and, in any event, the airline doesn't serve Great Falls.

Western Airlines was willing to help, allowing me to leave Great Falls on a stand-by basis and make my way to Denver, stand-by, via Salt Lake City. Never mind that Western's flight out of Utah later crossed a mountain jetstream so strong that the aircraft shook like a disco and the doors of its overhead baggage compartments started flying open.

(The pilot was comforting, stoic in the tradition of fighter-jocks possessing what the other Tom Wolfe calls the Right Stuff: "Ladies and gentlemen, we're flying upside down and backwards, and we're aimed at a mountain. This is only a minor inconvenience. please bear with us.")

Denver never looked so good.

Even Continental was looking better. I learned in Denver that the airline was still serving Fort Lauderdale and could fly me there—with a brief stop in Houston—rather than taking me directly to Miami.

I was waiting to board Continental's flight to Houston when I noticed the big, bold headlines bannered on the Denver newspapers: "Continental Pilots Strike." The articles were more hopeful, with an airline spokesman proclaiming that Continental's new, limited service would not be interrupted by the pilots' strike. I could imagine this Continental fellow, Bruce Hicks, beaming as he told the papers: "It is clear a vast majority of Continental's pilots are eager to fly."

Not mine.

"For passengers on Flight 434 to Houston," came the electrified announcement, "we have a plane, but we have no cockpit crew. We'll let you know when we're leaving, if we can find someone to fly the plane."

They found someone—he was well-dressed, with stripes on his sleeves, so I didn't ask any questions—three hours later. He piloted the plane to Houston, but landed there well after all the day's flights to Florida had departed. I would have to spend the night in Texas, as yet another kind but helpless Continental official explained to me, but the bankrupt airline wouldn't be able to pay for my night's lodging.

I have more than a little sympathy for the American labor movement. But it was at about that time, late last Saturday night, that I started leering at the picketing pilots pacing the halls of Houston's airport. They carried signs: "CAL Unfair to Pilots." They walked alongside flight attendants: "Continental Unfair to Flight Attendants."

I felt like carrying a sign on behalf of passengers.

The next morning, after sheepishly crossing the picket lines, I boarded Continental's plane bound for Fort Lauderdale. I noticed, as I passed the cockpit, that taped to the controls was a handwritten note from management to the crew: "Thank you for coming to work today."

Thank you indeed. I'm sure there are any number of compelling reasons for pilots striking, just as there are reasons for a major airline going bankrupt. But few things are so compelling—despite the lure of an endless vacation —as a voyager's desire to get home.

Reprinted with the permission of *The Miami Herald*.

•••

DATE: SUNDAY, MAY 1, 1983, P. 15D, 20D
SOURCE: THE ATLANTA JOURNAL-CONSTITUTION
AUTHOR: MARK C. WINNE

* * *

WHAT IT'S LIKE TO WATCH A MAN DIE IN ELECTRIC CHAIR

On April 15, 1983, John Louis Evans III became the first person in 18 years to be executed in Alabama. Mark C. Winne, a staff writer with the Atlanta Journal-Constitution, was among those who witnessed the execution on closed-circuit television.

The day before was clear. The day after will be clear. But on the night of the electrocution, there is a pounding rain and thunder.

There is a loud, wet scramble as reporters get off the two yellow school buses that have carried us to Holman Prison. Inside, we maneuver to get in line to be frisked and to get a good seat in front of the three closed-circuit, color TV sets.

Rarely, after all, do you get a chance to see a man die.

For days we had waited for the courts to finish with the case, to find out if they really would electrocute John Louis Evans III. Sometimes out of the monotony have come tasteless puns, soon regretted, about "electrifying suspense" and the like. But that was when the execution seemed as though it would never happen, that at some level a judge would stop it.

Small talk dies suddenly when the color test patterns flicker and there before us sits Evans, strapped in the bulky, lemon-yellow electric chair.

That's when the change starts in you, when you cease to think of the chair as a modern, efficient way to carry out a court sentence. Soon you will know it is more modern than the hangman's noose only because electricity is involved. You will know it is less efficient than the guillotine or the firing squad.

Shorn of his thick, black hair, the killer has lost his boyish look. He grins faintly, placidly, and you think the priest and the family were telling the truth, that Evans was ready to die if he had to, a devout Catholic.

The straps criss-crossing his white prison clothes make his thin frame look even skinnier. He wears white socks but no shoes, and one pant leg is rolled up to allow an electrode to be strapped onto his ankle.

He does not move. He could, just a little, at least drum his fingers. But he does not. He stares straight ahead with that grin. He nods at two witnesses appearing behind a window.

Two guards, in powder blue-over-blue uniforms, stand on either side.

You are not allowed to have anything with you but your clothes in the prison, not even watches. So there is no way to be sure of the time, and when you are staring at a man staring back at you as he waits to die, the time goes slowly. But it has to be 15 or 20 minutes he's sitting there, waiting, staring.

You wince, and you think of the phrase "cruel and unusual" while you watch.

The quiet in the prison is broken by the low strains of a spiritual sung in a distant cell.

Suddenly the guards are pulling tight on the strap across Evans' chest. They strap the headgear onto him. The peaceful scene explodes. His eyes are confused, panicky as the guards pull the chin strap tight. They are like that when you last see them, as one of the guards drapes a black shroud before his face and ties the drawstring behind.

You pray. You say the same prayer over again, and the story you've dogged for two days fades. You just want someone to step across that TV picture and announce that a call has come from the governor stopping it all.

One of the guards leaves the room. The other holds up a sign that looks like a yellow ping-pong paddle and said "ready"; then he assumes parade rest facing Evans.

Evans' chest heaves and his fists clench and his skin is bluish. You wince.

Neon red flashes from beneath the shroud. A fiery halo, you say to yourself. Then yellowish smoke drifts upward from his face, drifts like smoke from a crowded ashtray in a bar. The electrode on his leg explodes.

It seems longer than the 30 seconds you have been told it will last. But you do not have your watch; you wouldn't look if you did.

His abdomen throbs; his body quivers. For an instant, you think he has survived. It's nerves; you think next about the chicken with its head cut off.

His body is limp.

A brown curtain falls over the camera lens.

Huh-hupp! is the signal for the prison riot squad to form a corridor to the prison door through which the reporters are ushered. Their faces are blank. Many are shaken. A TV anchorwoman is helped from the room. Later, as speakers are marched to the microphones in front of her in the clamor of the press room, she sits wide-eyed, her hand over her mouth. When she leaves that night, she is still pale.

You run through the hard rain to the bus, and German shepherd guard dogs bark wildly as, against that backdrop, you hear Taps, trumpeted from an inmate dormitory in the distance.

In the press hut you find out it took 14 minutes to kill Evans, two more jolts after they shut off the camera. What he's just seen registers in the face of progressive young Alabama Prison Commissioner Fred Smith, calm and cordial in the days leading up to the execution, but distant as he stands before the microphones and the feeding frenzy of TV cameras.

Among the newsmen dictating their stories is Mark Harris, 25, who will forever remember April 22 as the first time he learned he was going to be a father and the first time he saw a man put to death.

You call your paper. You tell your editor you will never forget it. Then you dictate your story.

Later, early in the morning in the only big motel in town, Evans' family and friends mingle in the hallways with the reporters. Many are drinking. Everybody is tired, but nobody can sleep.

The prison chaplain is there and tells you about a videotape that Evans—now four hours dead—made before he died, pleading with school children not to take his path. You slip into a small motel office room, and there is another color, closed-circuit TV, much like the one you last saw John Evans on.

The chaplain turns it on, and there is Evans again. This time he has hair.

"My name is John Evans. I'm on Death Row in Alabama, and I'm scheduled to be executed in about four days," he says in a close-up.

Next day you drive an hour or so to the Florida beach and stare at the rolling surf at night while the wind blows, and you are still thinking about what you saw.

Reprinted with the permission of the *Atlanta Journal-Constitution*.

A Professional's Point of View

By John Mack Carter
Good Housekeeping

To my way of thinking, the personal experience feature is the core of magazine journalism, one of the hallmarks that sets us apart from the news media. In one form or another—the first person article, the case history, anecdotes, nostalgia—I consider personal experience the most important part of the mix of features in *Good Housekeeping*. In *Good Housekeeping* these articles may take any of 10 different formats:

1. *The exclusive celebrity interview.* Two examples of this type of article that we've run in *GH:* "My 12 Years with Prince Charles" by Stephen Barry and "Diana's Life as a Wife, Princess and Mother."

2. *Crime and suspense.* Two examples:

"Shattered Night," the trial of the wife of a famous heart surgeon who, after suffering years of physical and psychological abuse, shot and killed her husband.

"Who Killed Patricia Gilmore?" This young woman was killed by her former boy friend after the authorities failed to take his threats seriously.

3. *Weight loss stories.* We look for new but sound breakthroughs on weight-loss products, techniques or diets. An example: "I Lost 100 Pounds Through Hypnosis."

4. *A miracle or legal first.* Two examples:
"A New Life for My Joi." This is the story of the first pancreas transplant as a treatment for severe diabetes.
"The 14 Million Dollar Woman." Story of Dorothy Thompson, who initiated and won a landmark anti-discrimination suit against the U.S. government.

5. *A woman's personal courage triumphs over a difficult challenge.* Example: "Alice Williams' Impossible Dream." Inspiring story of how a sharecropper's daughter, the only one among her siblings to graduate high school, managed to put her own 11 children through college.

6. *A provocative issue.* Examples:
"Doctors and Rape." The trial of a young nurse who accused three doctors of raping her.
"Malpractice." A doctor and expert witness opens his casebook on malpractice suits. Some of which have made medical and legal history.

7. *Personal stories of medical oddities.* Examples:
"I Froze to Death—But Lived." A young girl, caught in a Minnesota blizzard,

was frozen literally as stiff as a board—but much to her doctor's amazement, she recovered fully.

"My Heart Stopped While My Baby Was Being Born." Doctors thought there was a high probability that neither Laura Spitler nor her baby would survive—but they both beat the odds.

8. *Unique family lifestyle.* Examples:

"A Very Different Kind of Family." A fascinating glimpse into what it was like growing up in a polygamous Mormon household with 47 brothers and sisters.

"His, Mine . . . Ours." What happened when a mother of two married a widower with four—and got his former mother-in-law as well.

9. *The brief, personal, nostalgic essay.* Examples:

"A Spoonful of Love." The precious gifts passed down from mother to daughter.

"Watch Out, Great Grandma is Coming . . ." An anecdotal tale of multigenerational life.

10. *A woman's problem and how she solves it.* Examples:

"My Husband Was a Tightwad."

"I Fell in Love With My Doctor." (Carter, 1988, personal communication)

* * *

John Mack Carter is editor-in-chief of *Good Housekeeping* magazine, a position he has held with Hearst Magazines in New York since 1975. He has also been director of new magazine development for Hearst Corporation since 1979. He has edited two other major women's magazines—*Ladies' Home Journal* and *McCall's.* He was also editor-in-chief and chairman of *American Home* and *American Home Crafts* magazines. He was also associate editor of *Better Homes & Gardens.* He is host of the cable television program, "Good Housekeeping's A Better Way."

14

Writing Humor in Feature Articles

The market for high quality prose humor is always strong. A creative, truly funny writer can just about fill in the blanks on his or her own paycheck for full-time work or free-lance assignments.

Some publications in the United States specialize in humor, but most simply use it along with other content. Regardless, if you have an eye and ear for funny stories, and you have an ability to express things in a humorous way, it might be a specialization for you. Some magazines and newspapers use humor as spot features; others use it as a regular item in columns or departments. Still others will use humor only as fill material.

To be successful as a humorist such as the *Atlanta Constitution's* Lewis Grizzard, or the *San Francisco Chronicle's* Alice Kahn, whose syndicated columns and books have grown in popularity in the 1980s, or Art Buchwald, whose time-tested books and syndicated national political commentary column have been popular for three decades, takes basic hard work. Yes, you have to have something funny to say, but you must also have the wide-ranging experiences and unique perspective to make it work.

Most writing experts say that writing humor is among the toughest types of writing. Because humor writing has this reputation, few people try it and, of course, even fewer succeed. Hollywood writer Larry Wilde (1976) says humor writers are "hypersensitive, indulgent, indefatigable, disciplined, sentimental, highly intelligent, and well-educated individuals. Their influence on society is immeasurable. They are the word-picture painters, word coiners, phrase makers, colloquial-expression designers of our times" (p. 6).

This chapter cannot teach you *everything* about humor writing; in fact, entire books are devoted to this subject; for example, see Gene Perret's *How to Write and Sell (Your Sense of) Humor*. But this chapter will show you the basic elements of writing funny stories, columns, and other material. And although humor can be both fiction and nonfiction, spoken or written, the focus here is written nonfiction. This chapter will look at the formulas that make writers such as syndicated newspaper and magazine humorist Dave Barry, who won the 1988 Pulitzer Prize for commentary, so successful. Although you might not become an Erma Bombeck or an Art Buchwald, you will learn about writing briefs and brights as well as the longer humor columns and articles in this chapter. You will see how proven humorists have built their reputations—one funny word at a time.

WHAT'S HUMOR?

What is funny to you? Or to someone else? Is there a difference? Webster's New World Dictionary (1966) says humor is a person's disposition or temperament, sort of a state of mind. The dictionary continues to define humor as whim or fancy. Then it adds, well into the definition, "the quality that makes something seem funny, amusing, or ludicrous; comicality. . . . the ability to perceive, appreciate, or express what is funny. . ." (p. 708).

Scholars have been studying humor since the days of the Greek philosophers. Humor takes many different forms. As a writer, your humor can be jokes, brief fillers or sketches, essays, columns, and the normal feature article. Today's scholars have gotten no further than those of centuries ago. Humor remains an elusive concept and there is still no agreement on how humor should be defined.

The bottom line is simple enough—what is humorous is different to each individual. Humor historians Walter Blair and Hamlin Hill (1978) put it this way: "Laughter is a highly subjective response. So writers who are foolhardy enough to discuss the humor which does or doesn't produce it are an endangered species" (p. VII).

DRAWING IDEAS FROM REAL LIFE

Some of the funniest stories we find to write about are not made up. When we hear or read one, it might seem as if some very creative person just thought it up, but the best is what happens on a daily basis.

Just keep yourself on alert for the possibilities.

Humor writer Mary Ognibene (1975) says her humorous articles are based on her own experiences. "The only humor I can write is based on the idea that every dumb thing that happens to me also happens to everybody else. I add a little exaggeration and the formula seems to work" (p. 1), she explains.

Some writers feel that finding ideas is the most demanding part of the job of the humor writer. That's how humor columnist Richard Benedetto (1975) sees things. "The hardest part of column writing is coming up with ideas. I pound the pavement and stay awake nights trying to find them. And once one is selected, I begin to worry about the next one. Readers, colleagues and friends often offer suggestions, which are sometimes used" (p. 5), he says.

Syndicated columnist Art Buchwald uses the daily newspaper for most of his ideas. A new Buchwald column, usually about 600 words, begins when he reads the newspaper. Often he will see something he will file away for later use. Then he looks for the news peg for whatever idea he has filed away—in other words a reason for writing about that subject. Then he writes. And he repeats this process three times a week, or more than 150 times a year.

Lewis Grizzard's columns and books focus on his own experiences in Georgia. They focus on family members, his dogs, his former family members (such as his *three* former wives), life in the South, landlords, neighbors, religion, relationships, Northerners, politics, and much more. He tells short anecdotes and long stories. But he bases his material on what he sees and hears.

New Orleans Times-Picayune columnist Angus Lind also uses real stories, but has even advertised for humorous stories from readers. His strategy works because his readers call—even long distance from around Louisiana—to tell him of their experiences. Lind takes the best material for his column.

Good, funny writing, in sum, takes advantage of our unusual and ordinary experiences. Journalism professor Shirley Biagi (1981) says humor writing depends on a writer's ability to form images and word pictures along with the surprise or unexpected finish or resolution of the story. The strategy keys on building up to the end by taking a small step at a time to tell the story, allowing momentum to grow. By using a combination of little jokes, she says, you can then break the punchline.

Tom Ladwig (1987), writing for the *Columbia Missourian,* simply told a funny story and let situations in the story do the job. The story was based on a series of incidents involving a Missouri couple who took a trip filled with strange, but true incidents and coincidences:

1. At a drive-through wildlife attraction, an elephant sits on the couple's camper.
2. The couple's wrecked car is mistaken by police for a vehicle involved in a hit-and-run accident as the couple tries to drive home.
3. The investigating officer does not believe the explanation that an elephant damaged the car.
4. After the elephant story is checked out by police, the husband is left behind at a gas station by his wife—she thought he was asleep in the back of their camper.

5. The same police officer drives by and sees the husband sitting on the side of the road.
6. The officer drives the husband home and the husband arrives home before his spouse does.
7. Without his house keys, the husband sits in front of the house waiting for his wife to arrive.
8. He waves at his wife when she pulls into the driveway. She is startled to see him and drives through the garage door.

As Ladwig tells the story, it grows increasingly funny from the first step to the conclusion. And it is quite entertaining reading. His eye for a good story and his ability to re-tell it won Ladwig first place in the 1987 humorous column category of the National Newspaper Association writing contest.

MAJOR HUMOR TECHNIQUES

The market for humor is ready and waiting for copy that is entertaining and an escape for readers from their day-to-day concerns. And the pay is not so bad, either—some magazines pay $100 to $400 per item for brights and even more for longer pieces.

Topically, most publications do not want off-color or sexist humor. Taking shots at others, such as telling ethnic jokes, is not published today, either. So, a smart professional humor writer will stay away from techniques that use these out-of-favor subjects and approaches.

Humorist Patrick McManus (Finley, 1988), author of books and articles, offers four major tips for writing short (up to 1,500 words) humor. First, he says the idea should be covered by a single theme. Second, develop the characters in the story. Third, list the bits of humor—the jokes, in other words—you can fit into your prescribed length in words. And fourth, start writing and rewrite frequently. Concentrate on the lead, since it is often the hardest part. But McManus says you should make it funny to alert readers that the piece will be funny. He then recommends using exaggeration, but it should be appropriate exaggeration.

The best humor writers employ nine standard techniques in writing humor: satire, parody, exaggeration, contrast, understatement, asides, irony, grammatical emphasis, and puns. These are the major tools humor writers use to achieve their goal of entertaining readers.

Satire

Writers often ridicule a subject's vices, excesses, abuses, follies, or stupidities. This is satire, a form of criticism common in humor writing today. When someone prominent is caught in the act, perhaps drinking a little too much or using an illegal drug, and the story is reported in a serious way, it does not take long before humorists take the poor victim's mistakes as fair material for their writing. Satire often becomes the approach used to criticize a gun-toting leading citizen who takes a position for gun control, for example. Portraying the individual as using his weapon to protect himself against overly aggressive children who want their weekly allowances might get the point across. Several church group leaders, such as Jim and Tammy Bakker, Oral Roberts, and Jimmy Swaggert, have been satirized for their excesses in either fund-raising techniques, their personal lifestyles, or their atypical sexual behavior.

Dave Barry (1986) uses satire in his account of a lunch date with Sophia Loren. Barry got to take his peek at the world of the rich and famous and told his readers about it. Using satire, he makes fun of himself by writing that he was "working" when he lunched with the movie star (and a lot of other people). He satirizes the lifestyle of the luxury residential complex that the luncheon event and Loren promoted. He pokes fun at the free food and champagne, the high prices of the exclusive apartments, the press kit descriptions, and even the press itself. When it comes time for him to ask her a question, he asks her about cockroaches in her own luxury apartment at the complex.

Parody

At times, there is an opportunity to imitate the style of an individual, place, object, or institution. This is parody. To do parody well, you must study the subject you plan to write about. Once you have mastered the characteristic style of the person or other subject, you take a nonsensical approach to the subject. This works best with serious subjects such as political leaders or revered institutions. For example, a local humor columnist might use parody to write about a local public official who has made a bad political decision or squandered public resources. Or parody can simply involve an embarrassing revelation. President Reagan, late in his second term, was parodied by writers after his former Chief of Staff Donald Regan wrote in a book that the President and his wife, Nancy Reagan, used astrology in making some of their scheduling decisions.

Exaggeration

In telling funny stories, a useful technique is to enlarge, distort, and overemphasize to make a point. Although the cockroach on your kitchen table might not be quite equal in size to your Irish Setter, it makes the point better when you stretch the fact a little. This emphasizes your perspective and conveys to readers that the insect in your kitchen really did scare you into jumping onto a chair and crying out for help. Remember that when you more than make a point using a technique like exaggeration, you make a promise with readers to have a reason for it. Exaggeration and overstatement for nothing more than the purpose of overstating often do not work.

Contrast

This can also be described as incongruity. In using contrast, you establish a lack of harmony with the world; you show unreasonable and unsuitable situations. There are times when something that is expected and routine becomes something completely unexpected and non-routine. For example, a story about a business trip that was well-planned in advance with hotel and rental car reservations, airline bookings, and so forth turns into humor when the realities of the trip include an airline strike, rental car breakdown, no hotel reservations, and just plain bad timing (for example, you finally arrive at the hotel at 11:15 p.m., hungry and tired and find out that room service closed at 11 p.m.).

Understatement

Just like exaggeration, understatement works to create emphasis and reaction on the part of the reader. An intentional, softer comment will draw attention when it is contrasted with the expected. If, for example, you were referring to the real summer heat that the local readers know was 98 degrees with 80 percent humidity by saying, "It was a little warm outside yesterday," then you have understated the case dramatically and no doubt drawn a reaction from your reader.

Asides

Many humor writers like to use parentheses in writing to communicate with readers on a quasi-private level. This is a technique often used in acting that permits the actor to communicate only with the audience. In writing, humorists who use asides are attempting the same technique as if to privately communicate with you (and not the book's editor). Did you notice? The previous sentence contained an aside. You don't have to use parentheses all the time. Some writers prefer dashes or other typographic devices to accomplish the same thing. Some writers will even use footnotes for the same effect. Dave Barry likes to use asides in his writing. In his column about the Astrology Lady at the White House, (Barry, 1988) he makes several "personal" comments to readers. Barry also likes to make asides by writing what might appear to be an in-house note to an editor about the content of the column and leaving it in the text.

Irony

Similar to contrast, irony is a technique that employs contradictions through writing tone and subject, for example. It focuses on the direct opposite of what is usual or expected. The distance between what happened and what should have happened or what is said and what is intended is irony. Writers using irony set up the story they tell by leading the reader to expect one type of outcome through a combination of circumstances or steps involving the principals of the story. Then the reader is stunned by the opposite or inappropriate outcome. This technique is used often in writing brights, which will be discussed later in this chapter.

Grammatical Emphasis

Some writers will make points in their humor writing by intentionally overusing and abusing English grammar. One such technique is overuse of exclamation marks (e.g., multiple exclamation marks after a word in the middle of a sentence). Another is capitalizing nouns (e.g., Campaign Trail) used in generic references rather than specific contexts. These tricks draw readers' attention to certain words and terms in an extreme fashion and help place focus where the writer wants it. Other writers intentionally invent words when they cannot find the right word to express their feelings (e.g., "they will 'Pepsify' the South"). These diversions from the ordinary uses of grammar are functional and help the writer as he or she tells the story.

Puns, Other Techniques

For many centuries, humor writers have used puns for a good laugh from readers. This device uses plays on words to provide double meaning. No doubt you can think of countless puns you encounter in everyday conversation, reading, and your own writing.

There are other techniques humor writers use. For example, Art Buchwald likes to use dialogue in his columns, creating fictitious conversations that *might* have occurred. In his column about Larry Speakes, President Reagan's former press secretary, Buchwald uses dialogue to describe a conversation about direct quotes that could have occurred in the White House. You might recall that Speakes admitted in a book written after he left the White House that he had made up quotes as press secretary that he attributed to the President.

The effect is humor. Buchwald's mythical conversation between Speakes and the President points to all the troubles resulting from Speakes' revelation.

BRIGHTS AND HUMOROUS SHORT ITEMS

Much humor published in American newspapers and magazines takes the form of short, brief stories that fit in various places throughout the publication. Some newspapers like to run front page one-line chuckles and editorial page one-paragraph funny stories. Other publications incorporate such short humorous material into regular news or columns. Some publications simply use these funny feature articles as fill material when it is needed to complete a page or a specific space. Magazines such as *Reader's Digest* use regular humor features such as "Humor in Uniform" and "Campus Comedy" that are collections of brights about American military and college life. And they're very popular. Research at *Reader's Digest* shows these sections are among the most popular in the entire magazine. They can be lucrative also: *Reader's Digest* pays $400 for published stories.

These brights, as many people refer to them, are typically amusing stories that offer, as writer Daniel Williamson (1975) defines them, "a humorous and unusual quirk" (p. 117). These items can come from reporters on the police beat, the courts, meetings, or from callers.

University of Houston professor Louis Alexander (1975) says the main purpose of a bright is "to change the pace and tone of the newspaper, the magazine, or the broadcast. Being so short, a brite [sic] makes a fine filler; fits anywhere to complete a page, round out the makeup of a section or fill out a broadcast. And in this process, brites accomplish their main purpose: they provide variety" (p. 30).

Author and comedy writer Gene Perret (1987) offers three reasons for writing these short humorous anecdotes:

1. It's easy and takes little time.
2. It's quick and fast writing.
3. It's fun and a challenge.

Brights are particularly popular with the news services, which use them for both the newspaper wires and the broadcast wires. They are then used by editors as a counterpoint to the day's usually serious news.

The writing style dictates that these items remain brief, using the most concise writing. People and places cannot be thoroughly described or themes developed in detail. The usual bright is a couple of sentences to a couple of paragraphs in length. Usually, this means no less than 50 words but no more than 300 words.

With such short, funny items, structure is important. Brief and to-the-point leads work best for brights. They must be terse, Williamson advises. They should be fast-moving, and skeletonlike. Most briefs are written in inverted pyramid form, but some stories lend themselves to chronological writing also.

Structure is dominated by a strong lead and an even stronger ending. The best material goes last. This should be an unexpected outcome, a surprise finish. If readers will expect one sort of resolution, the bright will strike them as funny because it does the opposite.

Some brights will not have a punchline finish. Brights without a punchline must leave readers wondering why something happened, who was involved, or simply what happened. This is usually a finish forced on writers because no resolution is available. For example, did the man ever get his keys out of the car? Did the child get the ink off her face? Did the student pay the overdue book fine?

Finding brights is easy, writer Gene Perret (1984) says. His advice is to review your own personal stories, to trade stories at gatherings, read a great deal and remember what you read, stay aware of what is going on in your community, and be alert to what is happening around you.

Brights have a "twist," as some humor writers explain them. This twist is the uncommon point of the story, the writer's statement about human nature. It can be the punchline described in the preceding paragraph. Louis Alexander describes the main characteristics of brights:

1. They make fun of human nature and human errors.
2. They must have a newspeg (be about someone and be recent).
3. The situation should be unusual.
4. They must be cleverly written.
5. The item should end with a punchline.
6. There should be good transition elements.

Brights, it should be added, should not be written with the solution in the lead. This spoils the effect for readers and destroys the value of the item. A well-thought-out bright will hold its best for last.

In addition, Alexander recommends avoiding the inverted pyramid structure in writing brights. You write a bright much like you tell a joke. Not all brights have to be funny. If brights are not going to bring a laugh, they should draw out sympathy or another emotion. They can draw their reaction from the reader's intellect.

Brights are not always time-bound. Some editors compile them for use in columns and other regular features. The entertainment value of brights is more important than the time element, yet a timely bright is even more valuable when it is available.

Perret (1987) recommends another approach—writing the bright backwards. Begin with the ending when you write. Then build toward that ending and be compact. The beginning, he advises, should be "a short explanation of why you're telling this story" (p. 29).

The good bright writer is also a good reporter. The funny story, as tempting as it may be, cannot invent facts or even stretch them for the effect the stretching might bring. Stick to the facts and good reporting.

Now let's look at three brights from an issue of *Reader's Digest* to see how they achieve these goals:

From "All in a Day's Work"
As a new real estate agent, I had just been given my first beeper. Eager to show it off, I went to visit my mother. She was much impressed and jotted down the number in case she ever had to reach me. Then she invited me to dinner. While she finished preparing the meal, I went shopping. I was waiting in a checkout line when I got my first "beep." Feeling important, and as everyone in line looked on,

I pushed the beeper's call button to hear my mother's voice loud and clear: "SUPPER'S READY!" (Angel Bain, p.104)

Reader's Digest seeks brights like that one. In the *Writer's Market* (Neff, 1988), potential contributors are told about sections such as "All in a Day's Work," "Campus Comedy," "Humor in Uniform," and "Life-in-these-United States": "Contributions must be true, unpublished stories from one's own experience, revealing adult human nature, and providing appealing or humorous sidelights on the American scene" (p. 317). Readers are also advised in each issue what editors look for, because many contributors are magazine readers as well as professional feature writers. A maximum length is 300 words for *Reader's Digest*.

Does this bright achieve its goals? Structurally, yes. It sets the situation up and then delivers a surprise ending. It contains sound description of what happened in chronological order. But there are no lengthy direct quotes. We might have anticipated a call while in an embarrassing situation, but probably few readers will guess what the message might be. Here is another example:

From "Campus Comedy"
Once when I was doing homework while on my job at the North Texas State University racquetball courts, a student walked up to me to check in. He showed me his ID card, then asked what I was reading.

"American literature . . . Walt Whitman," I replied.

"Little guy with curly hair?" he asked. "Worst teacher I ever had. Gave me a D." (Daniel W. Ferguson, p. 122)

This bright is just a moment in time, but a funny one. The very short item stands solely on its dialogue recreation. The quotes are critical since the answer of the student is the punchline. Try writing this bright without the quotes and it just does not have the same impact.

From "Campus Comedy"
While waiting for an early-morning class to begin at California State University in Chico, I overheard another student talk about a big party he had attended the night before. That he'd slept late and rushed to make it to class was obvious. We all had our calculators sitting on our desks. He reached into his book bag and pulled out the remote control to his VCR! (Kimberly Ledesma, p. 121)

The third bright is purely descriptive and is accomplished in only four sentences. The behavior is the important point here, and the author's description of the behavior does not reveal the mistake the student made in his rush to attend class until the final word. This is the timing and delivery that is important to successful brights.

SUBMITTING BRIGHTS FOR PUBLICATION

Gene Perret (1984), who has written humor for Bob Hope and Carol Burnett, recommends three rules for submitting short humorous anecdotes and other similar material for publication:

1. *Send your submissions in batches.* No less than five should be in each envelope you send, although you can submit as many as a dozen each time. Giving the editor a few to read through each time helps your percentages.

2. *Send each anecdote on a separate page.* On each sheet, include your name, address, phone number and Social Security number (the last will help speed payment). . . .

3. *Neatly type all submissions.* Don't cut corners because it's "only" an anecdote. Be professional. Buyers don't want to read through hand written or messy submissions. Type everything with a fresh ribbon, and double-space submissions for easier editing. The usual SASE [self-addressed, stamped envelope] is not required because most periodicals don't acknowledge these submissions except with an acceptance check.

HUMOR COLUMNS

Art Buchwald's long-running political satire column is one of the leading examples of how to succeed at humor column writing. Buchwald's humor focuses on big government but does not get inappropriate for family consumption. The column on Larry Speakes and Ronald Reagan is just one example of this approach. Buchwald writes a regular column that is produced 3 days a week.

Buchwald's ability to regularly produce amusing material is rare. What is funny varies, depending on the reader, so Buchwald says he writes to please himself. He says he likes to laugh at his own material and tries not to think whether a reader will think it is funny or not.

Although many humorists are syndicated and write from an independent base like Buchwald, major newspapers and magazines often have a humor columnist on staff. Many of the most popular "local" humorists have become syndicated and their followings have grown from regional to the national level.

Gannett's long-time Oregon columnist John Terry (1975) says humor columns can cease to be an extension of the writer and take on their own identity. "It's the column that demands to be written; I am merely the instrument of its handiwork" (p. 12).

Most columnists will focus on their own experiences, observations, or current events. The usual run of current events involving our community leaders provides enough material for most humorists—stories such as the varied troubles of evangelists Jim and Tammy Bakker, President Reagan and Nancy Reagan's use of astrology in White House decision making, Gary Hart's 1988 presidential campaign and his personal involvement with a model, and other unusual national stories.

For almost 7 years, William Geist wrote real-life humor for *The New York Times*. Before that, he wrote a column for *The Chicago Tribune*. Although he has moved on to write books and humor for the *CBS News Sunday Morning* program, he still writes about the people, the environment and scenery around him, and the most commonplace activities he experiences. He looks around for ideas in his neighborhood, says writer Peter Spielmann, who profiled Geist for *Writer's Digest* in 1988.

Geist explained how he finds material for his regular regimen of writing: "I always look for a story where there's a conflicting sense of values or ethnic groups, or anything where something doesn't fit, is out of whack, in order to get insights on what people are really like" (Spielmann, 1988, p. 30). An example: he focused on class conflict when he wrote about "driveway dress codes" in suburbia—all brought about by a New Jersey community's ordinance preventing certain vehicles (e.g., service trucks) from being parked in driveways overnight.

THE DIFFICULTY OF WRITING HUMOR

It is worthwhile to once again remind you that humor writing is not easy. Most professional writers agree and are often frustrated by even attempting to describe how they do it or how you should do it. Some say it cannot be taught. Here's how *Writer's Digest* columnist Art Spikol (1986) sums up writing humor:

> It's hard to write humor. I can teach any half-decent writer to write a salable magazine article, but I can't teach anyone to write funny. That ability really comes from an inner voice, and that inner voice may not necessarily be there when you need it. After a few years of developing the muscle, you'll be able to flex it at will—but you'll never get that far if you're not somebody who thinks funny to begin with. (p. 18)

Spikol is right. You need that certain unusual perspective on life to write quality humor. And you need a mind for it as well—you must know your market and what makes it tick. If you write for a general audience as most newspaper writers do, then you have a different humor challenge from those who write for specialized magazines. Those who write humor for specialized magazines know the "inside" issues and concerns that inside jokes can be built upon. As Spikol says, humor is not written in a vacuum.

And there's no substitute for grand creativity. A very creative individual has an edge in writing humor. Stephen Doig's inspired April Fool's Day hoax displays this. Topically, it is perfect for the South Florida market. The subject misleads the reader into thinking the story is genuine. It is presented as a real news story. Doig's genius in creating this article with its tricks and other devices made the article a success. It is amusing, entertaining, and clever. Readers appreciate such efforts and respond.

Although well-known humor writers get the best publication breaks, it is not impossible for you. And you might want to start at a low-pressure level by writing humor when you are inspired to be funny. By writing infrequently and thinking small in the beginning, you will gain confidence one step at a time. Small newspapers, such as your community or neighborhood weeklies, and small magazines or newsletters, will be easier market to crack. Dave Barry and Lewis Grizzard did not become successes overnight. Their careers developed slowly and methodically at local levels into their national superstar levels today.

And once success as a humor writer is achieved, it must be maintained through hard work. Inspiration, as Dave Barry told *Writer's Digest* writer Marshall Cook (1987), is not enough if you make a living off the writing. "I write seven days a week," Barry said. "If I don't write, I feel guilty. There's real work out there, and I'm not doing it. The least I can do is write" (p. 29).

HOW PROFESSIONALS WROTE IT

DATE: MONDAY, OCTOBER 5, 1987
SOURCE: COLUMBIA MISSOURIAN (AS REPRINTED IN *PUBLISHER'S AUXILIARY*), VOL. 123, NO. 20, P. 20.
AUTHOR: TOM LADWIG

* * *

THE BADDEST OF BAD DAYS GIVES COUPLE A GOOD STORY

This story is intended for those among us who think we've had a bad day.

It doesn't seem to have one whit of historical significance, but it is a story that probably will be told and retold.

Adam (not his real name) is a man of the cloth. He and his wife were missionaries for many years, and he now teaches in a bible college in southeast Missouri.

For the first time in many years, they have weekends free. To enjoy them more, Adam purchased a small pickup and had a camper shell installed. They explore the Ozarks and occasionally help a fellow minister when he needs a Sunday off.

They filled in for a colleague one Sunday last summer. They started home early Monday and passed one of those tourist attractions where you see all sorts of wild animals in a pseudo-natural setting.

It was early, and it seemed like fun so they drove in. After buying their tickets they saw all the animals they wanted to see from the safety of their pickup camper.

As they neared the end of the road, they found a huge elephant standing in the middle. Adam, a calm man, edged the truck closer. The elephant didn't budge. Adam edged closer.

Possibly patience and prayer would have worked better, but Adam honked. The elephant did move. It sat down, right on the hood of the truck.

The rear end of the camper went into air and Adam, now in desperation, honked and honked. The proprietors came and sent the elephant keeper who finally convinced his charge to leave.

Of course the management arranged for the damage to be repaired and left Adam their business card with the insurance firm's telephone number. The motor still ran and Adam decided to limp home.

They had driven about 20 miles on the four-lane when they passed a wrecked car. Seeing there were other travelers assisting they drove on.

Four miles down the road, a highway patrol car approached and as it came abeam, wheeled across the median and flagged them down with siren and lights.

The trooper approached and told Adam he was investigating a hit-run-accident a few miles back and asked Adam how his truck came to be damaged.

Adam said: "Officer, you're not going to believe this. An elephant sat on my hood." The trooper said: "You're right, I don't believe it. Get out."

It took a while for Adam's story to check out. The trooper, a 20-year veteran, still shaking his head in disbelief, told them they were free to go.

By this time Adam's head ached. He asked his wife to drive while he rested in the camper. They made good progress. Adam's wife made a rest stop at a service station. Adam awakened and decided this was a good idea.

When Adam returned he found the camper gone, his wife obviously thinking him still asleep in the camper. He walked to the highway and sat on the curb to plot his next move. While there, the same patrolman drove by. Seeing Adam, he stopped and asked: "What now?"

Adam explained. The trooper said he was going towards Adam's hometown and could drop him off. They took off and somehow arrived before Adam's wife and the pickup camper.

It was still daylight, and Adam, the keys to the house still in the truck, thanked the trooper and said he would just sit and wait.

It wasn't but a few minutes before Mrs. A turned into the drive. As she approached the house, she caught sight of Adam waving from the porch. She jerked her head violently back toward the camper. And while in the position, her battered pickup slammed through the garage door.

Fortunately, Adam's wife was not injured. And nothing unusual happened to Adam and his wife for the remainder of that day. Or since for that matter.

Reprinted with the permission of the *Columbia Missourian*.

• • •

DATE: FRIDAY, SEPTEMBER 12, 1986
SOURCE: THE MIAMI HERALD, P. 1B
AUTHOR: DAVE BARRY, MIAMI HERALD TROPIC COLUMNIST

* * *

DAVE TO SOPHIA: 'CHOW, BELLA'

My original plan was not to have lunch with Sophia Loren. My original plan was to eat a chicken salad sandwich, then go pick up my son at kindergarten. In fact, I had actually purchased the chicken salad sandwich at *The Miami Herald* cafeteria when a person in the Business Section asked me if I wanted to have lunch with Sophia Loren. "Sure," I said. This kind of thing happens all the time in the news game.

So I called my wife. "Could you pick up Robby?" I asked. "I'm going to go have lunch with Sophia Loren."

"Sure," she said, in a sweet and kind and totally understanding voice. She will get even.

The reason I was invited to lunch with Sophia Loren was that she was promoting something. Somebody is always promoting something in the news business, and it is our job, as communications professionals, to go and find out what it is, even if this means eating a lot of free food. In this case, Sophia Loren was promoting something up in North Dade called "Williams Island," which, according to the press packet, is "a luxury, 80-acre island resort residence community on protected waters just off the Intracoastal Waterway." It's very nice. I would recommend Williams Island as a potential residence for anybody, whether he had $250 million or just $245 million.

No, seriously, the brochure says they have "residential offerings" there starting at a very affordable $180,000, which I bet you could round up just by walking around and picking up the money that blows off the balconies of the nicer units. One of those units is occupied, when she's in town, by world-famous raving-beauty movie actress Sophia Loren, who also does promotional work for them in exchange for money. (Yes! Even Sophia Loren!)

We had lunch at the restaurant on Williams Island, the Island Club. They have a new kind of Very Trendy food there called "tapas," which also was being promoted. According to Richard Lamondin, director of marketing and sales for Williams Island, "The Tapas Experience is now one of the North American rages."

So we media people all sat down at our assigned tables and had the Tapas Experience, which consists of eating things off little plates. I thought they were great, except this one plate that I swear to God had a small dead octopus on it. Probably it was a prank. Probably back in the kitchen, they said: "Look what Lester found in the protected waters just off the Intracoastal Waterway! Yuck! Let's see if the news media will eat it, because it's free food!"

After the Tapas Experience, they served us lamb chops, during which Sophia Loren herself came over to our table and sat down to chat with us personally. You ladies have heard, of course, that Sophia Loren is very, very beautiful, especially for a woman of 51, but let me tell you something: When she is close, when you really get a look at her, she is Beyond Perfect. I'm sorry, ladies, but there you have it. Genetics. If it makes you feel any better, there is probably some area in which you are superior to Sophia Loren, such as playing the accordion.

So after we had just looked at her for a minute, we asked her some questions. This is where I would hate to be a famous movie actress, because she got asked, for example: "Is there any message you would want to give to the women of the world?" Think about that. There you are, trying to eat your lamb chop, and you have to come up with a message for the women of the world. I know if it was me, I'd blow it. I'd say something like, "Well, they should floss their teeth." But Sophia Loren, she was very poised. She said she felt the women of the world should be Generous. She came up with that right off the top of her head.

I had given careful thought to what question I would ask her. I wanted it to be the kind of question you, my readers, would want to ask in the astoundingly unlikely event you ever had a personal lunch with Sophia Loren.

"Have you found any large insects in your apartment?" I asked.

"Insects?" she said.

"Cockroaches," I said. "They get huge down here." I held my hands about a foot apart so she'd get the idea.

"Not yet," she said.

So there you have it: an exclusive interview with the lovely Miss Sophia Loren at her South Florida residence, the luxurious and cockroach-free Williams Island. If you want my opinion, you all should head over there as soon as possible and try the tapas and maybe purchase yourself a residence offering. And I don't say this just because they gave me a lot of free food. I say this because they also gave me champagne.

Reprinted with the permission of the author and *The Miami Herald.*

• • •

DATE: THURSDAY, MAY 12, 1988
SOURCE: THE MIAMI HERALD, P. 1B
AUTHOR: DAVE BARRY, MIAMI HERALD TROPIC COLUMNIST

* * *

ASTROLOGY LADY SURE CAN'T BE REAGAN'S WORST ADVISER

Well, according to White House Insiders—what few we have left—Nancy is just furious. And I believe it. I just hope that some third-rate power such as Uruguay doesn't get into a dispute with us over some minor matter such as limits on mackerel fishing, because in her current mood, Nancy could very well recommend solving it via nuclear weapons. That is how angry she is.

And I don't blame her. Because once again, a departed aide has betrayed the Reagan administration. You'd think the Reagans would have learned by now not to let aides depart. You'd think they'd have a little trapdoor installed in the Rose Garden, so that at the end of an aide's going-away party, they could push a button, and fwooosh!, the aide would go plummeting down to an underground pit inhabited by Michael Deaver, Larry Speakes, et al. (Yecch!) Makes me shudder just thinking about it!)

But unfortunately, White House aides continue to escape and betray the Reagans. When we say "betray," of course, we mean, "reveal to the voters what actually goes on in the White House." Recently, for example, former press secretary Speakes revealed that he had made up quotations that were attributed to the president, a charge that Reagan angrily denied, using cue cards.

But the latest, and most serious, betrayal comes from former White House chief of staff Donald Regan, who was forced to resign because his name kept getting everybody confused. Regan has just released a book entitled The President Routinely Acts on the Advice of His Wife's West Coast Astrology Loon.

Well, OK, that's not technically the title, but it is definitely the thrust of the book, as grasped by the voting public. And thus we have yet another in the series of Amazing White House Stories, contributing to the growing public perception that the Ship of State is being steered by Mr. Magoo and the Spider Woman.

But is this really fair? I think not. I mean, suppose the president really does permit astrology to influence his decisions. Does that make him any different from millions of us regular citizens who consult our newspaper horoscopes each day for advice on such matters as when to hold press conferences, or sign arms-reduction treaties with the Soviet Union? Of course not!

Besides which, if the president can't get advice from astrologers, who is he supposed to get advice from?

Should he turn to Attorney General Edwin "You'll Never Take Me Alive" Meese? Or the advisers who came up with the idea of sending the Navy to the Persian Gulf to engage in "Operation Form Big Targets"?

Or how about the strategists who came up with the brilliant plan to oust drug-running slimeball Manuel Noriega as ruler of Panama, a plan so perfectly conceived and executed that millions of years from now, when the rest of human civilization has evolved beyond recognition, Panama will still be ruled by drug-running slime-ball Manuel Noriega?

No, I think the astrology loon could well be our best hope for rational input into the White House. I personally would have no objection to giving her a Cabinet post.

I do feel, however, that her influence should remain limited to matters relating to the president's schedule. She should have nothing to do with policy. I feel very strongly that policy decisions, in accordance with both federal tradition and the U.S. Constitution should continue to be made by the Tarot Card Lady.

Reprinted with the permission of the author and *The Miami Herald*.

• • •

DATE: TUESDAY, APRIL 19, 1988
SOURCE: THE MIAMI NEWS, P. 17A.
AUTHOR: ART BUCHWALD, LOS ANGELES TIMES SYNDICATE

* * *

MOUTHPIECE ISSUES PEARLS OF WISDOM

WASHINGTON—Larry Speakes has been roundly criticized for putting words in President Reagan's mouth. As press secretary he made up quotes that he attributed to the president, causing damage to Mr. Reagan's reputation as commander-in-chief of everything he utters.

The White House press corps was not so much amazed at Speakes' resorting to such subterfuge as puzzled about why the president permitted it.

The best explanation is that President Reagan never worried about what Speakes said at his briefings as long as it sounded good to the public.

There were some close calls for the Gipper, however. One time Speakes came into the Oval office and said, "Sir, we have just secured Grenada. Is there any statement you'd like to make?"

"How about, 'Fourscore and seven years ago our forefathers brought forth a new nation and that is why we have nothing to fear but fear itself'?"

"It's a bit wordy," Larry said.

"Well, you have the idea, just kick it around and use anything you want to."

"I will say, 'This is one of the greatest victories against communism in our lifetime and is a signal to our foes that we will never negotiate out of fear nor fear to negotiate.' "

"That's fine. Good night."

"But, sir, it's 4 o'clock in the afternoon. You have to make a speech this evening at your state dinner for Margaret Thatcher."

"What are you going to tell the press I said?" the president asked.

"I might tell them that you said she has brought us nothing but blood, sweat and tears."

"I hadn't planned on saying that. Why can't you report when I made my toast I had no comment."

"The press doesn't like that. Don't worry, I'll think of something."

"You're very good, Larry."

"I see it this way, Mr. President. A press secretary's job is to make the president look better than he really is. If I can have you expounding brilliant things, we both win."

"How do we both win?"

"You come out of it as the Great Communicator, and I get a much higher advance on my book."

"Larry, are we doing anything wrong?"

"Of course not. I am your spokesman. What difference does it make if you say it or I say it, as long as you get the credit for it?"

"Suppose they find out the words aren't mine?"

"Only you and I know that, sir, and I sure as heck am not going to tell. Look, I won't make up quotes all the time. If you ever come up with anything original, I'll use it."

"And it won't hurt us when it comes out?"

"Not on your life. You don't think Abraham Lincoln said everything he was credited with?"

"Can I give you my statement now on how we won the war in Afghanistan?" the president asked.

"Try it out on me, and I'll see if I like it."

"You really take over, don't you, Larry?"

"Better me than Gorbachev."

Reprinted with the permission of the author and the Los Angeles Times Syndicate.

•••

DATE: WEDNESDAY, APRIL 1, 1987
SOURCE: THE MIAMI HERALD, P. 1B.
AUTHOR: ROLLO PIAF (STEPHEN K. DOIG), MIAMI HERALD

* * *

CODED MESSAGE SNIPE HUNTERS STUMBLE ON ARMS RIDDLE:
ATPHREIJLOFKOEOSLOSNDYAOYU

A couple of curious hunters who spotted a light flashing Morse code in the Everglades early this morning stumbled onto a cache of arms worth at least $411,987, according to puzzled authorities.

Police said Guff Gammon and Poisson D'Avril, both of rural Canard, were in the swamps southeast of Miami shortly after midnight, hunting pigeons and Florida snipe. Also, today is the first day of the short wild goose season.

"Right there on the horizon we saw this bright light flashing on and off," Gammon told reporters. "I thought it might be druggies, but Poisson here said we should go look."

Intrigued, the two men began wading cautiously in the moonshine toward the light. Suddenly, Gammon—a thimblerigger and ham radio operator—realized it was blinking out a cryptic repeating message.

"Luckily, I could read it easily, so Poiss wrote it on his pants leg," Gammon said, holding up a strip of cloth that read: ATPHREIJLOFKOEOSLOSNDY-AOYU. "We can't figure out what it means."

Finally, as Gammon and D'Avril drew closer, the light suddenly died. Seconds later, a camouflaged Loki Gull cargo helicopter roared straight up and away.

On the soggy hammock, stacked in the grass flattened by the departed whopper, were 41 wooden crates of arms. Each whitewashed crate, bearing only the inscription "HOCHS" stenciled in black paint, was filled with deadly Mannekin-Ulnas packed in greasy adulterine, ready for dissembling.

Overcoming their surprise, Gammon and D'Avril radioed police.

Later today, the arms and other evidence will be sent to the Federal Investigation Bureau lab for further prevarication, according to FIB agent Sham Kidder. He asked anyone who can crack the mysterious code to write him. Kidder added that he personally would read every other letter.

Reprinted with the permission of *The Miami Herald*.

This article appeared the following day:

DATE: THURSDAY, APRIL 2, 1987
SOURCE: THE MIAMI HERALD, P. 1B.
AUTHOR; HERALD STAFF

* * *

APRIL FOOL; ARMS TALE WAS A RUSE

The code has been broken.

In this space Wednesday, The Herald had a story about two hunters who found a cache of arms and a mysterious message:
ATPHREIJLOFKOEOSLOSNDYAOYU.

If you read every other letter, as the story hinted, you found: "April Fools Day" and "The jokes on you."

We tried to give you plenty of clues. For instance, the first letter of every paragraph also spelled "April Fool." All the names suggest something tricky. The money mentioned—$411,987—was also the date: 4/1/1987. The stenciled "HOCHS" could be pronounced "Hoax." There were a couple of deliberate typos, such as "whopper" and "FIB." Mannekin-Ulna, the supposed "arms" cache, means "mannequin armbone."

Even the byline, Rollo Piaf, was an anagram for April Fool. The "story" was written by Herald Science Writer Stephen K. Doig.

Happy April Fool's Day.

Reprinted with the permission of *The Miami Herald*.

A Professional's Point of View

By Alice Kahn
San Francisco Chronicle

I am often asked: "Alice, how can I join the exciting and glamorous world of article writing and hardly work at all and make tons of money?"

There are several foolproof methods of achieving this goal. The most common are the sleaze dig, the trend invention and the integrity-ectomy. Let me give you an example of each.

Recently a young woman called me and asked if she could interview me for a paper she was writing for her journalism class. It was a profile of John Raeside, editor of the *East Bay Express*, the paper where I got my break.

She asked me many probing and interesting questions about the influence of Raeside on my *oeuvre*. I was only too happy to go on at length about how much my old editor had encouraged me, how lucky I have been to work with supportive editors, the importance of including the writer in the editing process, etc. Obviously, time had glossed over whatever battles we had had, because I couldn't recall a single fault in my former editor other than his being born with the genetic defect of frugality.

After she asked me about Raeside's particular qualities, we got to the hidden agenda. "How long have you known him?" she asked.

"About six years," I answered.

And, lifting her shovel for the sleaze dig, she said, "And did you have what we might call a *personal* relationship?"

"Are you asking if I slept with him?"

"Just trying to dig something up," she said.

Now, I could understand, if she were interviewing me in person, how she might think a swell-looking babe like me would have no other way of succeeding than by sleeping with editors. But this was a phone interview.

I don't know what they're teaching them in journalism schools these days, but they'd better get one thing straight: "Bay Area Writer Sleeps With Editor" is not going to have the same market potential as "Liz Taylor Found in Pat Robertson's Love Nest."

Within hours of my conversation with the student journalist, I got a call from an experienced writer who is on the staff of a major metropolitan newspaper. She asked me if I could give her some "quotes" for a story she was doing. You see, she was on deadline, so she didn't want to have a discussion. Just gimme some quotes and keep your stinkin' ideas to yourself.

She said she was writing something about yuppie despair. She had a major trend going. That is, she had three yuppies who were willing to be desperate— on the record. Now she needed something from me as an expert on yuppies. I had written three articles on yuppies. I was an expert.

I said three things. Those became three quotes. A trend was born.

When the final call of the day came, I realized I needn't write any more. I could just fill requests. The person wanted to know what I thought of something or other. He was writing an article that consisted of nothing more than calling up other people and asking them what they think of something or other. He didn't even have the integrity to dream up a trend or fantasize someone's weird sex life.

Now, we here at The Alice Kahn Column consider ourselves a full-service agency. We are only too happy to oblige the readers by providing them with further information about the important subjects covered in this column. But I am serving notice on all writers of articles in search of a point that if you want me to pop open your idea, it's gonna cost you.

Henceforth, a 10 percent surcharge will be added to your bill for intellectual corkage. (Kahn, 1988, p. B4)

* * *

Alice Kahn is a syndicated columnist for the *San Francisco Chronicle*. She is author of two books, *Multiple sarcasm* (1985) and *My life as a gal* (1987), and she resides in Berkeley, Calif.

Reprinted with the permission of the author and the *San Francisco Chronicle*.

15

Writing Science and Technical Features

Writing about science and other technical subjects can be doubly rewarding. You can provide an educational service to readers who learn about the latest medical or engineering developments. And this in turn helps readers to live more complete and enjoyable lives. More and more, this is a major role of the feature writer in our society. Concern about AIDS in recent years, with the mix of rumor and fact, left the public confused about the truth about this disease. Governments around the world turned to the news media to help disseminate the known facts about AIDS and to educate the public about how to avoid the fatal epidemic. These public health information campaigns depended in part on science and technical writers for their success. The public's dependence on the news media for such valuable information underlines the significance of such feature writing. Through news stories, as well as through feature articles about discoveries about AIDS and other medical problems, the public is educated and better served.

You are part of a generation of science and high technology that pervade all aspects of your life. The same applies to today's magazine and newspaper readers. There are vital issues involving science today that never existed before and were not even in the minds of our best scientists a generation ago. Few people could have anticipated a medical problem such as AIDS, for example. The first computer was developed less than a half century ago. Manned aviation itself is less than a century old. It would have been hard for most scientists in the 1940s to imagine an energy source that could be as inexpensive or as dangerous as nuclear power. The list of these major developments is endless.

It is one of the news media's most important duties to provide the latest science and technology information to our communities. Certainly reporting about new developments that are life-saving techniques, or simply just time-saving, can be particularly satisfying for feature writers.

It can also be rewarding in another way. Writer Jacqui Banaszynski wrote a series of articles for the *St. Paul Pioneer Press* in 1987 about AIDS in America's heartland. She focused on the life and eventual death of an AIDS victim in telling the story from a compelling human perspective. She was able to write about difficult scientific subject matter in human terms. The effort earned Banaszynski the 1988 Pulitzer Prize for feature writing.

The excellence in *Baltimore Evening Sun* feature writer Jon Franklin's two stories about a new brain surgical technique not only told his readers about the procedure through detailed description of an operation on a 57-year-old woman, but won the 1979 Pulitzer Prize for feature writing. Why did both win? Because they had mastered science feature writing.

This chapter outlines the basics of writing science, technical, and other specialized features. Banaszynski and Franklin succeeded because of their abilities to take complicated subjects and write about them in an accurate manner that could be understood by readers without medical backgrounds. For example, Franklin's article displays the uncertainty and tension surrounding any surgical procedure that risks human life, particularly the drama of a revolutionary technique. The story is even more effective because of the humane approach to the article—readers get to know the patient and the neurosurgeons because Franklin develops their roles in the story beyond just name and identification. This type of science and technical writing is sensitive and dramatic through its narrative description. It's a good read. And that's what writing about complicated subject should do—allow readers to learn from, and enjoy, the subject.

DESCRIBING SCIENCE AND TECHNICAL FEATURES

Science and technical feature topics cover the universe, literally. Some of the hot topics in the 1990s will include medicine, computers, astronomy and space travel, psychology and psychiatry, nutrition and diet, sports and exercise science, geography and oceanography, meteorology, and biology. Take any of these topics, and each can be broken down into numerous subdivisions that are important topics themselves. In medicine, for example, focus will continue to be on drugs, AIDS, cancer, paralysis, burns, heart disease, children and childbirth, sleep, and sex.

The examples of science and technical writing accompanying this chapter illustrate the concerns of the 1990s about science and technical features for the general public. Certainly ecology and the environment, perhaps second only to human health and medicine, have been high-interest subjects in recent years.

The Boston Globe science writer Dianne Dumanoski's (1988) article on ozone loss is but one such article. Her story, telling about scientists who have identified possible ozone loss at the North Pole caused by man-made chemicals, should alert people to the need to find alternative chemicals to those used in refrigeration and air conditioning systems.

Knight-Ridder's Terry Bivens (1988), writing about the lack of sexual desire in some adults, shows one dimension of the vast human health and medicine subject category. On a subject that might not have been regarded as serious a few years ago, this article explains the sexuality problem and discusses possible solutions, particularly one new drug, for persons experiencing a dwindling interest in sex.

Susan Campbell (1988), a reporter for *The Hartford Courant*, tells a highly charged story about autism in a teenager and what one family and one institute have been doing about it. Through dialogue and detailed observation, readers are shown in Campbell's skilled writing how autistic children receive this controversial treatment program. Because the medical community does not seem to agree on how to treat autism, the article is dramatic and interesting.

There are more subjects in science and technical writing than there are sciences. It is up to you as a writer to determine those subjects that are marketable and appealing to your readers. You can be certain that subjects such as those already mentioned will appeal across the board. But you must also consider subjects of particular local interest. In Kentucky and West Virginia, for example, considerable concern remains about black-lung disease commonly found in coal mine workers. Although such a subject might not be interesting to most Southern Californians, articles about skin cancer caused by the sun will be.

WHAT IS SCIENCE AND TECHNICAL WRITING?

Science and technical writers, at least as a group, have been a recognized specialty in the news media since 1934. That was the year the National Association of Science Writers was founded. There are other groups of writers worldwide who concern themselves with technical material—groups such as the Council for the Advancement of Science Writing and the American Medical Writers Association. There are courses on the subject at many universities and colleges offered through journalism programs or various science departments. It is a *growing* specialization in feature and news writing.

Today, many newspapers have reporters assigned to specific science and technology beats. Among the most common beats are health and medicine, environment, aviation and transportation, and energy. With the growing interest in science and high technology, many major newspapers today have science and technology sections or pages on a regular basis.

Some magazines, with their well-defined markets, specialize in scientific content. Some are generally about science. They include publications such as *Discover, Omni, Popular Science, Science Digest,* and *Science,* the official publication of the American Association for the Advancement of Science. Other magazines have departments devoted to medicine, space, the environment, technology, and the like.

Thus, as you have probably deduced by now, science and technical writing is subdivided into specializations. Some writers are able to handle the general science assignment as it comes up, but most try to develop their own specialties within the science because of the difficulty of the subject matter.

The basic feature writing and reporting skills are no different in science and technical writing from other forms of feature writing. However, the growth in information and in interest in science requires it be treated as a specialization of newspaper and magazine feature writing.

But beyond the basics of writing and reporting, there is one critical difference. You must be able to gather this usually complex scientific information, digest and understand it, and then translate it into understandable information for the general public. This requires a feature writer willing to accept this challenge and able to meet it. You must often cope with a technical language unique to a specific science. You must be able to write along that fine line that keeps well-educated readers interested without losing the less-sophisticated ones. It is always a difficult assignment. But this is what Dumanoski, Bivens, and Campbell achieve in their stories.

You must also be able to define and explain. It is critical to maintain accuracy in use of unique scientific and technical terminology. Such words must be explained in your article; you must take the time and effort to define terms and then use them in precise fashion in your article. What does the story mean to the average person? How will the information in the article affect his or her life? Or the lives of succeeding generations? This determination of meaning often is the most difficult challenge of all science and technical writing.

And while you are faced with the challenge of writing about new scientific and technical developments that affect our lives, there is still another challenge. You must also be able to write about subjects that readers already know about in a manner that is appealing and new. This may be more difficult for a writer than a story dealing with new developments. Making the old and familiar seem new is a tough assignment.

The work of most science and technical writers is difficult to generalize about. Newspaper writers who specialize in science and technical writing many times have other duties. While a science writer for a small daily newspaper might focus on the medical beat, he or she might also have assignments to cover schools or city hall. Many science and technical writers for smaller magazines work free-lance and must be able to generate assignments on their own initiative and enterprise. This effort requires paying attention to developments by reading and talking to the leading information sources in the area.

Research about science and technical writing has determined that there are four factors that affect reader interest in science and technical subjects, according to Michael Shapiro, a science writing researcher at Cornell University. Two concepts do influence a person's interest in science articles, but two others seem less likely, Shapiro says in a 1988 study. The two that certainly affect interest are:

1. *Relevance of the Subject.* You must, as a writer, find a way to help readers see how the subject is important to them. If you do, this enhances readership.

2. *Entertainment Value of the Article.* The article must be prepared in such a manner that it satisfies readers' need for stimulation if you want a widely read article.

The two concepts that have traditionally been associated with readership but now seem less likely to influence interest are:

1. *Ease or Difficulty of the Subject Material:* Even though it seems that difficult subjects would be less inviting to readers, there is little evidence that interest in science articles is related to subject difficulty.

2. *Topic Familiarity.* Although many writers have believed that people turn to material they already know, this is true only for actively sought material. For casually encountered articles in newspapers and magazines, familiarity has little effect on interest.

WRITING FOR THE RIGHT AUDIENCE

You have an assignment. You must write about unhealthful high levels of asbestos found in local public elementary school classrooms. How much does your reader know about the complicated subject? How much do you have to explain and define as you write this article? You must make these types of decisions before you write one word.

Your science and technical writing approaches will vary considerably—depending on whether you write for a general audience or a specialized audience. We discuss both here.

The General Audience

Much of the science and technical writing you will do will be oriented to the general public. The wide range of educational levels will put a special demand on you to write in an interesting fashion for the reader with a professional degree as well as the reader who did not finish high school. But you must know as much as you can about this general audience because it might have special interests.

For the general audience, it is best to err on the side of stating the obvious with too much explanation. Remember, part of your work is educational, too.

The Specialized Audience

Some science and technical writing you may do will be designed for a specialized audience. Feature writers for sophisticated business and industry periodicals, for example, will prepare articles for those with high interest levels in a subject and, it is likely, high knowledge levels as well. Most specialized audience readers will have some experience with the subject themselves, either through their work or their education. This expertise on the part of readers requires that you have an even greater awareness of audience when you write. You do not want to make the mistake of assuming too little, and thus bore the reader. Nor do you want to assume the audience knows too much and turn it off by leaving too many vague explanations or unanswered questions. Some preliminary research about your readers may help solve this problem.

Most newspaper and magazine editors have a particular audience and subject range in mind for each article they accept. For example, *1989 Writer's Market* reports the editors of *Popular Science* seek applied science feature writing for their unique market:

> *Popular Science* is devoted to exploring (and explaining) to a nontechnical but knowledgeable readership the technical world around us. We cover the physical sciences, engineering and technology, and above all, products. We are largely a "thing"-oriented publication: things that fly or travel down a turnpike, or go on or under the sea, or cut wood, or reproduce music, or build buildings, or make pictures, or mow lawns. We are especially focused on the new, the ingenious and the useful. We are consumer-oriented and are interested in any product that adds to the enjoyment of the home, yard, car, boat, workshop, outdoor recreation. . . . Free-lancers should study the magazine to see what we want and avoid irrelevant submissions. No biology or life sciences. (Neff, 1988, p. 549)

KEY SOURCES FOR SCIENCE AND TECHNICAL ARTICLES

In science and technical article writing there is a vast, rich lode of sources for you to mine. These include organizations such as professional and trade associations, professional and trade groups' conventions and exhibitions, regular local and national professional meetings, articles in professional journals and business/industry publications, researchers at local and state universities and colleges, area research and technical institutes and centers, research groups and foundations, scientists on staffs of museums, and commercial research organizations—just to mention a few possibilities.

Specialized publications can be a good starting point. Familiarize yourself with those in the subject areas that interest you. There are numerous special handbooks, guidebooks, and directories available for reference. Many are written specifically for reporters and writers by specialists in a field. Some are produced by journalists for other journalists. For example, Edward Edelson (1985), science editor of the *New York Daily News*, wrote *The Journalist's Guide to Nuclear Energy* for the Atomic Industrial Forum, a collective of organizations involved in peaceful use of nuclear energy. Similarly, the Drug Abuse Council, a private foundation, sponsored the *Reporter's Guide: Drugs, Drug Abuse Issues, Resources* (1975). These books, and ones like them, contain explanations, definitions, diagrams, and other helpful resources for feature writers.

Many organizations and events are buffered by public relations specialists or other media liaisons whose job it is to provide writers with access to scientists and technicians with the expertise needed for your article. With this in mind, let's look at these major categories of science and technical sources in more detail.

BEST SOURCES

Organizations such as professional and trade associations
    Resource books prepared for the news media
    Professional associations and trade group conventions and exhibitions
    Professional meetings
    Professional journals
    Bibliographic indexes and abstracts
    On-line access bibliographic data base search services
    Business/industry publications
    Universities and colleges
    Research and technical institutes and centers
    Research groups and foundations
    Museums and libraries
    Commercial research organizations
    Information hotlines

Scientific Journals and Other Publications

The literature of a particular discipline or field is the best place to seek out story ideas. Most science and technical writers who specialize in a subject (medicine or environment, for example) read the major publications. When possible, it is advisable to subscribe to these publications. In medicine, two of the leading publications are the *Journal of the American Medical Association* and *The New England Journal of Medicine*. Yet there are dozens more of these highly specialized medical journals, magazines, and newsletters. General science and official organizational technical publications, such as *Science*, are also good for story prospects.

Professional and Technical Organizations

In science and technical subjects, professional organizations exist for exchange of new knowledge and for continuing education. Most leading researchers participate in these organizations in one way or another. Examples include the American Psychological Association, the American Chemical Society, and American Institute of Architects. These groups hold regional, national, and international gatherings on an annual basis, and they provide a perfect forum for story ideas. Most organizations also produce newsletters for members, or produce their own journals and magazines. If you can, subscribe to these publications, and they will be excellent sources for writers.

Conventions and Meetings

In addition to organizational meetings, industry-wide conventions or meetings are regularly scheduled to permit leading experts to gather and discuss the latest developments. These meetings may transcend organizational interests and provide even better opportunities for writers to develop story prospects and sources.

Universities and Colleges

You probably have one nearby. As you have learned from earlier chapters, major universities and colleges that have research missions (usually the larger state and private 4-year schools) will provide a ready series of sources for new information on just about any subject. This is particularly true about universities with medical and other professional schools and centers. A look at a current catalogue will let you know what programs exist at the university and, from that, what types of research are being conducted. For more specific information, contact individual departments or public relations offices. In addition to these sources, some universities and colleges have begun to offer science and technical writing programs. One such program, at Lehigh University in Pennsylvania, allows students to specialize in science writing.

Institutes, Centers, and Research Groups

Perhaps the best-known organization that supports science and technical development is the National Science Foundation. This is not only a national funding source for research, but it is also a source of information about the research it is funding. Other sources exist at institutes, centers, and groups that can provide the latest information on topics of current concern. For example, one major source for changing weather patterns is the Climate Research Group at the Scripps Institute of Oceanography in LaJolla, California. Scientists there can be available to discuss their most recent work in meteorology and other related subjects.

BEING A RESEARCH CONSUMER

Prof. Paul D. Leedy, a researcher at The American University in Washington, has written a helpful book to bring research literature to an understandable level for most feature writers. The critical considerations he outlines in his book, *How to read research and understand it,* include these points for a research consumer:

1. Determine and evaluate the source of the research and the purpose of the study.

2. Understand the research process, that is, know the basic scientific method: Curiosity, expectations, collecting facts, conclusions. This way you can judge whether the work is quality research or not.

3. Know where to find research reports, know their major parts, know how to study and make sense from them:
   a. Read the title
   b. Read the abstract or summary.
   c. Thumb through the report quickly, noting the main headings and sub-headings, to get the organization of the report as a whole.
   d. Go back to the beginning. Read the report carefully and in detail, noting the problem that was researched and the manner in which the data were collected and interpreted. Note exactly what the researcher has written. What you read, you may not agree with. Do not interpolate your own thoughts; do not infer anything more than is expressed on the page. In reading research, you have one responsibility: to know precisely what the researcher has said, and this must be uncolored by your own wishes.
   e. Read the conclusions. Then read the problem again. The conclusions should follow logically from the statement of the problem.

4. Understand how to interpret statistics, data tables, and graphs.

5. Be able to identify a fact.

PITFALLS IN SCIENCE AND TECHNICAL WRITING

Writing about science and technology, even with these sources available, can have its trying moments. As a feature writer involved in writing about complicated information, you must be able to discern fact from opinion. This can be done by using multiple expert sources and is often necessary when you write

SCIENTIFIC METHOD IN RESEARCH

The scientific research process involves six standard steps. Familiarity with the process will aid you in understanding what you write about:

1. *Focus:* Statement of the research problem and subject.
2. *Expectations:* Formulation of an hypothesis or educated guess about the outcome of the research being done.
3. *Evidence:* Collection of facts, or data, through observation.
4. *Analysis:* Organize data for interpretation and analysis.
5. *Meaning:* Reach conclusions about meaning of data.
6. *Confirmation and re-exploration:* Repeat the five-step process if necessary.

about research and similar work at the cutting edge of a subject where the lines between scientific opinion and fact are blurred.

Warren Burkett (1986), late author of *News Reporting: Science, Medicine, and High Technology*, advises all science feature writers to remember:

1. To plainly tell readers when a discovery or medical procedure is experimental, and thus not available as accepted medical practice. Or, put negatively, "Raise No False Hopes."

2. There is no drug without side effects, even when the public relations people tell you so; share this with readers.

3. To advise readers that just because something works in a lab experiment or on a few patients, there is no guide to whether or not it will work in a production process or become accepted medical practice. It usually takes about ten to fifteen years for a new science discovery to reach application and acceptance.

4. Be careful in using the word "breakthrough." Scientists, doctors, and experienced science writers object to use of this word, since it is usually misleading.

Science and technical feature writing runs the risk of being incomplete as well. At times, sources may be unwilling to discuss all aspects of their work. Incomplete reporting causes confusion and uncertainty, and this results in lack of clarity. At times, sources are unprepared to talk with reporters, or they cannot adequately explain their work to you. If this occurs, how can you expect to make sense of things for your readers? Remember, scientists can be skeptical about you and your effort to communicate their work to the world. You must make a concerted effort to gain their confidence and trust.

Science and technical writers can get involuntarily involved in the politics of the scientific community as well—especially when hard-to-get funding is at stake from public and private sources. Writers must be able to cut through the competitive nature and hype of some scientists and technicians to get at the heart of a matter.

Cures and solutions to difficult scientific problems must be viewed with skepticism on your part, too. At times, announcements of study results can be premature and create unjustified optimism in readers. Writers must be careful not to over-dramatize the importance of results of studies they report.

USING SCIENCE INFORMATION HOTLINES

presstime, the magazine of the American Newspaper Publishers Association, says one science information hotline is getting more frequent use.

The Media Resource Service that is operated by the Scientists' Institute for Public Information receives more than 70 calls a week. Established in 1980, the hotline helps when science based stories break in the United States and elsewhere. Such major stories as the Chernobyl nuclear plant meltdown and the Challenger space shuttle explosion create need for information from such services. Other subjects that have brought calls to the Media Resource Service include AIDS, superconductivity, and cancer.

Feature writers can call the service toll free by dialing 1-800-223-1730. The service will refer writers to experts who can help them. Callers will be given names and telephone numbers for their sources.

Still another caution about science sources is the illegitimate source. You will occasionally encounter sources who attempt to provide evidence about new discoveries that is faked or artificially enhanced. There are still individuals who try to gain attention through tricks and hoaxes played on the media.

It is important not to depend too much on the information provided by a single source. Science writers should go beyond press releases and research reports in collecting information. These sources are only starting points, really, and should be supplemented by interviews and other written sources where possible.

Public relations staffers for research companies involved in research and development of new products can be helpful to you, but they can also be a barrier. These individuals can stop you in your tracks from getting important information they see as negative for their clients. They will often have different ideas about how you should use new information. It is up to you to get around these barriers by talking to the scientists and managers directly whenever possible.

On occasion, it might be appropriate for you to review your story's first draft, or parts of it, with your primary source. This is done solely in the interest of *accuracy*. Although this is *not* normal procedure in most feature writing, it is sometimes necessary when writing highly technical subjects.

Finally, it is important to discuss sensationalism in science and technical writing. Despite your impressions about the value of the story and the enthusiasm of your sources, be careful about overly "hyping" the story. Because science writing is not often glamorous and does not often command page one or cover story status, there is a temptation to overwrite an article and exaggerate its importance to gain an editor's attention. For example, Jim Sibbison (1988), a U.S. correspondent for *The Lancet,* a British medical journal, says too many reporters are drawn into the magic of "breakthrough" medical reporting. Sibbison says, "Medical scientists often criticize the news media for proclaiming major breakthroughs on the strength of what are, in fact, no more than tentative findings. . . . But the scientists can't rightfully unload all the blame on the media. Some of them can, on occasion, be found egging on the press with exaggerations of their own" (p. 36). He adds an observation that seems to be central to the whole problem: good medical articles that are properly qualified tend to be of low news value. "Stories that say a salve performs miracles are more attractive than ones that say there may be flies in this particular ointment" (p. 39) Sibbison writes. There is a simple test that can be a solution to this problem, he advises: "If your story includes words or phrases such as 'for the first time,' 'cancer-causing peanut butter sandwiches,' 'dawn of a new age,' 'milestone,' or 'breakthrough,' a second scientist's opinion may be in order" (p. 39).

MAJOR SECTIONS OF A SCIENTIFIC JOURNAL ARTICLE

Most scientific journals that report the findings of new studies in a discipline will follow the same general model for articles. Some sections are more important than others. Here is a list of those sections and their value to science and technical feature article writers:

1. *Introduction and literature review.* This section can be skimmed, but usually has minimal value to you. In it, you will find out about the problem being studied, what has previously been done by other researchers on the subject, and justification for the present study.

2. *Statement of hypotheses or research questions.* This part is more important because it tells you the particular focus of the study. What does the researcher want to find and, in the case of hypotheses, expect to find?

3. *Method.* All research reports should have a section devoted to study procedures. What materials and methods were used in the study? What type of study (survey, experiment, and so on) was it? This section is valuable only if the procedures used are controversial, revolutionary, or otherwise noteworthy.

4. *Findings.* The findings are more valuable than the previous sections. Usually these are reported as text, but findings may also be placed in tables for quantitative studies. What did the study determine? The article should tell you in this section. What do you think of the findings yourself?

5. *Discussion.* Interpretation and conclusions may be as important to you as the findings. Much of the article's value depends on the quality of this section, because this is the place where the researcher tries to make sense of the findings. The key point here is for the researcher to describe the meaning of the findings and simply not re-tell them.

Other common parts include an abstract, author's identification, acknowledgments, and of course, data tables and appendices.

DEALING WITH QUANTITATIVE INFORMATION

One reason some writers shy away from science and technical writing is their aversion for anything involving numbers. This is especially true if the numbers are so small or so large most people cannot comprehend them.

Readers often have the same aversion to statistics. Articles with a large amount of numbers or statistics turn off certain readers. It is up to you to judge the right amount of quantitative information in your articles.

Often, this means finding ways to sugar-coat the statistical medicine for readers. The information may be critical to the article and you must use it. Getting creative helps retain readership. Here are some tips to beat the technical game:

1. Use *informational graphics,* a subject which we will discuss in more detail later in this chapter.

2. *Simplify numbers* by rounding off or shortening the detail of certain numbers. Although you cannot do this on all statistics, it can be done on very large or small numbers.

3. Put numbers in a *meaningful context* for readers with examples. If you have statistics for an entire state or country, reduce them to a level that makes more sense.

4. *Interpret* unusual statistics. Tell readers what they mean. Is a statistic good or bad? High or low?

A BASIC STRUCTURE FOR WRITING

When you sit down to write a science or technology article, the usual rules for writing and organization apply. But because of the unusual nature of the material involved, a little extra effort will make a difference.

Regardless of the organizational plan you choose, if you accomplish these four goals in the article, you will probably succeed:

1. *Get the reader's attention.* Using whatever lead you choose, draw the readers into the article. Make them want to read it. Create drama. Use tension. No matter what you do, do not lose your potential readers with a slow, unimaginative start.

2. *Get the reader personally involved.* After you have the readers' attention, show readers how this subject affects them. What does it mean to them? Can you help them identity with the subject? Have you written it in a personal way to appeal on an individual level? How can your readers benefit from the article's content?

3. *Illustrate your points.* If you achieve this goal, you are showing readers what you are writing about. Give examples and case studies. But try to provide situations that can be understood at your readers' level—whether the reader is the general public or the sophisticated specialist.

4. *Explain the meaning.* Tell readers what this development means. Do not leave your reader feeling, "So what?" when he or she puts down your article. This is the major point of your article, so make certain you have made this assessment at some point. Many writers recommend the "so what?" be placed near the end as part of the conclusion.

TECHNICAL AND INDUSTRIAL/BUSINESS TRADE PUBLICATIONS

Although technical and industrial/business trade publications might be an excellent source for some of your feature writing ideas, have you ever considered these publications as possible markets for your features?

If you have an interest in science and technology writing, then you should consider these publications as outlets for your work, especially if you want to be a free-lance writer. If you want full-time employment as a science and technical feature writer, then these publications will be your new home.

These publications are highly specialized and require that you have extensive knowledge of the subject as well. Alert students should consider a second major in addition to journalism that might create that specialization. For example, if you have an interest in transportation, a second major in engineering would be useful.

And for writers getting into the profession after their college experience, think about your undergraduate major as a possible specialization. It is not uncommon to have a "previous life" before an interest in journalism, and this experience can often be the ticket to a specialization in these highly defined publications.

As you read in the first chapter, there are many business–industry publications in the United States today. Thousands of such business periodicals means thousands of opportunities for a writer. *Writer's Digest* columnist Art Spikol

(March 1987) sums up your opportunities with these publications: "It's hard for me to think of any field of human endeavor for which a trade publication doesn't exist. And since many of you do something else with your time when you are not writing—like holding down full-time jobs—chances are you already know enough about something to come up with some articles you can sell to the trades themselves" (p. 18).

Some trade publications are in-house publications. That is, the publications represent and are published by institutions, organizations, corporations, and other businesses—each with special interests.

The nature of these publications reflects the sponsor or source, of course. In many cases, however, these publications are produced for the technical community of the organization and are often no different in subject matter and approach from non-in-house, or consumer, publications which frequently use scientific and technical articles.

Spikol says there are some differences, however, that you must remember if you consider writing for such a publication. "Of course, corporate publications are *supposed* to be different from consumer publications. What makes them different, are, among other things, the selling of advertising, the advocacy position (the corporate publication is supposed to enhance the corporation), the captive audience, the clearances required, the free distribution" (Spikol, September 1986, p. 16).

SCIENCE AND TECHNICAL WRITING REFERENCES

Alley, Michael, *The Craft of Scientific Writing*, Englewood Cliffs, NJ: Prentice-Hall, 1987.

American Psychological Association, *Publication Manual*, third edition, Washington: APA, 1983.

Andrews, Clarence A., *Technical and Business Writing*, Boston: Houghton Mifflin, 1975.

Bly, Robert W. and Gary Blake, *Technical Writing: Structure, Standards, and Style*, New York: McGraw-Hill, 1982.

Booth, Vernon, *Communicating in Science: Writing and Speaking*, New York: Cambridge University Press, 1985.

Burkett, Warren, *News Reporting: Science, Medicine, and High Technology*, Ames: Iowa State University Press, 1986.

Eisenberg, Anne, *Effective Technical Communication*, New York: McGraw-Hill, 1982.

Farr, A. D., *Science Writing for Beginners*, Boston: Blackwell Scientific, 1985.

Foster, John, *Science Writer's Guide*, New York: Columbia University Press, 1963.

Freeman, Joanna M., *Basic Technical and Business Writing*, Ames: Iowa State University Press, 1979.

Hirschhorn, Howard H., *Writing for Science, Industry, and Technology*, New York: Van Nostrand, 1980.

Houp, Kenneth W. and Thomas E. Pearsall, *Reporting Technical Information,* fifth edition, New York: Macmillan, 1984.

Katz, Michael J., *Elements of the Scientific Paper*, New Haven: Yale University Press, 1985.

King, Lester Snow, *Why Not Say It Clearly: a Guide to Scientific Writing*, Boston: Little, Brown, 1978.

Leedy, Paul D., *How to Read Research and Understand It*, Macmillan, New York, 1981.

Olsen, Leslie A. and Thomas N. Huckin, *Principles of Communication for Science and Technology*, New York: McGraw-Hill, 1983.

Sherman, Theodore A. and Simon S. Johnson, *Modern Technical Writing*, fourth edition, Englewood Cliffs, NJ: Prentice-Hall, 1983.

Turner, Maxine T., *Technical Writing: A Practical Approach*, Reston, VA: Reston Pub. 1984.

Warren, Thomas L., *Technical Writing: Purpose, Process, and Form*, Belmont, CA: Wadsworth, 1985.

ILLUSTRATIONS HELP TELL THE STORY

Visual communication techniques such as informational graphics help tell the science and technology stories that today contain complicated statistics, numbers, or other quantitative information. But this is only one important use of graphics and illustrations in science and technical writing.

Newspapers and magazines have new visual tools such as "infographics" to help explain complex issues. These illustrations combine factual information with visual techniques such as graphs, charts, maps, or "exploded" diagrams to tell a story. *USA Today* pioneered much of this and remains an innovator in the field.

With more and more publications using color, the value of these visual packages is growing. Because computers and photocopiers are aiding in the rapid preparation of these images as well, they can be more readily available on shorter notice.

At times, photographs can be the answer. At other times, posed photographs used as illustrations will make the point. Line art, such as drawings, maps, and graphs can show the interrelationships of parts, procedures, and plans. In many cases, it is appropriate and necessary for you as the writer to take the lead in suggesting such visual applications for an article.

These techniques are particularly helpful for science and technical writers. For example, in explaining how the space shuttle disaster occurred, many publications used color graphics to supplement features written weeks and months after the accident.

The principle is no different from certain types of service articles, such as the how-to article. To make information more understandable—something as routine as bypass surgery or something as unusual as a nuclear reactor fire and explosion—illustrations such as informational graphics are necessary to tell the story.

NATIONAL SCIENCE AND TECHNICAL EXPERTS

Jim Detjen (1988), a reporter for *The Philadelphia Inquirer*, suggests some leading national scientific organizations for assistance in science writing because, he says, they are particularly helpful to journalists. His list was published in the Summer 1988 issue of *IRE Journal*, the publication of the Investigative Reporters and Editors organization:

All Purpose Groups

American Assn. for Advancement of Science	202-326-6440
American Medical Writers Assn.	301-986-9119
National Assn. of Science Writers	516-757-5664
National Science Foundation	202-357-9498
U.S. Office of Technology Assessment	202-228-6204

Animal Rights

Humane Society of the U.S.	202-452-1100
Foundation for Biomedical Research	202-457-0654
People for the Ethical Treatment of Animals	202-726-0156

Astronomy and Science

American Astronomical Society	301-286-8607
Amer. Institute of Aeronautics & Astronautics	202-646-7432
Astronomical Society of the Pacific	415-661-8660
National Aeronautics and Space Administration	202-453-8364
Planetary Society	818-793-5100

Biomedical Ethics

University of Minnesota (Art Caplan)	612-625-4917
The Hastings Center	914-762-8500

Biotechnology and Genetic Engineering

Environmental Policy Institute	202-544-2600
Foundation on Economic Trends	202-466-2823
National Institute of Health	301-770-0131

Climate

Climate Research Institute	202-547-0104
National Center for Atmospheric Research	303-497-1150
National Oceanic and Atmospheric Administration	202-377-4190

Environmental

Environmental Defense Fund   202-387-3500
Greenpeace   202-462-1177
National Audubon Society   212-832-3200
National Resources Defense Council   202-783-7800
U.S. Environmental Protection Agency   202-382-4355
World Watch Institute   202-452-1999

Geology

U.S. Geological Survey   703-648-4460

Medical and Health Issues

American Cancer Society   212-599-3600
American Heart Association   214-706-1340
American Medical Association   312-645-4430
American Public Health Association   202-789-5663
Centers for Disease Control   404-329-3286
National Institutes of Health   301-496-5787

Nuclear Issues

Center for Defense Information (missiles)   202-862-0700
Government Accountability Project   415-397-2001
Nuclear Information and Resource Service   202-328-0002
Union of Concerned Scientists   202-332-0700
U.S. Council for Energy Awareness   202-293-0770
U.S. Nuclear Regulatory Commission   202-492-7000

Oceanography

Scripps Institute of Oceanography   619-534-3624
Woods Hole Oceanographic Institute   617-548-1400
                                                      (ext. 2270)

Paranormal Claims

Committee for the Scientific Investigation of
    Claims of the Paranormal   716-834-3222

HOW PROFESSIONALS WROTE IT

DATE: WEDNESDAY, MAY 18, 1988
SOURCE: THE MIAMI HERALD, P. 2E
AUTHOR: DIANNE DUMANOSKI, BOSTON GLOBE SERVICE

* * *

SCIENTISTS SEE 'ALARMING' HINTS OF NORTH POLE OZONE LOSS

SNOWMASS VILLAGE, Colo.—Scientists have found "important and alarming" indications that man-made chemicals might be attacking the Earth's protective ozone layer around the North Pole as well as in Antarctica.

This new information, which comes from tests made over northern Canada and in Greenland last winter, was released in Colorado at an international scientific meeting on ozone destruction.

The tests found elevated levels of chlorine monoxide and chlorine dioxide—chemicals linked to the ozone destruction over Antarctica that have caused the dramatic hole in the ozone layer there.

Much of the chlorine attacking the ozone layer comes from man-made chlorofluorocarbons, or CFCs, that are widely used to cool refrigerators and air conditioners, clean computer chips and manufacture foam cushions.

Ozone, which is a form of oxygen concentrated in the stratosphere, screens out most of the sun's harmful ultraviolet radiation and makes life on Earth possible.

Since scientists learned that the extreme cold over Antarctica is a key factor in the rapid ozone destruction there, it has been speculated that the same thing could occur around the North Pole. Losses at the North Pole could have serious implications for the ozone layer over population centers at higher latitudes in Europe, Canada, the United States and Soviet Union.

George Mount of the National Oceanic and Atmospheric Administration said a team working at Thule, Greenland, in late January and early February found levels of chlorine dioxide 10 times higher than expected. This implies, he said, that the chemical processes that have destroyed ozone over Antarctica might also be working in the Arctic, but less powerfully.

A team of scientists from Harvard University and the National Aeronautics and Space Administration, which made measurements from a plane that flew to the edge of a swirling air mass over the North Pole in February, found high levels of another chlorine compound associated with ozone destruction: chlorine monoxide.

William Brune of Harvard, who presented the findings, said the maximum chlorine monoxide level measured was 55 parts per trillion. The normal level of chlorine monoxide is around three to four parts per trillion.

The high level of chlorine monoxide over the Arctic is "cause for major concern," said James Anderson of Harvard, a leading figure in the search for the cause of the Antarctic ozone hole. Anderson worked with Brune on the Arctic study.

Though the Arctic levels are much lower than those found over Antarctica, Anderson said this work and the Thule data are "a very important and alarming discovery." Because of these measurements, he said, scientists have decided to mount a major research effort in the Arctic next winter.

These findings follow a report in March on global ozone trends that found unexpectedly high losses of ozone over populated regions in the Northern Hemisphere. This report indicated that three to four times more ozone had disappeared.

These findings follow a report in March on global ozone trends that found unexpectedly high losses of ozone over populated regions in the Northern Hemisphere. This report indicated that three to four times more ozone had disappeared than computer models had predicted. In the region that includes Boston, ozone levels are 4.7 percent lower than normal during winter months, according to the report.

More than a decade ago, two scientists, F. Sherwood Rowland and Mario Molina, first suggested that CFCs could make their way to the stratosphere and attack the ozone layer. Molina said the chemical evidence from the Arctic supports the theory that ozone destruction at the North Pole is causing the ozone loss in northern latitudes.

"By analogy with the Antarctic ozone hole, these are very strong, hints, so one has to worry," he said.

A satellite has been measuring ozone levels over the North Pole for nine years, but the record is not long enough to show whether ozone loss is occurring, according to Richard Stolarski of NASA.

Reprinted with the permission of *The Boston Globe.*

•••

DATE: WEDNESDAY, APRIL 1

DATE: WEDNESDAY, MAY 11, 1988
SOURCE: THE MIAMI HERALD, P. 2E
AUTHOR: TERRY BIVENS, PHILADELPHIA INQUIRER AND KNIGHT-RIDDER
NEWSPAPERS

* * *

NEW DRUG BREAKS GROUND IN SEARCH FOR APHRODISIAC

PHILADELPHIA—Forget the ground rhinoceros horn and Spanish fly. Listen to this Cheltenham, Pa., woman's experience with modern science's first attempt at an aphrodisiac:

"About five years ago, after the birth of my son, I completely lost my desire for sex," she recalled. "I went to a psychologist, a gynecologist, an endocrinologist. But nothing worked. This was an important part of my marriage, and suddenly it was gone."

Then last year, she heard about a program at the Philadelphia Medical Institute. Today, the woman and her husband behave like honeymooners. "I still can't believe it," she said.

The difference? A small but extraordinary pill—a pill under testing that could signal a new era for the nation's pharmaceutical industry and millions of troubled Americans.

Business and pleasure, it turns out, might mix after all. For the first time, major drug companies have turned their attention and research dollars toward a cure for the dwindling libido. Most likely, it will be the engineered product of a gleaming laboratory and, unlike those timeworn folk remedies, it might actually work.

"The Zeitgeist is here for a pharmaceutical treatment for sexual problems," said Leonard Derogatis, director of the division of medical psychology at Hahnemann University in Philadelphia and a key researcher in the field.

FIRST OF A KIND

Derogatis and Joseph Mendels, a psychiatrist and director of the Philadelphia Medical Institute, are doing ground-breaking work with an experimental drug that is thought to be the first designed specifically to enhance sexual desire. The compound is made by Eli Lilly & Co., an Indianapolis pharmaceutical firm, and is known only as LY163502. The Cheltenham woman, a 37-year-old elementary school teacher, has been involved in the clinical tests for about a year.

As a matter of policy, Lilly does not comment on a drug in the research stage. But experts believe that the company could be spending $20 million or more to test the drug at 14 centers nationwide, including the two in Philadelphia.

As does the teacher, many test subjects see the drug as nothing short of miraculous. Researchers say it is far too early to make an assessment, but there is clearly a guarded optimism. "The preliminary analysis looks good," Derogatis said.

Perhaps more important, LY163502 might be a harbinger of things to come. By Mendels' estimate, one in every four American adults now suffers from some form of sexual problem. The number is expected to increase substantially as the baby boom generation moves further into middle age.

ENORMOUS POTENTIAL

That kind of market is simply too large for drug companies to ignore, experts agreed.

"The market potential is enormous," Derogatis said. "And the science will improve as the resources of the big drug companies come into play."

Credit for the initial interest among the large firms usually goes to Burroughs-Wellcome Co., based in the Research Triangle Park of central North Carolina. About five years ago, researchers noted that patients given Wellbutrin, Burroughs' anti-depression drug, often boasted about their sexual prowess. Intrigued, Burroughs commissioned studies.

The first reports were enthusiastic. Researchers at the Crenshaw Clinic in San Diego reported in 1985 that 19 of 30 patients given Wellbutrin showed a marked improvement in their sexual activity. But soon afterward, Wellbutrin fell into a regulatory limbo.

A subsequent study done by Mendels in Philadelphia was inconclusive, although he acknowledged that some patients showed a marked improvement in sexual activity. A second shoe dropped when Burroughs was obliged to pull Wellbutrin from the market in 1986 after it caused seizures in some bulimic patients taking it for its anti-depressant properties.

Burroughs is retesting Wellbutrin for possible reintroduction as an anti-depressant. A company spokesman said it was unclear whether any further testing on its sexual potential would be funded.

TAKING NOTICE

"I don't think the issue is settled," Mendels said. "And in any event, it caused other firms to take notice."

Harold Lief, professor emeritus of psychiatry at the University of Pennsylvania, said that Pfizer Inc., a New York drug firm, called together several medical experts, including him, to discuss the subject in October.

Research is also continuing into another drug, yohimbine.

Derived from the bark of an African tree, yohimbine has helped some patients, researchers agreed.

Leland Ellis, co-director of the Northwest Center for Impotence in Seattle, said six of 18 patients given the drug in a study showed an increase in sexual activity. Ellis said researchers ascribed part of that reaction to the so-called placebo effect, or the tendency of test subjects to respond favorably to any drug, even a harmless sugar pill.

"Still, we can't rule out the possibility that it could have some effect," he said. "Certainly, if a patient believes it will help, it will help."

Yohimbine has run afoul of the federal Food and Drug Administration, however. The agency banned its sale in over-the-counter form several years ago; some of the early ads were apparently quite lurid. It is manufactured as a prescription medicine by Kramer Laboratories of Miami. A company spokesman said current annual sales amounted about $45,000.

"These plant products can't take the place of a medication," FDA spokesman Ed Nida said. "If people have a sexual problem, they should see a physician."

Even the most enthusiastic researchers concede that there are other, more general problems with the idea of a new age of chemically induced sexuality. Experts agreed that the development of a prescription aphrodisiac opens a Pandora's box of problems, technical and otherwise.

Financial analysts said the FDA can be expected to accord a low priority to approval of such a drug. Drugs aimed at more serious illnesses would inevitably leapfrog ahead on the agency's agenda.

"The FDA might easily regard such a product as hedonistic, and it would probably be put on the bottom of the pile for review and approval," said David Saks, owner of a River Vale, N.J., health care investment advisory firm. "The approval process would be long and extended."

Too, the market—though huge—is equally amorphous. Sexual dysfunctions, as they are known to physicians, range from physical infirmities to the highly subjective realm of individual perceptions and preferences. Designing a drug that works for a large portion of that spectrum is no easy task, especially because the FDA would be extremely wary of side effects.

There is also the potential for abuse. "There's no question that a lot of people would like to get their hands on something like this," Saks said. "There's bound to be a black market for any prescription drug."

A STRONG DEMAND

But researchers and financial analysts believe that the demand for such a product will inevitably overcome the obstacles. Mendels said preliminary results on the Lilly drug are "encouraging."

"It's not like a cure for cancer, but it's not an unimportant issue when you consider how many people are affected," Mendels said. "We know whatever we come up with will be controversial, but there's no question something will develop. Wellbutrin opened the door, and I expect we'll see more and more research by the major companies.

"It's about time, really. Right now the only recourse for people with sexual problems is to either do nothing or seek counseling. And to tell the truth, counseling isn't very successful for a lot of people."

The Cheltenham teacher would not argue.

"What's happened to me in the program is sensational," she said. "In fact, I'm nervous about going off the drug when the study ends. I don't ever want to be the way I was."

Reprinted with the permission of *The Philadelphia Inquirer.*

(SIDEBAR PUBLISHED WITH MAIN STORY)

* * *

POPULAR APHRODISIACS

VUKA-VUKA: Made of crushed beetles, it is popular as an aphrodisiac in Zimbabwe. Experts have warned that its use might damage the kidneys.

RHINO HORNS: In India's Assam state, illegal slaughter of the rare one-horned rhinoceros has been a problem. The horn, believed to be an aphrodisiac, has fetched up to $40,000 in Singapore, Hong Kong and Nepal.

DURIAN: In Malaysia, Singapore and Thailand, McDonald's fast-food restaurants have sold milk shakes flavored with durian, a "foul-smelling Southeast Asian fruit considered locally to be an aphrodisiac," Business Week magazine has reported.

SEA TURTLE EGGS: In parts of Florida, including Palm Beach County and the Treasure Coast, poachers of sea turtle eggs have been arrested. The eggs are considered an aphrodisiac in some Caribbean and Latin American cultures.

Reprinted with the permission of *The Miami Herald.*

• • •

DATE: WEDNESDAY, MARCH 9, 1988
SOURCE: THE MIAMI HERALD, P. 2E
AUTHOR: SUSAN CAMPBELL, HARTFORD COURANT

* * *

TRYING TO BRING AUTISTIC GIRL INTO REALITY

BOLTON, Conn.—In a stark upstairs bedroom a 14-year-old boy is standing on his head, trying to get a little girl to look him in the eye.

Eye contact is paramount. If the little girl looks out from her world of autism into the teen-ager's eye, she may try to communicate, and who knows where that could lead.

Today, Melissa Tyler, who is almost 4, is attentive while Jason Hyland bounces around the room, keeping step with her. She places a block in her mouth. He places a block in his. During a quieter moment, he crawls beside her as she heads toward a tiny table in the corner. She looks at him, occasionally. Once, she almost smiles. As he crawls, he chatters:

"Melissa, find the grape under the cup. Oh, you did! You are a good finder. All right, step right up, just like a carnival. Find the grape. Yeah, you found the grape!

"Can you say grape? Say grape. Melissa. Say grape. Say grape, Melis. Melis, want a grape? Say grape? Yeah, grape. Yeah, you're trying to get that little 'p' sound out!

"Hey, good looking, Melissa. You looked at me."

At the end of two hours, Hyland will have sweated through his Hartford Whalers shirt, relishing what they call a "happy high."

He is among 13 volunteers—including Melissa's parents, Grant and Pat Tyler, and her grandmother, Kay Donovan—who combine to spend eight frenetic hours a day, seven days a week, with Melissa in her room. They follow her lead and mimic her when she puts toys in her mouth, runs into a corner and skips aimlessly around the room. They talk to her and try to teach her simple words. They applaud her just for being in the room with them. They do everything they can to draw her out, and always, always, they try to get her to look at them.

There is a method to this madness.

The Tylers and friends want to walk Melissa through a second birth, to bring her out of her silent world of empty stares and repetitive movement.

When the Tylers—who also have a son, Kevin, 2—first suspected Melissa wasn't developing as quickly as other children her age, they took her to a neurologist, a geneticist, a psychologist, a pediatrician and an audiologist. They were told their daughter exhibited autistic behavior. In fact, she was exhibiting about 15 of the 19 activities most common to autistic children.

Grant, a former nurse who now sells heavy construction equipment, and Pat, who taught school and worked in banking, explored conventional therapy, but in late October they took Melissa to Option Institute and Fellowship, an 85-acre compound in Sheffield, Mass., run by author Barry Neil Kaufman and his wife, Suzi Lyte Kaufman.

The Tylers stayed at the compound for a week, during which time Melissa began trying to say words and give more sustained eye contact. The family came home determined to set up their own open-ended program—which they began to call "The Project"—using volunteers they would train to accept Melissa as she is, yet still encourage her to do things she hadn't done before.

They threw their considerable energy into creating an advertising blitz to find volunteers. They printed posters that read, "Help Create a Miracle." They spoke to any civic, educational and social group who would listen. They looked for people who would come for two two-hour sessions a week with Melissa in her room, and for a weekly two-hour meeting to discuss her activities.

Some friends tried to dissuade them from thinking people would commit six hours a week, but Pat Tyler said,, "I am absolutely clear that anyone who participates will see benefits in other areas of their lives."

Hyland heard Pat Tyler speak to his catechism class. When he told his parents he was interested, they said he was shouldering a huge responsibility.

"But I said I wanted to do it," he said. Now, some of his friends at school want to get involved with helping Melissa, he said.

On Melissa's door is a list of reminders. Volunteers are asked to applaud her efforts, request eye contact frequently and speak only short sentences. And most of all, they are asked to have fun as they career around the room trying to catch Melissa's attention.

The Tylers have carefully recorded Melissa's progress. Recently, they watched her pull Kevin's hair as he watched television. It was the first time she'd done anything sisterly toward him.

The volunteers who work with Melissa meet to discuss her progress and how they can help her do more.

Every volunteer contributes. Their observations are discussed and recorded on a master data sheet so they can compare her week's work. At a recent week's meeting, the volunteers calculated that Melissa's eye contact was up to 40 percent. Lately, it's been closer to 65 percent.

They decide at this meeting to have Melissa repeat three times any request she makes in her room. Right now, "es-es" is yes. "Ga" is juice.

But it's a start.

"Before 'es-es' she would say nothing," Pat Tyler said. "Before that she would cry."

Grant Tyler has learned that every moment can be useful.

"There was a time when I used to see Melissa go into the corner of the room, and I would almost stand there waiting for her to come out," he said. "Pretty soon, she would be done with that, and then I could participate with her again. I started to see that I could go into the corner with her and create my own fun.

"So the next time, I followed her there and made a big deal out of, 'Wow, what a great corner this is.' What I have found is I am able to generate a lot more creativity in myself. I could go into the corner and generate a whole happening."

Kate Godbout, a University of Connecticut senior, joined the group in mid-December after seeing one of Pat's posters on campus.

Reprinted with permission of *The Hartford Courant.*

(SIDEBAR WHICH WAS PUBLISHED WITH THE STORY)
'PLACE FOR MIRACLES' STARTED AFTER SUCCESS WITH FOUNDERS' SON

SHEFFIELD, Mass.—A sign on the grounds of the Option Institute announces that this is "a place for miracles."

Barry Neil Kaufman and Suzi Lyte Kaufman, the institute's founders, don't promise to heal special-needs children, but they do tell parents they can learn ways of accepting their children's differences.

The institute trains parents to live with their children by trusting the children, and at the same time presenting a world in which the children can function comfortably.

The Kaufmans have been called everything from flakes and fakes by some in the medical field, to good friends and messengers of hope by parents and others.

"The place for miracles is creating a happy environment," said Barry Kaufman, who has written seven books that have been translated into 18 languages. "From that, all those other things naturally improve."

Suzi Kaufman said they were heavily into what they call the Option Process by the time their third child, Raun, was diagnosed at 17 months old as having an IQ of less than 30. The boy did not use language and did not acknowledge the presence of other people.

The Kaufmans decided to bring their child out of his inability to communicate by making a bridge from his world to theirs. For 12 hours a day, Suzi Kaufman sat with Raun and rocked and spun with him. Finally, after Suzi had spun with him for two hours on the 11th day, he looked at her and allowed his arm to be stroked. By the 11th weeks, he waved to his father. At 19 months, he went running and crying to find his mother.

The Kaufmans found volunteers to encourage Raun for the next three years. Today, Raun, 15, is a straight-A student. He shows no sign of autism.

Word spread—particularly with the publication of Barry Kaufman's Book, *Son-Rise*, and a subsequent television movie—and the Kaufmans began working with families from around the country.

In 1983, they began holding workshops on special-needs children, personal growth and parent skills. The workshops cost from $375 to $6,200.

Some in the medical profession are skeptical. They say that the Option method is not scientific, and stories of miraculous recoveries that aren't validated scientifically might falsely raise parents' hopes.

But others say the intense methods the Kaufmans use to reach autistic children are not unlike those of some noted clinicians.

Reprinted with permission of *The Hartford Courant.*

(SECOND SIDEBAR)

TREATMENT, CAUSE ARE STILL PUZZLE

American psychiatrist Leo Kanner first described autism—one of the most studied and least understood of developmental disabilities—in 1943, after examining 11 children who he thought formed a distinct group. Their principal feature was their "inability to relate to people from the beginning of life," he wrote.

The Autism Society of America says the syndrome occurs in 15 of every 10,000 births. Children diagnosed as autistic—a general term that encompasses a variety of behaviors—are seen as anxious, hyperactive, unable to speak and out of touch with reality. About 80 percent are considered mentally retarded. However, some have distinct skills in music, or mathematics. Many are involved in repetitive behavior such as waving their hands for hours at a time. Others are more involved with an inanimate objects—say, a cup—than people.

In its milder form, autism resembles a learning disability. However, most cases of autism are more severe.

Autism—which can be diagnosed only through observation of a child's behavior—is believed to be a permanent handicap, and its origins are unknown.

Because it manifests itself differently in each person, a number of treatments are successful, but none is effective in every case.

"No one person can come out and say, 'This is the way to treat a child with autism,' " said M. Alex Geerstma, a pediatrician, whose patient, Melissa Tyler, has been in the Option Process.

Families should be skeptical of programs that promise quick fixes, or that recommend so much involvement with the child that other areas of their lives suffer, Geerstma said.

—Herald Staff

Reprinted with permission of *The Miami Herald*.

A Professional's Point of View

By Patrice Adcroft
Omni Magazine

Nobody but nobody wants to read technical writing. It does nothing that good writing ought to do: inform, entertain, move the reader in some way. Expose an idea to the air, convert a nonbeliever. Instill a sense of wonderment. Let the reader in on a universal truth.

What science writing should be is really up to you, the writer. Every piece

should carry with it some kind of agenda; a determination to arrive at something greater than just a set of facts. I can tell you what good science writing—good journalism—should not do: it should never intimidate, pontificate, or confuse. Even the most complex scientific break-through can be described in ordinary terms. Writers who rely on jargon are either (1) befuddled or (2) snobs. I wouldn't want my readers to have to put up with either of these.

Telling a good story is fundamental to good writing. Don't forget to leave a trail which guides the reader from lead to end. Just be sure that the trail consists of some-thing more substantive than bread-crumbs. The trail should be clearly marked, with a few resting places along the way where a reader can stop and catch his breath and reflect on what's been said.

I really care about the way an article sounds. If one of my editors is having trouble with an article, I'll tell him to read the piece aloud. Then he gets an idea of how it will sound in the reader's head. If a sentence just clunks along, or you can't get its meaning from one reading, there's a problem.

Science writers should know how to interview professionals. That means getting them to talk on the average person's level. If you don't understand a concept or formula, neither will the reader. I have something I call the amazing dumb animal question. When there's something terribly complex to grasp, the theory of chaos, for example, or automata, I preface my questions with: "OK. This may sound like a dumb animal question, but. . . ." I've asked bioengineers to compare artificial organs to washing machines, neurologists to compare the central nervous system to the New York subway lines. (The article was going in a publication geared for New Yorkers.) Always ask your source to compare whatever he's talking about to an everyday item. Seek out an image the reader can hang on to. This will make the item, concept, equation, live.

A few words about the best science/technology stories I've published: All contained some human element (a maverick scientist's struggle with a staid institu-tion, for example); all were clear, but not simple-minded; all took the reader on a journey which left him more aware of himself and the world around him. Many were cleverly packaged—an article on the future of films appeared as movie treatments, actually written by famous directors who were told to pretend that they had the most futuristic technology at their fingertips. Good science writing doesn't just report on a breakthrough and leave it at that; it investigates the consequences of the discovery or breakthrough. (Adcroft, personal communication, 1988)

* * *

Patrice Adcroft is the editor of *Omni* magazine, Omni Publications International, New York. She had been a senior editor before becoming the first woman in the editor's position of a national consumer science magazine. Before joining *Omni* in 1983, she was senior editor of *Family Weekly* at CBS. She has also been managing editor for Family Media's *Alive and Well,* and a staff writer for *Good Housekeeping.*

III

THE PROFESSIONAL LIFE

16

Free-Lance Writing

Now you are ready to write feature articles for pay. This chapter will show you how to get started as a free-lance writer. Many beginning magazine and newspaper feature writers work free-lance part-time while they do something else. Some writers are good enough that they can build a lucrative full-time career as free-lance feature writers. But to be realistic, it is not a safe bet that you will find your full-time career in free-lance feature writing—at least not in the beginning. If you follow the path of most feature writers, especially those writing for magazines, you will be a part-time writer who has a full-time career in another field. While this is frequently the case for magazines, which usually maintain small writing staffs, more and more newspapers are using free-lance writers for material as well. This is not only true for features desks, but also for features for the traditional spot news desks, such as the city desk and sports.

Your work as a free-lance feature writer will be tough and demanding. You are your own boss. This puts you in charge of marketing, preparing, and submitting your work. No one will do any of this for you. Some people find this working environment—the freedom and flexibility—to be to their liking. Others cannot handle it and prefer staff work. You will have to decide what is better for you.

Some writers feel there is no better time than now to be a free-lance feature writer. There are more magazines, therefore more markets, than ever before. There is greater specialization than the magazine industry has ever known. And although there may be fewer newspapers, there are more editions of the major dailies caused by zoning, or segmentation, of neighborhood coverage. The opinion that you are beginning at an ideal time is expressed by University of Texas professor Thomas Fensch, who says: "There are more magazines than ever before and you can find markets for everything you write. If you work hard, read compulsively, if you are curious and care about words, articles, books and people you can" (Fensch, 1984, p. 4).

Yet some writers say full-time free-lance writing has never been as tough as it is now. Reporter and researcher Melissa Ludke Lincoln (1981) takes this position. She argues that the pay is low, editors are hard to deal with, and making a living writing as a magazine writer is not easy. "The unpleasant fact is that scratching out a living as a free-lancer has never been harder than it is today" (p. 49) she says. Pay rates are consumed by inflation, larger-fee magazines have closed, and larger numbers of writers make life more competitive. Are you ready for that?

Whether free-lance writing becomes a good or bad experience, a full-time or part-time career, and a short-term or long-term commitment is completely up to you. Now that you know the basics of writing features, this chapter will tell you how to get into print. At this point you turn the corner to a professional writing life. You will learn the basics of *selling* here—of being your own agent. This chapter focuses on a wide variety of concerns about free-lance writing. You will learn about marketing your work. You will learn about query letters and

---

BEST SOURCES FOR FREE-LANCE WRITING MARKETS

Books

    Writer's Market, Writer's Digest Books, Cincinnati.
    MIMP: Magazine Industry Market Place, R.R. Bowker, New York.
    Ayer's Directory of Newspapers, Magazines and Trade Publications
    O'Dwyer's Directory of Public Relations Executives, J.R. O'Dwyer, New York.
    The Standard Directory of Advertisers
    Literary Market Place (agents)
    Working press of the Nation (Vols. 1, 2)
    Local telephone book Yellow Pages ("publishers").

Periodicals

    Writer's Digest, Writer's Digest Books, Cincinnati.
    The Writer
    The Writer's Handbook
    Standard Rate and Data Survey
    Reader's Guide to Periodical Literature, H.W. Wilson Co., New York.
    Business Periodicals Index, H.W. Wilson Co., New York
    Social Sciences Index, H.W. Wilson Co., New York
    Humanities Index, H.W. Wilson Co., New York.
    Popular Periodicals Index

proposals for articles, preparation of manuscripts, cover letters, photographs and other artwork, developing multiple articles from a single research effort, and the business side, such as expenses and getting paid. You will also understand the legal and ethical concerns of free-lance writers, too. And finally, you will learn about professional organizations, continuing education opportunities beyond college, and contests and awards for quality work.

FINDING THE RIGHT MARKET

In recent years, a number of market directories and listings have been published to assist writers in finding the best markets for their work.

But you still must be very resourceful to find the right market. You cannot depend just on directories. You must set up a network by developing your own contacts in the industry. The more people—especially editors—you know, the better. Attend professional meetings, for example.

Still, it is helpful to begin with published market directories. At the top of the list is *Writer's Market*, the No. 1 source for nonfiction, free-lance writers. This 1,000-plus-page volume is published each fall and lists more than 4,000 publications for articles, books, and other written works. Another popular directory is *MIMP: Magazine Industry Market Place*. There are also listings of magazines and newspapers published annually by *Folio* and *Editor and Publisher*. Special issues of these two publications, and of others, such as *Writer's Digest*, list syndicates, new markets, and other reference books.

A beginning writer in or near a metropolitan area really needs to go no further than the "publishers" section of the local telephone directory Yellow Pages for a starting point. This listing will tell you which newspapers and magazines maintain offices in your area. Even if you do not have such telephone directories, you can go to a nearby library that should have the directories or microfiche copies available to use.

You must be patient. You must also try to market several ideas at once. Sometimes you will develop an idea but not find the right market for the article at the beginning of the project. Put the topic on hold for a while, if you can. While you are working on other writing projects that have more easily found markets for, your solution to the tough one might come along—at an airport news stand, at a friend's home, a local library periodicals room, or somewhere else.

University of Nevada-Reno professor Myrick Land (1987) also advises that you diversify in your marketing strategy. Try different types of articles. "You have a wide range of choices as a free-lancer. Although you may decide later that you prefer to devote most of your time to medical articles or pieces about television personalities, during your early years it would be good to explore a variety of possibilities" (p. 151), he says.

If all else fails, try to locate people who work or are interested in the subject you have chosen for an article. Ask them what they read. Find out what their favorite publications are. Their answers could give you an idea for a new market.

This all boils down to persistence. If you keep trying, eventually the effort will be rewarded with an acceptance letter and, later, a tearsheet and check.

MARKETING THE IDEA: QUERY LETTERS, ARTICLE PROPOSALS

You must go further than just "discovering" a subject for an article before going into the marketplace to make the sale. Having a subject is simply not enough in today's writing world. As the American Society of Journalists and Authors, Inc., defines it, the idea is one step further toward the finished product. An idea is a subject combined with an approach, ASJA says. This is your property, even if you do not have the article written yet. Once you get a good article idea, you have to decide when and where it is best to market it.

Most writers will not just query a publication with a subject. Most professionals prepare a query letter or an article idea proposal. You will find some writers who combine a letter and proposal into a single document, but for your purposes, you should consider them separate steps. A query letter will be briefer, less detailed, and an abstract of a fuller proposal. If you have refined the idea, then develop a proposal that runs 500 to 750 words that will summarize what you plan to do. Your basic strategy is to develop the idea to describe to an editor what you will do, or have done, without writing or sending the entire article. This is a more detailed outline of the article you plan to write. Editors find proposals helpful in determining whether your work would fit their plans for an upcoming issue.

Some articles do not need a proposal or query. This is particularly the case for short articles because editors will want to see the completed work. For editorials, humorous anecdotes/briefs, and most other articles under 1,000 words, a query is not as useful as the finished piece, literary agent Lisa Collier Cool (June 1985) says.

Cool also stresses that query letters must be convincing. "*Before* you begin writing your query letter, think your article idea through carefully. Imagine you are describing the article to a friend. Could you get the point across in just a few words?" (p. 24), she asks. Cool says queries must meet certain physical standards for serious attention to be given to them:

1. High-quality computer printer copies (letter quality or near-letter quality preferred over dot matrix) or high-contrast photocopies are acceptable.
2. Type letters on personal stationery printed on business-size (8 ½ by 11 inches) paper.

3. Single-space the query letter. Double-space proposals.

4. Submit each idea separately. Do not submit ideas together.

5. Enclose a self-addressed, stamped envelope (SASE) if you want material returned.

6. If you expect calls and are away from the telephone often, use an answering machine.

7. Enclose a self-addressed, stamped manuscript arrival confirmation post card.

8. Be patient. Wait up to six weeks before follow up.

Some editors prefer only query letters on first contact. If their initial response to your letter is positive, you might be asked to produce a proposal. The problem with many query letters, says veteran free-lancer Lorene Hanley Duquin (1987), is that the letter writers do not know what they are really proposing. If so, how can you expect an editor to know?

Ideally, a query letter will also include the proposal. Or, if you prefer to be more highly organized, send a proposal with a covering query letter that introduces you to the editor by describing your qualifications and other recent articles you have written. This more personal approach establishes your credibility as a serious professional writer.

Duquin says a proposal is the result of a four-step system:

1. *Capture the Idea*. When an idea strikes you, write it down to save it. When the time comes, it will be there for you to take to the next step.

2. *Develop the Idea*. Get more information. Think about the idea. Some preliminary research will help. Get the basic facts. Conduct some interviews.

3. *Tailor the Idea*. Shape the proposal to the audience that you will try to reach. Decide who would be interested and devise a writing and reporting strategy that will take you to that goal.

4. *Test the Idea*. Ask yourself these questions: Do you really want to do this article now? Are you capable? What is the cost (in time and money)? Can you find other uses for the material?

Read and study the publication you plan to query *before* you prepare the proposal. Call the magazine to get the name (and right spelling) of the proper editor (they do change from time to time and you cannot completely depend on annual directories to be up-to-date).

Duquin says well-prepared and well-researched proposals get the best attention.

If you've done your homework, you should have all the elements of a good query. Most editors recognize the time and preparation I put into my proposals and they respond personally. . . . More often than not . . . the editor will like the idea, but sees potential trouble spots. Since my proposal is well-developed, the editor can point to those spots and give me the guidance I need to research and write an article that will fit perfectly into the magazine's format. (Duquin, 1987, p. 40)

Southern magazine editor James Morgan (1986) says salesmanship in free-lance writing is most importance for success. He points to the timing of being in the right place at the right time with the right product in the right presentation. You control the last "right" but cannot always control the first three, he says. In saying this, he advises to avoid gimmicks, sloppy presentations, and dry formality.

Cover letters and accompanying proposals must provide certain basics, regardless of how you organize the information. Here's a list of things to include in a query letter:

1. How to contact you (address *and* telephone).
2. Your background as a writer, free-lancer. (Do not reveal that you are a student or novice. Act professionally and you will be treated as a professional.)
3. Your unique qualifications to write about this subject/idea.
4. Your availability and prospects for completion of the assignment if you get it.
5. A request for a response.

If you are writing a separate query/cover letter with a proposal, then the letter should be short and to the point. Most are written in traditional business letter form, meaning single-spaced and limited to one page if possible. An appealing, curiosity-arousing opening will get an editor to read more. Letters with dull starts are often not completely read.

Proposals should also have at least seven common elements:

1. Summary of the idea and the approximate word length.
2. Examples or cases to illustrate your focus.
3. Primary expert sources you plan to interview.
4. Facts/statistics from authoritative sources.
5. Time factors affecting freshness of material.
6. Outline of article and tentative title (if possible).
7. Availability of photographs and other graphics.

A proposal should be prepared much like a manuscript. This means it should be typed, double-spaced, and free of errors. The depth of your proposal depends on the publication.

In essence, then, you have several options in querying. Some proposals will be contained in detailed query letters. Some will take the form of 2-to-4-page essays. And others may be detailed outlines with other supplemental materials such as letters and descriptive essays. Put simply, University of Texas professor Thomas Fensch advises, *"The query letter demands as much practice and attention as does the feature article"* (Fensch, 1984, p. 79).

WRITING A QUERY LETTER

Here's a successful magazine query letter written by Donna Barron, a free-lance feature writer based in Hollywood, Fla., to the editor of *Ladycom: The Military Lifestyle Magazine*. Following it is the response she received. At the end of the chapter is the article Barron sent that was accepted and published by the magazine.

Ms. Sheila Gibbons
Editor
Ladycom
Downey Communications, Inc.
1732 Wisconsin Avenue NW
Washington, D.C. 20007

Dear Ms. Gibbons:

About four years ago some friends and I organized a local woman's investment club. We were a combination of about 20 full-time housewives and full and part-time working women.

While we didn't consider ourselves trend setters at the time, the popularity of investment clubs is becoming increasingly apparent. According to Mr. Thomas E. O'Hara, chairman of the National Association of Investment Clubs, his organization currently lists some 6,000 member groups. However, he estimates that there may be as many as 15,000-20,000 additional investors groups which do not belong to NAIC.

Mr. O'Hara points out that 29 percent of the total NAIC membership is women and that 36 percent of member groups are all-female clubs. Investment clubs are particularly attractive to women for several reasons. They provide an opportunity to learn about investing and gain experience without risking large sums of money, their required monthly contributions of $10, $25, $50 (or more) offer a form of forced savings, and their social orientation presents a chance to interact and learn from one's peers.

If you think your readers would be interested in an article pointing out the pros and cons of investment clubs—particularly from a woman's point of view, how to set up and what one can reasonably expect to accomplish with such a group, I would be happy to prepare one for you. I plan to interview Mr. O'Hara at length and will incorporate the experiences of women's investment groups in different areas of the country.

I hope this idea interests you and look forward to hearing from you. I have enclosed a recent clip as an example of my work.

>   Sincerely,
>   Donna Barron

The reply:

Ladycom
The Military Lifestyle Magazine
1732 Wisconsin Ave., NW
Washington, D.C. 20007
202-944-4025

Thank you very much for your recent query to *Ladycom*. We think your article has merit and we would like to see your manuscript on speculation.

Please submit it for consideration and we will contact you if it is accepted. When you mail the manuscript, please include a stamped, self-addressed envelope so we may return your article to you if we cannot use it.

>   Hope M. Daniels, editor

P.S.—Can you keep it under 1200 words?

DRAFTING A PROPOSAL FOR AN ARTICLE

Miami-based free-lance writer and business editor Laurel Leff (1984) has sold articles to numerous national magazines. She is a former *Wall Street Journal* and *Miami Herald* staff reporter. Her basic strategy is to query and propose before preparing and researching the article or writing the manuscript. Here is a proposal for an article for what she calls "mid-career doldrums" that was prepared for *Glamour* magazine:

MID-CAREER DOLDRUMS PROPOSAL

After four years as an account executive with AT&T, Sherry, a 26-year-old graduate of a small northeastern business college, realized that her chances for promotion were dim. Although she had performed her job well and consistently received satisfactory evaluations, there were just too many young managers vying for too few positions. With her dreams of being a fast-rising executive shattered, Sherry decided to quit her job, marry her long-time boyfriend, and lead the life of a suburban housewife.

For six years, Ellen, an associate in a Miami law firm, worked nights and weekends toiling away on technical, uninteresting cases in the hopes of becoming a partner in the firm. But when it was her turn to be considered, the firm decided it would not add any more partners. Her work wasn't bad, the other lawyers assured her, the firm simply did not have the room to make offers to all its associates. After all those long hours, boring cases, and high expectations, Ellen had no choice but to leave the firm.

Ever since she can remember, Fran wanted to be a professor. She first tried college teaching, working in the political science department of a small midwestern college. But when it became clear that she school didn't have any tenured openings, Fran decided to go to law school to become a law professor. Three years and a masters degree in law later, Fran still doesn't have a teaching job.

Sherry, Ellen, and Fran are talented, well-educated, hardworking, and ambitious. Unfortunately for them, so are hundreds of other people who wanted the same jobs. The coming of age of the baby boom (78 million people or one-third of the present population is between the ages of 20 and 38) means everyone can't climb directly up corporate and professional ladders. Many young professionals have stellar credentials and excellent work records. They went to the top schools, worked long hours and demonstrated competence in their professions. But the sheer numbers of young adults vying for the same positions mean some will inevitably be disappointed.

I'd like to propose a story on what happens to people in their twenties and early thirties as they begin to stall or fall backwards in their careers. I would deal both with the psychological implications of what for many of these people is the first real failure in their lives as well as suggest ways to overcome the mid-career doldrums.

I begin by laying out the dimensions of a problem that seems to span all professions. There were 535,000 lawyers, for example, for only 416,000 jobs in 1980. For the best paying and most prestigious jobs, the competition was even more intense. Large law firms typically hire 25 associates per class, yet only one or two become partners in the firm. Corporations are bulging with middle managers, many of whom have MBAs. Despite obvious qualifications, many managers are finding themselves trapped for years in the same job because there are simply no positions to which they can be promoted. Arnold Weber, a labor economist, says there are twice as many competitors for every managerial opening as there were in 1975. Even engineers are finding jobs hard to come by these days. Carnegie Mellon University reports that its engineering graduates received 40% fewer jobs offers in 1983 than they did in 1982.

And the problem in all professions seems to be growing worse. The Bureau of Labor Statistics estimated in 1982 that the economy will generate 19 million new jobs between 1980 and 1990 but only 3.5 million of them will be in professional or technical occupations. The rest will be low-paying, dead end jobs that offer little hope for advancement. For middle managers in particular, studies predict that opportunities will increase by 20% during the 1980s, but the number of people qualified to fill those jobs will jump by 40%.

In the story, I would lay out these rather grim statistics but the emphasis would be on how women like Sherry, Ellen, Fran and others cope with the disappointment and what positive steps people can take to get their careers and their lives back in gear. I'd profile women who have recovered from their disappointments and are again satisfied with their jobs. Some have found new careers which turned out to better suit them, like the Atlanta lawyer who began breeding horses when she didn't make partner in her firm. Others have carved out a different niche in their professions. Ellen, for example, is now working as an instructor at a local law school. Still others have decided to abandon the corporate rat race altogether by going into business for themselves, like the executive who opened a small theater.

From talking with counselors who specialize in midcareer doldrums, I'd offer a few pointers on how to identify when your career has come to a halt and what you should do to get past that point. I'd also find the occupations with the best possibilities for career advancement. Finally, I'd take a look at some institutionalized programs that are designed to help the overqualified job candidate. Citibank, for example, recently offered 300 of its qualified professional-level employees who couldn't be placed in management the option of going through career counseling at the bank's expense. NYU offers a Careers in Business Program where Ph.D.s are retrained for jobs in banking, consulting, manufacturing and other industries. Of 209 Ph.D.s enrolled, 90% got jobs upon completion of the course. Similar programs are now being offered at Harvard, Virginia, Texas, and UCLA.

Given the job crunch at the top of most professions, it seems likely that many of Glamour's readers are now facing or will soon face similar problems. I think a piece that would offer concrete alternatives to wallowing in a going nowhere job would find an enthusiastic audience.

PREPARING YOUR SUBMISSION

Once the article has been queried, proposed, *accepted*, and written, you prepare it in final form for your editor. There is an art to preparing your manuscript to mail to your chosen publication.

Because you have already been told of acceptance or have been invited to submit the finished manuscript for full review, you have good reason to do this job well. How well you prepare the manuscript and package it is a strong indicator of the caliber of your work. And if you are sending the finished manuscript on speculation, that is, without any prior correspondence with the publication, you have an even better reason to attend to the details of mailing your article with professional care.

A cover letter is an important part of the final package you mail to the publication. It should be business-like and stick to the point, editors George Scithers and Sanford Meschkow (1985) recommend. It can sell the manuscript you send on speculation. It should make life easier for the editor handling your correspondence. This means you must remember to help editors. You should be as detailed as possible with descriptions or summaries of earlier correspondence (include correspondence dates). "How you handle these [speculation and sale] and similar situations in a cover letter can help build the impression in the editor's mind that you are a professional who understands at least some of the ins and outs of publishing and the author—editor relationship" (p. 43), Scithers and Meschkow (1985) say.

What exactly do you send? Here's a basic list of the materials which you enclose in your package to the editor:

1. *Cover letter*. This should describe what is enclosed and why. Remember not many editors will remember the details of your project. Help them. This letter should also serve as a memorandum that explains any particulars of the work you have submitted.

2. *Manuscript*. This should be in clean (error-free), typed, double- or triple-space form. Final copies should always be typed on plain white paper, 8 ½ by 11 inches, and most editors prefer the manuscript be printed by letter quality or near-letter quality printers if you use a computer and word processor.

3. *Art work*. This includes any visual elements to your story such as photographs (or negatives), tables, charts, illustrations/drawings, maps, diagrams, and so on. *No* marking should be included on any materials that may be reproduced in the publication. And it is also best not to write on the back of any art work. Clip explanatory notes if needed, but do not damage the art.

4. *Protective covering*. If you submit fragile materials such as original photographs or drawings, protect them with hard coverings such as cardboard or padding. These specially-made shipping containers can be purchased at most office supply stores.

5. *Return envelope and postage*. Especially if you are submitting material on speculation, you should include a self-addressed, stamped envelope for return of materials. Some editors will not return your manuscript and art work if you do not include the envelope with sufficient postage. An SASE is not needed when the article has already been accepted for publication, of course.

Use a large enough envelope to mail the set of materials so they will not be damaged. This means a minimum size 9- by 12-inch manila envelope, but if you have a large amount of material, an 11- by 14-inch envelope works better.

Author and professor Thomas Fensch offers these do's and don't's as you prepare to go to the post office:

Do:
Keep a copy of everything you send.
Keep records of your correspondence.
Follow up after sufficient time (he recommends 10 weeks for a monthly but less for a weekly).
Use special mail and delivery services if time is crucial or if safety of materials is in doubt.

Don't:
Call or write to see if materials were received.
Use old mailing materials or odd-size materials.
Fold materials.

Staple art work.

Send rare copies that cannot be replaced.

Send negatives without duplicates on file.

PHOTOGRAPHS AND ARTWORK

Although you might see yourself as a writer, you will also find yourself in a position to be a photographer, graphic artist, or some other form of visual communicator. This happens frequently when a magazine or newspaper does not, or cannot, provide a photographer for you. To strengthen your position to make a sale, you should consider the complete package of your assignment and whether photographs or other artwork will make a difference. If you can take your own photographs, it will help. But if you cannot, it is best not to submit below-par photographs with strong writing.

What you can often do to assist an editor is *suggest* visual elements of the total package. You know the material best and will be able to propose photograph subjects, graphs or tables, charts, maps, diagrams and such that a professional artist can prepare. You should not have to pay for this service, but you should suggest it to an editor at the time of the query.

It strengthens your article if you can propose visual approaches to telling the story. A free-lance travel story will not be as enticing without photographs of the palm-lined beach or snow-capped mountain range. A how-to article is far more understandable with diagrams.

As you begin to increase the frequency of your free-lance work, you may get acquainted with free-lance photographers and artists in your area. Teaming up with these individuals can create a strong offering to an editor that might mean more good opportunities for everyone involved.

Finally, do not forget that you will be expected to write the first drafts of the cutlines, or captions, of the artwork you submit. These can be short, simple, left to right identifications of people in the photographs, or they can be more thorough explanations of procedures and other subjects of the artwork. Your newspaper or magazine's style will dictate how you handle the cutlines—short or long, tight or descriptive, general or detailed—so be sure to familiarize yourself with the way the editor handles these important elements of your work. Always be sure to provide sources of photographs and other graphics for appropriate publication credit if you did not produce them yourself.

WRITING MULTIPLE ARTICLES
FROM THE SAME RESEARCH

A wise free-lance feature writer will be able to develop more than one distinct article from the research effort on a subject. If you can, you will get more income from your time and resources investment.

This is the result of organization and planning. If you are going to make a 500-mile trip for one article—and spend $500 to $1,000—can you develop a second article prospect for the same trip? Often it is no additional expense to add a second or even a third project; all you give up is additional time.

You should consider different markets. There are several ways to focus on a subject, as you know from earlier discussions. Each may represent an article prospect.

Focus on both general markets and specialized markets. A general market approach for an article on personal finance will vary a great deal from the specific market approach that a banking magazine would take.

Furthermore, consider proposing longer articles in parts. In this way, you are selling two separate, perhaps shorter, articles instead of one longer one. You might earn more for such a sale, but this depends on the rate structure of a publication.

You need the right topic to do this, however. Free-lance writer Tana Reiff (September 1987) tells of one such example:

> I have a friend who is a lawyer by vocation and a race-car driver by avocation. To promote his racing career, he writes articles for racing magazines. In the course of researching an article recently, he stumbled on a sports psychologist. What a great topic for multiple angles! He's starting with an article on mentally preparing for a race. After that, he'll apply mental preparation to virtually any sport he knows (p. 24).

EXPENSES AND GETTING PAID

You will encounter certain operating expenses when working on an article. As a free-lancer, you must arrange to get these costs paid by the publication that accepts your article or else the cost will come from your agreed fee.

If you have proposed an article, you should estimate expenses and include the estimate if the cost will be excessive. Typical writer's expenses include automobile and plane travel, parking, lodging, food, admissions and other fees, express mail and overnight delivery services, long-distance telephone tolls, and photocopying. You should expect your publication to pay reasonable expenses, but you should check these details when an assignment is made or when your proposal is accepted.

Professional writers should keep expense logs and receipts. There are two basic reasons for this: first, you must have a record if you expect someone else to pay for your expenses; second, if you do not get them paid, you can still claim certain business expenses as deductions on your federal and state income taxes if you have documentation.

Always discuss expenses with your editor in advance, especially if a major expense such as out-of-town travel is involved. You may be given a ceiling for expenses for an assignment, and you will be expected to keep within the limit. If you foresee going over the limit, ask about it first. Otherwise, you may find the expenses chipping away your income.

As you start writing for pay, you will notice variations in how and how fast you are paid. Checks are the standard, although some free-lance writers today trade for their services. Checks are issued at various times in the process, but most often at a point after the article is submitted and accepted for publication. On bigger projects, you may seek an advance or a partial payment in the middle of the project. You have to ask, though, since most editors will not usually offer such a convenience.

Most professional free-lancers will include an invoice with their final manuscript when it is submitted. You need to keep track of such matters, since you will likely have several projects going simultaneously and can lose track of time and of who has paid what after a while. Setting up a ledger or spreadsheet will help you do this.

Reminders are not out of line after a grace period. You should be patient up to 30 days. But after that time period passes, send a reminder by mailing a copy of the invoice to your editor. They get busy and occasionally forget, or in some cases, you might accidentally be forgotten.

Basically, as Tana Reiff says, your situation as a free-lance writer is no different from a one-person business. You should operate this way. Be your own accountant and practice the basics of good accounting.

LEGAL CONSIDERATIONS

You cannot exist in a legal vacuum as a free-lance writer. In addition to the general concerns all journalists must have about libel, privacy, copyright, open records, and open meetings, you must also consider still other legal issues related to free-lance writing.

This means knowing the details of obtaining permissions, payment for work particulars, reprint and other second sales rights, contracts, general letters of agreement, and author copyright.

Permissions

There are times in preparing an article that you will wish to use a long passage from another published and copyrighted work. When you quote other authors, composers, and artists, you must get permission from the source, or rights holder. There are generally four steps to getting permission: (a) Find the copyright owner, (b) write a permission request letter, (c) act on the reply to your letter (for example, pay a fee), and (d) credit the copyright holder in your article. For short passages, usually up to 100 words or a paragraph, you do not need permission. But you will certainly be asking for trouble if you fail to get permission wherever it is needed; it can help your professional image if you do.

Payment for Work

You are entitled to the money you have earned: it is that simple. But some careless editors and publishers do not quite see it that way. They delay or simply do not pay. The first step, of course, is to agree to a "kill" fee before the work is submitted or even written. If an editor changes his or her mind about your article, you should be compensated for the work put into it. If a completed assignment is not acceptable due to no fault of yours as the writer, the American Society of Journalists and Authors, Inc. (Bloom, Bode, & Olds, 1985), recommends you should be paid from half the agreed amount to the full amount. ASJA also advises that you seek a kill fee of one-third of your author's fee in advance. Most professionals agree, also, that you should be paid within a month of delivery, but ASJA says ten days is appropriate. This will vary from publication to publication. Upon delivery of your work to the editor, you should always ask how much time payment takes. ASJA also recommends in its code of ethics and fair practices: "No article payment should ever be subject to publication" (p. 12). If a publisher does not pay and you feel you are entitled to your fee, writer Dean R. Lambe (1986) suggests several points: (a) write a polite inquiry letter to the editor; (b) next, write the publisher (if different from the editor); (c) see a lawyer and he will write an inquiry letter; (d) take legal action through your lawyer; (e) if a bankruptcy has occurred, file a claim so you can get a share when assets are sold; and (f) share your grief with other writers through professional groups.

Reprint, Copyright, and Other Sales Rights

Traditionally, free-lance writers have sold only the one-time publication rights of their work. Reprint fees should be yours as author, ASJA suggests to its members. The publication that prints your article should refer inquiries to you as well, unless you waive these rights. You hold the copyright unless you grant it in writing to the publication. Any other rights are yours, ASJA believes, and it strongly urges writers not to sign any documents that transfer rights to a publisher.

Contracts

If you have a chance to reach a contractual agreement with a publisher, *read it* thoroughly before you sign it and return it. Contracts will specify certain arrangements between the author and publisher. The major concerns, says literary agent Lisa Collier Cool (November 1985), include publication fee, kill fee (guarantee), final manuscript length (usually in words), expenses, payment schedule, deadlines, advances, credits, serial rights, book publication rights (usually for collections of articles by popular and experienced magazine and newspaper feature writers), dramatic rights, commercial rights, information retrieval rights, and translations (from English to another language), and frequency of use by the publication (some editors will re-publish an article from time to time).

Letters of Agreement

A sample letter of agreement that originates with the author, especially when the publication does not issue any written confirmation of the assignment, is included in the appendices. This letter has been formulated by the American Society of Journalists and Authors, Inc., for use when contracts are not appropriate or when the author and publisher prefer not to work with formal contracts.

Author Copyright

Ownership of the work, including copyright, remains with you as author, according to the 1978 U. S. Copyright Law. You should know the law and its finer points such as those described in the sections above.

There are other considerations. Lawsuits can arise at any time caused by just about anything in a written work. The main causes will be claims for libel, defamation, and invasion of privacy, especially in articles that break new ground or are about controversial subjects. And as a writer, you must be concerned with the possibility of legal actions, whether the cases are legitimate or not.

If your work is *accurate*, then you will have little to worry about. Truth, of course, is the best defense against libel actions. Writer and University of Southern California journalism professor Bruce Henderson (1984) recommends nine ways to "bulletproof" a manuscript:

1. *The idea.* Check whether the story idea is a new one. Be certain you are not copying or plagiarizing a work. Check your own motivations for doing the article. If your work involves revenge or venting anger, forget it.

2. *The assignment contract.* Honor the commitments you make in writing and otherwise. Know what you are liable for, such as legal fees, according to the contract terms.

3. *Research.* Use written sources if possible to guard against legal claims. Keep accurate records on where you find all factual information you use in the article.

4. *Interviews.* Select qualified sources. Be sure sources have no grudges against your subject. Get second sources to verify. Identify sources, whenever possible, in the article. Conduct important interviews in person and tape record them.

5. *Note taking.* Be thorough in taking notes. Organize the notes after an interview or a records search. Note negative results—that you could not find something—when you can.

6. *Writing.* Tell only what you know. Do not guess or make up information to fill in holes. And if you are not completely certain of a fact, then avoid using it.

7. *Editing and fact-checking.* Do not change information in a story, even if an editor asks you to do so, unless the change is true and accurate. Be ready for a fact-checker to verify information in your story.

8. *Final checks.* Have a lawyer read your final manuscript if you think it might be troublesome. Seeking legal advice before publication is smart and safe.

9. *Lawsuit.* If you ever find yourself served with a suit, contact the publication immediately. The publisher will be directly involved also. Plan to work together.

ETHICS OF FREE-LANCE WRITING

Another important topic for free-lance writers is ethics. Even though certain practices in journalism are legal, they may not be ethical. That is, they may not be accepted behavior among professionals. There are numerous codes of professional standards in journalism. Among them are the codes of the Society of Professional Journalists and the American Society of Journalists and Authors, Inc. Both codes are included in the appendix. There are other codes, but all have a similar purpose: to set forward the right way to work as a professional journalist. The SPJ code sets general standards for all journalists and is a good overall model for you to study. ASJA's code focuses on ethical and economic issues that are the fundamental concerns of writers.

What should we be concerned about? Professional codes list more than two dozen different issues pertaining to the relations of writers to sources, editors, readers, and even other writers.

Most general codes such as the SPJ code, focus on responsibilities to the public, the need for honesty, freedom of the press, the need for fairness, elimination of conflicts of interest and acceptance of gifts in exchange for favors, and the desire to achieve objectivity. Specific writers' codes such as ASJA's are more detailed and propose fair practices in the relationships of writers and editors. ASJA's code, for example, addresses nearly two dozen separate situations ranging from subjects similar to those in the SPJ code, such as accuracy and conflicts of interest, to specific details of writers' publication and payment rights and expenses.

The mark of a professional is the level of his or her ethical behavior. Familiarity with the accepted performance standards in your profession will only help you in the long run. And since these are evolving standards, they are constantly changing. It is up to you to keep up with them as your professional career expands.

GOING FROM PART-TIME TO FULL-TIME
FREE-LANCE WRITER

Two of the hardest decisions a part-time free-lance writer will face are whether to, and when to, go full time. Beside giving up an existing career, these are decisions that may mean giving up a regular, steady income. Therefore, they should be made only after thoughtful deliberation and discussion with family and colleagues.

Michael A. Banks (1985), an author who quit a factory job to become a full-time free-lance writer, describes advantages and disadvantages to making the big switch.

Advantages. First, there is more time to plan and write. You can take on larger projects, such as booklets and even books. You work as much as you want because you control your time. There is no need for the physical and psychological transition time to go from job one to job two. And finally, Banks says, the full-time writing effort gives you a boost in self-esteem by giving you control of your own career and business.

Disadvantages. You may be the primary wage earner for you and your family. Some economic losses from giving up a steady income are severe and must be reckoned with. You must be able to manage money that comes in uneven surges. You must also endure the operating expenses of being a writer yourself. This means travel, telephone, equipment, and even ordinary office supplies. You may pressure yourself to be productive. Failure can take on a greater significance. There is no supervisory pressure in many cases, and you must be disciplined to produce. And, do not forget, you lose all non-paycheck benefits that come along with your job (e.g., health insurance, pensions and retirement, social security contributions made by your employer—now you must make them—paid vacations, bonuses, sick days, overtime, and so on).

The decision to go full time must be economic. Can you afford it? What is your part-time income? What would it be full time if you project it to the amount of time you gain by quitting the full-time job? What are your basic normal living expenses? Will you cover them? Can you make sacrifices of other things for a while?

Free-lancer Tana Reiff (September 1987) recommends diversification of your writing, also. The more you can write about different specialties, the more you will bring in fees. She also recommends diversity in the types of projects you write. Taking on both short and long assignments can keep a steadier supply of income in the mail, she says.

Prepare for the switch by planning ahead. Put aside extra money for the expected slow period at the beginning. Also save up some good writing ideas, Banks recommends. These will help you through tough times. And finally, he advises, do not "burn your bridges" at your job. Try to leave yourself an option to return if things just do not work out. Test your career change first by taking a 3- to 6-month leave, or accumulated vacation time in one big block, if it is possible.

PROFESSIONAL ORGANIZATIONS AND PROGRAMS

The best way to continue developing yourself as a free-lance writer is to become involved in professional organizations and attend workshops and conferences about writing. These groups and events have numerous benefits that far outweigh any disadvantages.

First, professional organizations offer you the chance to network, or meet other writers and editors. Many times these groups, such as the Society of Professional Journalists, offer special programs that provide continuing professional development beyond your college and university years. This might not seem important to you now, particularly if you are still in school, but it will become increasingly important as time passes beyond graduation day.

National organizations like SPJ, or the American Society of Journalists and Authors, Inc., offer guidance through regular contact with members. This comes through publications and local and national meetings. Many beginning writers, especially free-lancers, find the contacts made at these organizational meetings helpful for story ideas and opportunities to meet editors and other writers. Local press clubs in major cities such as New York or Washington are also gathering and meeting places for professional writers.

Most professional memberships are not too expensive, although they may seem so to beginning writers. Most organizations require national dues of less than $100 a year, and some require additional, minimal local chapter dues as well. These business expenses are tax deductible, of course, and are sometimes paid by employers.

Writers' clubs are another alternative. They are often organized in a community with the goal to further members' careers. These groups can be useful for a free-lance writer if the groups offer speakers, writing critique sessions, readings of works, field trips and professional contact opportunities. Some offer service to the community, such as helping local schools, as well. Many are organized by towns or neighborhoods. Some have grown as large as statewide groups and have subdivided. In Florida, for example, the Florida Freelance Writers Association organized, as it says in a recent brochure, to be "the link between Florida writers and editors, public relations directors and other buyers of the written word" (p. 1). This particular group operates a referral system for writer members, furnishes updated state market information, and offers continuing education programs.

Author Dennis Hensley (1986) recommends that you be selective about these clubs so you can find one that will really emphasize writing development over social activities. "Manuscript evaluating is one of the great services a writers club or critique group can provide—if it is done correctly. Too often members offer routine praise to each other and shy away from seriously analyzing one another's manuscripts" (p. 38), Hensley warns.

Some writers prefer not to join organizations. Some work in rural areas where local membership is not possible. Nevertheless, there are other options for continuing professional education. These come in the form of writers' classes, conferences, seminars, and workshops. *Writer's Digest* magazine annually lists the major gatherings of writers. In 1988 for example, *Writer's Digest* Assistant Editor Bill Strickland found more than 450 such events in the United States scheduled through spring 1989.

Such events offer hands-on writing practice and learning, lectures, opportunities to meet successful writers, and the chance to re-tool or learn new techniques while on the job. Most last only a few days and are often sponsored at schools or writers' groups. The chance to interact with other writers during these events may be the best experience—it gives you a chance to exchange ideas, critiques, and help one another in social and working session settings.

CONTESTS AND AWARDS

Some writers love contests and awards; other writers detest them. The idea of competition and the thought of recognition for excellence often appeal to writers who get little feedback on their work other than a sale. Winning some contests can be financially rewarding, but other contests simply offer recognition for quality work. Most are offered annually and are specialized by subject. The *1989 Writer's Market* lists about 200 contests, and *Editor & Publisher* annually lists even more for newspapers and magazines.

Contests can provide opportunities for beginning writers. Winning recognition in a contest means greater professional visibility. It means new opportunities. It is a way to be discovered within your specialization. But winning an award is not the solution to all your professional problems. It is only a step to the next level of excellence in your writing.

The key to entering contests is to know about these competitions well in advance of deadlines. By doing your homework ahead of time, you have the chance to prepare an entry in your best professional presentation. Meeting the deadline with a clean entry that follows entry rules carefully is a must for contest participants. Many organizations sponsoring contests and award programs publish the entry specifications and will provide them at no charge if you request them well in advance of the deadline.

You must always take the time to check for your eligibility as well. This should be outlined in the contest rules, but if you are not sure, always contact the sponsors.

HOW PROFESSIONALS WROTE IT

DATE: JUNE 1986
SOURCE: LADYCOM: MILITARY LIFESTYLE MAGAZINE, PP. 10, 72.
AUTHOR: DONNA BARRON, FREE-LANCE WRITER

•••

YOUR MONEY: JOIN THE CLUB FOR SOUND INVESTING

Emma Dimpfel signed up for her first investment club back in 1959 at the Washington, D.C., Naval Officers' wives' annual fall coffee.

"They were hoping to generate enough interest to put one or maybe two groups together, recalls Dimpfel. "Ninety-nine women signed up—enough to form six separate clubs."

Dimpfel, who currently belongs to three different investment clubs, says her group—the only one of the original six still in existence—has experienced almost 100 member changes in the past 25 years. Now comprised exclusively of retired officers' wives, it shows no signs of slowing up.

According to Thomas O'Hara, chairman of the National Association of Investment Clubs (NAIC), there are currently between 24,000 and 25,000 investment clubs in the United States. About 6,000 of these belong to NAIC.

Made up of friends, neighbors, or business acquaintances who choose to pool their knowledge and share financial risk, investment clubs provide an excellent training ground for beginners seeking a painless way to learn the rudiments of investing.

But this doesn't mean clubs don't appeal to seasoned investors as well. Some simply enjoy the social atmosphere and stimulation inherent in group investing. Others, especially those with heavy demands on their time, appreciate the increased research potential a group provides.

Many members use the presentations and recommendations made by fellow club members as a basis for deciding what to buy for themselves as well. According to an NAIC survey, investment club members invest three times as much personally as they do with their clubs.

"There's no question that it helps you get started on your personal portfolio," says Emma Dimpfel. "I figure I put three children through college on what I learned through my investment clubs."

Most members of those first Navy wives' groups knew little about investing and less about investment clubs, but with the certainty of transfers looming in many of their not-so-distant futures, they made it a point to learn very quickly.

By the time Cynthia Charles' husband was assigned to the Pentagon in the early 1960s, the officers' wives' investment clubs were processing new recruits like a well-oiled military machine.

"Setting up a group of military personnel or wives is not much different from organizing any other investment group," says Charles, who is currently chairperson of both the National Board of Directors and the Delaware Valley, Pa., Council of NAIC.

"The most important thing is to have someone who is familiar with how to start a club help the group get up and running quickly," she says. Her first club, she points out, was made up exclusively of wives of officers on three-year D.C. tours. They were anxious to get started right away.

"The Navy wives virtually got us together and organized in one day," she recalls. "They pushed us through the housekeeping part—choosing a name, electing officers, setting up a partnership agreement and an accounting system. When we had our first meeting we knew absolutely nothing, but we were so excited. Then they taught us how to study."

Charles, who has been quite active in organizing investment groups over the past 20 years, admits that it isn't quite that simple for most aspiring military investors. Few areas of the country have military investment groups as active as the one she first encountered. However, plenty of help is available if you just know where to look.

For those interested in setting up a new club or joining an existing one, Charles recommends contacting the national NAIC headquarters (1515 East Eleven Mile Rd., Royal Oak, MI 48067). The national organization can provide all the necessary information and can put you in touch with your local area NAIC council, which can provide additional guidance.

Regional councils are currently set up in 27 metropolitan areas. "The role of the council is to help in the educational process," says Anne Uno, president of the Washington, D.C., area council. Uno says her group provides stock analysis training classes, runs speakers programs and puts on an annual investors fair for local club members.

Council members also provide help with the often confusing tasks of establishing operating rules, hammering out a partnership agreement and setting up financial records.

Membership in NAIC costs $30 per club plus $6 per member and provides a subscription to the NAIC publication, Better Investing; a handbook on how to organize an investment club; and a $25,000 fidelity bond against theft of club funds. An Investors Manual, available for $8, contains detailed instructions for setting up a club and provides work sheets for analyzing stock performance.

A typical investment club includes 15 to 20 members who meet once a month and make a monthly contribution of between $20 and $45. Profits are not guaranteed, so the monthly figure decided upon should not exceed an amount all members can freely afford to lose.

The size of a group is an important consideration. Including more members than the norm may provide a more rapid buildup of funds, but it can also make finding a place to have meetings and reaching agreement on club policy and proposed stock purchases considerably more difficult and time-consuming.

Each club is unique, with some made up of all women, others all men and still others mixed. One particularly successful group that got its start at NAS [Naval Air Station] Willow Grove, Pa., is comprised of husbands and wives. Most clubs are set up as limited partnerships where each member pays taxes on only his particular share.

Some groups allow members who are transferred to maintain their membership by mail. Most prefer that participants remain part of the active educational process that goes on within the club and simply buy out the shares of the leaving members.

The key to military club longevity is definitely the inclusion of retired or reserve personnel or wives who can provide long-term continuity. However, many groups are content to confine their membership to active-duty people. Some even limit their existence to a single tour of duty.

Perhaps the most important step in setting up an investment club is recruiting compatible members. NAIC reports that about 50 percent of all new clubs fail in the first 18 months because of clashes over investment philosophy.

NAIC recommends these guidelines:

* Invest on a regular monthly basis, regardless of market conditions or what market analysts are saying.

* Reinvest dividends and capital gains. Putting profits back into your portfolio will help it grow more quickly.

* Seek out conservative growth stocks in companies with earnings that exceed their industry average.

* Diversify by choosing stock in companies of different sizes and in a variety of industries.

Once your membership is established, you'll need both a tax number for purchasing stock and a broker. Some groups choose to save money by using reduced commission discount brokers to handle transactions. Others prefer, at least in the beginning, to go with a full-service broker who's available and willing to answer their questions.

"In the beginning, you're learning by doing," says Charles, "and new clubs should use their broker as much as they can for advice. If you are willing to take a course, you'd be paying tuition, so just think of the broker's commission as tuition."

Reprinted with the permission of the author and *Ladycom: Military Lifestyle Magazine*.

A Professional's Point of View

By Art Spikol
Writer's Digest

So you want to be a free-lance writer. Well, I've done it for a while, and I've learned a few things. Here they are—hang 'em over your typewriter.

Don't talk your stories. If you let it come out of your mouth, chances are it won't come out of your fingertips.

Develop a sales approach. Not a canned pitch, but an effective demeanor for  dealing with editors. That demeanor may end up in a query letter or a phone call or a personal visit, but never lose sight of the goal: to sound responsible and competent.

If you want success, you can't be just a writer. The biggest cause of failure among would-be-writers is not wanting to deal with the business issues.

For instance, a businessperson doesn't write something first and worry about where to sell it afterwards.

To be businesslike, ask yourself what kind of magazine you want to sell to. And then what kind of articles that magazine uses. And then make sure that the publication hasn't recently printed an article like yours. And then convince an editor that you're the person to write it. Time *is* money; don't squander yours.

You'll have to sound not just like somebody who can write a good article, but somebody an editor wouldn't mind putting on a witness stand someday.

Because of litigious times, it may come to that.

If you don't make the sale, don't blame the editor. Editors know what to buy, and they know what their readers want. If you don't sell the article, it (or you) wasn't right for the publication.

Do your job like a pro. If you were a race car driver, neurosurgeon or astronaut, a mistake could be disastrous. The same applies to writing: misspell a word, punctuate incorrectly, fail to meet a deadline—and your credibility goes up in smoke. Ultimately, your career will follow it.

Take charge of your business. If, for instance, you wait ten weeks to get a yes or no from a publication, it's your fault, not the publication's. Take the idea elsewhere— maybe to two or three other markets. If you were trying to sell your car, would you offer it to one person at a time?

Don't quit your job. Sure, you want to be a free-lancer, but don't give up what you have. It will create too much finaneial pressure to enable you to succeed. Instead, first see if you have the discipline to spend one hour a day writing. If you can do that on a sustained basis, stretch it to two. See what happens—are you selling? Making contacts? Nothing magical happens when you quit your job—except that your income disappears.

Don't use best-case scenarios as a guide. You *can* earn about $25,000 to $35,000 a year if you write for magazines and hit the best of them every month at their highest rates. Or you can earn $8,000 a year, which is far more likely. Prepare for the worst.

Diversify. If you want to make a lot more than the above figures, take your writing talent down some more financially rewarding paths. Write newsletters, brochures, annual reports. Write advertising, film scripts, books. They all pay better—for less work—than magazine articles.

Finally, *Love writing.* Practically everybody I meet would like to be a writer, but not many actually want to write. The hard work is sitting down and putting the words on paper.

Now, close this book and do it. May your fingers have wings. (Spikol, personal communication, 1988)

* * *

Art Spikol is a Philadelphia-based contributing editor and columnist for *Writer's Digest*, Cincinnati. His column, "Nonfiction" is a monthly feature in the magazine. He is currently a free-lance writer and is also a former editor of *Philadelphia* magazine. He has written hundreds of magazine articles and columns. His first novel, *The Physalia Incident*, was published by Viking Press in 1988. He is also a graphic designer and president of an editorial consulting firm which produces corporate publications and newsletters.

Appendix A:
Code of Ethics
Society of Professional Journalists

The Society of Professional Journalists believes the duty of journalists is to serve the truth.

We believe the agencies of mass communication are carriers of public discussion and information, acting on their Constitutional mandate and freedom to learn and report the facts.

We believe in public enlightenment as the forerunner of justice, and in our Constitutional role to seek the truth as part of public's right to know the truth.

We believe those responsibilities carry obligations that require journalists to perform with intelligence, objectivity, accuracy, and fairness.

To these ends, we declare acceptance of the standards of practice here set forth:

*RESPONSIBILITY: The public's right to know of events of public importance and interest is the overriding mission of the mass media. The purpose of distributing news and enlightened opinion is to serve the general welfare. Journalists who use their professional status as representatives of the public for selfish or other unworthy motives violate a high trust.

*FREEDOM THE THE PRESS: Freedom of the press is to be guarded as an inalienable right of people in a free society. It carries with it the freedom and the responsibility to discuss, question, and challenge actions and utterances of our government and our public and private institutions. Journalists uphold the right to speak unpopular opinions and the privilege to agree with the majority.

*ETHICS: Journalists must be free of obligation to any interest other than the public's right to know the truth.

1. Gifts, favors, free travel, special treatment or privileges can compromise the integrity of journalists and their employers. Nothing of value should be accepted.

2. Secondary employment, political involvement, holding public office, and service in community organizations should be avoided if it compromises the integrity of journalists and their employers. Journalists and their employers should conduct their personal lives in a manner which protects them from conflict of interest, real or apparent. Their responsibilities to the public are paramount. That is the nature of their profession.

3. So-called news communications from private sources should not be published or broadcast without substantiation of their claims to news value.

4. Journalists will seek news that serves the public interest, despite the obstacles. They will make constant efforts to assure that the public's business is conducted in public inspection.

5. Journalists acknowledge the newsman's ethic of protecting confidential sources of information.

*ACCURACY AND OBJECTIVITY: Good faith with the public is the foundation of all worthy journalism.

1. Truth is our ultimate goal.

2. Objectivity in reporting the news is another goal, which serves as the mark of an experienced professional. It is a standard of performance toward which we strive. We honor those who achieve it.

3. There is no excuse for inaccuracies or lack of thoroughness.

4. Newspaper headlines should be fully warranted by the contents of the articles they accompany. Photographs and telecasts should give an accurate picture of an event and not highlight a minor incident out of context.

5. Sound practice makes clear distinction between news reports and expressions of opinion. News reports should be free of opinion or bias and represent all sides of an issue.

6. Partisanship in editorial comment which knowingly departs from the truth violates the spirit of American journalism.

7. Journalists recognize their responsibility for offering informed analysis, comment, and editorial opinion on public events and issues. They accept the obligation to present such material by individuals whose competence, experience, and judgment quality them for it.

8. Special articles or presentations devoted to advocacy or the writer's own conclusions and interpretations should be labeled as such.

*FAIR PLAY: Journalists at all times will show respect for the dignity, privacy, rights, and well-being of people encountered in the course of gathering and presenting the news.

1. The news media should not communicate unofficial charges affecting reputation or moral character without giving the accused a chance to reply.

2. The news media must guard against invading a person's right to privacy.

3. The media should not pander to morbid curiosity about details of vice and crime.

4. It is the duty of news media to make prompt and complete correction of their errors.

5. Journalists should be accountable to the public for their reports and the public should be encouraged to voice its grievances against the media. Open dialogue with our readers, viewers, and listeners should be fostered.

Reprinted with the permission of the Society of Professional Journalists

Adopted by the 1987 national convention, Chicago

Appendix B:
American Society of Journalists and Authors, Inc.
Code of Ethics and Fair Practices

Preamble

Over the years, an unwritten code governing editor–writer relationships has arisen. The American Society of Journalists and Authors has compiled the major principles and practices of that code that are generally recognized as fair and equitable.

The ASJA has also established a Committee on Editor–Writer Relations to investigate and mediate disagreements brought before it, either by members or by editors. In its activity this committee shall rely on the following guidelines.

1. Truthfulness, Accuracy, Editing

The writer shall at all times perform professionally and to the best of his or her ability, assuming primary responsibility for truth and accuracy. No writer shall deliberately write into an article a dishonest, distorted, or inaccurate statement.

Editors may correct or delete copy for purposes of style, grammar, conciseness, or arrangement, but may not change the intent or sense without the writer's permission.

2. Sources

A writer shall be prepared to support all statements made in his or her manuscript, if requested. It is understood, however, that the publisher shall respect any and all promises of confidentiality made by the writer in obtaining information.

3. Ideas

An idea shall be defined not as a subject alone but as a subject combined with an approach. A writer shall be considered to have a proprietary right to an idea suggested to an editor and to have priority in the development of it.

4. Acceptance of an Assignment

A request from an editor that the writer proceed with an idea, however worded and whether oral or written, shall be considered an assignment. (The word "assignment" here is understood to mean a definite order for an article.) It shall be the obligation of the writer to proceed as rapidly as possible toward the completion of an assignment, to meet a deadline mutually agreed upon, and not to agree to unreasonable deadlines.

5. Conflict of Interest

The writer shall reveal to the editor, before acceptance of an assignment, any actual or potential conflict of interest, including but not limited to any financial interest in any product, firm, or commercial venture relating to the subject of the article.

6. Report on Assignment

If in the course of research or during the writing of the article, the writer concludes that the assignment will not result in a satisfactory article, he or she shall be obliged to so inform the editor.

7. Withdrawal

Should a disagreement arise between the editor and writer as to the merit or handling of an assignment, the editor may remove the writer on payment of mutually satisfactory compensation for the effort already expended, or the writer may withdraw without compensation and, if the idea for the assignment originated with the writer, may take the idea elsewhere without penalty.

8. Agreements

The practice of written confirmation of all agreements between editors and writers is strongly recommended, and such confirmation may originate with the editor, the writer, or an agent. Such memorandum of confirmation should list all aspects of the assignment including subject, approach, length, special instructions, payments, deadline, and guarantee (if any). Failing prompt contradictory response to such a memorandum, both parties are entitled to assume that the terms set forth therein are binding.

9. Rewriting

No writer's work shall be rewritten without his or her advance consent. If an editor requests a writer to rewrite a manuscript, the writer shall be obliged to do so but shall alternatively be entitled to withdraw the manuscript and offer it elsewhere.

10. Bylines

Lacking any stipulation to the contrary, a byline is the author's unquestioned right. All advertisement of the article should also carry the author's name. If an author's byline is omitted from a published article, no matter what the cause or reason, the publisher shall be liable to compensate the author financially for the omission.

11. Updating

If delay in publication necessitates extensive updating of an article, such updating shall be done by the author, to whom additional compensation shall be paid.

12. Reversion of Rights

A writer is not paid by money alone. Part of the writer's compensation is the intangible value of timely publication. Consequently, if after six months the publisher has not accepted an article for publication, or within twelve months has not published an article, the manuscript and all rights therein should revert to the author without penalty or cost to the author.

13. Payment for Assignments

An assignment presumes an obligation upon the publisher to pay for the writer's work upon satisfactory completion of the assignment, according to the agreed terms. Should a manuscript that has been accepted, orally or in writing, by a publisher or any representative or employee of the publisher, later be deemed unacceptable, the publisher shall nevertheless be obliged to pay the writer in full according to the agreed terms.

If an editor withdraws or terminates an assignment, due to no fault of the writer, after work has begun but prior to completion of the manuscript, the writer is entitled to compensation for work already put in; such compensation shall be negotiated between editor and author and shall be commensurate with the amount of work already completed. If a completed assignment is not acceptable, due to no fault of the writer, the writer is nevertheless entitled to payment; such payment, in common practice, has varied from half the agreed-upon price to the full amount of that price.

14. Time of Payments

The writer is entitled to payment for an accepted article within ten days of delivery. No article payment should ever be subject to publication.

15. Expenses

Unless otherwise stipulated by the editor at the time of an assignment, a writer shall assume that normal, out-of-pocket expenses will be reimbursed by the publisher. Any extraordinary expenses anticipated by the writer shall be discussed with the editor prior to incurring them.

16. Insurance

A magazine that gives a writer an assignment involving any extraordinary hazard shall insure the writer against death or disability during the course of travel or the hazard, or, failing that, shall honor the cost of such temporary insurance as an expense account item.

17. Loss of Personal Belongings

If, as a result of circumstances or events directly connected with a perilous assignment and due to no fault of the writer, a writer suffers loss of personal belongings or professional equipment or incurs bodily injury, the publisher shall compensate the writer in full.

18. Copyright, Additional Rights

It shall be understood, unless otherwise stipulated in writing, that sale of an article manuscript entitles the purchaser to first North American publication rights only, and that all other rights are retained by the author. Under no circumstances shall an independent writer be required to sign a so-called "all rights transferred" or "work made for hire" agreement as a condition of assignment, of payment, or of publication.

19. Reprints

All revenues from reprints shall revert to the author exclusively, and it is incumbent upon a publication to refer all requests for reprint to the author. The author has a right to charge for such reprints and must request that the original publication be credited.

20. Agents

According to the Society of Authors' Representatives, the accepted fee for an agent's services has long been ten percent of the writer's receipts, except for foreign rights representation. An agent may not represent editors or publishers. In the absence of any agreement to the contrary, a writer shall not be obliged to pay an agent a fee on work negotiated, accomplished, and paid for without the assistance of the agent.

21. TV and Radio Promotion

The writer is entitled to be paid for personal participation in TV or radio programs promoting periodicals in which the writer's work appears.

22. Indemnity

No writer should be obliged to indemnify any magazine or book publisher against any claim, actions, or proceedings arising from an article or book.

23. Proofs

The editor shall submit edited proofs of the author's work to the author for approval, sufficiently in advance of publication that any errors may be brought to the editor's attention. If for any reason a publication is unable to so deliver or transmit proofs to the author, the author is entitled to review the proofs in the publication's office.

Source: Murray Teigh Bloom, Richard Bode, and Sally Wendkos Olds, eds., *The ASJA Handbook: A Writer's Guide to Ethical and Economic Issues*, American Society of Journalists and Authors, Inc., 1985, Suite 1907, 1501 Broadway, New York, NY 10036 (212) 997-0947.

Appendix C:
American Society of Journalists
and Authors, Inc.
Suggested Letter of Agreement

Originating with the writer to be used when publication does not issue written confirmation of assignment.

DATE
EDITOR'S NAME AND TITLE
PUBLICATION
ADDRESS

Dear EDITOR'S NAME:

This will confirm our agreement that I will research and write an article of approximately NUMBER words on the subject of BRIEF DESCRIPTION, in accord with our discussion of DATE.

The deadline for delivery of this article to you is DATE.

It is understood that my fee for this article shall be $ AMOUNT, with one-third payable in advance and the remainder upon acceptance (1). I will be responsible for up to two revisions.

The publication will be entitled to first North American rights in the article (2).

It is further understood that you shall reimburse me for routine expenses incurred in the researching and writing of the article, including long-distance telephone calls, and that extraordinary expenses, should any such be anticipated, will be discussed with you before they are incurred (3).

It is also agreed that you will submit proofs of the article for my examination, sufficiently in advance of publication to permit correction of errors.

This letter is intended to cover the main points of our agreement. Should any disagreement arise on these or other matters, we agree to rely upon the guidelines set forth in the Code of Ethics and Fair Practices of the American Society of Journalists and Authors. Should any controversy persist, such controversy shall be submitted to arbitration before the American Arbitration Association in accordance with its rules, and judgment confirming the arbitrator's award may be entered in any court of competent jurisdiction.

Please confirm our mutual understanding by signing the copy of this agreement and returning it to me.

Sincerely,

(SIGNED)

WRITER'S NAME

PUBLICATION

by_____
                    NAME AND TITLE

Date_____

1. If the publication absolutely refuses to pay the advance, you may want to substitute the following wording: "If this assignment does not work out, a sum of one-third the agreed-upon fee shall be paid to me."

2. If discussion included sale of other rights, this clause should specify basic fee for first North American rights, additional fees and express rights each covers, and total amount.

3. Any other conditions agreed upon, such as inclusion of travel expenses or a maximum dollar amount for which the writer will be compensated, should also be specified.

Source: Murray Teigh Bloom, Richard Bode, and Sally Wendkos Bode, eds., *The ASJA Handbook: A Writer's Guide to Ethical and Economic Issues*, American Society of Journalists and Authors, Inc., 1985, Suite 1907, 1501 Broadway, New York, NY 10036 (212) 997-0947.

Bibliography

BOOKS

Alexander, L. (1975). *Beyond the facts: A guide to the art of feature writing*, Houston: Gulf Publishing.

Atkin, B. J. (1986). Are you a 'magazine' person? In *Magazine publishing career directory 1986*. New York: Career Publishing.

Becker, S. L. (1987). *Discovering mass communication* (2nd ed.). Glenview, IL: Scott, Foresman.

Biagi, S. (1981). *How to write and sell magazine articles*. Englewood Cliffs, NJ: Prentice-Hall.

Biagi, S. (1986). *Interviews that work: A practical guide for journalists*. Belmont, CA: Wadsworth.

Blair, W., & Hill, H. (1978). *America's humor: From Poor Richard to Doonesbury*. New York: Oxford University Press.

Bleyer, W. G. (1913). *Newspaper writing and editing*. Boston: Houghton Mifflin.

Bloom, M., Bode, R., & Olds, S.W. (Eds.). (1985). *The ASJA handbook: A writer's guide to ethical and economic issues*. New York: American Society of Journalists and Authors.

Burkett, W. (1986). *News reporting: Science, medicine, and high technology*. Ames, IA: Iowa State University Press.

Carter, J. M. (1986). Magazines: The New "Hot" Medium. In *Magazine publishing career directory 1986*. New York: Career Publishing.

Drug Abuse Council (1975). *Reporter's guide: Drugs, drug abuse issues, resources*. Washington, DC: Author.

Edelson, E. (1985). *The journalist's guide to nuclear energy*. Bethesda, MD: Atomic Industrial Forum.

Fensch, T. (1984). *The hardest parts: Techniques for effective non-fiction*. Austin, TX: Lander Moore Books.

Flesch, R. (1946). *The art of plain talk*. New York: Harper.

Flesch, R. (1949). *The art of readable writing*. New York: Harper.

Fogel, S.J., & Rosin, M.B. (1987). *The yes-I-can guide to mastering real estate.* New York: Times Books/Random House.

Graham, B. P. (1982). *Magazine article writing: substance and style.* New York: Holt, Rinehart & Winston.

Gunning, R. (1968). *The technique of clear writing.* New York: McGraw-Hill.

Hohenberg, J. (1987). *Concise newswriting.* New York: Hastings House.

Horowitz, L. (1986). *A writer's guide to research.* Cincinnati, OH: Writer's Digest Books.

Hunt, T. (1972). *Reviewing for the mass media.* Radnor, PA: Chilton.

Kando, T. (1980). *Leisure and popular culture in transition* (2nd ed.). St. Louis: C.V. Mosby.

Kaplan, M. (1975). *Leisure: Theory and policy.* New York: Wiley.

Kelley, J. E. (1978). *Magazine writing today.* Cincinnati, OH: Writer's Digest Books.

Knight-Ridder, Inc. (1986). *The 1986 Pulitzer Prize winners.* Miami: Author.

Krech, D., Crutchfield R.S., & Livson, N. (1969). *Elements of psychology* (2nd ed.). New York: Knopf.

Kresch, S. (1986). The changing face of the industry. In *Magazine publishing career directory 1986.* New York: Career Publishing.

Kubis, P., & Howland, R. (1985). *The complete guide to writing fiction, nonfiction, and publishing.* Reston, VA: Reston Publishing.

Land, M. E. (1987). *Writing for magazines.* Englewood Cliffs, NJ: Prentice-Hall.

Leedy, P. D. (1981). *How to read research and understand it.* New York: Macmillan.

Meredith, S. (1987). *Writing to sell* (3rd rev. ed.). New York: Harper & Row.

Neff, G. T. (Ed.). (1987). *1988 Writer's market: Where & how to sell what you write* (59th ed.). Cincinnati, OH: Writer's Digest Books.

Neff, G. T. (Ed.). (1988). *1989: Writer's market: Where & how to sell what you write* (60th ed.). Cincinnati, OH: Writer's Digest Books.

Nelson, H. L., & Teeter, D. L. (1986). *Law of mass communications* (5th ed.). Mineola, NY: Foundation Press.

Patterson, B. R. (1986). *Write to be read: A practical guide to feature writing.* Ames, IA: Iowa State University Press.

Pember, D. R. (1987). *Mass media law* (4th ed.). Dubuque, IA: William C. Brown.

Plotnik, A. (1982). *The elements of editing: A modern guide for editors and journalists.* New York: Macmillan.

Rivers, W. L. (1975). *Finding facts: Interviewing, observing, using reference sources.* Englewood Cliffs: NJ: Prentice-Hall.

Rivers, W. L., & Work, A. R. (1986). *Free-lancer and staff writer. Newspaper features and magazine articles* (4th ed.). Belmont, CA: Wadsworth.

Rose, T. (Ed.). (1981). *U.S. News and World Report stylebook for writers and editors.* Washington, DC: U.S. News and World Report, Inc.

Ruehlmann, W. (1979). *Stalking the feature story.* New York: Vintage Books.

Schoenfeld, A. C., & Diegmueller, K. S. (1982). *Effective feature writing.* New York: Holt, Rinehart & Winston.

Sloan, W. D., McCrary, V., & Cleary, J. (1986). *The best of Pulitzer Prize news writing.* Columbus, OH: Publishing Horizons.

Smith, A. (1970). *The seasons: Life and its rhythms.* New York: Harcourt, Brace Jovanovich.

Southern California's Latino Community: A series of articles reprinted from the Los Angeles Times. (1984). *Los Angeles Times.*

Spikol, A. (1979). *Magazine writing.* Cincinnati, OH: Writer's Digest Books.

Strunk, W., & White, E. B. (1979). *The elements of style* (3rd ed.). New York: Macmillan.

Thorp, W. (1964). *American humorists.* Minneapolis: University of Minnesota Press.

Wardlow, E. (Ed.). (1985). *Effective writing and editing: A guidebook for newspapers.* Reston, VA: American Press Institute.

Webster's new world dictionary of the English language. (1966). Cleveland, OH: World Publishing.

Whiteaker, S. (1988). *English garden embroidery: 80 original needlepoint designs of flowers, fruit and animals*. New York: Ballantine.

Wilde, L. (1976). *How the great comedy writers create laughter*. Chicago: Nelson-Hall.

Williamson, D. R. (1975). *Feature writing for newspapers*. New York: Hastings House.

Wolfe, T. (1966). *The kandy-kolored tangerine-flake streamline baby*. New York: Pocket Books.

Yates, E. D. (1985). The writing craft (2nd ed.). Raleigh, NC: Contemporary Publishing.

Zinsser, W. (1980). *On writing well* (2nd ed.). New York: Harper & Row.

OTHER SOURCES

Associated Press Managing Editors Features Committee. (September 1987). Features grow up. *Report of the Features Committee*, Seattle, WA: Associated Press Managing Editors.

Blais, M. (1984). *Writer's writing: Before the first word*. Produced by Learning Designs, Inc., and Educational Broadcasting Corp., WNET-TV, New York, and funded by The Annenberg/CPB Project, Public Broadcasting System.

Business Press Educational Foundation (n.d.), *The exciting world of business magazines* (informational brochure). New York: Author.

de View, L. S. (1988, March). *The poet, the fiction writer, the journalist: Shared skills*. unpublished collection, *Florida Today*, Melbourne, FL, presented to the Writer's Workshop, School of Communication, University of Miami, FL.

Florida Freelance Writers Association. (1985) *FFWA: Florida Freelance Writers Association* (membership brochure). Fort Lauderdale, FL: Author.

Kilpatrick, J. J. (1985). *The art and the craft*. The Red Smith lecture in journalism, Department of American Studies, University of Notre Dame, South Bend, IN.

Quindlen, A. (1984). *Writer's writing: Before the first word*. Produced by Learning Designs, Inc., and Educational Broadcasting Corp., WNET-TV, New York, and funded by The Annenberg/CPB Project, Public Broadcasting System.

Shapiro, M. A. (1988, July). *Components of interest in television science stories*. Unpublished paper presented to the Theory and Methodology Division, Association for Education in Journalism and Mass Communication, annual convention, Portland, OR.

PERIODICALS

American Newspaper Publishers Association staff. (1987, April). *presstime: '87 Facts about newspapers* (pp. 2–14). Washington, DC: American Newspaper Publishers Association.

Associated Press staff. (1988, March 20). New travel magazines crowd publishing field. *The Miami Herald*, p. 13J.

Astor, D. (1988, September 10). Writer is a lampooner of baby boomers: Humor columnist Alice Kahn 'fluctuates between disgust and joy' as she comments on the trends and attitudes of a generation. *Editor and Publisher, 121*(37), 48–50.

Austin, D. (Ed.). (1986, October). *Tips to take home, 1986 APME changing newspapers committee report*. Cincinnati, OH: Associated Press Managing Editors.

Bain, A. (1988, June). All in a day's work. *Reader's Digest, 132*(794), 104.

Banaszynski, J. (1987, June 21, July 12, August 9). AIDS in the heartland. *St. Paul Pioneer Press Dispatch* (three-part series).

Banks, M. (1985, February). Breaking away! *Writer's Digest, 65*(2), 22–26.

Barnes, H. (1987, December 7). Selleck is an easygoing charmer in 'Three Men and a Baby.' *The Miami News*, p. 3C.

Barron, D. (1986, June). Your money: Join the club for sound investing. *Military Lifestyle*, 10, 72.

Barry, D. (1986, September 12). Dave to Sophia: 'Chow, bella.' *The Miami Herald*, p. 1B.

Barry, D. (1988, May 12). Astrology lady sure can't be Reagan's worst advisor. *The Miami Herald*, p. 1B.

Bartlett, S. (1988, February 1). Our intrepid reporter wheels and deals currencies: And learns tricks of the trader from a Citicorp game. *Business Week*, (3036) pp. 70–71.

Benedetto, R. (1975, March). The hardest part: Ideas. *Editorially Speaking: The Gannetteer, 30*(15), 5.

Bennett, P. (1987, September 13). Gangs divide and conquer children of Mexico City. *The Miami Herald*, p. 24A.

Berger, I. (1979, May). A writer's guide to tiny tape recorders. *Writer's Digest, 59*(5), 25–27.

Bernstein, P. (1979, May). Take care of your tape recorder—And it will take care of you. *Writer's Digest, 59*(5), 20–24.

Bivens, T. (1988, May 11). New drug breaks ground in search for aphrodisiac. *The Philadelphia Inquirer* and Knight-Ridder Newspapers (reprinted in *The Miami Herald*, p. 2E).

Blais, M. (1987, January 11). Dyeing for attention. *The Miami Herald*, Tropic, p. 15.

Blais, M. (1987, July 5). The promise. *The Miami Herald*, Tropic, p. 5.

Blais, M. (1987, August 23). Steam: the boiling point. *The Miami Herald*, Tropic, p. 8.

Bogus, R. (1983, August). Complaining for cash. *Writer's Digest, 63*(8), 40–41.

Boles, P. D. (1985, April). The elements of your personal writing style. *Writer's Digest, 65*(4), 24–28.

Briskin, J. (1979, February). Research is a snap. *Writer's Digest, 59*(2), 26–28.

Brody, J.E. (1982, July 6). Remembering the Hyatt disaster: Emotional scars persist a year later. *The New York Times*, pp. C1, C4.

Buchwald, A. (1988, April 19). Mouthpiece issues pearls of wisdom. *The Miami News*, p. 17A.

Buffum, C. (1983, October). Sunday best: Newspaper magazines and a parade of weekend reading. *Washington Journalism Review, 5*(8), 33–35.

Burka, P. (1984, June). The man in the black hat. *Texas Monthly, 12*(6), 128–133, 212–223, 230.

Burka, P. (1984, July). The man in the black hat. *Texas Monthly, 12*(7), 122–125, 175–187.

Burns, D. H. (1987, August 19). Authors prescribe dose of discipline in family formula. *The Orlando Sentinel*, pp. E1, E4,

Campbell, S. (1988, March 9). Trying to bring autistic girl into reality. *Hartford Courant* (reprinted in *The Miami Herald*, p. 2E).

Carlton, M. (1988, January 9). Scotland's Borrobol Lodge a birdwatcher's flight of fancy. *The Miami News*, p. 3C.

Carter, E. G. (1986, June). Conversations with the heartbreak kid. *Gentlemen's Quarterly*, pp. 220–224, 246–252.

Caruana, C. M. (1981, October). A basic reference bookshelf for writers. *Writer's Digest, 61*(10), 30–31.

Casey, K. (1985, September). Love & death in the Piney Woods: The tragic story of the coach, the principal, and the secretary. *Houston City Magazine, 9*(9), 82–89, 124–25.

Collins, M. (1987, August 31). Cover story: Time flies while Cosby, 50, has fun. *USA Today, 5*(247), 1–2.

Cook, M. (1986, March). Training your muse: Seven steps to harnessing your creativity. *Writer's Digest, 66*(3), 26–30.

Cook, M. (1987, June). Dave Barry claws his way to the top. *Writer's Digest, 67*(6), 28–30.

Cool, L. C. (1985, June). How to write irresistible query letters. *Writer's Digest, 65*(6), 24–27.

Cool, L. C. (1985, November). Making contract. *Writer's Digest, 65*(11), 39–41.

Curley, A. (1977, December 4). Goodby car, hello city buses, *The Milwaukee Journal*, pp. 1, 6.

Danville Commercial-News staff. (1977, May). Give a potpourri of people news to people in your community. *The Gannetteer, 30*(41), 4–5.

Detjen, J. (1988, Summer). Where to go for science experts. *IRE Journal, 11*(3), p. 3.

Dickson, F. A. (1979, March). Thinking ahead: 37 article ideas for fall and winter. *Writer's Digest, 59*(3), 2.

Dickson, F. A. (1980, April). Thinking ahead: 34 article ideas for fall and winter. *Writer's Digest, 60*(4), 33–35.

Dold, R. B. (1983, December 23). Wreathmaker's 15,000 'chores' instead are joy. *Chicago Tribune*.

Dudek, L. J. (1970, September). Newspaper critics critiqued: Are they qualified to judge theater, music, broadcasting? *The Quill, 58*(9), 30–31.

Dumanoski, D. (1988, May 18). Scientists see 'alarming' hints of North Pole ozone loss. *Boston Globe* (reprinted in *The Miami Herald*, p. 2E).

Dunlap, B. (1987, April 19). Beach puts terrific building in unfortunate location. *The Miami Herald*, p. 2K.

Dupler, S. (1987, November). Cover story: American hot wax. *Popular Mechanics, 164*(11), 79–81, 156.

Duquin, L. H. (1987, January). Shaping your article ideas to sell. *Writer's Digest, 67*(1), 37–40.

Eddy, B. (1979, February). Spelling: the curse of the working journalist. *The Quill, 67*(2), 15–17.

Editor & Publisher staff. (1987, December 26). Editor says travel writing is getting more credible. *Editor & Publisher, 120*(52), 13.

Emerson, C. (1986, February). Telling the tiny tale. *Writer's Digest, 66*(2), 36–39.

Eskilson, M. D. (1987, September). Chrysanthemums, a centuries-old favorite, make a comeback. *Flowers &, 8*(9), 48–51.

Ferguson, D. W. (1988, June). Campus comedy, *Reader's Digest, 132*(794), 122.

Figueroa, O. (1987, February 14). Some marry, others renew vows at North Miami Beach 'love-in'. *Miami News*, p. 1C.

Finley, M. (1988, July). Patrick F. McManus and the funny four. *Writer's Digest, 68*(7), 33–34.

Fiumara, G. (1987, March 3). Careers at home #2. *Family Circle*, pp. 24–25.

Flaherty, M. P., & Schneider, A. (1985, November 3–10). You grasp for trust. *The challenge of a miracle: Selling the gift* (reprinted from *The Pittsburgh Press*, Pittsburgh Press Co., eight-part series, pp. 46–47).

Fletcher, R. J., Jr. (1986, March). Trade secrets. *Writer's Digest, 66*(3), 42–44.

Franklin, J. (1978, December 12). Tales from the grey frontier. *Baltimore Evening Sun*, p. C-1.

Garateix, M. (1987, October 15). Volunteers help ease the aftershocks. *Los Angeles Times* (San Gabriel Valley ed.). pp. 1, 6.

Geczi, M. (1985, June). How to read an annual report, part 3: The balancing act. *Personal Investor, 1*(3), 34–38.

George, D. W. (1988, April 30). Travelers are willing to pay for inside scoop on destinations given in the latest newsletters. *The Miami News*, p. 3C.

Gilder, J. (1981, April). Creators on creating: Tom Wolfe. *Saturday Review, 8*, 40–44.

Goldberg, S., & Ezell, H. (1987, September 22). Enrollments likely to break records as frosh swell campuses. *Atlanta Constitution*, pp. 17A, 19A.

Grobel, L. (1978, January). A star interview is born. *Writer's Digest, 58*(1), 19–23.

Gruber, W. (1987, September 13). Some cave artists painted ceilings like Michelangelo. *The Miami Herald*, p. 13-J.

Hamilton, D. C. (1985, October 27). Sight & sound: The new member of the mid-'80s family. *Newsday*, pp. 3, 21.

Harris, B. (1982, July). The man who killed Braniff. *Texas Monthly, 10*(7), pp. 116–120, 183–189.

Henderson, B. (1984, April). How to 'bulletproof' your manuscripts. *Writer's Digest, 64*(4), 28–32.

Hensley, D. (1979, May). Pumping the profs. *Writer's Digest, 59*(5), 34.

Hensley, D. (1986, January). Getting the most out of your writers club. *Writer's Digest, 66*(1), 36–38.

Howell, W. J. (1973). Art versus entertainment in the mass media. *Education*, *94*(2), 177–81.

Hunter, J. D. (1983, February). Good writing is: Good journalism, good business, an art, good for you, all of the above. *The Bulletin of the American Society of Newspaper Editors*, (657) pp. 5–7.

Johnson, T. E., & Shapiro, D. (1988, January 11). A mass murder in Arkansas. *Newsweek*, *111*(2), 20.

Kahn, A. (1988, February 24). How to profit from the coming article-writing glut. *San Francisco Chronicle*, p. B4.

Kelton, N. (1988, January). How to write personal experience articles. *Writer's Digest*, *68*(1), 22–24.

Kleiman, C. (1981, October 4). The rescued: Family buried for hours feel closer than ever. *The Chicago Tribune*, p. 24A.

Kleiman, C. (1981, October 4). The rescuer: Those he couldn't save still haunt fire fighter. *The Chicago Tribune*, p. 24A.

Krajewski, R. (1983, September). A writer's guide to word-processing software. *Writer's Digest*, *63*(9), 40–42, 52–59.

Kreig, A. (1986, July). Death wish III. *Connecticut Magazine*, *49*(7), 71–73, 98–99, 123.

Ladwig, T. (1987, October 5). The baddest of bad days gives a couple a good story. *Columbia Missourian* (reprinted in *Publisher's Auxiliary*, 123 (20), p. 12).

Ledesma, K. (1988, June). Campus comedy. *Reader's Digest*, *132*(794), 121.

Lamb, D. R. (1986, April). What to do when the publisher won't pay. *Writer's Digest*, *66*(4), 36–38.

Lincoln, M. L. (1981, September-October). The free-lance life. *Columbia Journalism Review*, *20*(3), 49–54.

Luzadder, D. (1982, March 15). A fitful night for those whose dreams lie under the river. *Fort Wayne, Ind., News-Sentinel*.

MacDonald, D. (1987, September/October). The capybara: Giant among rodents. *Animal Kingdom*, *90*(5), 22–33.

Maier, F. (1987, September 12). A second chance at life. *Newsweek*. *110*(11), 52–61.

Markus, R. (1988, January 3). He's finally main man: Miami's Johnson gains a championship, respect. *Chicago Tribune*, Sect. 3, pp. 1, 10.

Marx, L. (1987, September). Jeffrey Arthur: From rock music star to a king of jingles. *Florida Trend*, *30*(5), 31–36.

McDaniel, D. (1986, December). 12 tips on profiles. *The Editors' Exchange*, American Society of Newspaper Editors, *9*(11), 4.

McGill, L. (1984, August). Give your how-to articles the voice of authority. *Writer's Digest*, *64*(8), 26–28.

McKinney, D. (1986, January). How to write true-life dramas. *Writer's Digest*, *66*(1), 24–28.

McVicker, M. F. (1987, August). The ABC's of accounting. *Flowers &*, *8*(8), 61–62, 88–96.

Marcus, D. (1986, May 19). 'Closed' signs mark a change of season. *The Miami Herald*, p. 1-B.

Miller, L. (1986, September). The expenses primer. *Writer's Digest*, *66*(9), 34–35.

Mitgang, H. (1987, April 3). Everyone wins in 'Johnson' expose, *The Miami News*, p. 7C.

Modzelewski, J. (1988, January 13). The $80,000 expense account. *The Miami News*, p. 1A.

Moorman, R. (1987, July). Stop, look & listen. *Air Line Pilot*, *56*(7), 18–22.

Morgan, J. (1986, July). The secrets of superlative salesmanship. *Writer's Digest*, *66*(7), 30–33.

Moroney, T. (1985, October). Swindled! *Boston Magazine*, *77*(10), 170–74, 218.

Morrow, S. B. (1987, September). Colossal cookies. *Bon Appetit*, *32*(9), 70–72, 74–78.

Moss, B. (1982, May 31). I never felt sorrow. *The Miami Herald*, p. 1D.

Nager, L. (1987, September 24). Jagger's older, wiser—but still a rocker. *The Miami News*, p. 2C.

Nordan, D. (1986, August). The legend of Stewart Avenue: To some it's seedy and suspect, to others it's a street of dreams. *Atlanta Magazine*, *26*(4), 32–35.

Ognibene, Mary. (1975, March). Funniest things are those that really happen. *Editorially speaking: The Gannetteer*, *30*(15), 3.

Osborne, P. B. (1987, April). Writing the 'art-of-living' article. *Writer's Digest*, *67*(4), 20–25.

Parker, C. E. (1975, December). 'Tis the season for seasonal articles. *Writer's Digest, 55*(12), 30–31, 44–45.

Patoski, J. N. (1987, October). Every bar but Hershey's. *Texas Monthly, 15*(10), 112, 177–78.

Perret, G. (1984, July). How to build humor, one chuckle at a time. *Writer's Digest, 64*(7), 30–32.

Perret, G. (1987, September). Short investments, sweet returns. *Writer's Digest, 67*(9), 27–29.

Pevsner, D. (1988, January 3). Travel Wise: Airlines toast new year with 2 outstanding bargains. *The Miami Herald*, p. 6J.

Piaf, R. (Stephen K. Doig). (1987, April 1). Coded message. *The Miami Herald*, p. 1B.

Plimpton, G. (1986, April). Life begins at Mach 2. *Popular Mechanics*, pp. 75–79, 152–153.

Provost, G. (1985, July). Mind games. *Writer's Digest, 65*(7), 24–26.

Queenan, J. M. (1987, August 31). Too late to say I'm sorry. *Newsweek, 110*(9), 7.

Reiff, T. (1987, September). How to keep the money coming. *Writer's Digest, 67*(9), 22–26.

Reiff, T. (1987, October). How to keep the money coming, part II. *Writer's Digest, 67*(10), 40–42.

Robertson, N. (1982, September 19). Toxic shock. *New York Times Magazine, 132*(45), Section 6, 30–34.

Romantini, W. (1987, May). So you wanna' be a food critic? *Milwaukee Magazine, 12*(5), 49–52.

Schaefer, J. (1987, July/August). Fiction is once again finding a place in the daily newspaper. *The Bulletin of the American Society of Newspaper Editors*, (697) pp. 12–13.

Schulman, C. (1984, February). Syndicates: How they work, and how they can work for you. *Writer's Digest, 64*(2), 31–34.

Schumacher, M. (1983, January). Johnny Deadline to the rescue. *Writer's Digest, 63*(1), 30–33.

Schwartz, M. (1984, February 4). Coming soon to late-night TV: The go directly to bed game. *The Miami News*, Television book, p. 2.

Schwartz, M. (1984, March 20). Jordan's queen still remains an all-American girl. *The Miami News*, p. 3C.

Schwartz, T. (1984, May). 12 money-making ideas for writers. *Writer's Digest, 64*(5), 37–38.

Scithers, G., & Meschkow, S. (1985, August). Invisible manuscript. *Writer's Digest, 65*(8), 28–29.

Scithers, G., & Meschkow, S. (1985, September). Under cover. *Writer's Digest, 65*(9), 42–43.

Seidman, M. & Strickland, B. (1988, May). The 1988 *Writer's Digest* guide to writers conferences, seminars and workshops. *Writer's Digest, 68*(5), 28–40.

Shannon, J. (1984, November). Typewriter as time machine: The secrets of selling seasonal material. *Writer's Digest, 64*(11), 33–34.

Shoup, M. (1987, August 30). Long-distance bicycling, you can if you want to. *The Philadelphia Inquirer*, p. R3.

Sibbison, J. (1988, July/August). Covering medical 'breakthroughs'. *Columbia Journalism Review, 27*(2), 36–39.

Silva, M. (1983, October 6). Take my plane ticket—please. *The Miami Herald*, p. 1B.

Singer, J. (1988, February 11). Parent survival: Lay down the law. *The Miami Herald*, p. 1B.

Sorrels, R. (1986, March). The sensous writer. *Writer's Digest, 66*(3), 38–41.

Spielmann, P. (1988, January). The real-life, stranger-than-fiction humor of William Geist. *Writer's Digest, 68*(1), 28–31.

Spikol, A. (1979, March). Non fiction: Profiles with punch. *Writer's Digest, 59*(3), 7–10.

Spikol, A. (1981, April). Non fiction: Source spots. *Writer's Digest, 61*(4), 6–8, 61.

Spikol, A. (1984, October). Non fiction: Service please. *Writer's Digest, 64*(10), 15–16.

Spikol, A. (1986, January). Non fiction: Make me laugh. *Writer's Digest, 66*(1), 16–19.

Spikol, A. (1986, July). Non fiction: Do you have what it takes to be a writer? *Writer's Digest, 66*(7), 20–24.

Spikol, A. (1986, September). Non fiction: Different worlds. *Writer's Digest, 66*(9), 16–18.

Spikol, A. (1987, March). Non fiction: Trading in on trade journals. *Writer's Digest, 67*(3), 16, 18.

Spikol, A. (1987, September). Non fiction: Before the interview. *Writer's Digest, 67*(9), 8–10.

Stager, C. (1987, September). Silent death from Cameroon's killer lake. *National Geographic, 172*(3), 404–20.

Strickland, B. (1987, May). The *Writer's Digest* guide to writers conferences, seminars and workshops. *Writer's Digest, 67*(5), 32–47.

Swanson, M. (1979, May). Covering the campuses. *Writer's Digest, 59*(5), 33, 35.

Swartz, M. (1988, February). Behind the lines: Celebrate with us. *Texas Monthly, 16*(2), 6–9.

Talese, G. (1966, April). Frank Sinatra has a cold. *Esquire, 65*, 89–98, 152.

Teer, J. (1973, January 20). Florida newsman discovers Samaritans still hard to find. *Editor & Publisher, 106*(3), 24.

Terry, J. (1975, March). The column has an identity of its own. *Editorially Speaking: The Gannetteer, 30*(15), 12.

The Miami Herald staff. (1987, April 2). Every fool has his day; this is yours. *The Miami Herald*, p. 1B.

The Miami Herald staff. (1987, February 12). Profile: W. Scott Piper III. *The Miami Herald*, p. 3F.

Towers, J.F., & Jenkins, P.J. (1987, December). The hazards of winter operations, part I, *Air Line Pilot*, pp. 12–16.

Towers, J.F., & Jenkins, P.J. (1988, January). The hazards of winter operations, part II, *Air Line Pilot*, pp. 34–37.

Turtle, C. (1986, November 2). System keeps tab on teachers. *The Miami Herald*, Miami Beach Neighbors ed., p. 16.

United Press International. (1987, July 23). Profile of Detroit: 20 years after riots old ills lingering, report says. *The Miami Herald*, p. 16A.

Wasik, J. (1987, August 3). Money matters: How to draft a complaint. *San Antonio Light*, pp. D1, D8.

Wilker, D. (1987, September 4). Veteran rocker Slick draws '60s faithful to Starship show. *The Miami News*, p. 8C.

Winne, M. C. (1983, May 1). What it's like to watch a man die in electric chair. *The Atlanta Journal and Constitution*, pp. 15-D, 20-D.

Wolfe, T. (1963, November). There goes (varoom! varoom!) that kandy-kolored tangerine-flake streamline baby. *Esquire, 60*(11), 114–18, 155–68.

Wooldridge, J. (1984, July 18). Do you know the correct way to cultivate a proper beard? *The Miami Herald*, p. 5E.

Writer's Digest staff. (1981, October). Browsing the reference bookstore. *Writer's Digest, 61*(10), 32–33.

Writer's Digest staff. (1985, December). Tip sheet: Four steps to getting permission to quote from another author's work. *Writer's Digest, 65*(12), 47.

Yankelovich, D. (1981, April). New rules in American life: Searching for self fulfillment in a world turned upside down. *Psychology Today, 15*(4), 35–91.

Author Index

Subject Index